INTERVENTIONS: NEW STUDIES IN MEDIEVAL CULTURE
Ethan Knapp, Series Editor

Eschatological Subjects

Divine and Literary Judgment in Fourteenth-Century French Poetry

J. M. Moreau

 The Ohio State University Press • *Columbus*

Copyright © 2014 by The Ohio State University.
All rights reserved.

Library of Congress Cataloging-in-Publication Data
Moreau, J. M. (John M.), 1983–
  Eschatological subjects : divine and literary judgment in fourteenth-century French poetry / J. M. Moreau. — First edition.
      pages cm. — (Interventions : new studies in medieval culture)
  Includes bibliographical references and index.
  ISBN-13: 978-0-8142-1269-1 (hardback)
  ISBN-10: 0-8142-1269-7 (cloth)
  ISBN-13: 978-0-8142-9373-7 (cd)
 1. French poetry—To 1500—History and criticism. 2. Eschatology in literature. 3. Judgment Day in literature. 4. French poetry—Appreciation—History—14th century. 5. Guillaume, de Deguileville, active 14th century—Criticism and interpretation. 6. Guillaume, de Machaut, approximately 1300–1377—Criticism and interpretation. 7. Froissart, Jean, 1338? –1410?—Criticism and interpretation. I. Title. II. Title: Divine and literary judgment in fourteenth-century French poetry.
  PQ193.E83 2014
  841'.109—dc23

2014008291

Cover design by Janna Thompson-Chordas
Text design by Juliet Williams
Type set in Adobe Garamond

♾ The paper used in this publication meets the minimum requirements of the American National Standard for Information Sciences—Permanence of Paper for Printed Library Materials. ANSI Z39.48–1992.

9 8 7 6 5 4 3 2 1

CONTENTS

Acknowledgments   vii

INTRODUCTION
Literature as Eschatological Scene   1

    I. *La scène judiciaire:* Big and Little Judges   1
    II. The Eschatological *Procès*   25
    III. Scope of the Book and Chapter Outline   28

CHAPTER 1
Representation in Heaven: The Thirteenth- and Fourteenth-Century *Rhetor Divinus*   34

    I. *Quid sum miser tunc dicturus?*   34
    II. From Legal Subject to Eschatological Subject   38
    III. Human Rights and the Devil's Rights: The Virgin's Divine Advocacy   44
    IV. Divine Rhetoric in Action: The *Puys*   57

CHAPTER 2
A Particular Judgment: The Case of Deguileville's *Pèlerinage de l'âme*   63

    I. Introduction   63
    II. *Des ouvrages quë il a fait:* The First Two *Pèlerinages*   70
    III. Preliminary Judgments   80
    IV. Satan v. Guillermus de Deguilevilla   88

CHAPTER 3
Post-Apocalyptic Judgment: Machaut's *Jugement dou roy de Navarre*   102

   I. Introduction   102
   II. The Judgment of the Living and the Dead   108
   III. Bonneurté's Case and Guillaume's *Livres*   121
   IV. Judgment in the Court of Charles de Navarre   131

CHAPTER 4
The Judgment of Jupiter: Froissart's *Joli buisson de Jonece*   144

   I. Introduction   144
   II. Froissart's Judgment of Paris, or a Portrait of the Artist as a Young Machaut   151
   III. God's Capital, Venus's Gifts, and the Judgment of the Patron   166
   IV. Recollection and Redemption in Froissart's "Lay de Nostre Dame"   177

CONCLUSION
In Lieu of a Last Judgment: Beyond the Fourteenth Century   189

Bibliography   209
Index   228

ACKNOWLEDGMENTS

This book is ultimately the product of a dissertation completed in the Department of French and Italian at Princeton University. It could not have been written without the support of numerous people. Chief among them is my reader Sarah Kay, whose piercing insight, selfless dedication and tireless good humor helped to keep me going through thick and thin. Simone Marchesi, who read early drafts of the project, also played a pivotal role in its evolution. I have also to acknowledge those who made it financially possible for me to conduct research, including the Department of French and Italian, the Center for the Study of Religion, and the Donald and Mary Hyde Fellowship at Princeton, the Cogut Center for the Humanities at Brown University, and the Andrew W. Mellon Foundation. In addition, I am grateful to the editorial staff at The Ohio State University Press for their very hard work. Last but not least, this project would not have been at all possible without the patient encouragement of my wife Samantha Mahar. To all those who have lent a hand, and to you, the reader, thank you.

INTRODUCTION

Literature as Eschatological Scene

I. *La scène judiciaire*: Big and Little Judges[1]

When Jean-Jacques Rousseau's *Confessions* appeared posthumously in 1782, the book met readers with an imagined scene of the author's judgment before God:

> Que la trompette du Jugement dernier sonne quand elle voudra; je viendrai ce livre à la main me présenter devant le souverain juge. Je dirai hautement: 'Voilà ce que j'ai fait, ce que j'ai pensé, ce que je fus. J'ai dit le bien et le mal avec la même franchise. Je n'ai rien tu de mauvais, rien ajouté de bon, et s'il m'est arrivé d'employer quelque ornement indifférent, ce n'a jamais été que pour remplir un vide occasionné par mon défaut de mémoire; j'ai pu supposer vrai ce que je savais avoir pu l'être, jamais ce que je savais être faux. Je me suis montré tel que je fus, méprisable et vil quand je l'ai été, bon, généreux, sublime, quand je l'ai été: j'ai dévoilé mon intérieur tel que tu l'as vu toi-même. Être éternel, rassemble autour de moi l'innombrable foule de mes semblables; qu'ils écoutent mes confessions, qu'ils gémissent de mes indignités, qu'ils rougissent de mes misères. Que chacun d'eux découvre

---

[1]. The section title is borrowed from Gisèle Mathieu-Castellani's *La scène judiciaire de l'autobiographie*. Paris: Presses Universitaires de France, 1996. Mathieu-Castellani's reading of Rousseau generally informs my own, and I first discuss her work in detail on page 3.

à son tour son cœur aux pieds de ton trône avec la même sincérité; et puis qu'un seul te dise, s'il l'ose: *Je fus meilleur que cet homme-là.*'²

Let the trumpet of the Last Judgment sound when it will; I shall arrive with this book in hand to present myself to the sovereign judge. I shall say loudly, 'Here is what I did, what I thought, what I was. I said the good and the bad with the same sincerity. I omitted nothing bad, added nothing good, and if it so happens that I employed some ornament or other, it was only to fill a gap caused by a lapse in memory; I supposed true what I knew could have been true, and never what I knew to be false. I showed myself such as I was, wretched and vile at times; good, generous, sublime at others. I revealed my interior just as you have seen it yourself. Eternal being, assemble around me the countless crowd of my peers; let them listen to my confessions, let them cry at my indignities, let them blush at my misfortunes. Let each of them uncover his heart at the foot of your throne with the same sincerity; and then, let just one of them say to you, if he dares, *I was better than that man.*'³

Rousseau's appeal to the Almighty reminds us that the *Confessions* were written partly as a response to the author's most pitiless *human* judge, Voltaire, who had anonymously published *Le sentiment des citoyens* in 1764.⁴ In this short pamphlet, Voltaire revealed that Rousseau had left all of his children at a foundling hospital and, speaking in the collective voice of the citizens of Geneva, denounced his writings as blasphemous and seditious to the state.

The heavenly court scene which begins the *Confessions* is thus also a *mise en scène* of literary controversy, of the way the author must face the judgments of readers and critics in an endless trial process. On the one hand, as we are asked to make the right decision about whether Rousseau lived a good life, we assume the place of the divine judge to whom the book is addressed. On the other hand, the author insists on the validity of his own judgment. Rousseau promises that the version of his life contained in the book is just as God has seen it ("tel que tu l'as vu toi-même"), yet he reserves the right to employ "ornements" whenever the narrative happens to be held up by a "défaut de mémoire."

Championing his own perspective and asking that readers judge him less like Voltaire and more like a merciful God, Rousseau depicts a trial

---

2. Jean-Jacques Rousseau, *Les confessions.* Ed. Bernard Gagnebin, Marcel Raymond. Paris: Gallimard, 1973. 33–34.
3. Unless otherwise noted, all translations in this book are my own.
4. Voltaire, *Œuvres complètes.* 52 vols. Paris: Garnier Frères, 1877–85. XXV: 309–14.

somewhere between heaven and earth, in the elusive jurisdiction of authorial legacy. To readers as yet unknown, the author demands that he be tried as a unique human being with all of his particularities. But he also demands that he be judged as an author, within parameters specific to the activity of literary production: it is his book that will represent him, in both the artistic and judicial senses.[5]

Rousseau's imagined Judgment Day was part of a much wider trend of literary self-representation. In her admirable study, *La scène judiciaire de l'autobiographie,* Gisèle Mathieu-Castellani has documented how authors like Augustine, Montaigne, Rousseau, and Genet deployed the trope of the writing subject on trial before the readership. As Mathieu-Castellani argues, the *scène judiciaire* represents the act of literary self-disclosure itself, and its reception by a literary public whose power to judge the author and his text always shares in something of the godly:

> Le souverain juge, le grand juge: l'entreprise de mise à nu sous le regard de l'Autre déclare ici sans détours et comme sans réticences sa visée: le tribunal imaginaire, présidé par Celui qui voit tout, jusques à nos plus secrètes ordures, autorise à la fois l'exaltation et la sourde angoisse. Encore reste-t-il en ce cas à régler la relation instable entre le grand Juge et les petits juges qui liront un texte écrit pour un autre qu'eux, et tout de même pour eux.[6]

> The sovereign judge, the big judge: the enterprise of laying oneself bare in the gaze of the other announces its objective here without equivocation or reserve: the imaginary tribunal, presided over by He who sees all, even our most shameful secrets, authorizes at once exaltation and deep anguish. Here we are still left with the problem of resolving the unstable relationship between the big Judge and the little judges who will read a text written for another than them, and yet also for them.

The "relation instable" that Mathieu-Castellani posits between God and readers—between the "grand juge" and the "petits juges"—suggests a means of imagining eschatological judgment that is particular to literary self-representation. The process of writing about oneself is directed toward an eventual judgment which, whether pronounced by God, the reader, or both at once, is anticipated only insofar as it is the judgment of the absolutely other and cannot properly be anticipated. Inasmuch as

---

5. For Mathieu-Castellani, the *scène judiciaire de l'autobiographie* is a "modèle omniprésent de représentation aux deux sens du terme" (*La scène judiciaire,* 36).

6. *Mathieu-Castellani, La scène judiciaire,* 39. Mathieu-Castellani speaks at greatest length of the relation between God and the reader in her fourth chapter, "Le regard du juge," 115–33.

this judgment is "l'entreprise de mise à nu sous le regard de l'Autre," the conditions for that *mise à nu* will be dependent upon the other's particular reading of the text, which lies beyond the subject's grasp. As it submits the text to the judgment of a potentially infinite number of readers, most of whom the author will never know, the literary tribunal opens onto an ever-changing future, with definitive meaning about the text, and about the subject who writes, always just out of reach. While readers' judgments are less immutable than the judgment of God, they may be no less exacting, for they constantly expose the text and its author to new opinions and perspectives.[7]

The ways in which authors of different periods have enacted such literary scenes of divine judgment has much to reveal about how these authors conceived of the reception of their work, their authority, and their relationship to audiences real and imagined. One period of literature which has been left mostly unexplored in this regard, even in Mathieu-Castellani's excellent book, is the Middle Ages.[8] Medieval Christianity placed an unprecedented emphasis on the direct individual experience of God's scrutiny, an emphasis readily appreciated in writings of all kinds from the period. I understand medieval "literature" to include all written texts, but with a particular conception of the literary as a function of the author's self-awareness as an artist recognizable to his public. In the later Middle Ages especially, literary self-consciousness was brought to a fine point, as poets displayed an intense focus on the reception of their work, and on their connections to audiences. As a result, later medieval literature is an excellent place to find scenes where the author performs his trial before the imperious readership. What makes *scènes judiciaires* from the period all the more remarkable is the extent to which their literary judgments are saturated with eschatological significance.

In the later Middle Ages, the omnipresence of eschatological representation gave authors occasion to reflect not only upon the fate of their bodies and souls, but also upon the value of their own literary production. Thirteenth- and fourteenth-century authors, much like Rousseau after them, used imagined representations of divine judgment to dramatize the

---

7. For Mathieu-Castellani, writing about oneself is "un procès interminable" (*La scène judiciaire*, 225).

8. One exception is Philippe Maupeu's account of the fourteenth-century poet Guillaume de Deguileville and his influence on later French poetry, *Pèlerins de vie humaine: autobiographie et allégorie narrative, de Guillaume de Deguileville à Octovien de Saint-Gelais*. Paris: Champion, 2009. In this very thorough study (24 n2, 257, 265), Maupeu briefly considers Mathieu-Castellani's "scène judiciaire" as a model of autobiographical representation in Deguileville. See also below, Chapter 2, 85.

unending evaluation and reinterpretation which their work would undergo in the hands of readers, and the way in which their own judgment would be subject to challenge by judges both *petits* and *grands*.

In this book, I consider four major examples of later medieval poets in France who used scenes of divine judgment in order to frame their own literary production and to explore problems inherent in submitting their work to a literary public. I deal in turn with thirteenth- and fourteenth-century rhetoricians and Marian devotional poets, with Guillaume de Deguileville's *Pèlerinage de l'âme* (c. 1356), with Guillaume de Machaut's *Jugement dou roy de Navarre* (c. 1349), and with Jean Froissart's *Joli buisson de Jonece* (1372–73).

My project concerns both the rhetorical and the ethical aspects of the trope of divine judgment as reader-reception. First, I outline the specificity of the eschatological judgment scene as a rhetorical device used to stage the relationship of author and reader in later medieval literature. Second, and at the same time, my effort is to show how this rhetorical device expresses ethical concerns specific to literature, and to the respective duties of author and audience. While later medieval authors used scenes of divine judgment to defend their work to the reader, or to guide the reader's understanding of the work, exposing themselves to the scrutiny of a divine audience was also a symbolic way for these poets to defer judgment to a higher interpretive power, and a greater authority. The conceit of a divine judgment on the author is an ethical gesture, in that it represents the responsibility of facing one's audience, the anxiety of responding to criticism about one's writing.

In this gesture, divine and earthly audiences cannot always be neatly disentangled; indeed, thirteenth- and fourteenth-century authors frequently suggested that there is a significant overlap between the judgment of the reader and the judgment of God. Through their interpretation of texts, readers were understood to participate in an ongoing process of ethical deliberation which could save or condemn the author. The judgments of readers—as fickle or shortsighted as they might be—would also have to be taken into account in one way or another, when the final trumpet blew. God's judgment was always taking place, made manifest in the encounter of the author with those who read his work.

But can the judgment of readers—or authors—ever be truly squared with the judgment of heaven? Medieval literature is, after all, full of meditations on the limits of human consciousness and its divorce from the divine mind. Most importantly, medieval discourse tends to place human judgment at a distance from divine judgment because of the problem of representation, the very nature of language: while human judgments are conducted through—and marred by—words, God's judgment will not be a matter of argumentation and verbal testimony, and will thus remain untainted by the imperfection of language.[9]

Yet later medieval depictions of divine judgment can hardly be considered monologic; instead, they possess the same will toward a divine-human judicial dialog first exemplified in the Judeo-Christian tradition by the Book of Job.[10] The period, rich in debate poetry, offers no scarcity of scenes in which human interlocutors and their saintly intercessors plead eloquently in the heavenly court. Reflecting the growth of legal studies,[11] thirteenth- and fourteenth-century texts imagine the trial proceedings of the Judgment with a complex deployment of the technical language and procedure of the courtroom—generally, the civil courtroom. As in the work of Marian devotional poets, discussed in Chapter 1, or in Guillaume de Deguileville's *Pèlerinage de l'âme,* discussed in Chapter 2, the heavenly court was frequently dramatized with the principal actors of the eschatological drama—Christ, Mary, Satan, and Mankind—cast in well-defined judicial roles: the judge, the advocate for the defense, the plaintiff, and the defendant.

Borrowing from the domain of human law to stage the operation of heavenly justice, later medieval poets confronted God's unchanging judgment with the innumerable legal uncertainties of the period, which has been described as an intense "conflict of jurisdictions," a turbulent mix of contradictory systems of deliberation.[12] Above all, the eschatological courtroom drama of the later Middle Ages ensured that language would per-

---

9. For example, see Aquinas, *Compendium theologiae.* Ed. Jean-Pierre Torrell. Paris: Cerf, 2007. 1.244. See also Aquinas, *ST Suppl.,* Q.88, arts. 2, 4 (In *Summa theologica.* Blackfriars edition. New York: McGraw-Hill, 1964–81).

10. On the importance of Job as a model for the literary judgment scene, see Mathieu-Castellani, *La scène judiciaire,* 9–11.

11. James A. Brundage considers that most of the elements necessary for the professionalization of the legal class had occurred by the end of the twelfth century (*The Medieval Origins of the Legal Profession: Canonists, Civilians, and Courts.* Chicago: University of Chicago Press, 2008. 217–18). See also Gillian-Rosemary Evans, *Law and Theology in the Middle Ages.* London: Routledge, 2002. 50. In Chapter 1, I provide a more detailed account of the impact which the rise in legal learning had on poetic subjectivity and its eschatological *mise en scène.*

12. The phrase is Esther Cohen's (*The Crossroads of Justice: Law and Culture in Late Medieval France.* New York: Brill, 1993. 17). The legal chaos of the period was one part of a more general "crisis of truth" often ascribed to the fourteenth century—a new set of anxieties regarding the nature of signs and their interpretation. See Laurence De Looze, *Pseudo-Autobiography in the Fourteenth Century: Juan Ruiz, Guillaume de Machaut, Jean Froissart, and Geoffrey Chaucer.* Gainesville: University Press of Florida, 1997. 8, 12; Rosemarie P. McGerr, *Chaucer's Open Books: Resistance to Closure in Medieval Discourse.* Gainesville: University Press of Florida, 1998; Richard Firth Green, *A Crisis of Truth: Literature and Law in Ricardian England.* Philadelphia: University of Pennsylvania Press, 1999.

sist in the scene of divine judgment, threatening claims to certainty by demanding that words be dealt with, just as they must be in earthly courts. In God's tribunal, the author's own particular use of language was put on trial, and the author claimed the right to use still more language to defend himself.

In later medieval representations of divine judgment, it is not only the legal side of earthly judgment that matters, but also judgment as a human faculty of mind employed to evaluate literature. In French, the word *jugement* has been in use at least since the thirteenth century to describe both an individual cognitive event—the formation of a personal opinion—and an official decision made by a judge.[13] In the later medieval period, *jugement* was often used to depict poets formulating opinions in their poetry, and readers making judgments in response. The ambiguity of the word also features in the eschatological scene of literature, where the audience's favorable reception of the author's poetry is sought at the same time as God's mercy. In the discursive play between the reader (*le petit juge*) and God (*le grand juge*)—the fourteenth-century author situated his anxiety about how the text would be received and interpreted.

In later medieval literature, the mix of divine and earthly jurisprudences to construct a literary courtroom does not entail a reading of the scene of judgment as satirical, parodic or carnivalesque. Indeed, none of the poets I consider in this book deviate appreciably from Christian teachings on divine judgment. Rather, each contributes to a tradition of eschatological representation that is specific to literature itself, to the ethical concerns unique to reading and writing. These authors all expand the boundaries of eschatological judgment to encompass the activity, and the relationships, most central to their lives as artists. Accordingly, they force the issue of how language and literary production can properly be evaluated by a judgment that is supposed to transcend the contingency of words and subjective opinions.

Similarly, although all of the scenes of judgment examined in this study are staged through some kind of allegorical imagery, they are precisely not allegorical when it comes to the relationship of divine and human judgment. That is, the author's judgment by a divine audience does not simply stand in for his more human tribulations; nor, conversely, do the author's attempts at self-defense in the earthly court of opinion refer to an always

---

13. For instance, Brunetto Latini in his *Livres dou tresor* (c. 1268) uses *jugement* in the sense of an opinion (*Li livres dou tresor*. Ed. Francis J. Carmody. Berkeley: University of California Press, 1948. 1.1.4). This would tend to contradict Laurence De Looze's claim that *jugement* was primarily used in the juridical sense until about the 1360s (*Pseudo-Autobiography*, 16).

higher arena of moral deliberation. The medieval *scène judiciaire* is not allegorical in this way because it does not contain such a distinct separation of terms, which would allow us to speak of substitution or metaphor. Instead, as I maintain, later medieval authors intentionally conflated traditional aspects of divine and readerly judgment in order to figure the irreducible coexistence and interdependence of "big" and "little" judges in the ethical process of writing and reception.

Human and divine judgment seem to have enjoyed an especially close proximity in literature during the thirteenth and fourteenth centuries, when a number of convergent factors help to explain the importance of the trope of the eschatological scene as a commentary on the nature of authorship. On the most basic level, the trope represents the coming together of two great ethical discourses in later medieval Christian culture. The first is the general and pervasive call for individuals to accuse themselves in the here-and-now as before God, conducting a constant and rigorous judgment of the self to parallel his judgment. The second ethical discourse concerns literature and the specific responsibilities assigned to both author and reader.

As a phenomenon tied to the rise of lay confessional practice in the West, the increasingly personal nature of eschatological discourse in medieval Europe has been much discussed by historians.[14] In undertaking penance, individuals were taught to conduct a trial process just as rigorous as the Judgment they faced from on high. Through the self-judgment of the conscience, which would also be the principal witness for or against each sinner at the Judgment itself, human beings were provided a glimpse of the ongoing scrutiny of heaven and thus given the ability to avoid eternal condemnation.[15] A detailed meditation on individual judgment became a necessary part of devotion, and an integral component of what Michel Foucault and others have seen as the fashioning of the modern subject through the interiorized discourse of the confessional.[16]

---

14. See, for example, Philippe Ariès, *L'homme devant la mort*. Paris: Seuil, 1977; Jean Delumeau, *La peur en Occident: XIVe–XVIIIe siècles: une cité assiégée*. Paris: Fayard, 1978; Jacques Le Goff, *La naissance du Purgatoire*. Paris: Gallimard, 1981; Delumeau, *Le péché et la peur: la culpabilisation en Occident, XIIIe–XVIIIe siècles*. Paris: Fayard, 1983; Jacques Le Goff and René Remond, *Histoire de la France religieuse*. 4 vols. Paris: Seuil, 1988–92. II: 152–57.

15. See, for instance, Bernard de Clairvaux, *De conversione ad clericos*. Ed. J. Leclercq, H. Rochais, Ch. H. Talbot. Introduction, translation, and notes by Françoise Callerot, Jürgen Miethke, Christiane Jaquinod. Paris: Cerf, 2000. Bks. 2–3; Hughes de Saint-Victor, *De sacramentis christiane fidei*. Ed. Rainer Berndt. Aschendorff, Germany: Monasterii Westfalorum, 2008. 2.17.21.

16. See, especially, Marie-Dominique Chenu, *L'éveil de la conscience dans la civilisation médiévale*. Montréal: Institut d'Études Médiévales, 1969; Michel Foucault, *Histoire de la sexualité*. 3 vols. Paris: Gallimard, 1976. I. For an account of how confessional practice in the earlier Middle Ages

In doctrine, later medieval Christianity attached new importance to the particular judgment of the soul.¹⁷ Instead of looking toward the collective Last Judgment to follow the Resurrection at the end of time, individual penitents were urged to think upon their own ending day, the time directly after their death when they and they alone would be called to account. To house those masses who had been neither damned nor admitted immediate entrance to heaven at the particular judgment, purgatory gained new theological and popular prominence and put a new focus on the "citizen" of the otherworld¹⁸—a distinct, individual soul whose personal struggle back to God would become the centerpiece of Dante's *Commedia*.

What has often been overlooked by scholars is how the more general variety of personal eschatological discourse helped to shape literary treatments of the ethical problems specific to reading and writing. This second important set of ethical discourses—about literature—was fashioned as authors of the period puzzled over and actively debated issues like the following: In order to be good, must poetry have an evangelical or devotional purpose? Who is responsible for determining the meaning of a text—the author or his readers? What is the proper use of allegory, and of personal narrative? When is the author obligated to retract and rewrite what he has already written, and how should he go about doing so? All of these questions, and many more, were posed repeatedly by authors throughout the Middle Ages, answered in a variety of different ways, and—with varying degrees of pious expression—treated as a subset of problems within the wider field of Christian ethics.

In the later Middle Ages, such problems of literary responsibility assumed new importance. European poets writing in the vernacular began to depict themselves as authors, which is to say, among other things, that they claimed responsibility for their own bodies of work as unified literary

---

contributed to an individuation of the subject, see Colin Morris, *The Discovery of the Individual, 1050–1200*. 2nd ed. Toronto: University of Toronto Press, 1987.

17. The general and particular judgments were usually thought of as complementary rather than contradictory, but the issue is complex. In some regards, it is true that, as Paul S. Fiddes notes, the particular judgment had come to dominate in the popular imagination by the end of the twelfth century (*The Promised End: Eschatology in Theology and Literature*. Oxford: Blackwell, 2000. 87). For the most nuanced and thorough account of the relationship of the two judgments, see Jérôme Baschet, "Jugement de l'âme, Jugement dernier: contradiction, compléméntarité, chevauchement?" *Revue Mabillon* 6 (1995): 159–203. Belief in the particular judgment was strengthened especially by the papal bull *Benedictus deus* (1336), issued by Benedict XII, in which it is affirmed that the divine vision is accessible to the just and purified dead before the General Resurrection.

18. The formulation ("citoyen de l'au-delà") is Jacques Le Goff's (*La naissance du Purgatoire*, 316). On the growing individual importance of death in medieval European culture, see Ariès, *L'homme devant la mort*.

objects. Later medieval poets asserted authorial status by having their texts compiled together under their own names as "complete-works" codices, by identifying their first-person narrators with themselves, and by sprinkling their narratives with myriad autobiographical details and allusions.

It was in the fourteenth and early fifteenth centuries especially that the great superstars of vernacular poetry exploded onto the European literary scene:[19] Dante, Petrarch and Boccaccio in Italy; Machaut, Froissart, Eustache Deschamps, Christine de Pizan, and Alain Chartier in France; Chaucer, Gower, and Lydgate in England. All of these poets may be defined as *authors* not only for their influence and their level of productivity, but also for the extent to which their work calls attention to its own status as a unique and proprietary literary object. By involving their first-person narrators directly in the plots of their own narratives, these poets created distinct personae for themselves. Through clever word play and more explicit means, they made frequent reference within the same narratives to their earlier works and to the development of their careers. Composing poetry itself became a narrative thread to rival the knightly *aventure* of the courtly romance. While the self-presentation of the vernacular writer began to take shape in the *poésie personnelle* of the thirteenth century, it developed into a true poetics of *auctoritas* in the fourteenth, in which the first-person subject assumed a much greater referential weight.[20] Although it can strike the modern reader as glibly self-promotional—and rightly so—such self-representation did not come entirely lightly. In an age when deep suspicion was attached to worldly literature and to writing about oneself, vernacular authors felt the need to use their self-representation in order to consider the validity of their projects and the nature of their responsibility to readers.

---

19. On the idea of medieval authorship in general, see Alastair Minnis, *Medieval Theory of Authorship: Scholastic Literary Attitudes in the Later Middle Ages*. London: Scolar Press, 1984. On the vernacular tradition, see especially 160–217. Daniel Hobbins's work on Jean Gerson also contains important insights into the nature of "authorship" and "literature" in a later medieval context (*Authorship and Publicity Before Print: Jean Gerson and the Transformation of Late Medieval Learning*. Philadelphia: University of Pennsylvania Press, 2009).

20. This important feature of late medieval vernacular narrative is largely quantitative, that is to say a function of the frequency and scope of self-referential discourse; it does not represent an absolute departure from earlier modes of literary subjectivity. Sarah Kay, for one, has argued persuasively for a more robust conception of authorial subjectivity in the lyric poetry of the twelfth-century troubadours (*Subjectivity in Troubadour Poetry*. Cambridge: Cambridge University Press, 1990). Likewise, the apologetic mode of self-presentation is not unique to the post-Lateran world, only more well-developed and more directly connected to eschatological judgment. On apologetic self-presentation in the earlier Middle Ages, see Jean-Charles Payen, *Le motif du repentir dans la littérature française médiévale, des origines à 1230*. Geneva: Droz, 1967. See especially Chapter 4, "La poésie personnelle de la conversion," 579–90.

In the thirteenth and fourteenth centuries, the concept of "pseudo-autobiography," such as it has been elaborated by the critics G. B. Gybbon-Monypenny and Laurence De Looze, is of particular importance.[21] As De Looze, especially, employs the term, pseudo-autobiography is a deeply self-referential mode of literary production, a style of narration in which the narrator is "a poet first" and in which the literary text "is not only about its own creation, but is also the creator's story of himself as creator in the act of creating."[22] According to De Looze, the pseudo-autobiographical mode of the later Middle Ages also depends upon a rhetorical posture in which the author presents his own life as being virtually indistinguishable from the material existence of the book.[23]

That which is "pseudo" about a pseudo-autobiographical text, then, has less to do with the relative truth value of self-representation than the degree to which the self-representational text acknowledges its status as an art object, and by the same token, invites readers to judge its veracity and meaning for themselves. The pseudo-autobiographical submits to judgment only, or at least primarily, the literary aspect of an individual existence, "the creator's story of himself as creator in the act of creating."[24] The process of writing thus assumes a greater ethical and existential weight, whereas the autobiographical mode claims to distribute its judgments more evenly across all aspects of a life.

Pseudo-self-presentation does not defer ethical responsibility away from its subject but places it more squarely onto the shoulders of a literary persona who must answer, above all, for what he has written. The author who portrays himself first and foremost as an author may not have to defend himself, as Rousseau does in his *Confessions*, for abandoning his children or being too eager to receive corporal punishment. What we as readers of later medieval narrative poetry are asked to judge instead are mostly the sins of a literary life: the inevitable errors or offensive material perceived in writing the poet has already produced, instances of bad judgment in matters of opinion, or simply of bad poetry.[25]

---

21. G. B. Gybbon-Monypenny, "Guillaume de Machaut's Erotic 'Autobiography': Precedents for the Form of the *Voir dit*," in *Studies in Medieval Literature and Languages in Memory of Frederick Whitehead*. Ed. W. Rothwell, et al. Manchester: Manchester University Press, 1973. 133–52; Laurence De Looze, *Pseudo-Autobiography*.

22. De Looze, *Pseudo-Autobiography*, 7.

23. Ibid., 8.

24. Ibid., 7.

25. Although "bad poetry" does not come up as an issue in this study, for an example, I would direct readers' attention to the Tale of Sir Thopas, told by Chaucer's own character in the *Canterbury Tales*, and to the highly unfavorable judgment it receives from the Host (*Canterbury Tales*. Ed. A. C. Cawley. New York: Alfred A. Knopf, 1992. 382–90).

Featuring prominently among the pseudo-autobiographical strategies of later medieval poets was the self-referential vision of divine judgment. Inserting himself into the heavenly court as a defendant, the poet both called attention to his status as an individual and created a powerful vehicle through which to navigate the most vexing ethical problems of poetry. Thus did the impulse to judge the self at all times—the famous eschatological anxiety of later medieval Europe—transpose questions about reading and writing into the imagined scene of Judgment.

In his groundbreaking study, *La subjectivité littéraire*, Michel Zink has argued that the thirteenth-century emphasis on personal conscience-examination is one of the major factors behind the rise to prominence in that century of French *trouvères* like Guillaume le Clerc, Rutebeuf and the Artois poets Adam de la Halle, Jean Bodel, and Baude Fastoul.[26] Zink notes that the literary personae these poets created for themselves were largely constructed through rhetorical gestures of confession and repentance, including meditations on the immanence of the speaker's Judgment.[27]

As the *je* became more important, so too did the use of penitential introspection, and thus of eschatological anticipation, as devices of self-representational framing. Following Michel Zink's lead, a number of critics have noted that fourteenth-century poets also frequently drew upon the language of sacramental confession in order to emphasize their roles as individual authors. In Jerry Root's repurposing of a phrase from Chaucer, confessional practice provided fourteenth-century authors with a "space to speke,"[28] that is, a way to situate their own presence in the text and to ground their authority in a discourse of truth-production. Through the familiar script of self-accusation was born an apologetic poetry in the fullest sense, which not only obliged its subject to indict himself, but also permitted his self-defense.

In my view, critics like Zink and Root have been extremely astute in documenting the use of confessional discourse as a privileged mode of authorial self-presentation in the later Middle Ages. Yet while this approach

---

26. Michel Zink, *La subjectivité littéraire: autour du siècle de saint Louis*. Paris: Presses Universitaires de France, 1985.

27. Ibid., 59–60, 199–200.

28. See Jerry Root, *'Space to Speke': The Confessional Subject in Medieval Literature*. New York: Peter Lang, 1997; Matthew Senior, *In the Grip of Minos: Confessional Discourse in Dante, Corneille, and Racine*. Columbus: The Ohio State University Press, 1994. See also Mary Flowers Braswell, *The Medieval Sinner: Characterization and Confession in the Literature of the English Middle Ages*. East Brunswick, NJ: Associated University Presses, 1983. For another study of the late medieval tradition in England, with particular reference to Lollardy, see Katherine C Little, *Confession and Resistance: Defining the Self in Late Medieval England*. Notre Dame, IN: University of Notre Dame Press, 2006.

has contributed vitally to our understanding of medieval subjectivity as a rhetorical construct, it has given relatively little attention to the ways in which the confessional act points to an ethical relationship outside of itself, in the impossible or miraculous dialog of the human subject with God. Confessional discourse does not fully account for the cataclysmic event of divine judgment always taking place, which Matthew Senior defines as the psychoanalytical "other scene" underlying confessional practice: "The confessant addresses his or her *pater peccavi* not just to the priest but most essentially to a transferential father in heaven. The other scene of Christian confession is the spiritual world of heaven and hell, time and eternity, sin and forgiveness."[29]

In later medieval texts, as in Rousseau's *Confessions*, eschatological judgment is also the ultimate other scene of literary self-disclosure, where the reader is offered something like a God's eye view of the writing subject and comes to act as a divine proxy, weighing the subject's worth *in loco Dei*. The ethical relationship of medieval authors and readers was thus transferential in much the same way as the structured dialog of priest and penitent. If he did not quite become God himself, the reader nevertheless entered into immediate proximity with the divine as he passed judgment on the work of literature and on the author.

How exactly are we to define the nature of the responsibilities assumed by medieval poets and audiences, responsibilities which were so readily translated into eschatological terms? The ethical *relationship* of author and reader becomes less theoretical and more concrete as soon as we remember that medieval authors were often much more intimately acquainted with their readers (or with a larger percentage of them) than is the case in modern print culture. As poets felt the need to respond to specific, critical readers, they introduced these *petits juges* into the lofty space of the cosmic courtroom.

In this regard, one factor most sets the thirteenth—and above all the fourteenth century—apart from the rest of medieval vernacular poetry. I refer to the new prominence assumed by powerful lay patrons. It was especially in their close dealings with patrons that poets entered into an immediate and quite literal relationship with their audiences, a relationship that often included a sustained critical dialog and sometimes extended to actual literary collaboration. The patron's court was a singular site of ethical conversation. In it, the poet's duties to his benefactors, and his ability to please, instruct, or otherwise serve them through writing, became primary

---

29. Senior, *In the Grip of Minos*, 10.

concerns. These concerns could be and were repositioned within the frame of eschatological judgment as the patron assumed the role of *petit juge*. I discuss this phenomenon notably in the cases of Guillaume de Machaut (Chapter 3) and Jean Froissart (Chapter 4).

This is not to say that the later medieval poet's conception of an ethical relationship to readers existed only within the exclusive luxury of the court. In later medieval France especially, the growing importance of patronage was seconded by the rapid development of the commercial book trade, catering to an expanding population of monied laypersons literate in the vernacular. Still, the scale of production remained modest enough that it is generally more accurate to speak of a small coterie readership, whose specific tastes, prejudices, and objections would have preoccupied the poet above all. The consolidation of a literary "public," however private it may have been in reality, brought its own ethical problems into the mix. For instance, as Guillaume de Deguileville must consider (Chapter 2), is a broad lay audience prepared to grasp complex religious allegory, and is the poet to blame if they should misunderstand it to the detriment of their souls?

Moreover, how should poets "package" and "sell" their work to such a public? The phenomenon of "complete-works" codices, to which I have already alluded, was largely an invention of the late thirteenth century and became especially widespread in the fourteenth century. Compilers of manuscripts, who in the fourteenth century were sometimes the authors themselves, began to organize vernacular poetry anthologies by author rather than by an overriding thematic or generic logic. Manuscripts containing the work of poets like Adam de la Halle, Rutebeuf, Watriquet de Couvin, Guillaume de Machaut, Guillaume de Deguileville, and Jean Froissart are some of the most important examples of single-author, complete-works books in the thirteenth and fourteenth centuries.[30]

Increasingly, the compiled corpus was used to give fantastic shape to its creator, by establishing a consistent first-person narrative persona which readers were encouraged to identify with the author, and by allowing them to follow the exploits of this self-representational narrator from poem to poem. Because poetic self-image went hand in hand with poetic authority, the establishment of a unified self-portrait through such compilations is also an important reason for my focus on the fourteenth century. An essential element in De Looze's definition of fourteenth-century pseudo-

---

30. On the development of single-author anthologies, see Sylvia Huot, *From Song to Book: The Poetics of Writing in Old French Lyric and Lyrical Narrative Poetry*. Ithaca, NY: Cornell University Press, 1987. 211–41.

autobiography, the uncanny overlap of the book and the individual human being who produced it has a special importance in the heavenly court, where it also confuses the boundaries between the author's text and the figurative record books of his soul and conscience.

These otherworldly texts were ubiquitous symbols in the later medieval eschatological tradition. They include first of all the Liber Vitae (Book of Life), which is referenced in Exodus (32:32–33), Isaiah (4:3), Daniel (7:10, 11:1), Revelation (5:1, 20:13–15), and in the Psalms (69:28, 139:16). In these sources the Liber appears as the great volume of revealed truth to be opened at the Last Judgment, the register of those who are to be saved, and from which the names of the wicked are to be "blotted out" (Ps. 69:28) at the end of time.[31]

A record of the spiritual collectivity, the Book of Life also had an individualized counterpart in medieval depictions of the Book of Conscience, a more personal set of accounts to be squared with the great Book.[32] In his *De conversione*, for instance, Bernard de Clairvaux compares the desire for repentance to an impossible attempt to expunge what has been written in the memory, just as a scribe might try to scratch out a mistake from an inferior grade of parchment:

> Quomodo enim a memoria mea excidet vita mea? Membrana vilis et tenuis atramentum forte ebibit; qua deinceps arte delebitur? Non enim superficie tenus tinxit; sed prorsus totam intinxit. Frustra conarer eradere: ante scinditur charta quam caracteres miseri deleantur.[33]

---

31. This conception of an eschatological master-text was consciously imitated in medieval practices of book production. For instance, beginning in the Carolingian period, the beneficiaries of the communal prayers of monasteries were inscribed in tomes entitled *libri vitae* and meant to correspond more or less exactly to the great Book of Judgment. See Le Goff, *Histoire de la France religieuse*, I: 212; Michel Lauwers, *La mémoire des ancêtres, le souci des morts: morts, rites et société au Moyen Âge: diocèse de Liège, XI–XIIIe siècles*. Paris: Beauchesne, 1997. 108–10. In post-conquest England, the Domesday Boke employed the same concept as an organizational principle for the comprehensive accounting of political subjects and their property. See Penn Szittya, "Domesday Bokes: The Apocalypse in Medieval English Literary Culture," in *The Apocalypse in the Middle Ages*. Ed. Richard K. Emmerson, Bernard McGinn. Ithaca, NY: Cornell University Press, 1992. 374–97. Richard K. Emmerson argues that the Apocalypse "may have influenced the medieval conception of 'the book' as a symbol of political, religious, and natural totality and unity" (in Emmerson's introduction to part 3 of *The Apocalypse in the Middle Ages*, 331).

32. Another important medieval source for the Book of Conscience was the *De miseria conditionis humane* of Lothario dei Segni (the future Pope Innocent III), notably 3.19. See Robert E. Lewis's edition and translation (Athens, GA: University of Georgia Press, 1978). On the idea of the Book of Conscience, see also Chenu, *Éveil*, 42–43; Mary Carruthers, *The Book of Memory: A Study of Memory in Medieval Culture*. 2nd ed. Cambridge: Cambridge University Press, 2008. 11.

33. Bernard de Clairvaux, *De conversione* 28.5–9.

For how might my life slip from my memory? The cheap, thin parchment totally absorbs the black ink; by what art may it thenceforth be deleted? For it does not only saturate the surface, but soaks through and stains the whole. In vain would I attempt to scratch it out: the document itself would be torn apart before the wretched letters were removed.

Following such personal conceptions of an eschatological text, the book as a symbol of universal totality and unity, a register of the Church or humanity, began to cede in the later medieval period to the idea that its composition and revision was more of an individual undertaking. As Phillipe Ariès argues, this shift would have been particularly palpable in the thirteenth century with the advent of obligatory lay confession. At this point, the *Liber vitae* was no longer only a *"census* de l'Église universelle," but "le registre où sont inscrits les affaires des hommes,"[34] an individualized accounting of souls. Even the illiterate were taught to symbolically draw up their book of accounts, as in the late fifteenth-century English morality play *Everyman*, where the title character frets about not having enough time to finish his "writing" before Death takes him.[35] In a less figurative sense, the last will and testament became a mandatory form of self-accounting at all levels of society in the later Middle Ages.[36]

The allegorical textuality of the Book of Conscience and Book of Life was also transferred to very concrete later medieval literary practices, including common conventions of authorial self-representation. The ambiguity between the author's book and the "text" of his soul was more than allegorical, as the book purported to be a relatively transparent reflection on the poet's life and career, providing the most direct evidence for or against the author. Acts of composition and compilation thus assumed serious consequences in this world and the next, making the author's lifelong work of assembling his book a fundamentally ethical enterprise.

In a number of ways, the thirteenth century anticipates the fourteenth-century tendency to conflate the author's corpus with the textual evidence

---

34. Ariès, *L'homme devant la mort*, 106–7.

35. "And also my writinge is full unredy," *Everyman*, v. 187. I cite the edition by John Conley, et al., *A Mirror of Everyman's Salvation: A Prose Translation of the Original* Everyman *Accompanied by* Elckerlijc *and the English* Everyman *Along with Notes*. Amsterdam: Rodopi, 1985. The English poem was based on the Dutch *Elckerlijc*.

36. See Jacques Chiffoleau, *La comptabilité de l'au-delà: les hommes, la mort et la religion dans la région d'Avignon à la fin du Moyen Âge (vers 1320–vers 1480)*. Rome: École Française de Rome, 1980. See also Le Goff, *La naissance du Purgatoire*, 315; Ariès, *L'homme devant la mort*, 188–97; Gérard Gros, "'Que feray je se n'ay argent?': une étude sur le Testament de Jean Régnier (*Fortunes et adversitez*, vers 3577–3774)," in *Fin des temps et temps de la fin dans l'univers médiéval*. Aix: Centre Universitaire d'Études et de Recherches Médiévales d'Aix, 1993. 211–24.

entered for and against the sinner before the divine tribunal. A good example of this trend is the *Besant de Dieu* (c. 1226–27), written by the Norman *trouvère* Guillaume le Clerc. *Besant* takes its title from the parable of the Talents (Old French *besants*, Byzantine coins) in the Gospel of Matthew (25:14–30).[37] In the parable, the return of Christ to judge the living and the dead is compared to the homecoming of a master who has left various sums of money with his servants, commanding them to invest and make a profit for him. Upon the master's return, two of the servants are rewarded for having increased their master's capital, while the third is reproached for having hidden the money away and letting it lie dormant.[38]

The parable's message is that all people should wisely invest the spiritual capital with which they have been entrusted, using their specific talents to serve God. Guillaume opens his *Besant* by confessing that he has thus far squandered the parabolic *besant* given to him, and will be called to account for it at the Judgment if he does not change his ways:

Car ge ne sai quant il vendra	For I know not when he will come
Ne a quele hore il me somondra	nor at what hour he will summon me
Que devant lui viengne a conter	to come before him and account,
Savoir com bien purra durer	to know how long will last
Le guäin que jeo li ai fait	the profit that I made for him on earth,
Et que de son avoir ai trait.	that I derived from his capital.
(vv. 5–10)	

The personal eschatological economy of sin and merit taught in Matthew inspires fear in Guillaume because of his writing, which he says, has until now been of no spiritual profit to readers:

Guillaume, uns clers qui fu normanz,	Guillaume, a clerk who was Norman,
Qui versefia en romanz,	who versified in *romans*,
Fablels e contes soleit dire.	and used to compose *fabliaux* and *contes*.
En fole e en vaine matire	In foolish and vain subject matter
Peccha sovent: Deus li pardont!	he sinned often: God forgive him!
(vv. 79–83)	

---

37. The Parable of the Minas (Lk. 19:12–27) is similar but, unlike the parable in Matthew, it does not specify that each servant receives a different amount from the master. It is thus less well-suited homiletically for stressing each individual's particular talent and responsibility.

38. I cite the edition of Guillaume le Clerc's *Besant de Dieu* by Pierre Ruelle. Brussels: Éditions de L'Université de Bruxelles, 1973. Zink (*La subjectivité*, 119–22) discusses *Besant* in terms of the discourse of conscience-examination.

Guillaume's authorship of such "fole et vaine matire" as his "romanz, fablels e contes" endangers his soul; not only that, but the poet's own corpus will provide the most damning evidence against him, as it reflects a net loss of divine investment.

Yet Guillaume hopes that his spiritual accounts may be put in order with his new poem, *Besant* itself, which is an unsparing denunciation of sin and contemporary social ills. This more pious work promises to put both the corpus and the divine balance sheet back in order by winning souls for God. In the composition of *Besant*, the gift of poetry—the Master's capital—will finally be employed to a good end, by calling readers to repentance and by expressing the author's own contrition:

Se Deus m'a doné de bien dire	If God has given me the grace
La grace, ne me dei targier,	of eloquence, I cannot hesitate
Mes son besant creistre e chargier.	but must make his *besant* multiply and yield fruit.
(vv. 2780–82)	

The conflation of literary works with otherworldly documents can also be seen in *Le miracle de Théophile* (early 1260s),[39] a mystery play by the prolific *trouvère* Rutebeuf (c. 1230–c. 1285). Theophile is an impoverished clerk who, desperate to improve his situation, sells his soul to the Devil. Tired of being cheated by unscrupulous soul-sellers, Satan reasonably demands that Theophile provide him with a written contract, which the clerk duly draws up himself, in his own blood. Later, Theophile repents and pleads for the assistance of the Virgin Mary, who snatches the contract back and saves his soul. The contract is not to be destroyed, however; rather, its meaning is transformed as it is read aloud by Theophile's bishop to his congregation as a cautionary exemplum intended to warn them (or rather us) to avoid similar deals with the Devil.

Theophile is of particular interest because the play coincides with the period in Rutebeuf's career usually understood as his "conversion." *Theophile* probably followed closely on the heels of two other pieces—*La repentance Rutebeuf* and *La vie de sainte Marie L'Egyptienne*—in which the poet more directly addresses his past, his supposed sins, and his prior body of work.[40] In his *Repentance*, Rutebeuf contemplates his Judgment with fear and trembling. This leads him to dramatically renounce the kind of

---

39. See the edition in Rutebeuf, *Œuvres complètes*. Ed. Michel Zink. Paris: Livre de Poche, 2001. 531–83.

40. Rutebeuf, *La repentance Rutebeuf*, in Zink, ed., *Œuvres complètes*, 331–39; *La vie de sainte Marie L'Egyptienne*, in Ibid., 453–529.

unwholesome poetry he had practiced for so long, and which he had written for worldly profit as, he says, a good clerk should not do (vv. 19–21). Rutebeuf laments, moreover, that he had used his poetic talents to please some people by attacking others, whose reputation he had thereby tarnished (vv. 37–42).

It is not entirely clear to which part of his previous writings Rutebeuf is referring; these verses may allude to the conflict of seculars and mendicants at the University of Paris, in which Rutebeuf had positioned himself against the friars, or to the *jongleur*'s and *trouvère*'s common tactic of insulting those absent from court behind their backs.[41] Whatever the case, if the Virgin does not take his side, and if he is not forgiven his vain and injurious past writing, the poet fears that this will mean a "mau marchié" ("bad deal," v. 12) for him on the Judgment Day (vv. 70–72), just as the clerk Theophile's bargain with the Devil brings short-term profit but long-term perdition. As is also the case for Theophile, Rutebeuf is well aware that his own offending documents cannot simply be destroyed or removed entirely from circulation. They must instead be supplemented and reinterpreted—recast, like Theophile's contract in blood, as examples to warn readers and aspiring poets alike against making the same mistakes.

In a very different way, Jean de Meun (c. 1240–c. 1305) also played on the equivalence between the author's work and his eschatological record.[42] Jean, one of the most influential French poets of the thirteenth century, owes his lasting importance to a continuation (c. 1270) he appended to another's text—Guillaume de Lorris's *Roman de la Rose* (c. 1230). While Guillaume's *Rose* begins as a lover's allegorical quest to obtain the object of his desire—a rose at the center of a walled pleasure garden—Jean greatly amplifies his source, transforming it into a satirical and burlesque encyclopedia of classical mythology, learned discourse, and contemporary sociosexual mores.

Nearing the end of Jean's *Rose*, the priest Genius delivers a sermon to the God of Love and his barons.[43] Genius is, among other things, a mitred bishop towering above his congregation from the pulpit and a walking, talking erection. In this capacity, he preaches passionately to his flock on the urgent necessity for sexual reproduction. Painting a hell-fire portrait of man's end, Genius warns that those who do not propagate the species will

---

41. On these points, see Ibid., 334–35 n1.
42. I cite the edition of the *Roman de la Rose* by Armand Strubel. Paris: Librairie Générale Française, 1992.
43. The figure of Genius is adapted from Alain de Lille's twelfth-century *De planctu Naturae*.

be tormented without cease, while those who do will be rewarded with a spot in paradise, which Genius describes as the magnificent *parc de l'agneau* (lamb's garden).[44]

Genius's sermon identifies procreative sex with writing: penises and vaginas become the *greffes* and *tables* (styli and tablets, v. 19549) with which Nature endowed human beings, and which must be employed productively. As Genius exhorts his listeners to perform their "œvres naturels" (v. 19693) diligently, then, he also highlights the writer's own works, demanded of him by God and Nature. The emphasis on writing is particularly striking given that Jean de Meun spends a good portion of Genius's section of the continuation comparing his own *Rose* to that of his predecessor, Guillaume de Lorris. While the *parc de l'agneau* is paradise, it is also a rewritten version of the *vergier de deduit* (garden of delight) in which Guillaume de Lorris had set the action of his original *Rose*, a re-troping of the classic *hortus conclusus*, or walled garden. The Lamb's garden, affirms Genius, is superior to Guillaume's orchard in that the latter is liable to lead the reader to hell with its seductive lies and vanities, its "truffles et fanffelues" (v. 20356). Jean's own *parc*, on the other hand, is the true and eternal paradise.

Genius's judgment against Guillaume's *vergier* is difficult to take seriously because this bawdy bishop claims that sex, chief among earthly delights, will lead to eternal life—just as long as it results in offspring. What seems more important than the sermon's dubious message, however, is the virtue which Genius's version of the *hortus conclusus* ascribes to itself as the emblem of a rewritten text. The *parc de l'agneau* is perhaps not an improvement on Guillaume's *vergier* in Christian moral terms, but because it represents Jean de Meun's new reworking and continuation of the original *Rose*, it is by definition artistically superior. In this, the exhortation to "multiply"[45] one's lineage by using one's stylus or tablet correctly, under forfeit of eternal death, is also the writer's particular labor (*œuvre naturelle*) of continually producing more and more by reworking earlier material. As an implicit apology for Jean's vast, sexually charged addition to Guillaume's *Rose*, Genius's sermon on the Judgment Day insists that reproduction is both the natural state of the poet and his God-given duty. A counterpoint to Guillaume le Clerc's Matthew-inspired mission to "multiply" what God has given to him by writing the *Besant de Dieu*, Genius

---

44. The lamb refers to the Lamb of God (*agnus Dei*), but also surely to those who sit on Christ's right hand, separated from the goats and saved by the blood of the Lamb. On the eschatological nature of Genius's address, see Alastair Minnis, *Magister Amoris: The* Roman de la Rose *and Vernacular Hermeneutics*. Oxford: Oxford University Press, 2001. 110–11.

45. See, for example, *Rose*, v. 19390: "Que leur lignage mouteplient."

has another kind of eternal life in view: that of fame, which depends both on the author's productive use of his stylus and on the continued reproduction of his words by copyists and other poets.

At or near the end of his life, in the late thirteenth or early fourteenth century, Jean de Meun apparently felt obliged to make a final addition to his own corpus, in the form of a last, poetic *Testament*.[46] Jean begins this much more sober work of Christian didacticism by repenting for the vain writings of his youth, including, by logical inference, the perennially controversial *Rose*. Jean concludes his last poem by praying that his name be entered "ou saint livre de vie," tying his poetic self-inventory directly to the great Book of Judgment.[47]

Like Rutebeuf, Guillaume le Clerc, and other thirteenth-century poets in northern France, Jean de Meun was an important innovator of literary voice, who put a marked emphasis on his own authorial presence in the text. And like Rutebeuf and Guillaume le Clerc, Jean de Meun adapted traditional aspects of eschatological representation in order to suggest strong comparisons between the evidentiary texts of divine judgment and his own body of work. Although none of these thirteenth-century poets are likely to have been anthologized in a single-author compilation during their lifetimes,[48] all of them nonetheless display an acute awareness of the permanence of earlier texts, both in their circulation among readers, and in the eschatological record.

Sylvia Huot, who is largely responsible for documenting the history of single-author compilations in the period, has also begun to uncover

---

46. See the edition by Silvia Buzzetti Gallarati, *Le testament Maistre Jehan de Meun: un caso letterario*. Alessandria: Edizioni dell'Orso, 1989. Huot (*From Song to Book*, 233) notes that the *Testament* is often appended to Jean's *Rose* and could be seen as a further continuation of it with the same first-person narrative voice.

47. v. 2120. As I discuss in Chapter 3 (139–40), Machaut makes a very similar gesture in the "Lay de plour" which follows and concludes his *Jugement dou roy de Navarre*. Responding to and adding further color to the *Rose*'s eschatological poetics, Jean Gerson would stage a rather entertaining trial in absentia of Jean de Meun long after his death, as part of the early fifteenth-century Querelle de la Rose, in which Gerson took sides with Christine de Pizan against the text. In his 1402 *Traictié d'une vision faite contre Le Ronmant de la rose,* Gerson states the case against Jean (thinly disguised as "Fol Amoureux") through the mouth of the personification Theological Eloquence, who concludes that the author would probably already have endured painful punishments for his work in purgatory (in *Debating the Roman de la Rose: A Critical Anthology*. Ed. Christine McWebb. Introduction and Latin translations by Earl Jeffrey Richards. New York: Routledge, 2007. 272–305). Gerson's opponent in the *Rose* debate, Pierre Col, replies by reasserting Jean de Meun's eternal place in the Lamb's Garden (In McWebb, ed., *Debating the Roman de la Rose*, 342).

48. Rutebeuf provides an early example of single-author compilation, but there is no evidence that complete-works compilations of his poetry were produced during his lifetime. See Huot, *From Song to Book*, 213–19. Parts of Jean de Meun's work were found together, but never in anything like a compilation anthology. See Huot, Ibid., 233–34.

to what extent these compilations reflect contemporary conceptions of the Book of Conscience.[49] As Huot argues, later medieval sources like the *Ovide moralisé* depicted the composition of the Book of Conscience as a process of careful, penitential revision carried out by the individual, in which the personal text must be collated against the perfect exemplar that is at once the Book of Christ's life and the Book of Life.[50] Beginning in the early fourteenth century, authors like Watriquet de Couvin would have adopted this conception of a personalized eschatological document in order to construct an implied image of spiritual wholeness in manuscripts containing their complete works. The book's boundedness reflected the discrete spiritual identity of its maker, whose artistic career could be traced as a meta-narrative linking otherwise disconnected episodes and otherwise unrelated genres.[51]

The single-author compilation made poetic fame, poetic self-fashioning, and poetic authority possible like never before in the vernacular. It allowed readers to identify the author as the sum of his work, and to identify him with his narrator, whose transformations and peregrinations from poem to poem invited rich comparisons with those of the historical poet. But the complete-works style of compilation also raised the stakes of the author's responsibility. Once in circulation, the Book reflected the permanence of the eschatological record, ensuring that no word the author wrote and no part of his career could be disowned or hidden from the reader's omniscient view. With the single-author compilation, Saint Bernard's metaphor of ink that cannot be scratched out of parchment took on a new and more literal significance, as authors were increasingly forced to confront the particularly indelible nature of written sins, which would be forever attached to the book bearing their name and made in their image. As I

---

49. Huot, "The Writer's Mirror: Watriquet de Couvin and the Development of the Author-Centered Book," in *Across Boundaries: The Book in Culture and Commerce*. Ed. Bill Bell, Philip Bennett, Jonquil Bevan. New Castle, DE: Oak Knoll, 2000. 29–46. Dante's *Commedia* also suggests such an eschatological text; see Robert Hollander "Dante's Book of the Dead: A Note on *Inferno* XXIX, 57." *Studi Danteschi* 54 (1982): 31–51. Sachi Shimomura has described the figurative, penitential process of textual revision, or *correctio,* in some detail as it occurs in sermons and romances of the period—see *Odd Bodies and Visible Ends in Medieval Literature*. New York: Palgrave MacMillan, 2006. 39–84. In her study of the poets of Arras, Carol Symes discusses how the correct recording of stories by the *jongleurs* reflects the divine balancing of accounts (*A Common Stage: Theater and Public Life in Medieval Arras*. Ithaca, NY: Cornell University Press, 2007. 98–99).

50. Huot ("The Writer's Mirror," 29, 31) specifically cites the *Ovide moralisé* V, vv. 2394–424, and another fourteenth-century text, the unedited *Livre de vie et aiguillon de vrai amour,* as sources for the individual composition of the Book of Conscience.

51. The emphasis on formal diversity is especially the case in Guillaume de Machaut's manuscripts. See Huot, *From Song to Book,* 232–38, 242–301. See also below, Chapter 3, 123–25.

show, Guillaume de Deguileville, Guillaume de Machaut, and Jean Froissart all used traditional aspects of eschatological representation in order to depict this problematic aspect of the corpus, and to narrate the difficulties inherent in making revisions and additions to their bodies of work over time.

Along with changing compilation practices, changing views of the poetic vocation itself influenced later medieval conceptions of poetic authority. In particular, our understanding of the ethical, eschatological space of medieval literature depends upon the growing later medieval consensus that writing vernacular poetry constituted a distinct kind of labor. Confessional practice in the thirteenth and fourteenth centuries was regularly shaped by a systematic exposition of the sins most common to specific vocations and classes,[52] and scenes of divine judgment from the period often portray the professions and estates—such as jurists, clerics, secular and religious potentates, and merchants—standing before the throne of God.[53] Because later medieval authors increasingly referred to composing poetry as a calling among others, they also depicted their judgment in heaven based on certain parameters of professional identity. The pseudo-autobiographical poet began to imagine himself tried as an author, among other types of people, their characteristic sins, and their specific social duties.

Weighing the deontological criteria of the poetic trade—or what Jean Froissart called "li mestiers gens" ("the noble profession")[54]—can thus tell us a lot about how its members imagined their judgment. Poetry, of course, was not a true profession in the later medieval period (if ever it has been one). Even the best-supported of court poets exercised a myriad of other tasks in the dispatch of their duties, and theorists of poetry drew upon numerous other vocations in order to find suitable analogies for their own. One has only to consider Chaucer's eclectic resumé, and his shadowy existence as he rides among a kaleidoscope of other social types in *The Canterbury Tales*. But it is precisely the poet's ill-defined identity as factotum which complicates his Judgment in the period: vernacular, Christian poetic authority was itself at stake in the eschatological trial scene, which attempted to define and codify the poet's work in both technical and ethical terms.

Of the various vocational models available to later medieval vernacular poets and likely to weigh on their Judgment, the most obvious by far is

---

52. See, for example, Chenu, *Éveil,* 45; Jacques Le Goff, *La civilisation de l'Occident médiéval.* Paris: Arthaud, 1964. 328–29; Le Goff, *Histoire de la France religieuse,* II: 103–4.

53. On the judgment of lawyers, see below, Chapter 1, 35.

54. Jean Froissart, *Le joli buisson de Jonece.* Ed. Anthime Fourrier. Geneva: Droz, 1975. v. 160.

pastoral care, or evangelical responsibility. Its use as a justification for writing well predates the later Middle Ages or the advent of vernacular poetry, and throughout the medieval period the poet's most common training was indeed clerical. In Guillaume le Clerc's *Besant de Dieu*, Rutebeuf's "conversion" poetry, and Jean de Meun's *Testament* (if not also his *Rose*), the poet's perceived duty to save souls through writing was already clearly expressed.

But the pastoral role was far from the only vocational standard which vernacular poets used to judge themselves and their work, or to justify their authority. In the thirteenth and fourteenth centuries, poets were nearly as likely to have received civil legal training as a clerical formation (and despite a ban on clerics practicing civil law, the two were far from mutually exclusive[55]). Moreover, classical legal rhetoric was a crucial influence on the development of vernacular poetics.[56] Thus, the advocate's profession also left its mark in important ways on the later medieval subject of poetry, and on authors' articulation of the vocation and its duties.

Given the already close connections between poetry and law, it was seemingly only a matter of time before the lawyer-poet would insert himself into the eschatological trial scene. In France especially, this occurred as poets cast themselves as members of a privileged class of person, the *rhetor divinus*, or divine rhetorician. Bringing together the abilities of the legal orator and the poet with the power of prayer, the *rhetor divinus* could use vernacular verse compositions in order to successfully petition heaven. Or so claimed, at least, a set of popular devotional practices and rhetorical principles which were developed beginning especially in the thirteenth century. Devotional poets of the 1200s and early 1300s saw themselves as active participants in the intercessory process of divine judgment, able to advocate on behalf of themselves and others for saintly assistance and divine mercy. For later fourteenth-century poets as for their predecessors, the *rhetor divinus* provided a model of the poet's spiritual and rhetorical authority—and a model of the poet's dual audience, composed at once of divine and human judges. But later fourteenth-century poets added a new dimension to this devotional trope by using it to defend and justify their bodies of work before heavenly and earthly audiences alike.

As fourteenth-century authors frequently remind us, medieval readers had their own unique responsibilities to fulfill. Whether envisioned primarily as souls to be saved or paying clients and consumers, readers were charged with correctly interpreting texts so as to seize their deepest

---

55. See Brundage, *Medieval Origins*, 134, 231, 469.
56. I discuss this strand of influence in more detail in Chapter 1, 38–43.

moral meanings and to avoid being led astray by appearances. The overlap of divine and readerly judgment did not mean that readers, like God, were immune from error, for medieval reading was a difficult process. It entailed a constant duty—with inevitable spiritual risk—to make interpretive choices, exercising sound judgment and a purified will at each turn of the page, and a well-trained memory to sort the good from the bad.[57] The reader's deontological imperative is often cited by medieval authors as they mount their eschatological self-defense, as a way of displacing responsibility for a text's perceived faults from its creator to its interpreters. As judges, medieval audiences were entrusted not only with making the right decisions about textual meaning, but also with fairly judging the author, his intentions, and his larger body of work. Failure to do so could result in damnation for the reader, just as much as for the poet.

The ethical space explored by this study cannot be defined with exact precision, because it belongs to what is, in the later Middle Ages, a new court of inquiry opened to deal with new and difficult problems posed by vernacular literary production and reception. There are no immutable laws to be delineated here, no unswerving code for ethical reading and writing, only a vast, anxious, and inconclusive dialog that finds its supreme expression—but no final verdict—in the eschatological *scène judiciaire*.

II. The Eschatological *Procès*

It may seem paradoxical that the inherently open-ended judgments of literature should have assumed a close and at times indistinguishable association with the highest and most authoritative courtroom of all. Yet medieval conceptions of divine judgment demand a rather different conception of the "eschatological" than is often understood in today's language. While divine judgment became ever more personalized in medieval discourse, its timeframe also became more immediate. The perception of medieval Europe as a hotbed of apocalypticism is certainly warranted: for many, the End of the World did always seem to be just on the horizon. But later medieval Christianity in particular also tended to emphasize the Judgment as an incessant trial process, in which the most mundane individual actions were constantly subject to the divine gaze. To borrow the same terms which Frank Kermode used to describe early Christianity, the later medieval expe-

---

57. On the ethics of reading, see especially Carruthers, *The Book of Memory*; John Dagenais, *The Ethics of Reading in Manuscript Culture: Glossing the Libro de buen amor.* Princeton: Princeton University Press, 1994.

rience of divine judgment was not so much imminent as immanent.[58] The eventual Judgment, after all, would be only the final reading of a verdict and sentence. Life was the trial.

Emblematically, by the beginning of the twelfth century the dominant source for eschatological representation was no longer the Book of Revelation. The surreal enigmas of John's vision on Patmos had yielded to the simple parables of the Gospel of Matthew, emphasizing personal responsibility and a present-time Kingdom-at-Hand.[59] When depicted in medieval texts, God's judgments of the saved and damned are usually drawn from Matthew 25:41–43, in which Christ speaks in the name of the least of his brethren to separate the just from the wicked.[60] Through the commandment to feed the poor and visit the prisoner, medieval audiences were reminded that God's judgment is always present in everyday human interactions, and that the time of judgment is always *now*.

As the poets in this study suggest, eschatological judgment also inheres in the present-time work of literary production; even through the most erratic or contradictory judgments of readers, God is trying the poet. In all of their capacity for change, audience opinion and taste impose ethical as well as aesthetic obligations on the artist. These are responsibilities in the truest sense, in that they enjoin the author to respond constantly to criticism, summoning him to a trial process that never provides the finality of the Last Judgment but always falls under the jurisdiction of the divine. By much the same logic through which Christ was expected to pronounce judgment in the name of the poor and the prisoner, the author became responsible to the reader—the exemplary Other—as before God. Or, to return to Mathieu-Castellani's characterization of the eschatological scene, God is represented as the *tiers* (third-party) abiding in the judgment of the reader: "Entre moi qui me confesse et toi lecteur qui entends mes confessions, Dieu, témoin, auditeur, spectateur, est le tiers toujours présent, dont la voix est requise." ("Between myself, who confesses, and you the reader who hears my confessions, God, witness, listener, spectator, is the third party always present, whose voice is required.")[61] Our customary understanding of the eschatological as pertaining to the chronologically "Last" Things should thus be tempered somewhat by a definition which takes

---

58. Frank Kermode, *The Sense of an Ending: Studies in the Theory of Fiction*. Rev. ed. Oxford: Oxford University Press, 2000. 46–47.

59. See Émile Mâle, *L'art religieux du XIIIe siècle en France*. 7th ed. Paris: Armand Colin, 1931. 369–93; Ariès, *L'homme devant la mort*, 105; Le Goff, *La naissance du Purgatoire*, 313–14.

60. On these verses as the sentences to be pronounced by Christ, see Peter Lombard, *Magistri Petri Lombardi Parisiensis episcopi Sententiae in IV libris distinctae*. 2 vols. 3rd ed. Grottaferrata, Editiones Collegii S. Bonaventurae ad Claras Aquas, 1971–81. 4.47.1, 4.47.4.

61. Mathieu-Castellani, *La scène judiciaire*, 60–61.

into account the ongoing, everyday quality of divine judgment in medieval thought and literature.

One such redefinition may be found in the work of twentieth-century philosopher Emmanuel Levinas, who saw the eschatological not in terms of a Last Judgment, but rather as the continual ethical encounter between human beings. For Levinas, the judgment of God can only take place through the judgment of the flesh-and-blood human other, just as in the medieval mindset, God is constantly scrutinizing us through the eyes of the poor and the prisoner. The eschatological trial is not, for Levinas, an *arrêt* (verdict, sentence, stopping-point), but a *procès* (trial, process) without end, in which the subject finds himself responsible to an infinitude of others. Levinas's divine judgment is, moreover, a *procès* which depends directly on its open-endedness, and most especially on the instability of language, which alone promises justice as it bridges the space between subject and other. The infinite trial scene described by Levinas is not, for its insistence on flux, a picture of divine indulgence or moral relativism; on the contrary, this is a fearful Judgment indeed. Answering to it constitutes an ethical labor whose duties, like those of writing, are never to be fully discharged. Indeed, they can only increase the harder one works to respond to the accusing other—or the more new writing one produces.

As Levinas explains, it is only in the space between the subject and the accusatory other that God's judgment can operate, because it is only in this space that the *tiers* (third party) can emerge. Although Mathieu-Castellani does not refer directly to Levinas in her own account of the *tiers*, the resemblance is strong. For Levinas as for Mathieu-Castellani, the divine third party represents at once the presence of God and the presence of all others whose judgment must be taken into account. My relationship with the singular other (the reader) is inevitably complicated as this particular being reminds me that I am also being judged by an infinity of other beings, whose claims against me will necessarily enter into conflict with each other. Doing my duty to one, I become guilty before many. This impasse guarantees that the eschatological trial, and the work of writing, will have no end.

A difficult *procès*, certainly, but the very process which breathes life into the subject in the first place. For Levinas, the subject simply does not exist prior to the other's judgment. The eschatological moment—the subject's devastating awareness of his ongoing judgment—is as creative as it is deliberative; it does not just evaluate my pre-existing moral worth, but "confirms"[62] my existence as a first-person consciousness, even as each new

---

62. Emmanuel Levinas, *Totalité et infini: essai sur l'extériorité*. The Hague: Martinus Nijhoff, 1971. Repr. Paris: Kluwer Academic, 2008. 276.

judgment simultaneously destabilizes my identity. As Levinas has it, playing on Latin grammar, I must be "accusative" before I can be "nominative."[63] In a similar way, the eschatological scene of medieval literature seems to have been a necessary rite of passage for the authorial subject, who never stops becoming himself as his corpus is exposed to the critical gaze of a multitude of readers, those whose work it is to accurately reconstruct and evaluate the author based on his book. Long dead, the medieval poet faces an ever-expanding public which today only continues to grow, and which only continues to find new grounds for critical inquiry—if not accusation.

In the conclusion to this book, I return in greater detail to Levinas's model of eschatological judgment, and throughout, I adopt Levinas's French term *procès* to refer to the particular conjunction of the poet's endless labor with the "other scene" of a continual, eschatological trial process. This is not to suggest any exact correspondences between medieval representations of judgment and the thought of Levinas.[64] Instead, via such a non-medieval philosophical paradigm, I wish to evoke the commonality of medieval and post-modern depictions of the subject as a being created first and foremost in the other's judgment. In both instances, ethics—predicated on the self's relationship to the other—come before ontological being, predicated on the self's relationship to the self. In their respectively ante-Cartesian and anti-Cartesian historical contexts, later medieval poets and post-war philosophers like Levinas put the subject on trial in more ways than one: questioning or rejecting its primacy, they also described the emergence of the subject as a constant process of accusation and response, and a process which could bring the defendant into dialog with the divine through his most everyday negotiations of ethical problems.

III. Scope of the Book and Chapter Outline

I have chosen to focus primarily on fourteenth-century authors because of the new and powerful ways in which poets of that century grappled with the ethical dilemmas of writing and reading vernacular poetry, and with the problematic status of authority itself. I have chosen, more particularly, to focus on French authors of the fourteenth century, as they represent

---

63. Emmanuel Levinas, *Autrement qu'être ou au-delà de l'essence*. The Hague: Martinus Nijhoff, 1978. Repr. Paris: Kluwer Academic, 1991. 26.

64. Some interesting work has been done on Levinas and medieval literature, notably by the editors and contributors of *Levinas and Medieval Literature: The 'Difficult Reading' of English and Rabbinic Texts*. Ed. Ann W. Astell, J. A. Jackson. Pittsburgh: Duquesne University Press, 2009.

a relatively limited corpus, whose treatment of judgment is nevertheless indicative of trends in European literature as a whole. Dante, whom I discuss briefly in Chapter 1, also conflated divine and readerly judgment, often in strikingly similar ways to the French poets.[65] Petrarch, whom I do not discuss here at any length, played frequently on the overlap between the Audience and the Almighty, while also cultivating an aesthetic of shifting judgments.[66] Chaucer's *Canterbury Tales*, which I will likewise not attempt to integrate into this study, repeatedly invite comparisons between human judgment of the tales and divine judgment of their tellers—most especially the author himself.[67] But Machaut, Froissart (in his poetic works, at least), and especially Deguileville, have been much less studied than either Chaucer or the major Italian poets, including in their use of judgment and eschatological motifs. Thus, by exploring the changing dimensions of the eschatological scene of literature in fourteenth-century France, I also hope to offer the reader some new perspectives on the development of vernacular poetry and poetic self-representation in that time and place.

Because the focus of this book is on poetic self-representation, it is largely concerned with the loosely defined French narrative genre known as the *dit*. Usually in octosyllabic rhyming couplets and recounted from a first-person perspective, the *dit* is, simply put, the most personal and most pseudo-autobiographically charged of all fourteenth-century forms.[68] I do not mean to suggest that other genres of later medieval poetry do not allow for poetic self-reflection, or eschatological meditation. But it is consistently to the *dit* that fourteenth-century French authors turned when they wanted to show themselves at work, staging acts of writing and interactions with readers as central plot points. It is thus also in the *dit* that later medieval expressions of eschatological anxiety intersect most abundantly with personal narratives concerning the construction and compilation of an *œuvre*, and concerning the defense of literary authority.

---

65. See below, Chapter 1, 40–42.
66. See, however, below in Chapter 4, 183. *Rime sparse*, also known as the *Canzoniere*, or *Rerum vulgarium fragmenta*, provides especially good examples of these aspects of Petrarch. See especially *canzone* 360. I cite Gianfranco Contini's edition of *Petrarch's Songbook: Rerum Vulgarium Fragmenta*. Binghamton, NY: Medieval and Renaissance Texts and Studies 15, 1995.
67. Likewise, Chaucer's prologue to *The Legend of Good Women* is an excellent example of the English poet's mixing of divine and literary judgment. See below, Chapter 3, n3.
68. For discussion of the *dit* as a genre and how it relates to the later medieval poetics of self and compilation, see Huot, *From Song to Book*, 212–13; Jacqueline Cerquiglini, "Le Clerc et l'écriture: le *Voir dit* de Guillaume de Machaut et la définition du dit," in *Literatur in der Gesellschaft des Spätmittelalters*. Ed. Hans Ulrich Gumbrecht, with Ursula Link-Heer and Peter M. Spangenberg. Grundriss der romanischen Literatur des Mittelalters, Begleitreihe, vol. 1. Heidelberg: Carl Winter, 1980. 151–68.

In order to understand fourteenth-century French authors' specific narrative deployments of divine judgment scenes within the *dit* form, however, it is first necessary to explore in greater detail some of the larger historical and cultural trends, and some of the other genres, which influenced these poets. Chapter 1 encompasses thirteenth- as well as fourteenth-century texts and takes in a relatively broad European context, by tracing some of the most important rhetorical models that poets adopted and reworked in order to represent themselves speaking in their own defense before God. This chapter concerns above all the question of defining the poetic vocation—that is, how vernacular authors in the thirteenth and early fourteenth centuries began to represent themselves as members of an exceptional class of society. In the tradition of Marian devotional verse, especially as it developed in France, poets rallied around the image of the *rhetor divinus*, who possessed the unique ability to move God with prayer—even prayers made by laypersons, in the vernacular, and in verse forms not traditionally used in the liturgy. The *rhetor divinus*, in turn, was largely modelled on the popular veneration of the Virgin Mary as a legal advocate for sinners, whose passionate defense speeches to the heavenly court inspired poets to aim for a similarly effective divine rhetoric. In order to show the importance of the *rhetor divinus* model in the development of the eschatological subject, I pay particular attention here to dramatic and dialogic representations of the Virgin's advocacy, as well as to the tradition of poetic confraternities which emerged first in northern France for the purpose of promoting Marian devotional composition.

As I discuss in Chapter 2, the models of textuality and legal subjectivity found in the French Marian devotional tradition greatly influenced the poetry of the Cistercian monk Guillaume de Deguileville, who cast himself as the accused party in the heavenly court in order to establish a first-person defense of his writing. Deguileville's 1356 *Pèlerinage de l'âme* (*Pilgrimage of the Soul*) begins with an incomparable eschatological scene, as the author's narrator and literary persona "Guillermus de Deguilevilla" faces a lawsuit brought by Satan, who claims his soul in punishment for Guillermus's many sins. Guillermus, however, proves capable of defending himself, and manages to win his case against the Devil by imitating the rhetorical talents of the lawyerly Virgin Mary. As I show, Deguileville used his narrator's trial to represent his very own battles against critical readers unhappy with the alleged failings of his first major poem, *Le Pèlerinage de vie humaine* (c. 1330–31). Through his unique courtroom scene, the poet made a dramatic, if coded, response to audience accusations. *Pèlerinage de l'âme* is a rich example of how fourteenth-century authors built on preexisting representational models to figure the subject in judgment. Within the devotional tradition, it represents a distinct change in emphasis from the allegorical Book of the Conscience—traditionally used by Satan as evidence against sinners—and toward the more personalized, literal book that is the author's compiled corpus. With Deguileville, we have one of the earliest and most readily discernible examples of the poet who, like Rousseau some four centuries later, holds his life's work conspicuously in hand as he appears in self-defense before his creator.

In some contrast to Deguileville stands the matter of Chapter 3, Guillaume de Machaut's *Jugement dou roy de Behaingne* (mid-1330s) and its sequel, the *Jugement dou roy de Navarre* (c. 1349–50). Written in a playful, courtly mode, these two poems may not be especially pious, but they are nonetheless eschatological. For like Guillaume de Deguileville, Guillaume de Machaut also used a scene of divine judgment to revisit an earlier poem, the *Jugement dou roy de Behaingne*, with a piece composed near the mid-century, the *Jugement dou roy de Navarre*. At the beginning of *Navarre,* in the midst of the terrible plague year 1349, Machaut's narrator Guillaume contemplates the impending Judgment Day and considers how he himself will have to stand before the throne of God to answer for his sins. Machaut's narrator is, at least temporarily, spared this final reckoning and given a new chance at life. Yet he will not escape the severe judgment of the reader, who symbolically replaces the divine judge. Summoning Machaut's narrator, whom she calls "Guillaume," a certain mysterious Dame Bonneurté (Lady Happiness) accuses him of having slandered women in his *Jugement dou roy de Behaingne*. Bonneurté, who is partly identifiable with Machaut's patroness Bonne de Luxembourg, brings Guillaume to the court of another of the poet's patrons, Charles de Navarre, who is asked to determine whether Machaut's previous judgment about women was defamatory. In an absurd trial, Guillaume loses to his critic Bonneurté, but is then "sentenced" by Charles to write more poetry, effectively receiving a new commission. *Navarre* is one of Machaut's funniest poems, and yet beneath its self-conscious irony lies an admission that there is something of the divine in readers—and especially in patrons—which calls the writer to ethical responsibility for what he has written, and which must be taken seriously. In this chapter, I first examine how the Last Judgment scene of the text's prologue is used to set up—and thus ultimately frustrate—reader expectations for definitive judgment. I then argue that such ideals of definitive judgment are replaced with a different kind of eschatological representation, a *procès* in which the poet is called to account by the reader, who constantly provokes additions to the author's corpus by taking issue with earlier writing.

If Deguileville and Machaut can be seen as two extremes on a spectrum of devotional and courtly registers, Machaut's immediate poetic heir Jean Froissart falls somewhere between the two. Froissart's own narrative of changing judgments, the diptych *Espinette amoureuse* (c. 1369) and *Joli buisson de Jonece* (c. 1373), is the focal point of Chapter 4. Just like Deguileville and Machaut, Froissart had occasion to return to an earlier work of poetry in a later text, revisiting his courtly love romp *L'espinette amoureuse* in *Le joli buisson de Jonece*, at the time of the author's ordination as a priest. Through the transports of memory and dreaming, Froissart's narrator relives the earlier time of *Espinette*; he comes face to face with his younger self and with that self's bad judgments as a love poet and a lover. At the end of *Buisson* occurs arguably the most dramatic moment of the poem, in a sustained meditation on the Last Judgment. Here the narrator's awareness of his Judgment leads him to condemn his youthful obsession with frivolous love poetry and to announce his new allegiance to God, the Church and the Virgin Mary. My approach is to examine how Froissart employed this judgment scene to stage his own revision of judgments about the ethical value of love poetry, and about the poet's ethical duty to his readers. Developing issues of patronage already raised by his master Machaut, Froissart also introduces economic problems into the divine court of literary ethics. As I show, the eschatological judgment from which Froissart's narrator reviews his literary career is anything but simple, because while it appears on the surface merely to reject erotic poetry, the looming specter of Judgment also demands that the poet reconcile himself to patrons, who have already paid generously for such writing. Seemingly, if Froissart does not renounce his literary past, he will be damned for persisting in his error and allowing readers to persist in theirs; but if he does renounce his literary past, he sins no less against audience members, by leaving them with a spiritually defective product in exchange for their money. Froissart's solution to this quandary is to transform his Last Judgment meditation into a hermeneutic frame in which he can suggest a new interpretation of his erotic work—namely, spiritual allegory. By adding such an after-the-fact gloss, Froissart is able to justify the continued existence of otherwise questionable material in his corpus, while allowing readers to enjoy, in good conscience, the early Froissart along with the late.

In the concluding chapter, "In Lieu of a Last Judgment," I begin by considering the posterity of the eschatological scene of literature as it was reshaped in the fifteenth century and in the early modern period more generally. 1400 makes a powerfully symbolic, albeit approximate *terminus ad quem* for this study because the turn of the century was the most intense period of creativity for Christine de Pizan (1364–c. 1430), whose treatment of judgment sets her distinctly apart from her forerunners. As Douglas Kelly has already shown in detail,[69] Christine represents a new insistence on the autonomy of the individual author's judgments, and on the power of subjective opinion. Looking briefly at Christine and other examples from the fifteenth century and early modern period, my concern is to show how this novel and broadly "humanistic" treatment of judgment represents a movement away from the eschatological anxiety displayed especially by fourteenth-century authors, whose judgment must always defer to readers and to prior authority.

In some ways, the eschatological scene of fourteenth-century poetry suggests stronger similarities with postmodern conceptions of subjectivity, like Levinas's, than with early modern ones like Christine de Pizan's. In the fourteenth century, the authorial subject was still described largely by reference to a dense network of others calling the subject to responsibility, rather than by reference to a primary and autonomous self. In the twentieth century, numerous thinkers developed a vast critique of the Cartesian model of subjectivity, redefining the subject as an effect of the other, rather than a self-sufficient cause. Nowhere is this critique more powerfully—or, I think, more medievally—expressed than in the Levinasian idea that divine judgment is the act of subject creation through a process of accusation and response originating in exteriority and in the ethical relationship. In the final section of this book, therefore, I return in greatest detail to Levinas's definition of the eschatological encounter as it suggests rich analogies with the Judgment scenes of later medieval poetry, and with that poetry's narratives of literary self-formation.

---

69. Douglas Kelly, *Christine de Pizan's Changing Opinion: A Quest for Certainty in the Midst of Chaos.* Cambridge: D. S. Brewer, 2007.

CHAPTER 1

Representation in Heaven
The Thirteenth- and Fourteenth-Century *Rhetor Divinus*

I. *Quid sum miser tunc dicturus?*

The thirteenth-century *Dies irae* hymn, one of the period's most well-known liturgical meditations on the Judgment Day, asks this haunting question: "Quid sum miser tunc dicturus?"[1] What am *I*, the wretched one, to say *then*, at the Resurrection and Judgment? What words can possibly excuse or explain my sins? Although posed from a rather different perspective, these are also the principle questions of this chapter, which considers some of the concrete rhetorical strategies used in later medieval texts to imagine the human subject appearing on trial before God.

In its context, of course, the big question of the *Dies irae* hymn—"What am I to say?"—is not intended to elicit a positive response, but rather to strike fear into the hearts of listeners, inspiring sincere repentance. In doctrinal terms, the correct answer to the question of what I can say is precisely nothing—the human subject can never justify himself in the eyes of his creator, and language in particular has no power to alter the course of divine decisions, to enable self-defense.[2] Not only is pleading impossible

---

1. *Missale romanum*, missae defunctorum 117, v. 19. The hymn is traditionally attributed to Tommaso da Celano.
2. See, for instance, Aquinas, *Compendium theologiae* 1.244; *ST Suppl.*, Q.88, arts. 2, 4; Hughes de Saint Victor, *De sacramentis* 2.17.8.

at the Judgment, but the time for asking forgiveness has forever passed. At that terrible hour, only the conscience can speak, and it does so only to provide a transparent record of good and evil deeds.

The question which comes next in the *Dies irae* is also worth considering:

> Quem patronum rogaturus,   What advocate shall I seek,
> Cum vix iustus sit securus?[3]   When even the just man is hardly safe?

Here again, the anticipated answer is wholly negative: no one else will be able to speak for me at the Judgment; there will be no possibility to hire a clever lawyer, unlike in earthly courts. For moralists writing against perceived abuses of language, lawyers have seemingly always occupied a special place in hell, but the vilification of the profession is all the more evident in literature of the later Middle Ages, when the expanding civil law appeared to threaten the traditional jurisdiction of episcopal courts and canon lawyers. In the thirteenth and fourteenth centuries, advocates were liable to find themselves compared to prostitutes for representing guilty or dishonest clients[4] and were regularly singled out in confessional manuals and sermons for the category of sins of the tongue (*peccata linguae*), due to their supposed mendacity, their abuses of rhetoric, and their tendency to argue frivolous distinctions.[5] Moralizing portrayals of divine judgment in the period vividly reflect this anti-legalistic attitude, and the inability of lawyers to speak in their own defense before God is a common topos of eschatological representation. For example, the influential early thirteenth-century collections of *exempla* for preaching by Étienne de Bourbon and Jacques de Vitry both contain anecdotes of jurists who attempt unsuccessfully to delay their death and judgment by petitioning for an appeal.[6]

---

3. vv. 20–21.
4. See Brundage, *Medieval Origins*, 480.
5. See Ibid., 483–84. Brundage cites in particular Robert of Flamborough's *Summa de poenitentia* (c. 1208–15), Cardinal Hostiensis's *Summa* (c. 1253), and the *Summa confessorum* of John of Fribourg (d. 1313).
6. Jacques de Vitry, *The Exempla or Illustrative Stories from the Sermons of Jacques de Vitry* (*Exempla ex sermonibus vulgaribus*). Ed. Thomas Frederick Crane. London: D. Nutt, 1890. 40.15.; Étienne de Bourbon, *Anecdotes historiques, légendes et apologues tirés du recueil inédit d'Étienne de Bourbon*. Ed. Richard Albert Lecoy de la Marche. Paris: Renouard, 1877. 439. See also the early fourteenth-century *Mystère du Jour du Jugement*, in which a lawyer disputes his Judgment in vain (*Le mystère du Jour du Jugement: texte original du XIVe siècle*. Ed. Jean-Pierre Perrot, Jean-Jacques Nonot. Besançon: Éditions Comp'Act, 2000). An anonymous thirteenth-century *fabliau*, *Le vilain qui conquist paradis par plait*, tells the story of a peasant soul who manages to talk his way into

How is it, then, that some thirteenth- and fourteenth-century poets had the gall to represent themselves speaking where they should not, defending themselves personally before the throne of Judgment with a full measure of rhetorical finesse and even legalese? For instance, the thirteenth-century Occitan troubadour Peire Cardenal (c. 1205–72) conceived his famous "sirventes novel" (1230s) as a prepared legal argument for the Judgment Day.[7] In the poem, Peire announces his plans to read the *sirventes,* or invective composition, to the heavenly court when he is summoned to answer for his sins there:

Un sirventes novel vueill comensar,	I wish to begin a new *sirventes*
Que retrairai al jor del jutjamén	that I will recite on the Judgment Day
A sel que-m fes e-m formet de nién.	to the one who made me from nothing.
S'el me cuja de ren arazonar	If he thinks he has a case against me,
E s'el me vol metre en la diablía	and if he wants to consign me to the devils,
Ieu li dirai: 'Seinher, merce, non sía!	I'll say, 'Lord, no way!
Qu'el mal segle tormentiei totz mos ans.	For I have already suffered all my days in this wicked world.
E guardas mi, si-us plats, dels tormentans.'	So spare me, please, from those tormentors.'
Tota sa cort farai meravillar	I will astonish all in his court
Cant auziran lo mieu plaideiamen;	when they hear my plea.
Qu'eu dic qu'el fa ves los sieus faillimen	I say that he does toward his own an injustice
Si los cuja delir ni enfernar.	if he plans to destroy them or send them to hell.

(vv. 1–12)

---

heaven like a lawyer or practitioner of Scholastic *disputatio*. But the most important argument the peasant employs is that he lived a virtuous and faithful life. In other words, it is not so much his command of rhetoric as its content which wins him Paradise; the peasant's divine "rhetoric" seems to occupy a mostly allegorical function, in contrast with many of the texts in this study. See the edition of *Vilain* in the *Nouveau recueil complet des Fabliaux*. Ed. Willem Nommen, Nico van den Boogaard. 10 vols. Assen, NL: Van Gorcum, 1983–98. V: 1–38. On this *fabliau*, see also Elizabeth Kinne, "Rhetorical Reasoning, Authority, and the Impossible Interlocutor in *Le vilain qui conquist paradis par plait*," in *The Old French Fabliaux: Essays on Comedy and Context*. Ed. Kristin L Burr, et al. Jefferson, NC: McFarland, 2007. 55–68.

7. The *sirventes* can be found in *Poésies complètes du troubadour Peire Cardenal (1180–1278): texte, traduction, commentaire, analyse des travaux antérieurs, lexique*. Ed. and trans. René Lavaud. Toulouse: Privat, 1957. 222–27. For more on this poem, see Catherine Léglu, "Moral and Satirical Poetry," in *The Troubadours: An Introduction*. Ed. Simon Gaunt, Sarah Kay. Cambridge: Cambridge University Press, 1999. 61–63.

Peire Cardenal, like many later medieval poets, had probably received some formal training in the law.[8] He was certainly familiar with basic legal terminology, using such terms as *arazonar* (to accuse or bring a claim against, v. 4)[9] and *plaideiamen* (plea, v. 10) to describe his anticipated confrontation with God.[10] At the end of the poem, Peire requests that the Virgin Mary bolster his arguments by providing a legal guarantee (*garentia*, v. 46) on his behalf to Christ.

About a century after Peire's death, in 1376, the Burgundian jurist and occasional poet Jean Le Fèvre (c. 1320–c. 1387) wrote his lively *Respit de la mort*.[11] Le Fèvre designed this poem as a petition for legal adjournment (*respit*) sought against his longtime creditor—God. The author confronts his formidable opponent with an abundance of rhetorical tropes and *exempla*, and inserts into the proceedings some of the real-life lawyers he knew from the Parliament of Paris. On the basis that those who suffer wartime damages are given temporary relief of their debts in French customary law, Jean contends that he has long been at war with the world, and should thus be afforded the same exception:

Je di que doy avoir souffrance;	I say that I must be awarded this delay,
car, par le coustume de France,	for by the custom of France,
stile et usage tout notoire,	in procedure well established,
dont je woeil interlocutoire,	and according to which I demand a decision,
se l'omme est damagié par guerre,	if a man incurs injury or damages in war,
il li loist bien de respit querre,	it is legitimate for him to seek delay,
quant en suppliant fait entendre	when in pleading humbly he makes it clear
que ait crediteur puissant d'attendre,	that he has a powerful creditor to deal with
et fait caucion juratoire	and does swear a solemn oath
pour obtenir la dilatoire.	to obtain the adjournment.
(vv. 2917–26)	

By the grace of God, Jean wins his adjournment; he is awarded more time to repent of his sins and live a better life before final judgment is passed, more time to pay back the master's capital with interest. As was the case for Peire Cardenal in the previous century, pleading successfully with God

---

8. See Paul Ourliac, "Troubadours et juristes." *Cahiers de civilisation médiévale* 8 (January–March 1965): 169.

9. On this and related Occitan legal terms, see Linda Paterson, *Troubadours and Eloquence*. Oxford: Clarendon Press, 1975. 12–13.

10. However, Cardenal criticizes the study of Roman law in other poems. See Ourliac, "Troubadours et juristes," 170.

11. I cite the edition of *Le Respit de la mort* by Geneviève Hasenohr-Esnos. Paris: Picard, 1969.

in a legal setting provided a clever way for this poet to call attention to his superior verbal abilities.

Peire Cardenal's *sirventes* and Jean Le Fèvre's plea for a respite are just two examples from the thirteenth and fourteenth centuries in which poets put the spotlight on themselves by imagining their own legal arguments before God. Each of these poets can be termed a *rhetor divinus* (divine rhetorician), according to a broad set of devotional traditions, common to the thirteenth and fourteenth centuries, which attributed to poets the miraculous ability to intervene in the drama of salvation by using rhetoric to advocate for others or on their own behalf.

What follows is an effort to trace how exactly it was that poets more generally came to occupy such a seemingly impossible rhetorical position as that of the *rhetor divinus*. Accordingly, this is also the most rhetorically focused chapter, which considers persuasive language itself, rather than a single author, as the object of eschatological judgment. The thirteenth- and fourteenth-century texts I discuss here vary significantly in terms of genre, including theological and rhetorical treatises, dialogic poetry, mystery plays, devotional lyric, and visionary narrative. Their languages include French, Tuscan, Latin, and Occitan. All of these texts reflect the theoretical development of vernacular poetics—second rhetoric—as it was shaped by official and unofficial belief systems which made the poet a participant in the unfolding cosmic *procès* of divine judgment. By taking a broader generic, geographical, and historical view of the eschatological scene than in later chapters, it becomes possible to see in greater detail how it was that fourteenth-century poets in France represented themselves—in both the legal and artistic senses of the word—at the center of the scene of Judgment.[12]

II. From Legal Subject to Eschatological Subject

Before he became a *rhetor divinus,* the medieval poet already bore a close resemblance to the lawyer. Indeed, poets' self-identification with courtroom rhetoric, and with the particular habitus of the legal profession, goes back to the very roots of the European vernacular tradition. Critics have long remarked, for instance, that the sexual entreaties of the twelfth-century Occitan troubadours—well before Peire Cardenal—echoed the technical

---

12. On this double sense of *représentation,* see, again, Mathieu-Castellani, *La scène judiciaire,* 36.

language of legal procedure,[13] as well as Ciceronian topical theory and strategies of exposition commonly used by jurists.[14]

By the middle of the thirteenth century, the tremendous growth of classical legal learning in northern Italy proved an important influence on that region's desire to establish a vernacular tradition worthy of succeeding the troubadours. Around 1260, the Florentine philosopher, scholar and rhetorician Brunetto Latini (c. 1220–1294) produced his consequential *Rettorica*. Written in Tuscan, it was the first vernacular translation of and commentary on Cicero's early work of legal rhetoric, *De inventione*. In his *Rettorica,* one of the most important additions that Latini made to Cicero's model of legal argumentation was in expanding its usual scope—from the courtrooms and the council chambers of Republican Rome and, later, the medieval city-states of northern Italy. Latini transferred the adversarial nature of these rhetorical contexts to a much wider variety of polemical positions, suitable for poets as well as lawyers. For Latini, the cases in which one might employ legal rhetoric included the lyric poet's conventional plea that his lady love him in return, rewarding his patient suffering with a merciful judgment:[15]

> Cosìe usatamente adviene che due persone si tramettono lettere l'uno all'altro o in latino o in proxa o in rima o in volgare o inn altro, nelle quali contendono d'alcuna cosa, e così fanno tencione. Altressi uno amante chiamando merzé alla sua donna dice parole e ragioni molte, et ella si difende in suo dire et inforza le sue ragioni et indebolisce quelle del pregatore. In

---

13. See Ourliac, "Troubadours et juristes"; R. Howard Bloch, *Medieval French Literature and Law*. Berkeley: University of California Press, 1977. 176; Kay, *Subjectivity,* 135–36; Eliza M. Ghil, "Imagery and Vocabulary," in *A Handbook of the Troubadours.* Ed. F. R. P. Akehurst, Judith M. Davis. Berkeley: University of California Press, 1995. 449; Catherine Léglu, "Defamation in the Troubadour *Sirventes.*" *Medium Aevum* 66.1 (1997): 28–41.

14. For discussions of the influence of formal rhetoric on medieval literature in the vernacular, see, among others: Douglas Kelly, "Topical Invention in Medieval French Literature," in *Medieval Eloquence: Studies in the Theory and Practice of Medieval Rhetoric.* Ed. James J. Murphy. Berkeley: University of California Press, 1978. 231–51; Kelly, *Medieval Imagination: Rhetoric and the Poetry of Courtly Love.* Madison: University of Wisconsin Press, 1978; Sarah Spence, "Rhetoric and Hermeneutics," in *The Troubadours: An Introduction.* Ed. Simon Gaunt, Sarah Kay. Cambridge: Cambridge University Press, 1999. 164–80, especially 164–66; Paterson, *Troubadours and Eloquence;* Nathaniel B. Smith, "Rhetoric," in Akehurst and Davis, eds., *A Handbook of the Troubadours,* 400–20; Simon Gaunt, *Troubadours and Irony.* Cambridge University Press, 1989. Virginia Cox notes the pervasive literary influence of Cicero, including on the Italian *novelle* ("Ciceronian Rhetoric in Italy, 1260–1350." *Rhetorica* 17.3 [Summer 1999]: 268–70).

15. See Cox, "Ciceronian Rhetoric in Italy," 255.

questi et in molti altri exempli si puote assai bene intendere che lla rettorica di Tullio non è pure ad insegnare piategiare alle corti di ragione.[16]

Thus it so happens regularly that two people send each other letters, either in prose or verse, in Latin or in the vernacular, or otherwise,[17] in which they disagree about something or other, and thus they engage in disputation. In the same way a lover petitioning his lady for mercy uses many different words and lines of reasoning, and she defends herself in her own speech and bolsters her own arguments and tries to undermine those of the plaintiff. In this and in many other examples it may well be understood that Cicero's rhetoric is not meant only for the purpose of teaching pleading in legal courts.

Latini expanded the rhetorical practice of *De inventione* from spoken and prose Latin to vernacular lyric composition ("o in latino o in proxa o in rima o in volgare o inn altro"), but he kept much of its juridical quality intact. With the emblematic example of the troubadour's plea for sexual mercy, he adapted the contours of Cicero's courtroom space to cover a much wider variety of argumentative situations in which the poet might find himself speaking.

In his own important treatise on vernacular rhetoric, Latini's student Dante Alighieri (c. 1265–1321) similarly affirmed that Italian poetry must be adaptable to different kinds of pleading—in both princely and legal courts[18]—before placing his poetic subject squarely before the heavenly court in his *Divina commedia*. As a poet whose judgments on society, on literature, and on himself are distinguishable only with great difficulty from the heavenly judgments filling the *Commedia*,[19] it is clear that Dante, before any of the major French authors considered here, already freely mixed the poetic with the legal and the eschatological. It is equally clear that Dante's masterpiece, taken as a whole, could not be a grander act of self-defense, or a more withering rebuke of his enemies. Moreover, as Albert Russell Ascoli has shown in some detail, Dante's first-person voice

---

16. Brunetto Latini, *Rettorica*. Ed. Francesco Maggini. Florence: Felice le Monnier, 1968. 76.14. On Latini's *tencione*, see Cox, "Ciceronian Rhetoric in Italy," 257–59. On the way this model can be seen to apply to Guillaume de Machaut and other poets, see Kelly, *Medieval Imagination*, 5, 11–12.

17. As Maggini (ed., Latini, *Rettorica*, 146 n1) explains, the "inn altro" refers to vernaculars which are not Italian, especially French and Occitan.

18. Dante, *De vulgari eloquentia*. Ed. and trans. Steven Botterill. New York: Cambridge University Press, 1996. 1.17.

19. Perhaps the best attempt to make this distinction has been undertaken by Teodolinda Barolini in *The Undivine Comedy: Detheologizing Dante*. Princeton: Princeton University Press, 1992.

and his authority as a witness to the afterworld are drawn on Ciceronian models of legal subjectivity.[20]

Yet in many ways, the differences between Dante's eschatological scene and those of the French authors I discuss later are more instructive than the similarities. It is striking that, as a *process,* divine judgment is rarely if ever on display in the *Commedia,* for Dante's divine tribunal takes place well beyond human law and human language. The judgments that we encounter in *Inferno* are the sentences meted out by Minos, not the condemnations by Christ which make those sentences necessary. The inmates of Dante's hell do not argue or try to appeal, but rather cannot stop accusing themselves for all eternity.[21] We as readers are not privy to the tribunal which has condemned them, or which peoples the mountain of purgatory, or which raises the just to the sphere of Jupiter, where, in the voice of Justinian's imperial eagle, they proclaim the vast inscrutability of God's justice:

> Però ne la giustizia sempiterna
> la vista che riceve il vostro mondo,
> com'occhio per lo mare entro s'interna;
> che, ben che de la proda veggia il fondo,
> in pelago nol vede; e nondimeno
> èli, ma cela lui l'esser profondo.
> (*Purgatorio* 19.58-63)[22]
>
> But of eternal justice the vision
> that your world receives is like an eye
> staring into the sea; though near shore
> it may glimpse the bottom,
> it penetrates not into the fathoms; and yet
> the sea floor is there, hidden by the deep.

And while Dante's narrator is able to peer into the folds of the celestial rose in *Paradiso* 30 and see the heavenly court just as it shall be assembled "a l'ultima giustizia" (*Paradiso* 30.45), he is not witness to its deliberations.

At the end of *Purgatorio,* when Beatrice comes to the narrator from the same court and judges him harshly, provoking his tearful shame and repentance, we have one of the most striking instances in which Latini's conjunction of the courtly with the juridical also abuts the eschatological. Beatrice's accusation is, moreover, a judgment on literature, since her claim is that Dante had abandoned her for another at the end of *La vita nuova* and in *Il convivio.* And Beatrice's is a judgment which serves to identify the poet through an assumed legal subjectivity: the only place where Dante's name appears in the *Commedia* is precisely at the head of his beloved's long

---

20. See Albert Russell Ascoli, *Dante and the Making of a Modern Author.* Cambridge: Cambridge University Press, 2008. 75, 103.

21. See Senior, *In the Grip of Minos,* 49.

22. I cite from the edition of the *Divina commedia* by Charles S. Singleton. Princeton, NJ: Princeton University Press, 1977.

indictment (*Purgatorio* 30.55). But Beatrice's reproach from heaven strikes dumb the voice of the poet—of the rhetorician—leaving him merely to sob in contrition. This was her merciful intention: to prevent her charge's condemnation at the Judgment by causing him to plead guilty now (*Purgatorio* 31.37–42). Neither Dante's theory of poetry nor his practice of it tend to suggest that the poet might also be able to engage in what Latini called *tencione* when appearing before God.

Dante's consistent lack of *procès* or pleading represents a sharp contrast with some French poets' tendency to provide detailed depictions of the technical apparatus of divine justice, and their tendency to plead in the heavenly court on their own behalf using elegant language and sophisticated arguments. Guillaume de Deguileville, to whom I devote the next chapter, shared many of his sources for otherworldly vision narrative with the Florentine.[23] Yet while Dante is undeniably the greater poet, Deguileville is a more active rhetorician in his own narrative, as he has his first-person narrator and namesake argue a stunning defense on behalf of his soul and on behalf of the author's body of work. Dante's rhetoric may be divine, but he does not cast his narrator as *rhetor divinus* in the same way. The reason, I think, has partly to do with differences in the development of second rhetoric that run across geographical and linguistic lines.

Certainly, the northern Italian tendency to classify vernacular poetry as a branch of legal rhetoric was echoed across the Alps. This was in part through the intermediary of Brunetto Latini himself. Latini wrote his *Rettorica* while exiled in France and during the same time produced a pioneering encyclopedia in Picard French—the *Livres dou Tresor* (1260)—whose sections on rhetoric would have been an important source for many thirteenth-century French poets' knowledge of Cicero.[24] However, northern France could not boast quite the same pervasive atmosphere of official legal culture as Italy or Occitania. In Paris, the papal decretal *Super specula* forbade the teaching of Roman civil law beginning in 1219, and for the next two centuries the law faculty there practically ceased to exist.[25] As a result, with the exception of Orléans, the region was somewhat slower in developing an influential class of jurists in the same way as Bologna, Florence, Toulouse, or Montpellier.[26]

---

23. On similarities, see Ursula Peters and Andreas Kablitz, "The *Pèlerinage* Corpus: A Tradition of Textual Transformation Across Western Europe," in *The Pèlerinage Allegories of Guillaume de Deguileville: Tradition, Authority and Influence.* Ed. Marco Nievergelt, Stephanie A. Viereck Gibbs Kamath. Cambridge: D. S. Brewer, 2013. 43–44.

24. See, again, Carmody's edition of *Li Livres dou Tresor*.

25. See Brundage, *Medieval Origins*, 231.

26. See Ibid., 231.

Likewise, northern France would wait much longer to compose vernacular *artes poeticae* than its Mediterranean neighbors—until Eustache Deschamps 1392 *Art de dictier,* which treats poetry as a branch of music rather than of rhetoric. It is therefore difficult to trace transalpine influence on the fourteenth-century French study of versification, or even to approach this study at all as a discrete object. If we want to understand how thirteenth- and fourteenth-century French poets conceived of their vocational identity and their authority as rhetoricians, we have no formal corpus of poetic instruction upon which to draw. Instead, we must consider a rather different cultural context in which second rhetoric was conceived as a form of legal speaking—as well as an instrument of divine justice.

In the course of the later Middle Ages, elements of the cult of Marian devotion were gradually transformed by poets into a new model of the poet as rhetorician, distinct from although frequently overlapping with more worldly comparisons of the poet and the lawyer like Latini's. In northern France, this new model was institutionalized not primarily by learned texts, but rather by lay confraternal societies formed for the purpose of promoting Marian devotion through vernacular composition and the staging of mystery plays. By establishing rules for fixed lyric forms, these confraternities became, almost by default, some of the most important French theorists of second rhetoric, which they, too, conceived largely as an extension of legal oratory.

But the confraternities did more than simply graft vernacular composition onto the established structures of legal pleading, as had their Italian counterparts. Because they presupposed a lack of distinction between devotional poetry and prayer, the confraternities also deployed legal rhetoric as a tool in the process of salvation. Conceiving of their devotional composition as one part in the complex drama of intercession, Marian poets had special reason to locate their authority in the heavenly court, where they became active participants with each line of verse requesting saintly and divine assistance. Poets were given some theological justification for this conception of authority by, among others, the bishop of Paris and influential theologian Guillaume d'Auvergne (c. 1180–1249), whose *Rhetorica divina* (mid-1200s) counsels those who pray to use Ciceronian legal rhetoric as a model for successfully petitioning heaven.[27]

It would be an oversight to deny that Dante was himself a major Marian poet, or that the rise of Tuscan as a literary language went hand in hand with the development of devotional poetry in the vernacular. But what is

---

27. See below, 54–56.

unique to French poetry in the period is that so much of it drew its authority—explicitly or implicitly—from the confraternities, which like no other body of rhetorical expertise in the later Middle Ages, tied together the seemingly disparate identities of poet, lawyer, and divine interlocutor into the singular image of the *rhetor divinus*. Drawing on the Marian and confraternal traditions, later authors of the French fourteenth century would appropriate elements of these traditions as they sought to represent their rhetorical mastery and poetic authority.

The confraternities' own authority derives from the Virgin, and in particular from the popular cult devoted to Mary's manifestation as Advocata Nostra—a sly and oratorically skilled defense lawyer engaged in the perpetual trial proceedings brought against mankind by Satan. Advocata Nostra's legal and rhetorical heroism is especially well developed in the so-called Devil's Rights genre of theatre and dialogic poetry, a genre which became an important part of the confraternities' dramatic repertoire. While the Advocata Nostra motif is not unique to the confraternal tradition, the tradition does furnish some of the motif's richest examples. Most importantly, the confraternal poets of northern France provide compelling instances in which the poet's own work is linked, directly or indirectly, to the Virgin's legal expertise. Putting rhetoric to work for divine justice, Advocata Nostra offered a ready model for poets aspiring to move heaven with their own well-crafted lyric arguments. I therefore begin this brief history of the French *rhetor divinus* tradition with Advocata Nostra as she appears in the Devil's Rights, before turning to the confraternal poets themselves.

III. Human Rights and the Devil's Rights: The Virgin's Divine Advocacy

The Devil's Rights genre employs the narrative structure of legal procedure and the technical vocabulary of the law to stage Satan's arguments that humanity became his rightful property as a result of Adam and Eve's transgression in Eden. The thirteenth-century Latin prose *Conflictus inter Deum et Diabolum,* which uses Justinian's *Corpus iuris civilis* to weigh the Devil's claims against mankind, is the earliest known example to feature such a law-court setting.[28] The tradition which grew out of the *Conflictus*

---

28. C. W. Marx notes that this is the earliest known example of the Devil's Rights dispute tied to "specific legal arguments" (*The Devil's Rights and the Redemption in the Literature of Medieval England.* Rochester, NY: D. S. Brewer, 1995. 60). Marx has also produced "An Edition and Study of the *Conflictus inter Deum et Diabolum.*" *Medium Aevum* 59.1 (1990): 16–40.

in the course of the next century made two innovations especially crucial to understanding how this version of the eschatological scene would be used by later poets. First, whereas the *Conflictus* had cast the argument as a direct dispute between God and the Devil, the later tradition gave a more pronounced role to humanity as the defendant in the case, rather than casting human beings merely as disputed pieces of property. Second, to allow humanity legal representation, the tradition came to introduce the Virgin as man's advocate. Both of these later tendencies may be observed in the Latin *Processus Sathane infernalis contra genus humanum* (c. 1320)[29] and its Anglo-Norman adaptation *L'advocacie Nostre Dame* (also c. 1320).[30]

In the Anglo-Norman *Advocacie,* Satan appears before the heavenly court (*la court des cyex*) to demand possession of mankind.[31] The angel Gabriel sounds his horn to summon humanity to the Judgment, yet not a soul comes forward to speak in man's defense. Satan claims that he should win on the grounds that the defendant failed to appear. However, Christ reminds the court that his justice is perfectly balanced with mercy, and delays the trial until the following day—Good Friday—so that humanity can secure suitable representation. Mary, who arrives in court the next morning, counters Satan's claim by arguing that he never took lawful possession of mankind, since he caused the Fall through malice and deceit. In a passionate display of maternal sentiment, the Virgin then tearfully reminds the judge—Christ her son—that he died to redeem mankind from original sin and thus definitively dispossess Satan.

Needless to say, Mary wins the case. Beyond the text's dramatization of the Redemption, the way its characters use language also reveals much about the status of legal and rhetorical learning in the early fourteenth century. Satan is depicted as well-read and articulate:

Là vint Sathan très bien matin,	In came Satan early that morning,
Qui bien sceit franchois et latin	he who knows French and Latin so well

---

29. This dating is given by Scott L. Taylor, "Reason, Rhetoric, and Redemption: The Teaching of Law and the *Planctus Mariae* in the Late Middle Ages," in *Medieval Education*. Ed. Ronald B. Begley, Joseph W. Koterski. New York: Fordham University Press, 2005. 70.

30. As Marx notes in his edition of *Conflictus* (24), variations on the basic pattern of the dispute were numerous. I cite from the edition entitled *Our Lady's Lawsuits in L'advocacie Nostre Dame (Our Lady's Advocacy) and La chapelerie Nostre Dame de Baiex (The Benefice of Our Lady's Chapel in Bayeux)*. Ed. and trans. Judith M. Davis, F. R. P. Akehurst. Based on the text edited by Gérard Gros. Tempe: Arizona Center for Medieval and Renaissance Studies, 2011.

31. On *L'advocacie*'s pervasive use of legal form, see Jody Enders, *Rhetoric and the Origins of Medieval Drama*. Ithaca, NY: Cornell University Press, 1992. 222–33. See also Brundage, *Medieval Origins*, 477.

Et sceit respondre et opposer	and knows how to respond and argue
Et toute Escripture gloser.	and gloss all of Scripture.
(vv. 447–50)	

As Mary admits, her opponent is extremely knowledgeable in all legal matters, both civil and canon:

Il sceit assez canon et loy	He knows canon and code enough
Pour troubler .I. bon jugement.	to confuse any good judgment.
(vv. 762–63)	

And as Christ himself concedes from the seat of judgment, not only does Satan "parle courtoisement" (v. 1630), but his claim against humanity does in fact seem reasonable ("y semble que rèson requière," v. 1631).

What is most striking about this depiction of the Devil as a lawyer is that here we do not necessarily recognize the voice of the tempter and the Father of Lies. Instead, Satan's case is grounded in Scripture and generally displays a concern with justice and with the accurate interpretation of authoritative texts. Most notably, the Devil cites Genesis to argue that Adam and Eve's disobedience put them and all their progeny into his possession:

Dist Sathan: 'C'est droit qu'i me vaille.	Said Satan, 'The law is on my side here.
Quant Adan et Eve feïs	When you made Adam and Eve
Et en paradis les meïs,	and put them in the Garden, you told them
Tu deïs que des fruyz menjassent,	they could eat from all the trees except one
De tous, fors qu'à .I. n'atouchassent;	that you forbid them to touch.
Ton commandement bien oïrent	They heard your commandment
Mès de touz poins désobéirent	but disobeyed it in every respect,
Et contre ton vouloir péchièrent,	sinned against your will,
Quer par lour folie mengièrent	and in their folly ate
Le piere pomme du pourpris,	the worst fruit in the garden,
Et pour ce furent il pourpris	and for this they were struck
De maladie si cruel	with a condition so vile
Qu'el doit estre perpétuel	that it must perpetuate itself
En toute leur postérité.	in all succeeding generations.
N'es tu justice et vérité?	Are you not justice and truth?
Fey donc tes paroles estables	Keep your words unchanging
Ou tu n'es mi véritables,	and put to eternal condemnation

Et met à condempnatïon	Adam and his line,
Adam et sa successïon.'	or else you will not be truthful.'
(vv. 1160–78)	

Satan goes so far here as to impute that God would be going back on his own precedent ("Fey donc tes paroles estables," v. 1175) if he failed to judge in the Devil's favor and condemn the human race based on his word in Genesis 2:17: the prohibition, on certain pain of death, against eating from the Tree of Knowledge of Good and Evil.

Elsewhere in the *Advocacie,* Satan calls upon strong precedent to object to Mary's presence in the court: she ought not to be allowed to plead, on the grounds that she is a woman, and on the grounds that she is directly related to the trial judge, Christ (vv. 860–72). But Mary adroitly defends her right to act as counsel by citing exceptions from Roman law sources.[32] And who, indeed, could be more exceptional? Not only is Mary the virgin mother of God, but she claims the right to speak where language—and lawyers—are supposed to fall silent.

In the end, Mary prevails due to a sharp technical knowledge of the law, but most of all thanks to her plainly superior rhetorical skills. While Satan stakes his entire argument on the established precedent of Genesis, Mary bests him by employing pathos to bring the heavenly court to mercy. In so doing, she turns her supposed frailty as a woman to her advantage, and she takes a cue from the classical rhetorical tradition, which emphasized the importance of producing an emotional response in courtroom audiences through body language and other physical techniques of delivery (*actio*):[33]

Lors la peüst l'en regarder,	Then one could see her
Aussi simple comme une teutre,	as simple as dove,
Et ensemble ses mains déteutre,	twisting her hands together,
Trembler, frémir et sanglouter,	shivering, shaking and sobbing,
Eschaufer, suer, dégouter!	her body burning and sweating.

---

32. In the Latin *Processus,* Mary cites the *Decrees, Decretals* and *Pandects* (see Taylor, "Reason, Rhetoric, and Redemption," 73). In the *Advocacie,* she brings up exceptions from Justinian's *Digeste* (v. 1089) and Gratian's *Décrétale* (v. 1235).

33. On Mary's successful use of gesture and pathos as adopted from legal rhetoric, see Enders, *Rhetoric and the Origins of Medieval Drama,* 228–30. Mary's rhetorical use of pathos is also discussed by Taylor, "Reason, Rhetoric, and Redemption," 74, and by George R. Keiser, "The Middle English *Planctus Mariae* and the Rhetoric of Pathos," in *The Popular Literature of Medieval England.* Ed. Thomas J. Heffernan. Knoxville: University of Tennessee Press, 1985. 167–93.

Elle estoit si lasse et si vaine	She was so weak and forlorn
Que sus lie n'avoit nerf ne vaine	that in her body she had no nerve or vein
À quoy l'en ne s'aperchëust	from which one could not see
Que grant angoisse au cuer eüst.	that her heart was torn with anguish.
(vv. 1396–404)	

Turning toward her son the judge, the Virgin calls on him to honor his filial obligations and acquit mankind, ripping open her shirt to make this point all the more vividly:[34]

Ha, beau douz filz, je suy ta mère,	Oh, good sweet son, I am your mother,
Qui te portey .IX. mois entiers:	who carried you nine long months.
Tu me dois oïr volontiers.	You must gladly listen to me;
Je t'enffantey mout povrement	I delivered you humbly
Et te nourri mout doucement.	and nursed you sweetly.
Ta mère suy, mère m'apèles.	Your mother I am, mother you call me.
Beau filz, regarde les mamèles	Beautiful son, look at my breasts,
De quoy aleitier te souloie,	with which I used to feed you,
Et ces mains, dont bien te savoie	and these hands with which
Souef remuer et berchier.	I used to gently cradle and rock you.
(vv. 1458–67)	

It would seem Satan was justified in claiming that Mary's presence as counsel would prejudice the proceedings, but he can do nothing to prevent it. While the Adversary knows the letter of the law backwards and forwards, he is no match for the Virgin because he cannot arouse compassion in the courtroom.

The conflict between Mary's ability to provoke an emotional response through her bare-breasted *planctus,* and the Devil's purely textual knowledge of the law, expresses an old theme of eschatological representation. Characteristically, the Devil incarnated an Hebraic or Pharisaic rigidity in his insistence on the literal interpretation of Scripture and of the spiritual account-books of individual lives. As discussed by Michael Camille, the scribe-demon Tutivillus was a frequent presence in medieval scenes of eschatological judgment, where his fixation on unchanging textual truth speaks to contemporary distrust of the written word as deathly.[35] The Old

---

34. This gesture was used to arouse pity in classical depictions of courtroom rhetoric long before its appearance in the Devil's Rights tradition. See Marilyn Yalom, *A History of the Breast.* New York: Alfred A. Knopf-Random House, 1997. 19–20; Sarah Jane Boss, *Empress and Handmaid: On Nature and Gender in the Cult of the Virgin Mary.* New York: Cassell, 2000. 37.

35. Michael Camille, "The Devil's Writing: Diabolic Literacy in Medieval Art," in *World Art:*

Testament legalism of Satan or Tutivillus could only be defeated by grace, through which Christ's New Law erases, or radically rewrites, the record of sin.[36]

The Virgin's substitution of new law for old may also be understood in terms of emerging medieval judicial practices. As Scott L. Taylor has established, the Latin *Processus* upon which *Advocacie* is based was actually used as a model of trial procedure in early fourteenth-century legal education. In particular, as Taylor argues, Mary would have served as an ideal example of the Bolognese approach to the law, the *mos italicus,* which stressed a methodological consideration of personal legal subjectivity (*status* or *condicio hominum*) and privileged equity over strict custom.[37] The *Processus* and its Anglo-Norman adaptation employed the image of Advocata Nostra to highlight contemporary points of judicial ethics, especially the need to arrive at an equitable decision beyond the letter of the law, and the right of all legal subjects—even of wretched mankind—to answer the charges against them.[38] As Taylor suggests, this makes the Devil's Rights as much about human law as divine jurisprudence.

Or rather, the Devil's Rights evoke a forum for eschatological justice situated somewhere between heaven and earth, in which the ability of mankind to face its accuser becomes an ethical imperative. In this context, persuasive language is fully incorporated into the eschatological scene as a means of revealing God's ineffable mercy, and as an instrument for bringing that mercy about. The Virgin's rhetoric affirms that God's judgment is supremely just only inasmuch as it allows the human subject representation and the possibility of going beyond the law to claim an exceptional pardon. Language, in all of its capacity for emotional manipulation, becomes the guarantor of heavenly justice, inasmuch as it allows the scene of Judgment to transform the meaning of established texts—that of the Fall, or of an individual's transgressions.[39]

Themes of Unity in Diversity: Acts of the XXVIth International Congress of the History of Art. Ed. Irving Lavin. 3 vols. University Park: University of Pennsylvania Press, 1989. II: 355–60, especially 356.

36. See Camille, "The Devil's Writing"; Carol Zaleski, *Otherworldly Journeys: Accounts of Near-Death Experience in Medieval and Modern Times.* New York: Oxford University Press, 1987. 71.

37. Taylor, "Reason, Rhetoric, and Redemption," 71. See also John Moreau, "'*Ce mauvais tabellion*': Satanic and Marian Textuality in Deguileville's *Pèlerinage de l'âme,*" in Nievergelt and Kamath, eds., *The Pèlerinage Allegories of Guillaume de Deguileville,* 119.

38. As Taylor ("Reason, Rhetoric, and Redemption," 68) explains, due process, including right to petition, opportunity to be heard and proper evidence, was a contemporary issue, stemming from the controversy over Henry II's justification of the trial in absentia of Robert of Naples, and the responses against it by Pope Clement V.

39. As Jody Enders has argued, Mary's feminine style of pleading also served to rehabilitate legal rhetoric, which had been criticized as effeminate by Quintilian and Lucian (*Rhetoric and the*

The transformative power of the Virgin's rhetoric can also be appreciated in cases where the Advocata intercedes on behalf of specific human beings rather than on behalf of mankind in general. A vivid example may be found in the *Miracle de Pierre le changeur*,[40] an early fourteenth-century mystery play whose eschatological narrative closely follows older versions of the Devil's Rights. The back-story of the *Miracle* is that the rich merchant Pierre never did a good deed in his entire life. This well-known fact about the man prompts two beggars to wager a pot of wine: the first beggar says that he will succeed in convincing Pierre to spare him something to eat, while the second bets that he will be refused. As it happens, Pierre throws a stale loaf of bread at the first beggar, not out of charity, but because he is unable to find a more suitable object with which to bash the man's head in. The unrepentant Pierre says quite specifically that it was not his intention to feed the beggar but rather to kill him:

Certes c'estoit tout mon desir	All I wanted to do
Que du main tel cop li donnasse	was to hit him so hard
Qu'en la place mort le jettasse.	as to knock him dead.
(vv. 230–32)	

Apparently, the loaf is not quite stale enough to serve Pierre's purpose. The beggar catches it and, perhaps less than honestly, uses the bread as evidence of Pierre's charity; he brings it to his compatriot so that he can collect on the bet and drink his pot of wine. In the meantime, Pierre has suddenly fallen gravely ill, and although he is not yet dead, a group of devils has already assembled before the heavenly court to claim the wicked man's soul as their own.

Satan might appear to have an open and shut case here, except that the Virgin quickly arrives on the scene to provide the defense. Ever the lawyer, she asks the angels—her crack legal team—if there isn't the least shred of evidence which would help their client. Frustrated, one of the angels informs Mary of the facts weighing against them: not only did Pierre never perform a single good deed, but his very last act—throwing the loaf at the beggar—was yet another instance of his total lack of human compassion:

Origins of Medieval Drama, 223). For Enders, Mary redeems the power of gesture and pathos (*actio*), making them not effeminate, but positively feminine and identified with mercy and goodness (233).

40. *Miracle de Pierre le changeur*, in *Miracles de Nostre Dame par personnages*. Ed. Gaston Paris, Ulysse Robert, François Bonnardot. 8 vols. Paris: Firmin Didot & Cie, 1881.VI: 224–300.

Si ne scé de quoy s'aquitta,	I don't know how he can be let off,
Au povre lors un pain jetta	for he threw at the poor man a loaf
Non pas de bonne voulenté,	not out of good will,
Non, mais a dire verité,	but to tell you the truth,
Par grant despit et par grant ire.	with great scorn and anger.
(vv. 501–5)	

However, despite Pierre's thoroughly bad intentions, it turns out that his final act is enough to get him off the hook, just as it is enough to win the beggar his wine. Mary begins her defense by launching into a moving *planctus* reminding God that he died on the cross for humanity (vv. 517–57). In this, she follows the basic pattern of Ciceronian rhetorical theory by starting her argument with a direct attempt to influence the emotional state of her audience—an *exordium*. Only afterward does she proceed to the facts of the case, introducing the loaf as evidence that Pierre has not completely lost the capacity for good. The bread constitutes a legal exception—seemingly, a dubious one—to Satan's contention that Pierre never performed a good deed:

Oultre, sire, vezci un pain	Besides, my lord, here is a loaf
Qu'il a a un povre donné,	that he gave to a poor man
Pour ce qu'il l'ot araisonné	because he asked him for it
Et de dire s'esvertuoit	and was trying to tell him
Que famine trop le grevoit;	that hunger was crushing him.
Si li doit estre de prouffit	This must count in his favor
Plus que touz les maux c'onques fist	more than all the wicked deeds he did
Ny en jonnesce n'en viel aage	in youth and in old age—
Ne li doivent estre a damage;	they must not count against him now;
C'est tout certain.	that's completely certain.
(vv. 548–57)	

Won over by her emotional appeal, God agrees with Mary's claim that throwing the loaf at the beggar constituted an act of charity outweighing all of the defendant's previous sins. Pierre is given a second chance; he is brought back to life, and devotes the rest of his time on earth to performing charitable acts. He becomes a holy man and even sells himself into slavery to a Muslim in Jerusalem, who is so moved by his example of self-sacrifice that he too converts to Christianity. Mary's subtle massaging of established textual fact for the sake of divine mercy exploits the two senses in which Pierre is a *changeur*; as the play becomes a narrative of personal conversion and redemption, the spiritual book of accounts of this money-changer is dramatically rewritten.

As is true of the Devil's Rights tradition more generally, Mary's judicial activities in *Pierre* include some of the same things for which earthly lawyers were frequently condemned in the Middle Ages as in the twenty-first century: the representation of a guilty client, the exploitation of emotional rhetoric, and the distortion of facts.[41] In Mary's exceptional case, however, these are not sins, but instruments of God's will in sparing his elect, and signs of the way God's grace triumphs over the Old Law, miraculously rewriting the bare, immovable facts to which the Devil lays claim.[42]

That the Virgin's rhetoric could wield such decisive power was a theologically sound idea, though not an entirely unproblematic one. While the Church encouraged devotion to the Virgin and other saints on all levels of society, theologians stressed that the ability of these *advocati* to intercede on behalf of human beings did not constitute an undue influence on God's will. Some Christian thinkers limited saintly intercession to the period during an individual's life on earth: after the separation of body and soul, even the Mother of God would be unable to persuade her son to change his mind.[43] Other theologians, particularly in the later Middle Ages, were less intent on removing the possibility of intercession from the Judgment and more insistent upon the idea that saintly intercession never actually changes God's mind.

For Aquinas and Bonaventure, among others, the intervention of the saints is possible as an instrument provided by God to save his elect; it does not introduce a new opinion into the heavenly court or influence God's

---

41. On another important depiction of the Virgin as a tricky lawyer, and the Devil as a more ostensibly ethical, truth-oriented figure, see Patricia Fagan's article on the *Cantigas de Santa Maria*, "El Mal Rey y la Ley: The Devil as Lawyer in the Divine Court of the *CSM*." *Romance Review* 5.1 (Spring 1995): 47–53. As Fagan writes, "The Devil is ironically the fair prosecutor who argues cogently for just retribution of unrepentant sinners, whereas Mary is the flagrant transgressor of the law who tips the scales of justice in favor of her remorseless supplicants" (48). The saints and angels, as well as the Devil, were often depicted tampering with the scales of justice. On this point, see Zaleski, *Otherworldly Journeys*, 71; Catherine Oakes, "The Scales: An Iconographic Motif of Justice, Redemption and Intercession." *Maria* 1 (2000): 11–36. Mary's representation of a guilty client is taken to an extreme in the late fifteenth-century Occitan mystery play *Lo Jutgamen General*, where the Virgin agrees to represent the devils themselves but loses her case; see the edition by Moshe Lazar, *Le Jugement Dernier/Lo Jutgamen General: drame provençal du XVe*. Paris: Klincksieck, 1971.

42. On *Pierre*, see also Moreau, "'Ce mauvais tabellion,'" 118–19.

43. See, for example, Augustine, *De civitate Dei*. Ed. Bernard Dombert, Alphonse Kalb. 2 vols. Stuttgart: Teubner, 1993. 21.18. On this thorny issue in the earlier Middle Ages, see Delumeau, *Le péché et la peur*, 453; Megan McLaughlin, *Consorting with Saints: Prayer for the Dead in Early Medieval France*. Ithaca, NY: Cornell University Press, 1994. 209–10; Richard Bauckham, *The Fate of the Dead: Studies on the Jewish and Christian Apocalypses*. Leiden: Brill, 1998. 142–48.

judgment, but is instead another effect of the Aristotelian first cause, the original divine will.⁴⁴ Considering that the saints are in perfect accord with God's plan, Aquinas affirms that their pleas are effective not in moving the Almighty to a new judgment, but rather in carrying out the creator's eternal design, confirming the immutable judgment made from God's position of eternal simultaneity, the *nunc stans*:

> Ad secundum dicendum quod sancti impetrant illud quod Deus vult fieri per orationes eorum. Et hoc petunt quod aestimant eorum orationibus implendum secundum Dei voluntatem.⁴⁵

> To this second proposition it is to be said that the saints succeed in obtaining that which God wants to accomplish by means of their prayers. And they petition for that which they deem will be granted through their prayers according to God's will.

In other words, if God is persuaded to mercy by the rhetoric of the saints, it is because he intends from all time to be persuaded to mercy by the rhetoric of the saints. Conceived like this, the petitions of such advocates possess real instrumentality without ever changing the course of individual or collective salvation.

A fourteenth-century mystery play, *Le Jour du Jugement,* confronts the problem of persuasion in a similar way, by having the lawyer-Virgin make the following disclaimer in the midst of her arguments:

Biau doux Filz, riens ne vous demande	Good sweet Son, I demand nothing
Qui soit contre vo voulentez:	which might contradict your will:
Je vous pri cil soient rentez	I pray you that those who have loved me
En paradis qui m'ont amee.⁴⁶	be granted tenure in heaven.

Of course, the disclaimer is not without its own rhetorical power, since it performatively reminds God of his own will. In theological and popular sources alike, the caveat that the saints' pleas do not technically change God's mind did not have the effect of discouraging depictions of Mary and

---

44. For a more detailed discussion of this intellectual current, see Barbara Faes de Mottoni, "Quelques aspects de la doctrine de l'intercession dans la théologie de Bonaventure et de Thomas d'Aquin," in *L'intercession du Moyen Âge à l'époque moderne: autour d'une pratique sociale.* Ed. Jean-Marie Moeglin. Geneva: Droz, 2004. 105–26, especially 121–22. As Faes de Mottoni explains (121), this attitude can be traced in part to Augustine's *De praedestinatione sanctorum.*

45. Aquinas, *Summa theologica,* IIa IIae, Q. 83, art. 11.

46. *Le mystère du Jour du Jugement,* vv. 1834–37.

other saints as *advocati* engaged in legal and rhetorical disputation. On the contrary, it only seemed to confirm the existence of such heavenly rhetoric as both an instrument of salvation and a sign of election.[47]

But the idea that rhetoric could play an essential part of the eschatological *procès* was not limited to the saints. A closely connected logic made it possible for human beings to think of their own prayers as both rhetorical acts and acts with real consequences for eschatological justice. To some extent, this way of thinking is visible beginning as early as Tertullian and Origen, but nowhere before or since was it developed to the same level of detail as in *Rhetorica divina* (*Divine Rhetoric*), a treatise on prayer written around the middle of the thirteenth century by Guillaume d'Auvergne, the bishop of Paris.[48] In line with contemporary intercessory doctrine, Guillaume d'Auvergne stresses that prayer does not actually change God's mind, but is only part of the same divine-willed process of salvation, a necessary response to the eternal Word that commanded it.[49] Prayer is nevertheless indispensible to salvation in its capacity to bring human souls back to God, and for Guillaume d'Auvergne what best defines successful prayer is its close resemblance to classical judicial rhetoric.[50]

In order to teach Christians the right way to plead for saintly intercession and divine mercy, Guillaume draws on the familiar model of the courtroom speaker found in Cicero's *De inventione* and in the first book

---

47. From this perspective, what would prevent God from allowing the most egregious sinner to act as an advocate at the Judgment? Such is the question raised by Boccaccio's Panfilo, who begins the first day of the *Decameron* by telling of the wicked Ser'Ciappelletto, known especially for his delight in providing false testimony in court. After giving a bogus and self-serving confession on his deathbed, Ciappelletto becomes a popular saint to whom the people of Burgundy pray for assistance. Panfilo chalks this up not to the triumph of dishonest men in the world, but rather to the inscrutable mercy of God's judgment, which discerns the sincerity of our prayers even when they are channeled through the most unworthy of advocates (Giovanni Boccaccio, *Decameron*. Ed. Cesare Segre. Milan: Mursia, 1966. 1.1).

48. The text can also be termed an *ars orandi*. As its modern editor Roland J. Teske points out, however, this is a problematic generic designation, given that the "*Rhetorica divina* is the fullest and perhaps only full exemplification of the genre" (*Rhetorica divina, seu ars oratoria eloquentiae divinae*. Leuven: Peeters, 2013. 3). For a good overview of scholarship on the classical, Patristic and medieval tradition of identifying oratory with prayer, see Teske's introduction, 1–10. See also Jean-Yves Tilliette, "Oraison et art oratoire: les sources et les propos de la *Rhetorica divina*," in *Autour de Guillaume d'Auvergne († 1249)*. Ed. Franco Morenzoni, Jean-Yves Tilliette. Turnhout: Brepols, 2005. 203–15, especially 203–4; Jean-Luc Solère, "De l'orateur à l'orant: la 'rhétorique divine' dans la culture chrétienne occidentale." *Revue de l'histoire des religions* 211.2 (1994): 187–224, especially 200–1.

49. See Solère, "De l'orateur à l'orant," 191.

50. The other perfections of prayer are its likeness to a messenger, its aspect of song, prayer as "the calves of our lips," prayer as the smoke of incense, prayer as a sacrifice, and prayer as a wrestling match against God.

of the pseudo-Ciceronian *Ad Herrenium*. Just like Cicero's forensic orator, the Christian pray-er, or more appropriately, *orant*,[51] should model his discourse on a six-part structure. He should begin with an exordium designed to capture the court's sympathy, then relate a narrative of the events to be adjudicated, then petition for a specific judgment, then make an emphatic confirmation of that petition, and then refute his opponent's case, before finally concluding his arguments.

There are naturally a few differences between Cicero's ideal legal subject and Guillaume's. For one thing, the praying subject's "opponent" is not a real interlocutor, but rather the sin which keeps human beings apart from God, who, Guillaume maintains, is always already on the side of the sincerely repentant. In fact, by exposing and denouncing his sins, the sinner can hope to separate himself from them, becoming a kind of prosecutor in God's own service as much as a defendant.[52] For another thing, Guillaume consistently reminds us that the orant is never actually moving God to mercy of his own agency, but only justly fulfilling the role which has been assigned to him from all time by the divine will. The rhetoric of prayer changes not so much its object, but rather its subject, as it prepares the human being to receive God's grace in the appropriate attitude of humility.[53] Moreover, there is only one good argument for the human subject to make in his defense—this is an unsparing confession of sins, for only by pleading guilty now can the *orant* hope to escape a fiery judgment later.

Yet as much as Guillaume is compelled by theological necessity to restrict the possibilities for human agency in prayer, the reminder that no persuasion is taking place actually gives him freer rein to describe the miraculous possibilities of human rhetoric as an instrument of the divine will. Guillaume's mystical side embraces the image of the heroic *orant* who, like the Virgin of the Devil's Rights tradition, can subject God to a kind of rhetorical "violence" by using Ciceronian *actio* to throw his entire body into the delivery of the argument:

> Est aliud adjutorium validissimum et inexpugnabile orationum, lacrimositas sive lacrimis profluvium. Dicit enim expositor libri Tobiae, quia oratio Deum lenit; lacrimae vero cogunt ipsum misereri. Lacrimosa igitur oratio

---

51. That is, the word is the most appropriate one for expressing how oratory and prayer are conflated in Guillaume's thought.

52. See, for example, Guillaume d'Auvergne, *Rhetorica divina*, ch. 9 (ed. Teske, 84).

53. See Solère, "De l'orateur à l'orant," 207. Solère describes the violent relationship between God and man in Guillaume d'Auvergne's conception of their dialog as "une lutte courtoise avec Dieu" ("De l'orateur à l'orant," 223).

> non solum placida seu placita est Deo, immo etiam violenta in ipsum, cum ei cedere vel succumbere necesse habeat invincibilis usque quaque omnipotentia creatoris victa.[54]

> There is another most strong and matchless thing that helps prayers: teary eyes and weeping. For the expositor of the Book of Tobias says that prayer softens God, but tears truly force him to mercy. Tearful prayer is therefore not only pleasing or agreeable to God, but even violent toward him, because the omnipotence of the creator, utterly invincible, must necessarily yield and surrender to it, defeated.

God's "defeat" is both willed by the creator and utterly necessary; it is the culmination of an eschatological *procès* that God has chosen to conduct in the perfected form of a rhetorical dialog. By the same token, God willed that human beings be able to learn successful participation in this dialog, and that they do so through the initially pagan template of Ciceronian legal oratory. For Guillaume d'Auvergne, as for those who created the Devil's Rights, then, rhetoric had a more than allegorical importance in the heavenly court: it described a real set of practices that human beings could use to mount a successful self-defense in heaven. While Brunetto Latini's *Rettorica* expanded the definition of Cicero's judicial rhetoric to encompass the *tencione* of frustrated lovers, *Rhetorica divina* glossed the teachings of *De inventione* to include prayer, thus inserting the Ciceronian model orator into an entirely different forum for disputation.

Guillaume wrote his Latin treatise especially for fellow clerics and monks, whose primary function in society was prayer. But the spirit of Guillaume's divine rhetoric also seems to echo in the work of vernacular devotional poets, especially those associated with the northern French confraternities. These poets, many of them anonymous amateurs, likewise envisioned prayer as a prescriptive, legalistic rhetoric—a craft whose technical principles could be practiced and mastered. The great difference is that the confraternal poets applied the idea of *rhetorica divina* to second rhetoric, concentrating on rules of verse rather than on structural principles of prose oratory. Nevertheless, these poets also celebrated the juridical aspect of the *rhetor divinus,* as they modeled their own work on the Virgin's exceptional powers of legal defense and, through their devotional compositions, participated in the very same intercessional *procès* as Advocata Nostra.

---

54. Guillaume d'Auvergne, *Rhetorica divina*, ch. 27 (ed. Teske, 200). In this one regard, Dante's tears in *Purgatorio* are evocative of Guillaume's *rhetor divinus.*

IV. Divine Rhetoric in Action: The *Puys*

In twelfth-century Arras, as Carol Symes has documented in brilliant detail, the confraternal order of the Carité de Notre Dame des Ardents began to put on its annual *puy*.[55] This was an event of public feasting and Marian devotional verse and theatre, including poetry contests judged by members of the Carité. The Carité was founded and governed by a group of the city's *jongleurs,* who were both minstrels and civic and household functionaries. By the time of the *puy*'s establishment, the economic and civic structure of the Artois region had given rise to favorable conditions for a sophisticated rhetorical culture in Picard French, in which verbal disputation and formal dialog were highly valued.[56] In this cultural context, the *jongleurs* of the Carité played an important role, and a virtuosic one. The *jongleurs* demonstrated their poetic skills by composing, reciting, and performing lyric and dramatic pieces in Picard. As they had received legal and notarial training and were skilled in drawing up court documents, they also frequently acted as mediators between various parties, and so gained substantial social prestige.[57] The *jongleurs*' understanding of law was, moreover, closely tied to "a self-conscious sense of theatricality," in which legal oratory, drama, and poetry became at times indistinguishable.[58]

It seems that the professional talents of which these urban notary-poets boasted as verbal factota—a mastery of legal terminology, formal rhetoric and vernacular verse—could also be extended to successful communication with the heavenly court. As Symes puts it, the confraternity was precisely a way for the *jongleurs* to "advertise their ability to act as intermediaries among different groups of people," while, through a certain Pauline logic, their alternate identities as motley fools also made them "piously receptive to the call of the divine."[59] Ultimately, the *jongleurs* claimed to receive their unusual civic prestige and their authority over the *puy* from an apparition of the Virgin to two of their number in 1105. With the aid of a miraculous candle they received from the Virgin, the minstrels are credited with help-

---

55. Symes, *A Common Stage.*
56. See Ibid., 27. Symes argues that the conjunction of legal, dramatic and poetic rhetoric in the Artois had much to do with the fact that Picard was "in precocious use" there "as a literary language," as "a language for the performance of plays," and as "a language of public record from the earliest years of the thirteenth century" (175). It is worth noting that one of Brunetto Latini's places of exile was Arras, and that he composed his *Tresor* in Picard French.
57. See Symes, *A Common Stage,* 42–43.
58. See Ibid., 176–77 (quote from 176). On the close connections between legal rhetoric and theatre, see also Enders, *Rhetoric and the Origins of Medieval Drama.*
59. Symes, *A Common Stage,* 85.

ing to save Arras from the devastating disease of ergotism, also known as Saint Anthony's, or Saint Martial's fire.[60]

The Arrageois Carité and its *puy* had a significant influence on the broader landscape of European vernacular poetry, inspiring similar organizations and annual Marian festivals in other northern-French cities like Rouen and Paris,[61] but also further afield—for example, in England and Castile.[62] The confraternities were arguably some of the most important rhetorical institutions of their time. By establishing standards for fixed-form composition in the vernacular which were then applied to particular lyric pieces during the annual judgments of the *puys,* these organizations contributed greatly to the development of poetry as second rhetoric.[63]

Wherever the confraternal tradition spread, it confirmed the vocational ideal of the poet as *rhetor divinus,* able to persuade saintly and divine audiences as well as earthly ones. Indeed, as Gérard Gros has shown, the *puys* could claim significant political clout precisely because of their well-known ability to pray effectively in verse.[64] Princes turned to poets involved with urban confraternal organizations as a means of obtaining an audience in heaven; in that, the *puys* functioned not unlike lay versions of monastic houses, intercessors with the intercessors and advocates among the saintly *advocati.* Their lyric prayers would move Mary and the host of saints to pity, and Christ to mercy.

Generally, the membership of the Arrageois-style confraternities which appeared throughout Europe in the later Middle Ages overlapped closely with that of specific trade guilds, from which each confraternity developed as an accessory organization. This makes the tradition a particularly interesting source for medieval views on the vocational identity of poets: although the confraternities were composed mostly of what we would consider amateur or occasional versifiers, their origin in the curious *jongleur*

---

60. The event is officially confirmed in an episcopal charter of 1241. See Ibid., 92.

61. For a good discussion of the confraternal tradition in Paris, see *Parisian Confraternity Drama of the Fourteenth Century: The Miracles de Nostre Dame par personages.* Ed. Donald Maddox, Sara Sturm-Maddox. Turnhout: Brepols, 2008. For the later tradition as it developed in Rouen, see Denis Hüe, *La poésie palinodique à Rouen, 1486–1550.* Paris: Champion, 2002.

62. Carol Symes has discussed the far-reaching influence of the *puy* of Arras, including in the court of Castille, where Alfonso X uses the story of the Virgin's blessing of the *jongleurs* in his own *Cantigas de Santa Maria* (*CSM* 259, cited by Symes in *A Common Stage,* 218 n105).

63. See Kelly, "Topical Invention," 233.

64. See Gérard Gros, *Le poète, la Vierge et le prince du puy: étude sur les puys marials de la France du nord du XIVe siècle à la Renaissance.* Paris: Klincksieck, 1992. 16, 32. See also Gros's similarly titled work *Le poète, la Vierge et le prince: étude sur la poésie mariale en milieu de cour aux XIVe et XV siècles.* Saint-Étienne: Publications de l'Université de Saint-Étienne, 1994.

class of Arras reveals points of permeability between poetry and a variety of other occupations.

As was the case with the *jongleur*-notaries of Arras, this permeability often included the legal profession and its accessory trades.[65] In the Occitan-speaking south, for example, the law faculty of the University of Toulouse adopted the *puy* model enthusiastically as it produced a sort of rulebook for Occitan devotional verse, the *Leys d'amors* (*The Laws of Love*, 1356).[66] The *Leys* address law students and aspiring Marian poets as one and the same audience, making more explicit than ever the need for the devotional poet to act as a kind of legal intermediary between earth and heaven. As a rulebook, the *Leys* might be thought of as the second rhetoric equivalent of Guillaume d'Auvergne's *Rhetorica divina*: they attempt to codify the best way for poets to achieve intercession, just as texts of legal rhetoric prescribe fixed models of argumentation designed to help lawyers win their cases. The *Leys* put a lawyerly stamp on devotional composition like never before, testifying to the historically more robust study of the civil law south of the Loire.[67] Nevertheless, this unique document had its origins in the peculiar mix of legal and divine oratory developed first in the north by the Artois *jongleurs,* among a rhetorical intelligentsia whose formal precepts were probably transmitted largely by mouth.

At the heart of this rhetorical culture, both oral and written, was the Virgin, venerated precisely as a divine rhetorician in so much of the devotional poetry and religious theatre produced and promoted by the confraternities; *Pierre le changeur,* for example, was originally staged at the Puy des Orfèvres, the annual festival of the powerful gold-workers' guild of Paris. Writing and performing mystery plays like *Pierre,* confraternal participants were not only praising Mary's capacity to argue for God's mercy, but also indirectly advertising their own exceptional powers of language, which could help to secure the Virgin's assistance. For confraternal poets,

---

65. In *Rhetoric and the Origins of Medieval Drama* (see especially 129–61), Enders discusses mystery plays and notes the importance of the Basoche, founded in 1303, which performed theatrical mock trials and was closely tied to confraternal organizations. As Enders points out, by the mid-fourteenth century, the Basoche had a partnership with the Confrérie de la Passion, and "in 1400 Paris lawyers formed the Communauté des Procureurs et Avocats au Parlement to replace the Confrérie de Saint Nicolas, named for the patron saint of law and drama—and apparently of legal drama as well" (134).

66. Catherine Léglu has argued convincingly for the direct influence of the *puy* of Arras on the Occitan Consistori; see "Languages in Conflict in Toulouse: *Las leys d'amor.*" *Modern Language Review* 103.2 (April 2008): 383–96, especially 383–84.

67. On the stronger tradition of legal learning in Occitania, see, for example, Brundage, *Medieval Origins*, 91, 350.

the Virgin was in this regard a true *patrona*—not only a patron or protector, but also a pattern or model who exemplified their own practice of divine rhetoric and heavenly mediation.

In that the purpose of the confraternities' art was nothing less than winning salvation—an oratorical "defeat" of God like that described by Guillaume d'Auvergne—the annual poetry contests which the confraternities adjudicated can be described with no exaggeration as formal decisions on what sort of poetry is most pleasing and most persuasive to the divine ear or the holy Advocata. The judgment of the *puys* suggests, implicitly but inescapably, a kind of divine judgment by proxy, in which the confraternities' authority is based on a special insight into the rhetoric most effective in securing mercy for the human defendant. Here then, the judgment of devotional poetry already suggests one way in which the judgment of the medieval reader or listener—the *petit juge*—became closely identifiable with the omniscient discernment of the *Grand Juge*. Here, ethics and rhetoric are inseparable, as the whole art of vernacular versification is turned toward the poet's ability to advocate for other people's souls and for his own.

Many poets who participated in the confraternities and their *puys* have remained anonymous to us. Others, like the Arrageois genius Adam de la Halle (c. 1240–c. 1287), were some of the most instrumental figures in what Michel Zink has rightly designated the personal turn of thirteenth-century French poetry.[68] In the following century, Guillaume de Machaut and Jean Froissart both competed successfully in various northern French *puys*.[69] The work of these poets vividly reflects the spirited rhetorical environment of the yearly gatherings, the fixed form lyrics, like the *chant royal* and *rondeau*, which they helped to popularize and codify, and the emphasis which the *puys* placed on lyric poetry as, at once, a species of prayer and an object of rhetorical judgment. As I suggest in the next chapter, although Guillaume de Deguileville was writing from a monastic rather than a civic perspective, he likewise fashioned his own lyric prayers to the saints within a framework of legal oratory evocative of the same traditions of divine rhetoric. Building upon images of the eschatological drama

---

68. Zink, *La subjectivité littéraire*. See Adam de la Halle, *Œuvres complètes*. Ed. Pierre-Yves Badel. Paris: Livre de Poche, 1995. As Sylvia Huot points out, Adam was also one of the first poets to produce single-author compilations (*From Song to Book*, 64–74).

69. See Daniel Poirion, *Le poète et le prince: l'évolution du lyrisme courtois de Guillaume de Machaut à Charles d'Orléans*. Paris: Presses Universitaires de France, 1965. 209; Gérard Gros, *Le poème du puy marial: étude sur le serventois et le chant royal du XIVe siècle à la Renaissance*. Paris: Klincksieck, 1996. 84–97; Jacqueline Cerquiglini-Toulet, *La couleur de la mélancholie: la fréquentation des livres au XIVe siècle, 1300–1415*. Paris: Hatier, 1993. 10–11.

largely established in the thirteenth century, Deguileville moved himself definitively to center stage in this drama—into the dual role of defendant and advocate.

Before considering the great pseudo-autobiographical narratives of fourteenth-century authors, however, it is necessary to make one final consideration. In this chapter, I have sketched the outlines of the heavenly court scene as it appeared in the thirteenth and early fourteenth centuries in France, showing how the devotional poet came to represent himself as a *rhetor divinus,* an active participant in the rigorous legal and rhetorical process of divine justice. One element is still missing from this scene as it would be staged by later fourteenth-century poets like Deguileville. This element concerns the text or texts at the center of the eschatological trial.

In thirteenth- and early fourteenth-century versions of the Devil's Rights, Satan and the scribe-demon Tutivillus draw their arguments from a seemingly incontrovertible body of spiritual record books, including the Book of Conscience and the damning evidence against mankind found in Scriptural sources like Genesis. The Virgin counters the Devil's arguments by citing other texts, especially the New Testament and the New Law. In the course of the fourteenth century, the set of written documents providing evidence for or against the human soul assumes another aspect entirely, as it becomes identifiable with the compiled corpus of the author. The poet's restless toil of composing, assembling, and defending a body of work over time was increasingly mirrored in the evidentiary texts at the center of the eschatological scene, and it was increasingly on behalf of a corpus-in-progress that fourteenth-century authors were moved to perform works of divine rhetoric. These developments in eschatological representation were anticipated in many ways by the poetics of Marian advocacy, which oppose the Satanic attachment to unchanging texts with the divine virtues of reinterpretation and rewriting; likewise, other thirteenth-century poets—such as Guillaume le Clerc, Rutebeuf, and Jean de Meun—began to suggest an equivalence between their writing and the permanent eschatological record.[70]

However, it was not until the practice of single-author compilation took firm root that poets would fully exploit correspondences between the legal documents fought over in the heavenly court and the literary document of the corpus. A new phenomenon at the beginning of the fourteenth century, and at first also a largely French phenomenon, complete-works codices of single vernacular authors quickly became commonplace in book produc-

---

70. See above, Introduction, 17–21.

tion, and they occupy a central place in claims that later medieval poets made to literary authority.

Guillaume de Deguileville's *Pèlerinage de l'âme* (c. 1356) was part of the emerging tradition of single-author manuscripts, and part of one of its most widely copied examples, Deguileville's triad of allegorical pilgrimage narratives. *Pèlerinage de l'âme* is itself a distinct rewriting of the Devil's Rights scenario (one source Dante did not share with Deguileville). Here, the author casts himself as both defendant and advocate, pleading eloquently on his own behalf before the heavenly court and managing to save his soul. As I demonstrate, Deguileville appropriates the judicial scene of the Devil's Rights, and makes the Virgin Mary's rhetoric his own, in order to stage the judgment of his work by readers and his own response to it. Deguileville thus effects a transformation of the heavenly court into a venue for considering the ethics of literature, a venue in which the author gives himself the opportunity to respond in the first person to the accusations weighing against his corpus.

CHAPTER 2

A Particular Judgment
The Case of Deguileville's *Pèlerinage de l'âme*

I. Introduction

As the Devil's Rights tradition shows, the courtroom drama is not a recent invention, nor is it confined to legal proceedings on earth. Texts like *L'advocacie Nostre Dame* and *Pierre le changeur* fill the scene of divine judgment with outraged prosecutors, silver-tongued attorneys, and controversial defendants whose eternal souls hang in the balance. In the middle of the fourteenth century, Guillaume de Deguileville (1295–after 1358), a Cistercian monk at the royal abbey of Chaalis,[1] developed in further detail the legal intrigue of this eschatological tradition.

Around 1356, Deguileville wrote his *Pèlerinage de l'âme* (*PA*).[2] The speaker of the poem—or self-designated *pèlerin*—narrates a dream in which he dies and travels through heaven, hell and purgatory. Deguileville's narrator-pilgrim is no passive observer of the world beyond, since the dream begins with his own soul's judgment in the heavenly court. At the conclusion of this trial scene, the soul is sentenced to a term in purgatory, from which the narrator has a close-up view of hell's punishments, before travel-

---

1. Deguileville may have been the prior of Chaalis. See Edmond Faral, "Guillaume de Digulleville: Moine de Chaalis," *Histoire littéraire de la France*. 43 vols. Paris: Imprimerie Nationale, 1865–2005. XXXIX: 8.

2. I cite from the only modern edition of *Le Pèlerinage de l'âme*, now in rare circulation (Ed. J. J. Sturzinger. London: Nichols, 1895).

ling upward again to discover heaven's mysteries. In my discussion of *PA*, however, I will focus mostly on the scene of the pilgrim's judgment, which occupies roughly the first quarter of this 11,000-verse poem.

The trial of Deguileville's narrator closely follows the pattern of the Devil's Rights.[3] *PA* begins as the narrator dies. His soul ascends from its body and immediately encounters its guardian angel, who intends to take it to heaven. But just as quickly, Satan appears and claims that the pilgrim's soul is rightfully his. Agreeing to present their cases to the heavenly court for judgment, the three then continue upward to the gates of paradise. When they arrive, a formal trial begins. Although the pilgrim's view of the courtroom is blocked by a large curtain, he can clearly hear the proceedings as a case is mounted against him.[4] Satan, aided by Raison, Justice and Verité, faces off against the pilgrim's defense team, led by Misericorde (Mercy). Both sides rely on the testimony of formidable witnesses: for the defense, the pilgrim's guardian angel, the Virgin Mary and Saint Benedict. The plaintiffs, on the other hand, need just one witness—the pilgrim's own conscience, in the form of the hideous worm-woman Synderesis.[5] The trial is adjudicated by the archangel Michael, whom God has appointed to preside over the judgment of souls prior to the Resurrection:

---

3. In particular, Faral notes the influence of *L'advocacie* on Deguileville ("Guillaume de Digulleville," 49 n4). See also Moreau, "'*Ce mauvais tabellion.*'" *L'advocacie* is the most important source for the trial scene, although not for the subsequent voyage through the afterworld. The most thorough account of the entire tradition of otherworldly voyage narrative, and Deguileville's place in it, is given by Fabienne Pomel, *Les voies de l'au-delà et l'essor de l'allégorie au Moyen Âge*. Paris: Champion, 2001. Michael Camille identified as influences on Deguileville Raoul de Houdenc's *Songe d'enfer* (1255) and the anonymous thirteenth-century *Voie de Paradis* ("The Illustrated Manuscripts of Guillaume de Deguileville's *Pèlerinages*, 1330–1426." 2 vols. Diss. Cambridge University, 1985. I: 7). See also the two articles by Stanley Leman Galpin: "On the Sources of Guillaume de Deguileville's *Pèlerinage de l'âme*." *PMLA* 25.2 (1910): 275–308; "Notes on the Sources of Deguileville's *Pèlerinage de l'âme*." *MLN* 28.1 (1913 January): 8–10.

4. Before his view is obstructed, however, the pilgrim is bathed in celestial light and feels intense joy—a momentary glimpse of the beatific vision which the 1336 bull *Benedictus Deus* had confirmed as doctrine. Through this gesture, the pilgrim is judged one of the saved before the trial even begins. At the end of the poem, once he has spent his term in purgatory, and immediately before waking up from his dream, the pilgrim is afforded another, slightly longer such vision (vv. 11002–13).

5. Conscience and synderesis are not exactly the same thing. Synderesis is usually understood in medieval discourse as the general inclination toward the good possessed by everybody and incapable of making a mistake. Conscience, on the other hand, consists in the application of this inclination to particular circumstances and can be mistaken. See Linda Hogan, *Confronting the Truth: Conscience in the Catholic Tradition*. Mahwah, NJ: Paulist Press, 2000. 66–87. See also Pomel, *Voies*, 355. I use the term "conscience" to translate the character Synderesis for the sake of convenience.

Jusqu'a tant quë au jugement	until such time as he [Christ]
Il descendra personnelment	will descend in person
Pour les grans assises tenir.	to hold his great tribunal.
(vv. 315–17)	

Deguileville's insistence on the particular judgment of the individual soul, before the *grans assises,* is crucial to an understanding of the author's importance in the history of eschatological representation and authorial subjectivity. The opening to *Pèlerinage de l'âme* was one of the first, and certainly one of the most influential, depictions of the particular judgment, which had assumed more doctrinal importance than ever by the middle of the fourteenth century, following the 1336 papal bull *Benedictus Deus.*[6] With the miracle play *Pierre le changeur* in the early fourteenth century, I have already discussed one dramatization of the particular judgment. But while *Pierre* illustrates a shift in the identity of the defendant from mankind to a specific man, Deguileville's most important addition to the Devil's Rights scenario was in making this individual defendant speak in the first person, and in the name of the author himself.

The resemblance of Deguileville and his defendant is confirmed during the trial when Justice enters into evidence against the pilgrim a letter which had been written to him by his mentor Grace Dieu (Grace of God).[7] As Justice alleges, Grace Dieu had sent the letter to warn the pilgrim that he must repent or risk damnation, but he took no heed of the admonition. We may be sure, Justice asserts, that this incriminating document was addressed to the pilgrim and to none other, since the first letters of its twenty-four stanzas spell out his Latinized name: *Guillermus de Deguilevilla* (vv. 1593–784). This is one of four acrostic signatures in Deguileville's body of work, and one of two such signatures to appear in a scene where the pilgrim is put on trial.[8] For Deguileville, authorial *subjectivity* is double-sided: the *Je* takes shape as a grammatical subject, but only as a response to the accusations of the other, to whose judgments it is always already subject.[9]

Not that the response comes easily. As in the Devil's Rights, the ability of the defendant to receive any kind of representation is a central point of

---

6. On the impact of the bull, see Camille, "The Illustrated Manuscripts," I: 123–24; Baschet, "Jugement de l'âme, Jugement dernier," 178.

7. For more on how this letter both accuses and individuates the pilgrim, see Pomel, *Voies,* 406.

8. The second of these scenes takes place in the 1355 version of *Pèlerinage de vie humaine,* and is discussed below, 84–87.

9. In a similar way, Dante names himself only once in the *Commedia*—at the head of Beatrice's long accusation against him (*Purgatorio* 30.55). See above, Chapter 1, 41–42.

contention in the trial. In *Pèlerinage de l'âme,* Satan and Justice both object vociferously to the defendant being allowed to argue now that the Judgment is at hand,[10] and they are especially concerned that the pilgrim's words will "toute exciter" (v. 1090), stirring up passion in the heavenly court, where it doesn't belong. But the plaintiffs' objections are neatly overruled. Saint Michael grants the defendant the right to respond and, indeed, places this decision beyond argument:

. . . Bien est chose digne	. . . It truly is a worthy thing
Que responde le pelerin	that the pilgrim speak for himself,
De sa voie et de son chemin,	responding about the path he has taken
Des ouvrages quë il a fait	and the deeds he has done,
Et que n'ait d'autre chose plait,	and that on this there be no more debate,
Car ceste court ainsi le veult.	because this court wills it thus. |//
(vv. 1119–24)

And in the end, Deguileville's pilgrim defends himself more than adequately. Although he initially admits to great anxiety about securing representation or assembling a defense (vv. 701–38), Guillermus manages to talk his way out of Satan's grip. In a first speech (vv. 739–1074), an elaborate, inset lyric-prayer, the pilgrim implores the heavenly court to provide him with their advocacy and the spiritual "alms" he needs to afford such high-powered attorneys as they. He calls directly upon individual members of the court, including Christ, Mary, and the Cistercian saints Benedict, Bernard and Guillaume de Bourges, pleading with them for assistance. Later, he takes the floor again (vv. 1406–84) to speak more directly in his defense: while recognizing that he did commit grave sins, in the same breath he displaces a large measure of responsibility for those sins onto Satan and the illusions of the world, whom he claims deceived him into wrongdoing. In response to Guillermus's pleas, Misericorde and the Virgin intercede with Christ on his behalf and Benedict provides the court with written evidence of the pilgrim's good deeds during his years as a Cistercian. Finally, Christ is moved to issue a special formal pardon ("Un don de grace especial," v. 2383) to all the wretched pilgrims of the world ("les pelerins chetis," v. 2381) who, like Deguileville's narrator, have recognized the error of their ways, even at the very end. Guillermus will go to purgatory, not hell.

While he uses it to request saintly assistance, it is the pilgrim's own legal and poetic rhetoric which really takes center stage in this eschato-

---

10. See, for example, *Pèlerinage de l'âme,* vv. 671–72, vv. 1077–84.

logical drama. Pleading eloquently with the saints, Deguileville's narrator showcases the verbal dexterity of the author himself, who, a fourteenth-century *rhetor divinus*, insists on his instrumentality in the process of intercession, and on the inseparability of prayer and second rhetoric. As prayer, the pilgrim's oratory reminds us that Deguileville was a Cistercian monk, part of whose job it was to pray for intercession. As second rhetoric, the pilgrim's speeches insist on his status as a poetic substitute for the author, skilled in the composition of devotional, vernacular verse. In particular, Guillermus's first address to the court (vv. 739–1074) is one of many inset lyric poems found throughout Deguileville's body of work, all of which serve to put into relief the pseudo-autobiographical presence of the poet.[11] As is the case with the narrators of Guillaume de Machaut and Jean Froissart, whom I discuss later, Deguileville's pilgrim symbolically performs the author's own act of poetic creation within the narrative.[12] For Deguileville as for his forerunners in the *puys* of northern France, the poetic, legal and eschatological aspects of rhetoric came together in the figure of Mary, advocate for mankind and patron of the Cistercian order. As Deguileville adapted the Devil's Rights model to the narrative of his own unique persona, he too saw the Virgin as the ultimate exemplar for using language persuasively, and it is the Virgin who is finally responsible for securing Christ's mercy in *Pèlerinage de l'âme*.

The difference with Deguileville, once again, concerns the voice of a first-person subject: as the defendant speaks for himself, the role of the saintly advocate is diminished. Indeed, as I have shown in a previous article, Deguileville went so far in *Pèlerinage de l'âme* as to reassign some of Mary's most powerful arguments from *L'advocacie Nostre Dame* to himself, and to reduce her presence to behind-the-scenes only.[13] While other poets had suggested that their powers of composition drew inspiration from the Virgin's lawyerly rhetoric, Deguileville stepped straight into the role of divine orator. In *PA*, this does not lessen Mary's importance, but rather shifts the dramatic focus to the Cistercian poet as intercessor with the intercessors.

---

11. The most famous of these inset lyrics is the ABC-poem from *Pèlerinage de vie humaine*, which Chaucer later adapted. On the importance of the ABC-poem, and on Deguileville's neglected lyric insertions in general, see Helen Phillips, "Chaucer and Deguileville: the ABC in Context." *Medium Ævum* 62.1 (Spring 1993): 1–19.

12. As Phillips writes, "Like many late mediaeval dream poems, the *Pèlerinage*, particularly [its second redaction], is a sophisticated lyrico-narrative hybrid, with the potentiality for raising provocative questions about relations between texts and life" ("Chaucer and Deguileville," 15). See also Denis Hüe, "L'apprentissage de la louange: pour une typologie de la prière dans les *Pèlerinages* de Guillaume de Digulleville," in *Guillaume de Digulleville: les* Pèlerinages *allégoriques*. Ed. Frédéric Duval, Fabienne Pomel. Rennes: Presses Universitaires de Rennes, 2008. 159–84.

13. Moreau, "'*Ce mauvais tabellion.*'"

The defendant Guillermus de Deguilevilla functions as a literary persona for the author through his name and through his identity as a divine rhetorician. As I demonstrate in this chapter, a still stronger resemblance between poet and narrator emerges once we consider how the heavenly trial scene allows Deguileville to address controversies involving his own writing. These controversies center around another long vision poem by Deguileville, the *Pèlerinage de vie humaine*, which had appeared prior to *PA* in two distinct versions (c. 1330–31 and 1355), and in which the same first-person speaker—the pilgrim Guillermus—had also been the narrator.[14] In the majority of manuscripts in which *PA* has been copied, it is preceded by the first version of *Pèlerinage de vie humaine*, although a small group of copies place after it the second; in turn, *PA* is often followed by Deguileville's third and final major poem, *Le Pèlerinage Jhesucrist*.[15] The three pilgrimage narratives constitute the bulk of Deguileville's extant work,[16] and their customary coexistence as a unified whole makes the Cistercian an important figure in the history of single-author compilation, even if it cannot be shown conclusively that he was directly involved in manuscript production.[17]

In *PA*, as he represents his namesake defeating the studied arguments of the Devil, Deguileville also speaks to readers—and to a readerly God—in order to defend himself against accusations surrounding *Pèlerinage de vie humaine*. In that, the poet's rhetoric constitutes a defense not only of the narrator or author's *anima*—his soul—but also of the *corpus*—the entire body of work for which that soul is answerable.[18] In *Pèlerinage de l'âme*,

---

14. He is not yet called Guillermus in the first version of *Pèlerinage de vie humaine*. The pilgrim is, however, named indirectly in *PVH1* through his father, Thomas de Deguileville (v. 5965).

15. For the most comprehensive summary of Deguileville's manuscripts, see Géraldine Veysseyre, Julia Drobinsky, and Émilie Fréger, "Liste des manuscrits des trois *Pèlerinages*," in Duval and Pomel, eds., *Guillaume de Digulleville: les* Pèlerinages *allégoriques*, 425–53. *Le Pèlerinage Jhesucrist* does not occur with the same frequency as *PVH* or even *PA*, and it is sometimes positioned as the first text in the trilogy rather than the last.

16. The only exception is Deguileville's minor work *Le roman de la fleur de lis*. See Arthur Piaget's edition, "Un roman inédit de Guillaume de Digulleville: *Le roman de la fleur de lis*." *Romania* 62 (1936): 317–58.

17. The most problematic aspect of this question is the dating of Deguileville's manuscripts, most of which were produced after the middle of the fourteenth century. On these dates, see, again Veysseyre, Drobinsky, and Fréger, "Liste des manuscrits des trois *Pèlerinages*." For a good analysis of how one manuscript may have reflected the author's designs, see Graham Robert Edwards, "Making Sense of Deguileville's Autobiographical Project: The Evidence of Paris, Bibliothèque nationale de France MS Latin 14845," in Nievergelt and Kamath, eds., *The Pèlerinage Allegories of Guillaume de Deguileville*, 129–50.

18. I owe much of my thinking about the pseudo-autobiographical corpus to Laurence De Looze, as I have discussed in the Introduction (11–12). Maupeu (*Pèlerins de vie humaine*, 193) makes a similar point about Deguileville when he compares the pilgrim's injured body to Alain de Lille's *liber experientiae* and later, to the broken book-body of Pierre Abelard (*Pèlerins de vie humaine*, 208).

as never before, the particular judgment became a forum for dramatizing the author's responsibility to readers, and his ensuing work of assembling a spiritually whole self-image through the composition of a unitary Book.[19]

The "other scene" of this heavenly trial—the way it reflects the ethical relationship between author and audience—is revealed through a complex and often puzzling set of allusions embedded in the text. In his thoroughly pseudo-autobiographical narrative, Deguileville suggested many points of comparison—often quite subtle—between the soul's judgment and the author's ongoing dialog with readers. Recall, for example, Saint Michael's judgment that the pilgrim be allowed to speak for himself and for the "ouvrages quë il a fait" (v. 1121). The archangel's use of the term "ouvrages" should be understood in its double sense—both morally consequential deeds and literary texts. Indeed, for Deguileville, this is less of a play on words than it is a matter of belief which invests literary production with ethical weight. In that he is a first-person narrator who speaks in Deguileville's name, the pilgrim must respond both for what he has done and for what the author has written. Thus, although Deguileville's work is steeped in complex allegorical imagery, the judgment of his narrator's soul by God does not function so much as an allegory for Deguileville's judgment by readers, as it demonstrates how divine and readerly deliberation inevitably come together in the later medieval author's trial.

Before it can be fully understood just how this trial stages the particular judgment of a literary controversy or the difficult elaboration of a poetic corpus, it is necessary to examine the case of Deguileville's first-person defendant in its entirety, which is to say Deguileville's *ouvrages*, the poetry he wrote before *PA*. To provide a thorough account of the potential literary judgments to which the defendant Guillermus de Deguilevilla may have been subject by the second half of the 1350s, when *PA* appeared, I turn now to Deguileville's two redactions of his *Pèlerinage de vie humaine*.

In addition to providing important context for the circulation and criticism of Deguileville's poetry, these earlier narratives already begin to describe the author's work and its reception through episodes of accusation, self-defense, and judgment. And well before he reaches the heavenly court, the narrator Guillermus expresses his awareness that the judgments of this world—literary as well as juridical—are forever exposed to the Judgment from on high. Punctuated with incriminations, justifications, and counteraccusations, *PVH1* and *PVH2* constitute a kind of case file,[20] which is to

---

19. On the idea of authorial responsibility in *PA*, see Pomel, *Voies*, 413–14.
20. Fabienne Pomel has investigated the thoroughly juridical character of the many documents

be reopened before the heavenly court in *Pèlerinage de l'âme,* and in which the author must face his divine and human judges all at once. The evolving narrative of the *Pèlerinages* gives us a consistent picture of Guillermus de Deguilevilla as a legal subject who must answer for the sins of the author.

I begin, therefore, by considering the apparent controversies of Deguileville's career, and the ways in which the Cistercian poet already used his earlier work to stage his relationship to readers and critics in terms of an ongoing legal and eschatological *procès*. Having taken into account the complex literary background of this case, I am then able to return to the scene of judgment in *PA* in the second half of the chapter, in order to demonstrate how Deguileville's earlier writing reemerges there as a matter for eschatological scrutiny and self-defense.

II. *Des ouvrages quë il a fait*: The First Two Pèlerinages

In 1330 or 1331, Deguileville completed the first version of a long allegorical dream vision, the *Pèlerinage de vie humaine* (*PVH1*). In *PVH1*, the author cast his first-person narrator (still unnamed) as a pilgrim on the way to the heavenly Jerusalem, just as he would do again in *PA*, when Guillermus is halted before the gates of the city of God by Satan's accusation. *PVH1* recounts the pilgrim's difficult journey through life, from birth to death. This includes, most memorably, his troubled wanderings on the left-hand side of the enormous Hedge of Penitence, which stretches the length of his pilgrimage route. On this, the wrong side of the hedge, the pilgrim is repeatedly attacked by vicious personifications of the seven deadly sins. At last, with the help of his patient guide Grace Dieu, the narrator makes it alive to the Ship of Religion—the monastic life—which promises to convey him safely across the perilous sea of worldly existence (La Mer du Monde) to the heavenly Jerusalem.

The first *Pèlerinage de vie humaine* became one of the most popular literary works of medieval Europe. In its original form, it was copied into no fewer than sixty-four extant manuscripts,[21] translated into numerous lan-

---

comprising Deguileville's body of work in "Les écrits pérégrins ou les voies de l'autorité chez Guillaume de Deguileville: Le modèle épistolaire et juridique," in Nievergelt and Kamath, eds., *The Pèlerinage Allegories of Guillaume de Deguileville,* 91–111. In the same volume, see also Moreau, "'*Ce mauvais tabellion.*'"

21. See Maupeu, *Pèlerins,* 270. See also Veysseyre, Drobinsky, and Fréger, "Liste des manuscrits des trois *Pèlerinages.*"

guages, regularly reworked in French verse and prose, and used as the basis for a vast tradition of allegorical texts.[22] But in 1355, a quarter of a century after *PVH* had first appeared—and immediately prior to the appearance of *PA*—the now sexagenarian Deguileville gave the world a drastic revision of *PVH1*. The second *Pèlerinage de vie humaine* (*PVH2*) is significantly longer than the first, and contains many noteworthy amplifications, additions, and omissions.[23]

In a new prologue, Deguileville introduces *PVH2* by explaining that, as is often the case when one dreams, he did not remember his vision all at once; only little by little did it come back to mind (vv. 1–8).[24] Claiming that *PVH1* was but a preliminary draft jotted down upon awaking, he laments that it had been copied widely before it was ready to be diffused. He blames this on a nameless person (later designated simply as "celui," v. 49) who had stolen the text from him:

Sans mon sceü et volenté	Without my knowledge or consent
Tout mon escript me fu osté,	my whole text was taken from me,
Par tout divulgué, et scet Dieu	made known everywhere, and God knows
Que je ne le tien pas a gieu,	that I do not consider this a pleasant thing,
Quar a mettre et a oster,	for much was left to add and to remove,
A corrigier et ordener	to correct and to put into good order,
Y avoit mout, si com perceu	as I realized after,
Apres quant bien esveilé fu.	when I had awakened fully.
(vv. 31–38)	

The author says that he made a thorough effort to search out the unauthorized, prematurely circulated copies of *PVH1* and correct them (vv. 39–42). This being unsuccessful, Deguileville wrote *PVH2*, which he describes as a sort of placard to be hung around the neck of the first version in order to announce the corrections to readers already familiar with the text of 1330–31:

---

22. The French portion of the tradition after Deguileville is discussed at greatest length by Maupeu in his *Pèlerins de vie humaine*. For the manuscript and early printed edition history, see 267–338. For later reworkings of Deguileville's allegory by other French authors, see 339–589.

23. For summaries of the changes made in the second redaction, see Faral, "Guillaume de Digulleville," 29–47; Maupeu, *Pèlerins de vie humaine*, 64.

24. Quotations and citations of the prologue are taken from Maupeu, *Pèlerins de vie humaine*, 55–57, where Maupeu has edited the first 94 lines of *PVH2*. All other quotations and verse citations from *PVH2* in this chapter are from my own close observations of the text as it appears in ms. BNF fr. 829.

Et iceluy amendement	And, as it is, this amendment
Quel qu'il soit et adrecement	and this putting-to-rights
Tout entour le coul li pendray,	I will hang around his neck,
Pour ce que veoir le vouray	for I would like it to be seen
Par tous les lieus ou a esté	in all the places he has been
Sans mon vouloir et sans mon gré.	without my consent or will.
(vv. 63–68)	

This strange image suggests that Deguileville conceived the revised *pèlerinage* as an act of literary penance, that his narrator was to perform a ritual return to the places he had already been—in the world of readers as much as along the allegorical hedgerow—to announce the sins he had committed in the first pilgrimage.

The revised prologue is startling and obscure. It has left Deguileville's modern interpreters with a host of questions. To begin with, for what must the pilgrim atone? I think the answer lies partly in the failure of the *PVHI* narrator to provide a suitable example for Christian readers. Not only does the pilgrim initially choose the wrong side of the hedgerow (that is, he avoids repentance), but while there, he repeatedly fails to ward off the attacks of the sins. And he consistently ignores the advice of Grace Dieu about how best to defend himself—notably, by donning his heavy spiritual armor, which the personification Memoire is good enough to carry for him everywhere he travels. The pilgrim is prevented by arming himself by the character Peresce (Sloth), who captured him at the beginning of his journey. If Deguileville's narrative is meant to represent the journey of a Christian through life, it cannot be thought very exemplary, except as a model of what not to do. For most of the poem, the pilgrim learns precious little from his long-suffering mentor Grace Dieu, displays an almost comical lack of resolve, and is literally beaten by the sins time and again. His entry onto the Ship of Religion seems like a last resort, born of a failure to exercise his free will and defend himself against Satan's influence in the world.

A negative model, or *repoussoir,* may have been what Deguileville had in mind with *PVHI*. In the poem's explicit, the author explains that his narrative has been a cautionary tale which Christian readers should use to avoid leaving the right-hand path to the city of God, presumably as his narrator-pilgrim had done:

Nulle erreur je ne vourroie	I should like to sow no error
Maintenir par nulle voie,	in any way, by any means,
Mes bien vourroie et ai voulu	but rather wish and have wanted

Que par le songe qu'ai vëu	that by the dream I have seen
Tous pelerins se radrecassent,	all pilgrims might find the right road,
Et de fourvoier se gardassent.	and that from detours they might turn away.
(vv. 13525–30)	

But perhaps *PVH1* had proved too much of a negative example. The author may have been motivated to return to his text in 1355 after twenty-five years because he felt readers were unable to separate the disastrous detours made by his first-person narrator from the overall spiritual lesson he intended the narrative to convey. The repeated failures of the narrator to keep to the straight and narrow may have offered a spectacle for prurient amusement which threatened to eclipse the text's didactic purpose.[25] Or more simply, Deguileville, older by a quarter of a century, may have felt that the original speaker was lacking in maturity and required some updating.

Whatever Deguileville's reasons for rewriting, his narrator comes off significantly better in the second version: unlike the narrator of *PVH1*, the revised pilgrim initially chooses the less attractive but correct (*droite*) path along the hedgerow—that of Labour—instead of opting for the seductive and spiritually lethal left-hand route of Huiseuse (Idleness). The narrator of *PVH2* only crosses to the hedgerow's *senestre* side later when Jeunece (Youth) forcibly carries the pilgrim there on her back. In addition, the pilgrim displays more bravery and resourcefulness during his time on the left side of the hedge. While he is beaten by all of the seven deadly sins in *PVH1*, he manages to fight most of them off in *PVH2* by heeding Grace Dieu's advice to don his armor, thus escaping from the clutches of Sloth.

It is not only a question in *PVH2* of greater spiritual brawn, but also of brains. In the first *Pèlerinage*, the pilgrim is forever asking Grace Dieu stupid questions and failing to grasp most of what she has to teach him. But in *PVH2*, the pilgrim is a more accomplished student. When he meets the rest of the sins who lie in wait for him after he breaks free of Sloth—and there are considerably more in the second version—he is able to defeat them by drawing on his impressive knowledge of doctrine.[26]

---

25. See Pierre-Yves Badel, *Le Roman de la Rose au XIVe siècle: étude de la réception de l'œuvre*. Geneva: Droz, 1980. 371.

26. The pilgrim refutes the claims of Astrologie and Idolatry, for example. See Philippe Maupeu, "La tentation autobiographique dans le songe allégorique édifiant de Guillaume de Deguileville: *Le pèlerinage de vie humaine*," in *Songes et songeurs (XIIIe–XVIIIe siècle)*. Ed. Nathalie Dauvois, Jean-Philippe Grosperrin. Québec: Les Presses de l'Université Laval, 2003. 65. As I discuss below (84–87), the pilgrim is viciously attacked by the same sins he first vanquished after escaping from Sloth—Envie, Trahison and Detraction, plus Conspiration—further along in *PVH2*. This, however, does not seem to be the pilgrim's fault, as it refers instead to treachery the author would have faced from among the brethren of Chaalis.

Improving his conduct from one version of the poem to another, the pilgrim becomes a more positive exemplar for readers to follow, his story no longer just a cautionary tale. But it is not the narrator alone who must make a revised pilgrimage to repent for his actions. Apostrophizing his original text in the new prologue, Deguileville designates the *Pèlerinage* itself as a pilgrim in the world:

Ne t'avoie pas apelé	Hadn't I called you
Pieça 'pelerin' et nommé	long ago 'pilgrim'
Afin qu'a cheval ne a pié	so that neither on horseback nor on foot
Alasses hors sans mon congié,	you would go forth without my leave,
Mes pour ce que te menasse	but rather that I might bring you
Avec moy quant je alasse	with me when I went
En Jerusalem la cité	into Jerusalem, that city
Ou d'aler estoie exité:	where I was stirred to go.
C'est ou je tent, ce est la fin	That's where I'm headed, and it's the end
Ou doit tendre tout pelerin.	to which every pilgrim should aspire.
(vv. 77–86)	

A wayward pilgrim, *PVH1* has strayed from its intended goal, or has been lured from the narrow path by those who copied and disseminated the text without the author's permission, before it had a chance to be perfected. Like the narrator, *PVH1* must also wear the penitential placard—the revision—to announce its errors to the world.

Deguileville himself is, however, the most important pilgrim to appear in these verses,[27] for it is he who will bring his book—his fellow pilgrim—with him to the heavenly city when he goes (vv. 81–82). The image implies that Deguileville's book will be opened and considered again at the Judgment. Like Rousseau four centuries later,[28] the author will stand before God with his work in hand. Or rather, he must stand with it hanging around his neck, and he fears that the unrevised poem may not represent him in the best light. He must regain control of his disobedient text and his defiant narrator, who are to accompany him to the New Jerusalem, and to whom he is bound for all eternity. Beginning all over again, the author must now

---

27. On the multivalent identity of Deguileville's pilgrim, see Maupeu, *Pèlerins de vie humaine*, 62. Similarly, Maupeu ("Tentation," 52) notes the three identities of the first-person subject: 1. dreaming narrator in bed at Chaalis, 2. allegorical dream-pilgrim, and 3. stand-in for the author. Maupeu (*Pèlerins de vie humaine*, 207–8) further points out that manuscript rubrics identify the narrator sometimes as "le pelerin," sometimes as "l'auteur" or "l'acteur."

28. See above, Introduction, 1–3, and below in the concluding chapter, 199–200.

guide his text and narrator back in the direction of his original intention in writing, that end "ou doit tendre tout pelerin" (v. 86).[29]

Whether or not his text had truly been taken from him, Deguileville insisted on the theme of authorial responsibility, on the poet's duty to answer even for the most unintended consequences of writing.[30] We must therefore consider what the author's perceived transgressions may have been, in addition to those of his narrator. Although his new prologue does not specify the nature of the *corrigenda,* the changes Deguileville made in *PVH2* have led scholars to a number of possible solutions. First, it has frequently been suggested that the 1355 revision may have been prompted by criticisms of Deguileville's poem by other monks in the abbey at Chaalis. As Fabienne Pomel notes, statements potentially critical of king and clergy have been omitted from the second version, while much more of the pilgrim's time is spent fighting enemies of the Church, with the addition of a host of personified sins not featured in *PVH1,* such as Hérésie, Nigromancie, Astrologie, Géomancie, Idolâtrie and Sorcerie.[31] In Pomel's words, "Guillaume aurait donc réécrit son texte pour le rendre plus conforme à une idéologie politique et religieuse, vraisemblablement à l'instigation de certains de ses proches ou supérieurs" ("Guillaume would thus have rewritten his text in order to make it conform better to a certain political and religious ideology, seemingly in response to certain of his peers or superiors.")[32] According to Philippe Maupeu, Deguileville's reasons for rewriting may have included a need for more doctrinal precision on matters concerning the Trinity, original sin, grace and free will.[33] While it is difficult to say with certainty what elements of *PVH1* would have prompted objections from Deguileville's readers, we may indeed consider many of the revisions as attempts to elaborate points of doctrine more clearly, if not to avoid charges of heterodoxy. The pilgrim's improved behavior—particularly his new ability to refute the personified enemies of the Church—seems to

---

29. Fabienne Pomel affirms that *PVH2* takes the form of a "pénitence rédemptrice pour son auteur" ("Enjeux d'un travail de réécriture: Les *incipits* du *Pèlerinage de vie humaine* de Guillaume de Digulleville et leurs remaniements ultérieurs." *Le Moyen Âge* 109.3–4 [2003]: 461).

30. Pomel writes that *PVH2* is part of the beginning of a "débat sur la responsabilité morale et idéologique de l'auteur et sur le statut du texte littéraire" ("Enjeux," 466). Pomel makes the same point elsewhere, more briefly, about *PA* (*Voies,* 413–14). See also Badel, *Le Roman de la Rose,* 371.

31. Pomel, "Enjeux," 460. See also Pomel, *Voies,* 246, 434–35; Maupeu, *Pèlerins de vie humaine,* 72–73; Maupeu, "Tentation," 51.

32. Pomel, "Enjeux," 460. See also Badel, *Le Roman de la Rose,* 367. Faral ("Guillaume de Digulleville," 33) has suggested that Deguileville's motives for revision may have been doctrinal in nature. On the question of orthodoxy, see also Maupeu, *Pèlerins de vie humaine,* 80–84.

33. Maupeu, *Pèlerins de vie humaine,* 83–84. See also Badel, *Le Roman de la Rose,* 375.

echo the position Deguileville himself may have needed to defend against critics.

In a broader sense, *PVH2* stands out as a more erudite work than *PVH1*, a facet of the revision which has likewise not gone unnoticed by prior scholarship.[34] The prologue of *PVH1* addresses a diverse congregation of listeners, rich and poor, male and female, lay and religious. As Deguileville announces it in the early 1330s, the endeavor of *pèlerinage* is the human condition in its entirety, the common legacy of the Fall and the collective journey back to God. Deguileville's audience is everyone, his pilgrim an allegorical stand-in for humankind facing tribulation. Apparently in order to reflect the author's project of lay evangelization, manuscript frontispieces for *PVH1* usually depict a tonsured speaker at a podium addressing a large crowd gathered outdoors.[35] *PVH1* is, furthermore, divided into four books which correspond to four days during which the dream vision is to be read aloud to the pilgrims of this world.[36]

These nods to orality and public preaching are by and large omitted in *PVH2*, which reads as being addressed to a more educated, more ecclesiastical (and more male) readership, rather than to a congregation of lay listeners. It is certainly questionable what use *PVH1* would have been to laypersons, since it highlights at every turn the inherent wickedness of worldly life and suggests that the pilgrim's debarkation onto the Ship of Religion is the only good solution to his problems. Now, the text seems destined more consciously for a monastic audience. *PVH2* includes several additions in Latin and macaronic verse as well as one in Latin prose, and introduces a host of theological topics not covered in *PVH1*. The new prologue no longer refers to a mixed audience of *pelerins et pelerines*, the text is no longer divided into four books/days, and the *PVH2* frontispiece is typically that of the tonsured author alone in his cell, dreaming of the heavenly Jerusalem in bed or writing at his desk. The enthusiastic worldliness of the pilgrim has been considerably toned down. It is the same worldliness which Deguileville makes an effort to disclaim in the new prologue, when he announces his intent to rescue and redeem the pilgrim following his premature wanderings outside the walls of Chaalis. We might well wonder if Deguileville had been criticized for public preaching or the suggestion of

---

34. On the more learned and writerly aspect of *PVH2*, see Faral, "Guillaume de Digulleville," 30–31; Pomel, "Enjeux," 462–63; Pomel, *Voies*, 246, 526–27, 529; Badel, *Le* Roman de la Rose, 367. On how this is reflected in manuscript illumination, see Camille, "The Illustrated Manuscripts," I: 77–78.

35. See Maupeu, *Pèlerins de vie humaine*, 270.

36. See Maupeu, "Tentation," 53, 56.

it, and thus now wished to portray himself as a more traditional, cloistered Cistercian.

Deguileville's efforts to move his narrator to the right side of the hedgerow, and to distance himself from suspicions of worldliness, are also reflected in an apparent about-face concerning one of his major source texts for *PVH1*—the *Roman de la Rose* of Guillaume de Lorris and Jean de Meun. Here the potential controversy of Deguileville's work may be considered in light of the ultimate literary controversy of the Middle Ages, the Querelle de la Rose. While it is difficult to speak of a fully blossomed Querelle in the 1350s, Deguileville's *PVH2* is the earliest known document providing evidence of readers' polemical reaction to the thirteenth-century text.[37]

In the prologue of *PVH1*, Deguileville had singled out the "biau roumans de la Rose" (v. 11) as his most important influence. The *Rose*'s intertextual presence in both versions of *PVH* cannot be ignored, beginning with the choice to frame the narrative as a first-person allegorical dream vision.[38] Some of Deguileville's personifications, like Huiseuse and Raison, are directly borrowed from Guillaume's *Rose*,[39] while their grotesque appearances—and the way they overwhelm the narrator along his journey—owe more to Jean's continuation than to Guillaume's beginning. Like the *Rose*'s narrator, called Amant, Deguileville's pilgrim has set his sights on a hard-won object on the other side of a heavy fortification. While for Amant, this object is the vaginal Rose, Guillaume de Deguileville's pilgrim strives instead for the heavenly Jerusalem. Deguileville's narrator particu-

---

37. Faral ("Guillaume de Digulleville," 37 n1) considers that *PVH2* is the first text that bears witness to the *Rose* controversy, later to escalate with Christine de Pizan and Jean Gerson. Badel (*Le Roman de la Rose*, 363, 372) offers the same opinion, as does Maupeu ("*Bivium*: l'écrivain nattier et le *Roman de la Rose*," in Duval and Pomel, eds., *Guillaume de Digulleville: les* Pèlerinages allégoriques. 32). John Fleming argues that *PVH2* does not provide evidence of a full-scale attack on the *Rose*, as, according to Fleming, the *Querelle de la Rose* cannot be said to begin until the polemics by Christine and Gerson ("The Moral Reputation of the *Roman de la Rose* before 1400." *Romance Philology* 18.4 [May 1965]). However, even Fleming concedes (433) a certain degree of criticism aimed at Jean de Meun by Deguileville.

38. For the most comprehensive accounts of Deguileville's use of the *Rose*, see Badel, *Le* Roman de la *Rose,* 362–76; Sylvia Huot, *The* Romance of the Rose *and its Medieval Readers: Interpretation, Reception, Manuscript Transmission.* Cambridge Studies in Medieval Literature 16. Cambridge: Cambridge University Press, 1993. 207–38. See also Maupeu's thorough treatment (*Pèlerins de vie humaine,* 53–55, 80–87, 98–107, 118–27). In Maupeu's opinion, the *Rose* may have been especially problematic for the critical eye it casts on those in religious orders (*Pèlerins de vie humaine,* 80–83, 120). On the *Rose*'s anti-clericism as a problem for Deguileville, see also Alan Murray Finlay Gunn, *The Mirror of Love: A Reinterpretation of* The Romance of the Rose. 2nd ed. Lubbock: Texas Tech Press, 1952. 34–36.

39. See Camille, "The Illustrated Manuscripts," I: 37; Maupeu, *Pèlerins de vie humaine,* 118–19.

larly resembles the final incarnation of Jean's Amant, who is transformed into a pilgrim at the end of the poem as he approaches the long awaited Rose. Amant carries a pilgrim's staff and purse (his genitals) and uses them to gain entrance to the Rose's reliquary, between whose columns (thighs) lies the object of his desire.[40]

For Deguileville's pilgrim, the staff is Hope, and the purse Faith. With *PVH1*, the author had meant to reappropriate and sanitize the popular image of Jean de Meun's erotic pilgrim for a Christian audience, producing what has been called a "contrepartie religieuse" and "édifiante" of the *Rose*.[41] But at times, Deguileville's protagonist of 1330–31 seems all too similar to the oversexed Amant, his tale not so much a moralizing *contrepartie* as another continuation. Both pilgrims fall under the violent influence of Venus and abandon the guidance of Raison, while Deguileville's narrator aggravates the situation by also departing from God's grace—his teacher Grace Dieu.

In its uncomfortably close resemblances to the *Rose*, then, *PVH1* may have provoked the censure of those who saw a potential moral threat in any such use of a profane text. Pierre-Yves Badel affirms that Deguileville's poem and its rewriting should be viewed in the context of a general suspicion which attached itself to late medieval vernacular literature, namely that "la littérature de fiction, plus apte à satisfaire les désirs des hommes qu'à exhorter les pécheurs à la repentance ou à édifier les croyants, a rencontré de réelles résistances et la réprobation de moines et de clercs qui refusaient tout compromis avec le monde" ("The literature of fiction, more apt to satisfy worldly desire than to exhort sinners to repentance or instruct believers, encountered considerable resistance and the disapproval of monks and clerics who refused all compromise with the world.")[42] In other words, in *PVH1*, Deguileville would have associated himself too closely with the seductive, purely entertaining aspects of the *Rose*, failing to produce a sufficiently edifying text or a suitably exemplary narrator.

Or, from the opposite perspective, by 1356 Deguileville may have felt diminished confidence in his audience's abilities to correctly interpret the ambiguities of a fictional, allegorical text; he may have felt that readers had failed to grasp his intentions. Whatever the reasons, modern critics have generally agreed that the revised *Pèlerinage* reflects Deguileville's attempts

---

40. Badel (*Le Roman de la Rose*, 65) notes the negative impact such parallels may have had on the reception of Deguileville's poem. See also Maupeu, *Pèlerins de vie humaine*, 85, 119.

41. Badel, *Le Roman de la Rose*, 365. The same terminology is later reconsidered by Steven Wright in "Deguileville's *Pèlerinage de vie humaine* as 'contrepartie édifiante' of the *Roman de la Rose.*" *Philological Quarterly* 68.4 (1989): 399–422.

42. Badel, *Le Roman de la Rose*, 371.

to put distance between himself and the *Rose*.⁴³ While the prologue of the first version begins by crediting the "biau roumans de la Rose" (v. 11), the 1356 prologue omits all mention of the text. In the second redaction, Deguileville's narrator now refuses to enter the left-hand path attended by Huiseuse, the very same character who guards the gate to the pleasure garden into which Amant enters as Guillaume de Lorris's *Rose* begins.⁴⁴ And in an added dialog between the pilgrim and Venus, the rewritten pilgrim denounces both the goddess of love and Jean de Meun, whom Venus claims as "her clerk" ("mon clerc escrivain," *PVH2*, v. 8632):

Toy donc, dis, et ton escrivain	You then, I say, and your writer too,
Estes de grant mauvaistié plain.	are full of great evil.
(vv. 8765–66)	

These conspicuous revisions strongly suggest that the *Rose* in its most thoroughly profane aspect had proven an undesirable influence on the reception of Deguileville's text, despite the author's intentions in adapting it to Christian allegory.

Deguileville thus had numerous possible reasons for facing censure, all of which could have prompted his rewriting of *PVH*. All of the potential criticisms of *PVH1*, moreover, speak to an underlying conception of the ethical relationship between author and reader. For Deguileville, this relationship was conceived, above all, as pastoral and didactic, as his expressed goal was to keep pilgrims on the right track and away from spiritual detours (*PVH1*, vv. 13525–30). In *PVH2*, the author seems to have shied away from the image of public preacher, and purposefully limited his audience. These gestures, too, may articulate a certain pastoral obligation, inasmuch as they speak to Deguileville's concern that the uninitiated had not understood his allegory and risked being led astray by appearances.

But while he assumes a heavy responsibility toward readers and describes his rewriting as a literary penance, Deguileville's attitude toward

---

43. See Pomel, "Enjeux," 64–66; Pomel, *Voies*, 246; Pomel, "Le *Roman de la Rose* comme voie de paradis: transposition, parodie et moralisation de Guillaume de Lorris à Jean Molinet," in *De la Rose: texte, image, fortune*. Ed. Catherine Bel, Herman Braet. Dudley, MA: Peeters, 2006. 355–76, especially 365–66, 372; Badel, *Le* Roman de la Rose, 375; Maupeu, *Pèlerins de vie humaine*, 120; Maupeu, "Tentation," 54–55.

44. Deguileville's Huiseuse declares her love of "roumans et choses mencongables" (*PVH1*, v. 6856). On the diverging path (*bivium*) of Huiseuse and Labour, see Maupeu, *Pèlerins de vie humaine*, 122–26. Maupeu (126) sees the figure of Labour (represented as a *nattier*, or weaver) as an emblem of the good writer, while Huiseuse becomes a potential allegory for the first *PVH1*, which had made too many concessions to the worldly pleasures of reading. See also Maupeu, "*Bivium*," especially 22–32.

the various criticisms surrounding his work can hardly be defined as submissive. Instead, Deguileville's approach is best understood as apologetic in the fullest sense: as a carefully crafted defense of his project, in opposition to certain kinds of reading and certain kinds of readers. As we will see, Deguileville gave this apologetic rhetoric its most grandiose expression in *Pèlerinage de l'âme,* by implanting it into a representation of eschatological judgment. Yet the trial scene of *PA* is only the most dramatic legal episode in Deguileville's body of work. Well before the pilgrim appears in Saint Michael's court, he is already the object of an ongoing series of judgments, at once legal and eschatological, staged in both versions of *PVH*. In these instances of judgment, the author's efforts at self-defense are already addressed to God and the reader at once, preparing us for the way in which the trial scene of *PA* works to apply spiritual justice to literary problems.

III. Preliminary Judgments

In both versions of *PVH,* as he is just starting out on his journey, the pilgrim encounters the hulking *villain* Rude Entendement (Vulgar Understanding):[45]

Un grant villain mal faconne,	A large, awkwardly shaped peasant,
Ensourcillie et reboule,	with a lumpy body and a leering brow,
Qui un baston de cournoullier	who carried a club of dogwood
Portoit et bien mal pautonnier	and seemed truly ignoble
Sembloit estre et mal pelerin.	to me and a bad pilgrim too.
(*PVH1,* vv. 5095–99)	

Lumbering at the pilgrim, Rude Entendement accuses him of presumption ("outrecuidance," v. 5120), since he is carrying a pilgrim's staff and purse despite Christ's directive to his apostles (Matt. 10:10, Lk. 9:3) not to carry these items when they go out into the world.

The pilgrim describes the scene as a legal dispute. Just as he will be initially dumbstruck at the beginning of his trial in *PA,* the pilgrim cannot come up with the words to counter Rude Entendement's accusation, and

---

45. In *PVH1,* the scene occurs at vv. 5093–632; in *PVH2,* at vv. 6880–7217. Rude Entendement resembles the character Dangier from the *Roman de la Rose,* who is first described in Guillaume de Lorris's text as a hulking and poorly-shaped villain (vv. 2918–22). On this episode in Deguileville, its treatment of allegory and its correspondences to the *Rose,* see Huot, *Medieval Readers,* 218–20; Stephanie A. Viereck Gibbs Kamath, "Unveiling the 'I': Allegory and Authorship in the Franco-English Tradition, 1270–1450." Diss. University of Pennsylvania, 2006. 49–53.

complains that he will not be able to find a suitable advocate to speak for him:

Quant ces paroles j'entendi,	When I heard these words,
Plus que devant fu esbahi;	I was even more startled than before,
Quar response nulle n'avoie	for I had no response
Ne que respondre ne savoie.	and did not know how to answer.
Un advocat eusse loue	I would have happily hired a lawyer
Volentiers, se l'eusse trouve,	if I could have found one,
Quar bien en avoie mestier,	for I truly did need one,
Se l'eusse sceu ou pourchacier.	had I only known where to seek one out.
(vv. 5139–46)[46]	

The pilgrim need not worry, however, for the personified lady Raison quickly appears and accuses Rude Entendement of waylaying pilgrims. Although not an advocate, Raison is identified as an *enquesteresse* ("officer of inquest," v. 5176), and her legal action, which is carried out under orders from the court of heaven, protects the pilgrim against the accusations of Rude Entendement.

Raison, heaven's *enquesteresse*, proceeds to serve Rude Entendement a kind of cease and desist order from Grace Dieu, and because this peasant is illiterate, the pilgrim must read it aloud to him (vv. 5219–56): the letter commands Rude Entendement to stop bullying pilgrims with his heavy club, Stubbornness (*Obstination*), and to stop trying to take away their staffs and purses. Grace Dieu's letter concludes by threatening to summon Rude Entendement to judgment before God should he fail to heed her injunction:

Et se de rien il s'opposoit	And should he refuse anything
Ou obeir il ne vouloit,	or not wish to obey,
Jour li donnasses competent	may you give him his day in court
Aus assises du jugement.	before the seat of Judgment.
(vv. 5249–52)	

---

46. Soon after his meeting with Rude Entendement, the pilgrim complains that his own body has begun a vicious trial against him:

Contre moy pour guerroier	To make war against me
Il est advocat devenu.	he has become a lawyer.
(*PVH1*, vv. 6772–73)	

Grace Dieu had already identified the pilgrim's body as his "*grans anemis*" (*PVH1*, v. 5748). Thus, Guillermus's body (his *corpus*) is closely connected to the Enemy, Satan, who will sue him in *PA*.

Rude Entendement, however, refuses to listen to Raison, questioning her authority over him by bringing up the contemporary scholastic debate over names and things. Rude Entendement claims that Raison is a false name, since millers habitually cheat their customers by using a deceptive measure (*raison*) for grain. Raison calmly explains that it is one thing to be her and quite another to have her name (vv. 5293–94). But Rude Entendement will not relent and continues to assert that Raison must also be false, since she shares her name with the miller's measure (vv. 5315–36). Raison retorts that Rude Entendement obviously knows how to put forward subtle arguments and nice examples (vv. 5341–42), but that his own name is perfectly apt, since his understanding of the world is severely limited. This shuts him up for a time, and he can only sneer and grind his teeth (vv. 5392–94) at Raison and the pilgrim.

The debate about names recalls a well-known—indeed, notorious—section of Jean de Meun's *Roman de la Rose*, where Jean's own version of Raison argues with Amant concerning her prerogative to name things as she sees fit. In the *Rose*, the word in question is not *raison*, but *couilles* ("balls," v. 5533), which Raison had used when she told Amant the story of Saturn's castration. When Amant objects to Raison's use of such a vulgar term, she defends herself by noting that God endowed her with the power to name, and that names in themselves are not the same as what they describe. Thus, Raison says, she might just as well have called testicles "reliques"—the word would still refer to exactly the same thing (vv. 7100–20).

In the argument Deguileville stages between Raison and Rude Entendement, the issue is quite similar: whether or not the signifier should be identified absolutely with the signified. Raison says no, while the stubborn peasant continues to insist otherwise. Since he cannot read and lacks a basic understanding of sign theory, Rude Entendement is also poorly disposed to comprehend Scripture, and he brings the discussion back to the accusation he had first made against the pilgrim: that Christ prohibited his apostles from carrying a staff or purse. Raison reviews the relevant passage of the New Testament and reminds Rude Entendement that shortly before Christ's death, he had changed his commandment (Lk. 22:36) to reflect the new and more difficult circumstances in which the apostles would find themselves: they should now take along a purse and a sword if they have them. The pilgrim is therefore perfectly in the right (vv. 5419–704). Ever obstinate, Rude Entendement refuses to acknowledge that God could ever change his commands (vv. 5517–26), and Raison again criticizes his inability to read Scripture deeply (vv. 5527–40). When Rude Entendement still fails to understand, and refuses to stop threatening pilgrims, Raison notes that he is only capable of digesting the outer covering of things, their chaff ("hauton," v. 5587). By this, Raison means that Rude Entendement does not know how to properly sift the outer covering of words from their true intention and meaning. He is a bad interpreter of everyday reality and Scripture, because he puts more stock in the forms and names things take than in what they are meant to signify.

By the same token, it is clear that Rude Entendement represents a certain undesirable reading of Deguileville's text, a reading that would confuse the covering of allegory—the signifying integumentum or chaff—with its deepest signification, or grain.[47] The rude peasant is identifiable with readers, particularly among the laity, who would either accuse Deguileville's allegorical narrative of being too worldly, or who would find in it only matter for amusement and fail to profit from the salutary substance that it encloses. The identification of Rude Entendement with irresponsible readers is especially pertinent given that the episode evokes Jean de Meun's *Rose* and Reason's treatment of names and allegory in that text. While Rude Entendement objects to the pilgrim's carrying a staff and purse because of his bad reading of Scripture, it is difficult to put out of mind the erotic signification which attaches to these objects at the end of Jean's *Rose* and which would have been their most immediate reference for many medieval readers.

Raison's condemnation of Rude Entendement, who sees only the surface elements of Deguileville's narrative, cautions readers against the same kind of superficiality which would lead them to snickeringly identify the pilgrim's staff and purse as a penis and testicles, or perhaps to enjoy the pilgrim's spiritual mistakes more than his successes. When Raison finally tires of arguing with Rude Entendement, she makes good on Grace Dieu's command to summon him to God's judgment if he won't stop attacking pilgrims:

'O,' dist Raison, 'maintenant voi	'Oh,' said Raison, 'now I see
Que plus n'ai a parler a toi	that I have nothing more to say to you,
Fors toi citer tant seulement	except only to bring you
Aus assises du jugement,	before the seat of judgment.
Je t'i semont sans plus targier,	I do hereby summon you without delay—
Viens i sans nul autre envoier!'	you will go there with no other in your place!'
(vv. 5627–32)	

---

47. On Rude Entendement as a figure for the bad reader, see Maupeu, *Pèlerins de vie humaine*, 127, 135. See also Moreau, "'*Ce mauvais tabellion*,'" 123.

At the Judgment, the winnowing time, Raison is confident that Rude Entendement will be condemned once and for all, and burned with the chaff.[48] That Rude Entendement's accusation against the pilgrim is turned around on him insists that literature is an enterprise with reciprocal, if asymmetrical, ethical demands. While the author's intentions are a matter for judgment on earth and in heaven, audience members are warned that reading or understanding texts in the manner of Rude Entendement may bring dire consequences for them in the next world. The scene begins to construct in Deguileville's corpus as a whole an eschatological context for judgment on the literary work, in which divine scrutiny is immanent, and in which the author already prepares his rejoinder against the real or potential accusations of readers.

The apologetic character of Deguileville's text—the way the narrator finds himself in the middle of controversies about the author and his work—is still more evident in the second *Pèlerinage de vie humaine,* as is the tendency to measure the judgment of readers against the judgment of God. When read in its entirety, *PVH2* stands out not so much as a penitential work—as its prologue might suggest—but rather as a document written by Deguileville in his own defense. At times, *PVH2* even becomes a raging tirade directed against the author's unnamed critics, those who, like Rude Entendement, had failed to appreciate the spiritual value of *PVH1*.

The combative aspect of the rewritten text is most evident in a startling new scene added to the Ship of Religion section of *PVH2*. Once aboard ship, the pilgrim tells us that he wants to recount something that really happened to him and to none other. In order to make this pseudo-autobiographical identification as clear as possible, he will narrate the episode in a French and Latin macaronic poem spelling out his name—*Guillermus de Deguilevilla*—with the first letters of twenty-four eight-line stanzas. As he will do in the heavenly trial scene of *PA,* Deguileville winks at the connection between his narrator and himself by framing the inset narrative with a signature-acrostic. This is the first time the poet names himself directly in his work, and it signals an important change of tone from *PVH1,* where the pilgrim's resemblance to the author is somewhat less obvious.[49]

The story told by the acrostic poem of *PVH2* is this: after Guillermus had already been on the ship for some time, he was brutally attacked by a cabal of personified sins—Envie, Traison, Detraction and Conspiration.

---

48. For the origins of this eschatological image, see Matt. 3:12, Lk. 3:17.
49. See Maupeu, *Pèlerins de vie humaine,* 203–6.

The sins set out to destroy the pilgrim and succeeded in badly injuring his leg, killing his trusty horse Renommé (Good Name), and forcing his exile from the ship (he is later reinstated). Although we know nothing about any real events this mysterious episode may reference, the episode makes several allusions to a legal case—perhaps one brought under canon law at the abbey of Chaalis—and a case which the pilgrim lost to his opponents.[50] For instance, the pilgrim describes how the personification Conspiration (or "Scilla") "pursued" him like a helpless beast:

Me persequens indefesse	Pursuing me without relent,
La tres cruelle veneresse,	the very cruel huntress
Ac violenter me subesse	let her dogs loose
Fist a ses chiens hors de lesse,	in order to bring me down violently,
Sicque clamare necesse	so that I had to cry out
Bien me fut, pour yssir de presse,	in order to free myself,
Sed si potuit prodesse,	but whether this was successful
N'est pas bien ceste chose expresse.	is not completely clear.
(vv. 16206–13)	

Although Deguileville colors his scene with hunting images, evocative of the Acteon myth, to accentuate the violence done to his person and his good name, the verb *persequens* (v. 16206) also suggests that Guillermus de Deguilevilla was the defendant in a legal action that his detractors brought against him. It seems, moreover, that he either spoke out on his own behalf (*clamare,* v. 16210) or initiated a counter-suit against his opponents. Later in the acrostic poem, the juridical aspect of the attack against Guillermus is further supported by mention of Detraction and her accomplice Murmure swearing testimony ("asseruntque de iure," v. 16234) damaging to the pilgrim and to others in the monastery.

To describe the added scene, Philippe Maupeu has adopted Gisèle Mathieu-Castellani's expression "scène judiciaire de l'autobiographie," which informs my own reading of the fourteenth-century poets in this study.[51] Indeed, the judgment of *PVH2* seems to refer at once to the real-

---

50. Faral thinks it evident that Deguileville had to face "accusations en quelque sorte officielles" ("Guillaume de Digulleville,"10). On the question of a possible excommunication, see Faral, "Guillaume de Digulleville,"10; Maupeu, *Pèlerins de vie humaine,* 91. Maupeu (Ibid., 92–93) further speculates that the accusation against the pilgrim may have been that of necromancy.

51. "Sur la 'scène judiciaire' de l'autobiographie, comme l'écrit Gisèle Mathieu-Castellani, l'auteur revendique en son nom propre l'aliénabilité de ses biens (littéraires) et la dignité due à sa personne" (Maupeu, *Pèlerins de vie humaine,* 214). Or, as Fabienne Pomel puts it, *PVH2* appears "comme un avocat de Guillaume en quête de réhabilitation" ("Enjeux," 460).

life legal struggles of Deguileville—whatever they may have been—and to the more figurative trial he faced at the hands of a readership much larger than his abbey. During the course of the episode, Deguileville provides several clues that the pilgrim was pursued by his enemies for literary transgressions. As Maupeu has shown, Deguileville's story of persecution at Chaalis is modeled partly on Pierre Abelard's *Historia calamitatum*, a narrative in which Abelard recounts a double misfortune: his castration and the 1121 burning of his *Theologia* for heretical propositions.[52] The parallels with Guillermus de Deguilevilla's own problems are interesting: Guillermus seems also to have been maliciously deprived of a lower body part or its use (his leg), while Deguileville begins *PVH2* by complaining of the loss of his book (to unnamed copyists). Moreover, the nature of the 1355 revisions hint that the first version of *PVH1* may have been accused of doctrinal imprecision, or even heterodoxy, as was the case with Abelard's burned book.

This is not the only reference Deguileville makes during the episode to another author's literary scandal. After he is savagely attacked and exiled from the ship, Guillermus is honored with a visit of consolation by none other than the poet Ovid. Ovid generously offers to the pilgrim his own *Ibis*, a series of acid curses in elegiac couplets, written during his exile on the Black Sea.[53] Guillermus places some of these donated Latin verses directly within his own narrative of personal tribulation (vv. 16109–25), making it likely that Deguileville identified with the Roman poet as one who had been harshly treated and banished for something he wrote, the infamous "carmen et error" ("poem and error") which got him sent to the edge of the empire.[54] It has generally been assumed that the *carmen et error* in question was Ovid's *Ars amatoria*, a satirical handbook on seduction. Particularly because the *Ars amatoria* was also a major source for Jean de Meun's *Rose*, it might be inferred that Deguileville was likewise facing official sanction, and was forced to leave the Cistercian order for a time, due to backlash against his worldly first *Pèlerinage*.[55]

52. Maupeu, *Pèlerins de vie humaine*, 207–15, 265.
53. See the edition of Ovid's *Ibis* by Robinson Ellis. Exeter, UK: Bristol Phoenix Press, 2008.
54. Ovid, *Tristia*. Ed. John Barrie Hall. Bibliotheca Scriptorum Graecorum et Romanorum Teubneriana. Stuttgart: Teubner, 1995. 2.207.
55. On Ovidian connections, see especially Pomel, "Les écrits pérégrins." While pleading with the Emperor Augustus in *Tristia* (2.103-6), the exiled Ovid compares himself to Acteon, who accidentally saw too much. Deguileville's mention of being hunted down by dogs also vividly recalls the Acteon myth. According to Simone Marchesi, Dante would have used Ovid's Acteon similarly, to identify himself as having been unjustly exiled from Florence in *Inferno* 21 and 22 ("Distilling

Crippled, ostracized, and humiliated, Deguileville cuts short Ovid's proposed poetic vengeance and takes solace instead in the faith that the false accusations against him at Chaalis will be rectified by God "au Jugement / que par devant le Roy atent" ("at the Judgment which awaits before the king," vv. 16132–33). Deguileville thus prepares us for *PA*, when the pilgrim's case is retried in heaven, albeit with Saint Michael presiding as God's lieutenant.[56] And at the end of the soul's trial in *PA*, Lady Justice will fulfill Guillermus's hope for exoneration, expressed near the end of his acrostic poem in *PVH2*:

Legi quodam volumine,	I read in a certain volume,
Quant fait est bien examiné	that when the facts are well examined
Justicie libramine,	in the scales of Justice,
Qui a tort, est tantost miné;	Whosoever is at fault is just as soon destroyed;
Et iustus non redit sine	And the just man does not remain without
Honneur quant le plait est finé.	honor when the plea is finished.
(vv. 16326–31)	

Although Justice is Guillermus's opponent and Satan's ally in the heavenly court, her scales cannot lie, and the judgment will indeed be returned in Guillermus's favor after the arguments have concluded ("quant le plait est finé," v. 16331), just as he predicts.

Deguilleville, apparently obliged to the readership to correct his mistakes after twenty-five years, also uses the occasion to replay an obscure legal event. In the recounting of the event, he pleads his innocence, lashes out at his unnamed critics, and finally, promises an appeal—a sequel—before the gates of paradise. The higher Judgment which the pilgrim awaits is focused especially on literary production, and it will provide the author with a new opportunity to respond to the criticisms of his audience. As I now turn back to reexamine the trial scene of *PA*, when Guillermus's appeal is heard, it is possible to show in greater detail how Deguileville's pilgrim speaks for the author's larger body of work.

Ovid: Dante's Exile and Some Metamorphic Nomenclature in Hell," in *Writers Reading Writers: Intercultural Studies in Medieval and Early Modern Literature in Honor of Robert Hollander*. Newark: DE: University of Delaware Press, 2007. 21–39).

56. Maupeu has noted this continuity, although without developing the idea further: "C'est ce nouveau procès qui attend l'âme du pèlerin dans le *Pèlerinage de l'ame*" (*Pèlerins de vie humaine*, 94 n1).

IV. Satan v. Guillermus de Deguilevilla

PA picks up where *PVH*, in both of its redactions, leaves off. Aboard the Ship of Religion, the pilgrim falls ill and is visited by Death, sickle in hand and open casket at the ready to collect his body. Grace Dieu, at the pilgrim's bedside, informs him that his soul will soon be judged worthy or unworthy to enter the long-awaited city of God. The dreamer does not proceed directly to his judgment, but awakens to the sound of the abbey bells chiming matins, at which point *PVH* ends. As *PA* begins, Guillermus has returned to bed, full of anxiety over the fleeting nature of human existence. He tosses over onto his other side ("sus l'autre couste," v. 24) and has another dream.[57] Thus begins the particular judgment scene, where the soul of Guillermus de Deguilevilla must answer for all three manifestations of the pilgrim: author, text, and narrator. As the "other side" ("l'autre couste") of the first dream vision and its *re*-vision, the eschatological scene of *PA* stages a retrial of the pilgrim's case in a new and more perfect forum.

I have already outlined the basic shape of this judgment scene, which Deguileville adapted from the Devil's Rights tradition with a first-person narrator who shares both his name and his ability to use language persuasively. Resemblances run much deeper than that, however, because Deguileville cleverly included a number of specific allusions to his own career and reception in this reworking of the Devil's Rights trial scene. These allusions further confuse the boundaries between the narrator's soul and the author's. Moreover, they conflate Deguileville's evolving corpus with the traditional documents of the eschatological record, such as the Book of Conscience. As it becomes a dispute about the historical author's guilt or innocence, Guillermus's cosmic trial also points to issues surrounding the reproduction and compilation of his work in manuscript form, and the author's ability or inability to control the circulation of his writing.

First, it is important to note that the evidence introduced by Satan and Justice against the pilgrim is drawn directly from the events of *PVH1*, which most often precedes *PA* in manuscripts.[58] As Satan claims,

Onques bien ne pelerina,	Never did he make a good pilgrimage,
Par bonne voie onques n'ala,	Never did he take the good path,
Par Orgueil et par Envie,	But through Pride and through Envy,
Par Venus et Gloutonnie;	Through Lust and Gluttony,

---

57. This prologue to *PA* does not occur in all manuscripts. For example, BNF fr. 829 transitions more swiftly between *PVH* (in its second version) and *PA*.

58. On this point, see Moreau, "'*Ce mauvais tabellion*,'" 119–22.

Ire, Avarice, Paresse	Through Wrath, Greed and Sloth,
A este tous jours s'adrece.	Was always his way.
(vv. 685–90)	

The Devil is not making things up. As readers follow Guillermus on his continued pilgrimage from the hedgerow to the gates of heaven, from one text to the next in the compiled corpus, they are forced to acknowledge the truth of Satan's position: in *PVH1*, the pilgrim really did fail to take the good path—the right side of the Hedge of Penitence—time and again, and was defeated with little resistance by all of the seven deadly sins. Likewise, Justice recalls how Grace Dieu had instructed the pilgrim precisely on how to use his spiritual armor, which he also failed to do:

Quel excusance puet avoir,	What excuse can he have,
Quant Grace Dieu en son manoir	when Grace Dieu in her house
Les armëures li bailla	gave him his armor
Et l'aprist et endoctrina	and taught and instructed him
Comment soustenir les devoit	in how to wear it,
Et comment armer s'en devoit	and how he should put it on
Contre tous ses adversaires,	against all his adversaries,
Et coment ne prisa gaires	and how he did not care at all
Quanque li dist, car n'en fist rien.	about anything she said, for he did nothing.
Je le vi et m'en souvient bien.	I saw it and remember well.
(vv. 1559–68)	

Deguileville's medieval reader, too, would have remembered how the pilgrim failed to act on Grace Dieu's instructions about his armor.

But this is only part of the story, or rather a different story entirely for that smaller group of medieval readers who would have traced the pilgrim's adventures in the compiled corpus from *PVH2* to *PA*, instead of from *PVH1*. In *PVH2*, the pilgrim is still beaten by Gluttony and Venus, and then captured by Peresce; but soon he remembers Grace Dieu's teachings and breaks free of Sloth (vv. 10448–93). Confronted with Envie, Orgueil and their kind, the pilgrim manages to resist them; these personifications only succeed in harming him after he has boarded the Ship of Religion. And here, we recall, the attack seems not to be the pilgrim's fault, but is rather the result of an evil conspiracy against him reflecting events in Deguileville's own life.[59] After defeating Envie and Orgueil along the hedgerow, the pil-

---

59. See Maupeu, *Pèlerins de vie humaine*, 191.

grim of 1355 also withstands Ire and escapes from Avarice, before going on to triumph over the enemies of the Church. Satan and Justice left these details conveniently out of their account.

The tendency of the plaintiffs to rely primarily on the narrative of *PVH1* for their evidence stands out sharply, since *PVH2* had appeared so soon before *PA* to offer an alternative version of the pilgrim's life. One conclusion that might be drawn from this bias is that the heavenly trial was for Deguileville a way of staging the confrontation of his two *Pèlerinages* as they were received by readers. After all, despite any attempts the author made to the contrary, *PVH1* not only stayed in circulation but remained much more popular than *PVH2*. The earlier version's centrality to the accusations against the pilgrim attests to the fact that most readers, like Satan and Justice, would have known only the original—especially in 1356.[60]

In the legacy of his wayward text, which he cannot expunge from the literary or eschatological record, Deguileville also faces his personal book of spiritual accounts, equally indelible. The Book of Conscience motif appears most powerfully in *PA* through the star witness for the prosecution, the worm Synderesis, who represents the pilgrim's own neglected conscience.[61] Like the accusations of Satan and Justice, Synderesis's testimony is also seemingly drawn from the events of *PVH1*. Unlike the speeches of Satan and Justice, however, the narrator does not reproduce most of what Synderesis says verbatim. This is because, the narrator claims, it would take him too long, and would cause him unnecessary anguish:

Et saches bien certainement	And know in certainty
Quë onques tant celeement	that there was nothing I ever thought or said,
Rien je ne pensai ne ne dis	no matter how secretly,
Et onques nul mal je ne fis	and no sin I ever committed
Que ne dëist en presence	that she did not bring up
De tous et en audience.	in the presence of everyone assembled.
Longuement le mist a dire,	She took a long time to say it,
Et je aussi a ce escrire	and I would take
Trop longuement y mectroie,	too long to write it all down.
Faire aussi ne le vourroie,	Moreover, I wouldn't want to do so,
Car ce seroit irrision	for it would be harmful
A moi et grant confusion.	to me and disturbing.
(vv. 1373–84)	

---

60. See Moreau, "'*Ce mauvais tabellion*,'" 122.
61. For more on Synderesis, see Pomel, *Voies*, 354–56.

Yet a more likely reason for the narrator skipping over Synderesis's testimony is that this information would be superfluous to the reader, who has been following the pilgrim throughout his journey from *PVH*. Synderesis's testimony is already written down and available for all to read: it is the pilgrim's own first-person narrative which now stands before the court (*en audience*) to accuse him.

Synderesis is a dark reflection of Deguileville's tripartite image as a *pèlerin*: author, narrator and book bound together and responsible for each other. The pilgrim describes her as a shriveled hag's head perched atop a worm's tail. Her teeth have been worn down to nothing from gnawing at the pilgrim's unrepentant heart. Her repulsive, flapping gums are living proof that the pilgrim had been repeatedly warned by his own conscience but failed to pay attention. She is hideous only because, as she tells the pilgrim, he has made her so:

Mes tu t'es tout deffigure,	But it was you who disfigured,
Deffourme et defaiture	deformed and defaced yourself,
Par mains peches et par divers,	by many and diverse sins,
Par mauvais dis et fais pervers.	by bad things said and perverse works.
(vv. 1317–20)	

Synderesis claims that her profound ugliness is a transparent record of the pilgrim's soul, his personal Book of Conscience, which overlaps significantly with Deguileville's own book. If the pilgrim-narrator had committed "many and diverse sins," isn't the author just as responsible for his conduct?

In this sense, Synderesis's choice of words in the above passage—"par mauvais dis et fais pervers" (v. 1320)—makes a good pun. As the plural of *dit*, "dis" can mean "things said," denoting the ways in which Deguileville's narrator may have committed various sins of the tongue, such as blasphemy. But *dit* is also a medieval designation of poetic genre which, although fairly loosely applied in the thirteenth and fourteenth centuries, always means some kind of a first-person narrative poem, usually in octosyllabic rhyming couplets. Very often in fourteenth-century literature, *dits* appear in the form of dream visions and contain intercalated lyric poetry. According to these characteristics, all of Deguileville's extant works are *dits*, as are the texts by Machaut and Froissart that I examine in the chapters to follow.[62] As part of Synderesis's testimony, then, the term has particular

---

62. Along with the two versions of *PVH* and the *Pèlerinage Jhesucrist,* Deguileville's *Roman de la fleur de lis* can be classified as a *dit*. Jean de Meun more explicitly used the term *dis* to repent for earlier writing—namely, the *Rose*—in his *Testament* (v. 5). See above, Introduction, 21.

resonance not only for the sinful things the narrator may have said, but also for the *mauvais dis* of the author, and especially for Deguileville's first redaction of *PVH*.

Synderesis's ugliness is both the mirror image of the pilgrim-soul's spiritual deficiency and a startling image of the work of art looking back at its creator, a first-person record which now stands to condemn the author "through his own words" (Matt. 12:37). Inasmuch as she is a personification of the poet's conscience, she is also a figure of Deguileville's earlier work, which continues to circulate despite any efforts that he may have made to stop it. Synderesis is a *ver*: she is the proverbial worm of conscience which gnaws at the sinner's heart, warning him to repent before it is too late. But she is also a *vers* (verse) of the pilgrim's own making which has returned to bear witness against him.

As we trace the contours of Deguileville's heavenly courtroom scene, it is essential to consider that Synderesis's testimony is recorded dutifully by the court's *tabellion*, or notary. Surprisingly, this is a role fulfilled by Satan, who is also the lead plaintiff suing for ownership of Guillermus's soul:[63]

Le Sathanas de bout en bout	The Adversary from end to end
En .i. grant papier escrit tout.	on a great scroll of paper wrote everything.
Aussi tost com celle parloit,	As soon as she [Synderesis] would speak
Tout aussi tost il escrisoit.	just as quickly would he write it down.

(vv. 1385–88)

One might well object that it would prejudice the court's record to allow the plaintiff to transcribe it; but like Synderesis, Satan protests his objectivity: he is "tant seulement tabellion," just writing down exactly what the pilgrim's own conscience testifies (v. 1360).

This is not the first time that Deguileville, or his narrator, claim to have problems with scribes. In his new prologue to *PVH2*, remember, the author had accused a nameless person of having copied and circulated *PVH1* before it was ready. There is an echo of the same wicked copyist in Deguileville's Satan, who duplicates the events of the pilgrim's life (the first *Pèlerinage de vie humaine*) for all to read, just as soon as Synderesis utters them. As he copies from the mouth of conscience, Deguileville's Satan recalls an ethical question which had already been broached in the prologue to *PVH2*: if *PVH1* confused readers or caused scandal, who is at fault: the anonymous

---

63. On Deguileville's Satan as *tabellion*, see Camille, "The Devil's Writing," 356; Moreau, "'Ce mauvais tabellion.'"

scribe who allegedly stole Deguileville's draft, or the author whose own troubled conscience produced it? Is Satan merely a stenographer, as he says—"tant seulement tabellion"? Or is he to blame for making public what should have remained private?[64]

Deguileville's judgment scene raises many such questions about the ethical stakes of the author's literary enterprise, more than it can claim to answer with certainty. In any event, the representation of the Devil as "just a scribe" highlights yet another of Deguileville's borrowings consistent with the Devil's Rights tradition: Satan's association with a strict, immutable interpretation of texts and individual lives, as opposed to Mary's more creative, "lawyerly" interpretation of them.[65] The Devil's Rights tradition characterizes the Adversary as a Pharisaical proponent of an unchanging Law and a rigid depiction of individual conduct. As he relies more heavily on the evidence of *PVH1*, the un-retouched version of the pilgrim's life, Deguileville's Satan too proves himself a stickler for the letter of the law and for the oldest textual precedent available. The pilgrim's life *was* the narrative of *PVH1* and nothing more can be added to it.

Satan's traditional literalism, represented in his role as *tabellion*, may also have relevance for the particular problem of allegorical narrative. The inability of readers to interpret the allegorical lessons of Deguileville's first *Pèlerinage*, specifically in its liberal borrowings from the *Rose*, may well have been foremost on the minds of the author's critics.[66] If so, Satan's characteristic inability to distinguish sign and signifier—which he shares to some extent with the chaff-eating *villain* Rude Entendement—may refer to the tendency of Deguileville's enemies, or his most problematic readers, to neglect the deeper meaning of allegory.[67]

In *PA*, as in the Rude Entendement episode of *PVH*, the archetypal bad reader finds his accusations turned back against him, since Guillermus claims that Satan deceived him into sinning:

Car ce mauvais tabellion	For this wicked scribe
Qui ores a mes maux escris	who has written down my wrongdoings
M'a en tout temps si de pres prins	has always taken such evil advantage of me
Que pas n'ai ëu grant lesir	that I have not had much freedom
De bien deles le mal choisir.	to choose the good instead of the evil.

(vv. 1426–30)

---

64. See Moreau, "'*Ce mauvais tabellion*,'" 124.
65. See Ibid.
66. See, again, Badel, *Le* Roman de la *Rose*, 371.
67. See Moreau, "'*Ce mauvais tabellion*,'" 123.

The defendant's specific strategy of counteraccusation is drawn from *L'advocacie Nostre Dame,* where the Virgin contends that the Devil wrongfully acquired his rights over mankind by tricking Adam and Eve. But although the pilgrim is ostensibly referring to Satan, the Devil also reveals the more human faces of the reader and copyist, who are implicated for perpetuating a worldly or overly literal reading of *PVH1*.[68]

While the plaintiffs assert the chain of events contained in the original text, Deguileville's defendant shifts the blame to his accusers through a series of implicit references to the revised narrative of *PVH2*, especially including his unjust condemnation and exile.[69] For example:

Par mes annemis decëu,	By my enemies I was deceived,
Si comme tu Dieux l'as scëu,	just as you knew, God,
Et pour qui sui en jugement,	and for this reason I now stand in judgment,
Puis qu'en povrete sui chëu	since into poverty I fell,
Et qu'ai trouve ve et hëu	and since I found misfortune and anguish,
Qui me maistroient durement.	which roughly governed me.
(vv. 751–56)	

Although the pilgrim's ostensible line of argumentation is that he was deceived by Satan and his minions, his "annemis" could also be Envie, Treason, Detraction, and Conspiration, those false accusers who set upon Guillermus in *PVH2*.[70] In the same vein, Guillermus reminds the court of the crutch ("potence," *PA*, v. 763; "jambe de fust," *PVH2*, v. 16079) he is now obliged to use after being attacked by Envie, Traison, Detraction, and Conspiration. He then tells the court that he has been reduced to begging, since his enemies have broken his "instrument" (his leg? his book? his quill?):

Point ne scai d'autre vielle,	I know no other instrument—
Mes annemis l'ont quassee.	My enemies have smashed mine.
(vv. 785–86)	

As his foes cite the first draft of Deguileville's poem—the most incriminating version of the pilgrim's life—Guillermus displaces culpability onto his

---

68. See Ibid.
69. See Ibid., 126–27.
70. As Satan reminds us in his own arguments, Envie and Traison are his "creatures" (*PA*, vv. 108–9). See also Moreau, "'*Ce mauvais tabellion,*'" 126–27.

detractors, suggesting that the negative image of himself and his *Pèlerinage* was their fault as readers, and perhaps as copyists.

Along with Deguileville's debt to the Devil's Rights, there is evidence that he also knew Guillaume d'Auvergne's *Rhetorica divina*, which I have discussed in the previous chapter as a text of primary importance for understanding how prayer and the rhetoric of legal self-defense became closely associated in later medieval discourse.[71] As Deguileville was a Cistercian, he had good reason to identify with *Rhetorica divina*, which treats the order and its most important abbot, Bernard de Clairvaux, as exemplary practitioners of divine rhetoric.[72] I have noted at least two allegorical images, both of them occurring in *PVH*, that Deguileville probably drew from *Rhetorica divina:* the personified representation of Prayer as a messenger sent to God,[73] and the pilgrim's immersion in a bath of tears flowing from the rock of penitence—a bath which directly follows Deguileville's most well-known act of divine rhetoric, his "ABC-prayer" addressed to the Virgin.[74]

While such borrowed images suggest the familiarity of Deguileville the author with *Rhetorica divina*, Guillermus's strategies of self-defense in *PA* also seem to take inspiration from that Latin text. This is especially the case in that Guillermus throws himself on the mercy of the court, pleading guilty just as *Rhetorica divina* advises; and just as Guillaume d'Auvergne describes, an impassioned guilty plea before the heavenly court causes the subject to be separated from his sins as he becomes their accuser. Through divine grace, the defendant adopts a prosecutorial role in the service of divine justice, just as Guillermus turns the accusation back against his *annemis*.[75]

But while Deguileville is clearly working within the *rhetor divinus* tradition, he has gone much further in his practice of it than Guillaume d'Auvergne's *Rhetorica divina* recommends. Self-defense is no longer just

---

71. See Chapter 1, 54–56.

72. See, for example, Guillaume d'Auvergne, *Rhetorica divina*, ch. 29 (ed. Teske, 224–25); ch. 36 (258–59); ch. 45 (346–47). See also Francesco Santi, "Guglielmo D'Auvergne e l'Ordine dei Domenicani tra Filosofia Naturale e Tradizione Magica," in Morenzoni and Tillette, eds., *Autour de Guillaume d'Auvergne (†1249)*, 148.

73. See Guillaume d'Auvergne, *Rhetorica divina*, ch. 39 (ed. Teske, 268–97). On Guillaume d'Auvergne as the probable originator of this trope, see Barbara H. Jaye in the coauthored book with Marianne J. Briscoe, *Artes praedicandi/Artes orandi*. Turnhout: Brepols, 1992. 96. For the occurrence in Deguileville, see *PVH1*, vv. 12883–942.

74. See Guillaume d'Auvergne, *Rhetorica divina*, ch. 27 (ed. Teske, 208–9) and ch. 28 (220–21); Guillaume de Deguileville, *PVH1*, vv. 10894–1342.

75. See above, Chapter 1, 55.

an unsparing and tearful confession because the defendant's opponents are no longer just his sins, or even just the Devil; rather, they insistently point to the presence of real accusers in Deguileville's world, as obscure as their identity remains.

As they contest the plaintiffs' side of the story, Guillermus's arguments for his soul also make a case for the validity of Deguileville's rewritten text, and thus for the preferability of manuscript compilations that contain the newly "authorized" *PVH2*. It is especially striking, for instance, that one of the major issues of the trial in the heavenly court is whether the pilgrim's requests for mercy come too late.[76] As Justice claims, "Trop tart vient a faire son cri" ("He comes too late with his plea," v. 1098). The accusation that the pilgrim has run out of time to excuse or amend himself refers not only to the fact that he is supposedly dead, but also calls to mind Deguileville's tardy revision of *PVH1*, some twenty-five years after the original. In his opening address to the court, the pilgrim himself admits that he has been negligent about repenting ("Et trop a tart a merci vieng," v. 825), but he claims that there were extenuating circumstances, since he was coerced and deceived into sinning by Satan.

The heated conflict of two texts, two versions of the same life, is also reflected in the final section of the trial, where it is precisely a question of weighing documents against each other.[77] After arguments have been made and witnesses heard, written records are collected on all sides. Justice stands atop a high platform and readies her balance scale, fulfilling the pilgrim's pronouncement of faith in divine judgment, made in *PVH2* after his crushing defeat on the Ship of Religion (*PVH2*, vv. 16326–31).[78] In the left-hand pan of Justice's scale is placed the record of everything the pilgrim's soul did wrong, Synderesis's testimony which Satan has transcribed onto a long scroll. Into the right-hand pan are placed documents in the soul's favor, notably Saint Benedict's written testimony for his Cistercian son Guillermus. At first, the scales tip dangerously to the left, and things do not look good for the pilgrim. But at last, Misericorde produces Christ's special letter of pardon, which outweighs all of his sins.[79]

---

76. See Moreau, "'*Ce mauvais tabellion*,'" 124.

77. Another notable writerly detail is that, according to the Devil, the pilgrim's sins are written on his face ("Escrit li est emmi le vis," v. 620), like the seven P's traced on the face of Dante's narrator in *Purgatorio* 9.112-14.

78. For the quote, see above in this chapter, 87.

79. The ritual weighing of souls, or *psychostasis*, has a long history which well predates the Christian tradition. As Catherine Oakes shows, *psychostasis* was depicted especially frequently in Cistercian manuscripts, including in *PA* ("The Scales," 26). See also Oakes, *Ora Pro Nobis: The Virgin as Intercessor in Medieval Art and Devotion*. London: Harvey Miller, 2008. 129–66; Zaleski,

Following Christ's directive for clemency, Michael consigns the pilgrim to a term in purgatory, until such time as the disputing parties Mercy and Justice are reconciled.[80] The sentence is faithfully carried out, although this enrages Satan and Justice, who promise to appeal at the "grant jugement derrain" (v. 2616), when the pilgrim's body and soul will be reunited and judged together by Christ himself. After being led away by his guardian angel, the pilgrim is immersed in purgatorial fire; but Deguileville does not spend many verses documenting his suffering. Instead, the narrator's sentence becomes an occasion for visiting all the realms of the afterworld under his angel's guidance. He spends the rest of *PA* detailing the terrible punishments meted out to sinners in hell and examining celestial mysteries such as the Redemption and the liturgical calendar. Effectively, although the pilgrim must endure purifying flame, the outcome of the trial is also a triumphant gesture which authorizes the poet to keep working. As is the case in Dante's eschatological saga, Deguileville strives for paradise but is most at home in purgatory. It is a space for constant change where, as in earthly life, more poetry is always to come, where authors and their texts must pass continually through a refiner's fire of revision and recompilation.

Nor does Deguileville stop at defending his name through this otherworldly trial; he also makes sure that those who wronged him are properly dealt with. When the pilgrim's guardian angel shows him the torments of hell, he sees Envie and her children being tortured (vv. 4565–694); these are the same personifications who attacked the pilgrim aboard ship. Further along in hell, Trahison is depicted as falsely donning the robes of religion ("en religion vestue," v. 4814; "de faus mantel affublee," v. 4816), lending additional support to the idea that the author had been betrayed by members of the community at Chaalis and that he intended *PA* to help clear his name and punish his opponents.

For the enemies who pursued him and who remain nameless today, Deguileville asks no mercy. Like Rude Entendement, the classic bad reader,

---

The Fate of the Dead, 70–71; Samuel George Frederick Brandon, *The Judgment of the Dead: The Idea of Life after Death in the Major Religions.* New York: Scribner, 1967. 79, 120–28, including mention of *PA* (126); Robert Easting, "Personal Apocalypses: Judgement in Some Other-World Visions," in *Prophecy, Apocalypse and the Day of Doom: Proceedings of the 2000 Harlaxton Symposium.* Ed. Nigel Morgan. Donington, UK: Shaun Tyas, 2004. 81; Pamela Sheingorn, "'For God is Such a Doomsman': Origins and Development of the Theme of Last Judgment," in *Homo, Memento Finis: The Iconography of Just Judgment in Medieval Art and Drama.* Ed. David Bevington. Kalamazoo: Medieval Institute Publications, Western Michigan University, 1985. 45.

80. This is a common topos of eschatological representation, particularly in the Procès de Paradis genre. Psalm 85 refers to the reconciliation of mercy and truth. Aquinas asserts that justice and mercy must be present in equal measure in each act of God's judgment (*Summa theologica,* Ia, Q.21, art. 4).

they are to be burned with the chaff. But for himself, the author speaks eloquently in order to offer a more transformative version of events. Just as in the Devil's Rights, lawyerly pleading causes the account books of individual lives to be radically rewritten, confounding the strict legalism of Satan. Following Saint Michael's judgment that the pilgrim be granted a forum in which to respond for his *ouvrages,* Deguileville demands that he too, be allowed to represent himself in the court of reader opinion. Although he takes a much more hell-fire approach to the ethics of *reading,* Deguileville suggests that it is only right for the author to be allowed to make major changes in his work, even twenty-five years after the fact.

Today, Deguileville's trial is still ongoing, in process, in the always evolving interpretation of the readership. From this perspective, it is crucial to remember that *PA* does not depict the Last Judgment, the "grans assises," or "Jugement / que par devant le Roy atent" that is anticipated several times in both versions of *PVH* and in *PA* itself. The judgment scene here represents only the particular judgment of the soul, or rather, only a dream of it, experienced by the narrator while sleeping in his cell at Chaalis, after having been reinstated into the order. It is a vision of how his life would be judged only were he to die then, at the moment of the dream. Deguileville reminds us often of this provisional aspect of his judgment scene, as when the angel Cherubin expresses anxiety over the possibility of *getting it wrong*:

Quant ci apres le temps venra	When afterward the time will come
Que notre bon roy jugera	for our good king to judge
Et tendra ses assises grans	and hold his great tribunal
Et se monsterra tous puissans,	and show himself all-powerful,
Honte seroit, se retraictier	it would be a shame if it were necessary
Failloit ce quë as a jugier.	to retract the judgment that you have to make now.
(vv. 521–26)	

Although it vindicates the pilgrim in a higher court than the one he faced at Chaalis, and confirms his privileged status as divine rhetorician, the trial scene of *PA* is not the last judgment to which the pilgrim-soul will be subject. For soon he will enter into a bitter dispute with his body over which of them are most at fault for sin (vv. 4052–352)—a reworking of the prolific medieval genre of body-soul debates.[81] The resolution of this disagreement is likewise put off to the Resurrection, when body and soul will be reunited

---

81. An overview of the tradition is given by Théodor Batiouchkof, "Le débat de l'âme et du corps." *Romania* 20 (1891): 1–55, 513–78.

and stand judgment as one. Nor was this Deguileville's last pilgrimage, for he would follow *PA* in 1358 with his *Pèlerinage Jhesucrist*, a text that repeats the scenario of a legal dispute between Justice and Mercy, and between the Old and New Laws, all over again in its dramatization of the Redemption.[82]

By repeatedly calling attention to the provisional nature of the divine judgment to which he is exposed, Deguileville suggests that literature is likewise an ongoing process of evaluation and reevaluation, no less eschatological for being resistant to closure. Literature belongs to the judgment of each moment, during which texts are constantly held up to scrutiny, subject to the changing opinions of readers, and of the author himself. Impishly—if not impiously—writing himself a favorable judgment on high and torturing his most critical readers in hell, Deguileville also acknowledged literature as a serious ethical enterprise. In more than an allegorical sense, writing is eschatological: its effect on the audience must be measured before the author can be justly evaluated by God, and so the author must be answerable to the particular judgments of all his readers—the Satans, the Trahisons and the Rude Entendements of the world included. Faced with a formidable collection of adversaries, Deguileville's means of defense lay in the ability he claimed to keep writing, to alter what he had made previously and to transform his own textual image in response to accusation. Even if Deguileville had little control over his text once it entered readers' hands, and even if he failed to change the course of its circulation, his efforts to advocate on behalf of his body of work constitute a unique and compelling justification of poetic authority. It is an authority that rests in part on the miraculous oratorical expertise inherited from the thirteenth-century *rhetor divinus,* and in part on the author's hyper-awareness of his compiled corpus as an extension of himself.

While *PA* is an exceptional example of heavenly rhetoric used to defend a literary text, Guillermus's trial and its outcome are also indicative of much wider trends at work in the development of later medieval vernacular poetry. The trial demonstrates that, in the fourteenth century, the concept of vernacular poetic authority was both ethically important enough and contentious enough to figure at the center of the scene of divine judgment. At the same time, the trial insists on the need for authority to be constantly performed as it is claimed. The highly stylized legal and rhetorical performance of Deguileville's narrator reveals at least four crucial, if often implicit bases for literary authority which underlie so many other later

---

82. See Agnès Le Bouteiller, "Le Procès de Paradis du *Pèlerinage de Jésus-Christ:* un débat allégorique, juridique et théologique porté au seuil de la dramatisation," in Duval and Pomel, eds., *Guillaume de Digulleville: les* Pèlerinages *allégoriques,* 131–58.

medieval texts. First, there is the creation of a pseudo-autobiographical, first-person persona whom audiences can identify with the flesh-and-blood author and who must stand trial in his place. Second, this persona allows the author to embed performances of poetry, rhetoric, and prayer within the text, simultaneously establishing his technical expertise and spiritual worthiness. Third, the first-person persona allows the author to conduct an ethical dialog with audiences, who perform necessary interpretive work on the text and must ultimately pass the judgments through which the author's identity is confirmed. Fourth and finally, the audience's recognition of the authorial persona, and its continued participation in the negotiation of meaning, allow the emergence of an *œuvre* which reflects the life of the author and testifies to his coherence through time as an individual artist.

Because of the vagaries of medieval book production, reception, and taste, and because of the embryonic nature of vernacular poetics, the question of just what should constitute the *œuvre*—and just who is responsible for it—inevitably becomes the most difficult point for judgment. While the author must recognize that his authority derives from that of his judges, and that his legacy is dependent on their reading of the text, he must also work to balance the public's reception with a carefully crafted program of intention, guarding the text from those who would seek to deform its essential meaning and—most problematically of all—reserving the right to alter and build upon his own work once it has already been absorbed by the public.

•

Deguileville's *Pèlerinage de l'âme* was the popular apogee of one major strand of eschatological representation, the Devil's Rights. Likewise, Deguileville exploited more fully than perhaps anyone else the dramatic and literary possibilities of the vernacular poet as *rhetor divinus*. But as the most personalized example of the celestial legal drama, *PA* stands in relative contrast with the texts I explore in the second half of this study, narrative *dits* by Guillaume de Machaut and Jean Froissart. That is because these authors did not make the same use of the heavenly court as a representational space. Instead, their scenes of judgment invest earthly acts of reading and writing with eschatological qualities. Rather than projecting the specific ethical problems of the author-reader relationship into a traditional *mise en scène* of divine judgment like the Devil's Rights, these authors showed the Judgment to be always already at work behind the author-reader relationship. In particular, the texts I examine next take us from the heavenly court, and its saintly patrons, to earthly courts and their princely and aristocratic patrons. Because of this difference, which represents something of a new development in literary treatments of divine judgment, I consider Guillaume de Machaut's *Jugement dou roy de Navarre* after Deguileville's *PA*, even though the former poem is older by half a dozen years.

For not staging their judgments directly in the heavenly tribunal, the courtly poets Machaut and Froissart drew a significant measure of inspiration from the kind of eschatological scene imagined by Deguileville. Like Deguileville, these poets portrayed the author's dialog with the reader—and especially with the patron—as an encounter with the world beyond, with the immanence of the divine judge, always present as the third party (*tiers*) between poet and audience. Like Deguileville, they also depicted the judgment of readers with strong parallels to God's own reading of human souls as texts. This aspect is particularly important for Machaut because of the revolutionary way that the poet's manuscript compilations privilege a unified conception of authority and narrative voice.[83] More even than Deguileville, Machaut expressed anxiety over the difficult *procès* of assembling an authoritative and coherent corpus, and like Deguileville he did so through reference to judgments both human and divine which obliged the author to become an advocate for his body of work. If Machaut was less of a *rhetor divinus* than Deguileville, this participant in the *puys* of northern France nevertheless preserved a strong element of legal rhetoric in his verse, in which the divine tribunal remains the "other scene" of both courtroom pleading and readerly accusation.

---

83. Here, I draw especially on the pioneering studies by Kevin Brownlee (*Poetic Identity in Guillaume de Machaut*. Madison: University of Wisconsin Press, 1984) and Sylvia Huot (*From Song to Book*).

CHAPTER 3

Post-Apocalyptic Judgment
Machaut's *Jugement dou roy de Navarre*

I. Introduction

Guillaume de Machaut (c. 1300–1377) is usually, and with justice, considered the greatest French poet and composer of the fourteenth century. Machaut's prolific poetic corpus combined lyric and narrative forms in innovative ways, his manuscripts were some of the earliest and most influential single-author compilations, and his music pushed the limits of polyphony, culminating in his celebrated *Messe de Notre Dame* (1360–65). The poet, who was canon at Reims, worked in the devotional and liturgical tradition but made his name among the secular elite of Europe with a substantial body of courtly-themed narrative *dits*.

One such *dit,* Machaut's *Jugement dou roy de Navarre* (or *JRN,* c. 1349–50)[1] begins with a frightening scene of divine judgment, which is customarily read as the poem's prologue. During the plague year 1349, Machaut's narrator finds himself shut up in his room alone facing what seems to be the end of the world. The narrator assumes the role of apocalyptic prophet and judge as he condemns broad categories of human beings and laments the world's fall into iniquity. He then turns his accusations inward as he awaits the judgment of his own soul. Ultimately, however, the Doomsday

---

1. I cite the editions of Guillaume de Machaut's *Jugement dou roy de Behaingne* and *Jugement dou roy de Navarre* by R. Barton Palmer. New York: Garland, 1984 and 1988 respectively.

is postponed indefinitely; the world does not end, and the narrator does not die. Instead, the dark prologue serves to introduce a different sort of judgment. Rejoicing in his new lease on life, Machaut's narrator decides to go out hunting; he is then unexpectedly summoned before a mysterious woman, Dame Bonneurté (Lady Happiness). Calling him "Guillaume" for the first time,[2] Bonneurté accuses the narrator of having libeled women in a poem that Machaut had written some ten or fifteen years earlier, the *Jugement dou roy de Behaingne* (or *JRB*, mid-1330s). In *JRB*, Machaut had recounted the dispute of two aristocratic interlocutors: a knight dumped by his lady for another man, and a lady mourning her lover's death. The knight and the lady had each argued that his or her own heartbreak was worse, and in order to settle the disagreement, Machaut's narrator had brought the two before the poet's real-life patron, Jean de Luxembourg, the King of Bohemia. Upon hearing the case, Jean had judged in favor of the knight, deeming his pain to be greater than that of the bereaved lady.

Now, in *JRN,* Dame Bonneurté confronts Guillaume with her accusation: the judgment of *JRB* is an insult to female emotional experience and to women in general—it must be withdrawn immediately. When Guillaume steadfastly refuses to overturn his judgment, Bonneurté conducts him to the court of his new patron, Charles de Navarre, where an absurd trial takes place to determine whether Guillaume has in fact wronged women. Against Bonneurté and her lively entourage of personified virtues, Guillaume attempts to defend his literary reputation. Both sides argue their cases with a barrage of historical and mythological exempla, all of which seem quite irrelevant. The principle issue of the case is quickly lost from view as the dispute becomes more about the relative fidelity of the sexes. As for the defendant, the court is prejudiced against Guillaume from the beginning, and he has little chance of receiving a favorable judgment there. In the end, he loses and must make amends to Bonneurté and womankind—by writing still more poetry. Symbolically, Machaut undertakes this penance himself by assuming the voice of the grieving lady whose plight had so outraged Bonneurté; in the "Lay de plour" ("The Lay of Tears"), added to the end of *JRN* in several manuscripts, the speaker is a woman mourning her lover's death.[3]

---

2. Specifically, it is Bonneurté's messenger who first summons the narrator as "Guillaumes de Machaut" (v. 573).

3. See Lawrence Earp, *Guillaume de Machaut: A Guide to Research*. New York: Garland, 1995. 238, 365. The "Lay de plour" appears after *JRN* in manuscripts *Vg, B, E,* and *M* (in the last instance, it also appears a second time in the *lays* section of the manuscript). All of these manuscripts were compiled after the late 1360s (See Earp, *A Guide to Research,* 77–97). The controversy over an allegedly misogynistic text, and Machaut's reparation for it, would have been likely inspirations

Like Deguileville's two versions of *Pèlerinage de vie humaine* and his *Pèlerinage de l'âme*, Machaut's *Jugement* poems narrate a movement through a number of different scenes of judgment, one of which is explicitly the judgment of heaven and which serves as a point of comparison for the others. Perhaps not surprisingly, critics have tended to approach *JRN*'s two momentous judgments—the interrupted scene of divine judgment at the beginning of the poem, and the literary judgment at the end—in terms of a sharp dichotomy. D. G. Lanoue and Jerry Root, for example, have each identified in the movement from *JRN*'s prologue to its final scene the opposition of divine and human judgment respectively.[4] As Root has it, in *JRN* Machaut "finds himself caught between two orders of sovereignty, one secular the other spiritual."[5] While Machaut's narrator laments the injustice of the world in his apocalyptic prologue and envisions the final Judgment as the only solution to human misbehavior, the "secular" turn of the rest of the poem seems precisely to illustrate the vain and limited nature of human judgment by performing a preposterous trial about love poetry in a kangaroo court.

In my view, such a traditional reading does not fully account for the subtle and unexpected ways in which Machaut used these scenes of judgment to stage the process of writing and reader reception. It is far from clear that the poet intended the apocalyptic vision of the prologue to mark opposition between a perfect divine judgment and an imperfect human judgment. Moreover, the dichotomy often imposed upon the two great judgment scenes of *JRN* takes for granted that there is nothing of the eschatological in the audience's judgment, that the secular order of reader sovereignty does not overlap with its spiritual counterpart. There is certainly a juxtaposition of judgments at work in *JRN*, but not strictly speaking of the divine and human. Rather, as I demonstrate in this chapter, the most dramatic movement between the poem's curious prologue and its (ir)resolution in the court of Charles de Navarre might better be conceived as a transformation of the eschatological itself.

---

for Chaucer's prologue to *The Legend of Good Women* (c. 1385), where the poet is judged in the court of the god of love and his queen Alceste for having maligned women in *Troilus and Criseyde* and in his translation of the *Roman de la Rose*, then given the penance of writing an anthology of virtuous women. See *The Legend of Good Women*. Ed. Janet Cowen, George Kane. East Lansing, MI: Colleagues Press, 1995. Just as Machaut's Bonneurté can be identified with the poet's patron Bonne de Luxembourg, Chaucer's Alceste is often understood to be a stand-in for Queen Anne of Bohemia, who would have commissioned the poem, according to John Lydgate (See Lydgate, *The Fall of Princes*. Ed. Henry Bergen. London: Early English Text Society, 1924. 1.330–36).

4. D. G. Lanoue, "History as Apocalypse: The 'Prologue' of Machaut's *Jugement dou roy de Navarre*." *Philological Quarterly* 60.1 (1981 Winter): 1–12; Root, 'Space to Speke,' 122–29.

5. Root, 'Space to Speke,' 128.

That is, Machaut replaces the collective and final judgment of the Apocalypse with a more personal and less conclusive vision of the poet's answerability, enacted through the meeting of the individual author with the indignant reader, to whom he is suddenly obliged to respond as before God. While *JRN* is one of Machaut's funniest poems precisely because of its element of legal farce, the eschatological persists in this literary trial scene in a different form; divine judgment is manifest in the reader's summons and accusation, and in the author's "condemnation" by his new patron. Bonneurté's case preserves a definite seriousness about the duties of an author to his audience—however ill-defined these duties may remain at the end of the text. Juxtaposed as it is with the Judgment of all men, her accusation is staged as a sudden appearance to the particular sinner (Guillaume) of the divine gaze to which he is always exposed.

As Machaut replaces the Apocalypse with his own ordeal, he brings the Judgment into the ongoing present, showing it to be no longer imminent but immanent.[6] When Guillaume does not die in the plague as he had feared, he realizes instead that he is forever being judged by God through the eyes of a powerful human third party, akin to the un-fed poor and the un-visited prisoner of the Gospel of Matthew. The somewhat irreverent humor of replacing these categories of other human beings with the offended female reader is certainly not lost; as *JRN* entertains the audience, however, it also entertains seriously the various problems of authorial responsibility. It is these ethical problems that keep Machaut's poetic persona Guillaume on the defensive and that take the place of the more conventional incriminations he imagined to be hanging over his head as he contemplated the judgment of his soul in the prologue. The trial scene of *JRN* interrupts the apocalyptic episode but stages, nonetheless, the divine judgment of the author, obliging him to respond for what he has written to a moral and deliberative force greater than himself—the readership.

Unlike the final judgment imagined by Machaut's narrator at the poem's opening, the judgment to which Dame Bonneurté brings him in the court of Charles de Navarre is by design ongoing, its parameters always shifting and a definitive decision always just out of reach. *JRN*'s trial is, above all, subject to the problems of language. The only convincing argument made by either the defense or the prosecution seems to be that the meaning of any written text changes according to who is reading it and when. As I argue in this chapter, however, the inconclusive nature of the trial does not so much illustrate the imperfection and corruption of human judgment

---

6. See Kermode, *The Sense of an Ending*, 46–47.

as it proposes a different kind of justice, even more demanding in its way than the Doomsday scenario at the beginning of the poem. Bonneurté's case against Guillaume suggests that there can never be a definitive verdict about the meaning or value of a text, and that the author's energy will always be directed to answering the accusations of readers, who continually demand that earlier writing be reexamined. Bonneurté uses the trial not only to force Guillaume to rewrite himself, but to demonstrate the ethical and artistic need for the author to change his judgments frequently in response to changing points of view. This impulse to constant revision turns the narrator away from his attempt to find certainty in judgment, symbolized by his apocalyptic vision. He is brought, instead, to embrace flexibility of opinion as the best way of dealing with the vagaries of literary reception and of human life in general. As eschatological vision becomes pseudo-autobiographical *scène judiciaire,* Machaut suggests that the poet falls under a special category of divine judgment, one in which the letter kills and revision gives life. As for Deguileville, Machaut makes of his trial scene not a ceremony of final revelation but an opportunity for the poet to defend the very act of rewriting, as he considers the coherence of his body of work, which was probably compiled into Machaut's first complete-works manuscript around the time of *JRN*'s completion.[7]

In the case of *JRN*, the impulse toward revising the corpus seems to have been borne of the circumstances of history, as the poem marks a major political shift in Machaut's career—his departure from service to the House of France, represented by the patron-judge Jean de Luxembourg, and his new allegiance to that house's great enemy, the House of Évreux, incarnated by the patron-judge Charles de Navarre. As I outline in the course of this chapter, the back-story to the change of judgments from *JRB* to *JRN* has much more at stake than the absurd problem of quantifying heartache. Namely, the suit brought by Bonneurté also recalls a troubling series of events then taking place in the courts of Machaut's two rival patrons, a true story of political intrigue, sex and murder which can be partially uncovered by clues Machaut scattered throughout his poetry.[8]*

The potentially explosive historical allusions contained in *JRN* provide another reason to be cautious when treating the comedy of *JRN*, for it is a comedy which was certainly intended to perform some degree of reflection on Machaut's own difficult circumstances and on the difficult circumstances of fourteenth-century Europe in general. In the poet's dramatic

---

7. See below in this chapter, 123–25.
8. See below in this chapter, 118–20.

change of judgment, we witness the author faced with the chaos of history and the sudden prospect of leaving old friends and comfortable political alliances behind. In this, Machaut's self-abasing/self-promoting portrayal of himself on trial before his audience also serves the more serious purpose of inquiring into the ethical problems of the author changing—or not changing—his opinions over time. As Machaut stages a self-defense before the imperious reader, he suggests not that his narrator's awareness of divine judgment was wrong, but that his expectation of final certainty was misguided. As a poetic persona for the author, Guillaume is subject to the judgment of the living, in which there cannot yet be any conclusions because texts—the literal book of the author and the figurative Book of Conscience—have yet to be completed. In order for the author to fulfill his responsibility to the reader, and thus to God, he must be ever answerable for his work, rewriting it when new and unexpected judgments arise.

The author's obligation to question and transform his opinions is performed through the sharp narrative movement from judgment to judgment in *JRB* and *JRN*. *JRN* begins with a classic, apocalyptic vision of divine revelation—a claim on the narrator's part to final moral certainty which is later echoed by his refusal to recant when faced with Bonneurté. The narrator's faith in definitive judgments—his own and God's—is soon frustrated, however, by a much less stable model of deliberation, which leads him to rewrite his work and, much like Deguileville, to affirm that the author's labor, if it is to be ethical, can be nothing other than a constant process of revision. The judgment which follows the prologue, brought to bear by Bonneurté and Charles de Navarre, shows the narrator's desire for firmness of opinion to be flawed, as it asserts that he must change his mind over time in order to do justice to his readers and to himself. In the complex trajectory from the courtly judgment of *JRB*, to the Apocalypse, to a reader's lawsuit, Machaut's *Jugement* poems do not so much represent the dichotomy of heaven's immutable judgment and man's corrupted powers as they suggest an attempt to distance ethical discourse from ideals of absolute and trans-historical truth.

Following this narrative sequence, the chapter proceeds by examining in turn each of the three major judgment scenes of Machaut's two *Jugement* poems as they respond to each other. First, and in relative brevity, I consider the initial judgment of *JRB*, the opinion about male and female suffering which Bonneurté later demands Guillaume overturn. This courtly case provides a vivid contrast to the second scene of judgment, in *JRN*'s prologue, which shatters the innocent tone of *JRB*. I next examine this episode in detail to show how Guillaume employs apocalyptic discourse and how this discourse serves to characterize his vain desire for certainty. Last, in Bonneurté's confrontation with Guillaume and in the trial scene that follows it, I trace a movement of the anticipated Judgment away from the final, collective Apocalypse and toward the continual ethical process of reading and writing—the continuous metamorphosis of the author's corpus. The latter judgment might be termed "post-apocalyptic," in that it follows immediately upon and gives the lie to the narrator's account of Doomsday, challenging his claims to an objective and conclusive vision of truth, or a definitive text. As it emphasizes the immanence, rather than the imminence of Judgment, Guillaume's trial at the hands of Bonneurté remains eschatological, but it transforms the expected day of reckoning into a continually unfolding negotiation of meaning. This, the judgment of the living author, is no less exacting in its own way than the terrible *dies irae* which precedes it; on the contrary, as it reveals God's judgment on earth, Bonneurté's suit against the poet ensures that his duty can never be complete, that the special nature of literary responsibility will compel him to face accusations without end as he composes and compiles his body of work.

II. The Judgment of the Living and the Dead

Le jugement dou roy de Behaingne begins on an idyllic day in the Easter season as the narrator lies in a bush, eavesdropping on a knight and a lady as they argue about which of the two suffers more: the lady, whose lover has died, or the knight, whose lady has left him for another man. Both make impassioned pleas but neither succeeds in convincing the other that his or her own heartbreak is greater. Eventually, they conclude that they require a skilled arbiter to decide the issue, and at this moment the narrator pops conveniently from his leafy hiding place. Making his presence known to the two parties, he tells them that he has heard the entire argument and can think of no better judge to settle the matter than his own patron, Jean de Luxembourg, the King of Bohemia (vv. 1296–306).[9] Impressed by the narrator's glowing recommendation, the knight and the lady agree to present their case to Jean of Luxembourg and defer to his judgment. Making their way to the king's splendid castle at Durbui (in the present-day

---

9. As Douglas Kelly has demonstrated, Machaut's relationships with his many patrons must be taken into account if we are to understand the terms of his artistic production ("The Genius of the Patron: The Prince, the Poet, and Fourteenth-Century Invention," in *Chaucer's French Contemporaries: The Poetry/Poetics of Self and Tradition*. Ed. R. Barton Palmer. New York: AMS, 1999. 1–27).

Belgian province of Luxembourg), the narrator and disputants are warmly welcomed by Jean and his magical court of sixteen personified virtues, figures like Love, Boldness, Generosity and Beauty (vv. 1476–85). After the parties have presented their arguments, the king modestly declares himself inferior to the task of judging this unusual case, but the personified virtues come swiftly to his aid, leading him to decide that the knight's heartbreak is greater than the lady's (vv. 1949–56). After pronouncing judgment, Jean magnanimously invites both sides to remain at his court to feast and make merry for eight days, at the end of which time he sends them off with rich parting gifts.

JRB stages a typically courtly judgment, drawn from various traditions of medieval debate poetry.[10] Among other things, Machaut amplified the gesture, already familiar from the *jeux-partis* of the *trouvères,* in which the dispute is submitted to the judgment of a specific patron. Machaut's idealization of Jean de Luxembourg's jurisprudence and generosity is clear; he even characterizes him as "l'Espée de Justise" ("the sword of justice," v. 1306), which is to say the magnificent instrument of God's judgment on earth. *JRB* is hardly an isolated incident of such praise; even well after Jean's death, Machaut continued to single this patron out for special tribute as a selfless and just ruler.[11] Nevertheless, Machaut does not allow the king of Bohemia to pronounce an immutable, perfect judgment. Jean's verdict is revisited and overturned in the second of Machaut's two judgment poems, the *Jugement dou roy de Navarre* (*JRN,* c. 1349–50). *JRN* is both a continuation and a symbolic rewriting of *JRB.* The latter poem's title is often given as the *Jugement dou roy de Navarre contre le jugement dou roy de Behaingne,*[12] and it only occurs in manuscripts immediately after *JRB.*[13]

While *JRB* stages a courtly trial scene, the meaning of judgment itself changes in the prologue to *JRN*. Whereas, conventionally for a courtly piece, *JRB* is set "Au temps pascour que toute riens s'esgaie" ("In the Easter season when all rejoices," v. 1)—*JRN* begins as summer fades quickly into November 9, 1349, a chilly day on which the north wind "cuts down flower

---

10. On Machaut's debt to the love debate tradition, see *The Love Debate Poems of Christine de Pizan.* Ed. Barbara K. Altmann. Gainesville: University Press of Florida, 1998. 16. See also William Calin, *A Poet at the Fountain: Essays on the Narrative Verse of Guillaume de Machaut.* Lexington: University of Kentucky Press, 1974. 39–40.

11. For example, in Machaut's later *Confort d'ami* (*Comfort for a Friend,* 1357). See the edition by R. Barton Palmer (New York: Garland, 1992).

12. (*The Judgment of the King of Navarre Against The Judgment of the King of Bohemia*). From my own study of the manuscripts, this expanded title occurs in BNF fr. 843, BNF fr. 1584, BNF fr. 1585, BNF fr. 1587, BNF fr. 9221, and BNF fr. 22545.

13. See Earp's painstaking descriptions of the manuscripts in *A Guide to Research,* 73–128.

buds with its cold sword" (vv. 34–36), and on which the contagion of the Black Death has forced the narrator to take refuge inside his room.[14] This is a far cry from his playful hiding place in the bush at the beginning of *JRB*, and it serves to introduce a lengthy diatribe on the vanity and transience of human life, the iniquity of the world, and the End at hand.[15]

Machaut's own perspective had certainly changed considerably when he wrote *JRN*. To begin with, Jean de Luxembourg, his longtime patron and the exalted judge of *JRB*, had died only a few years earlier in 1346 at the Battle of Crécy. *JRN* was most likely begun under the patronage of Jean's daughter Bonne, and the character Dame Bonneurté, who appears just after the prologue, may also have been created as an homage to the noblewoman.[16] Bonne had herself perished in September 1349, just prior to the time-frame of the poem.[17] Although Bonne's death is not explicitly mentioned in *JRN*, the prologue's sustained meditation on the passing of earthly beauty strongly suggests it, as do lengthy references to the Black Death, from which she was thought to have died.[18]

The overall tone of *JRN*'s prologue has as much to do with the transience of judgment as it does with the transience of earthly life. As Machaut's "sword of Justice" and his daughter pass with the fair season, the more innocent, courtly trial of *JRB* cedes to a cosmic day of wrath. Machaut fills his November scene with apocalyptic imagery, including echoes of Revelation.[19] His narrator speaks at length not only of the plague, but of the endless war, social strife, religious conflict, ominous astrological signs and devastating earthquakes of the years 1348 and 1349. Most importantly, he begins his invective by lamenting the world's fall from justice:[20]

---

14. Machaut's juxtaposition of plague and pastoral imagery is discussed by Ardis Butterfield, "Pastoral and the Politics of Plague in Machaut and Chaucer." *Studies in the Age of Chaucer* 16 (1994): 3–27.

15. Machaut's choice of theme is appropriate to the season: while the Last Judgment had no assigned place per se in medieval liturgy, it was often associated with Advent and particularly with November, since waiting for Christ's birth was also to await his second coming as judge. See David Bevington's introduction to *Homo, Memento Finis*, 3.

16. On the identity of Bonneurté as Bonne, see Calin, *A Poet at the Fountain*, 4–41; Root, 'Space to Speke,' 121; Jacqueline Cerquiglini, *'Un engin si soutil': Guillaume de Machaut et l'écriture au XIVe siècle*. Geneva: Slatkine, 1985.

17. See Earp, *A Guide to Research*, 25. See also Poirion, *Le poète et le prince*, 194, 201 n28.

18. Lanoue ("History," 4) suggests that Bonne's death may be behind the tragic vision of the prologue. See also Butterfield, "Pastoral and the Politics of Plague," 16. However, as I discuss later in this chapter (118–20), it is far from certain that the plague is what killed her.

19. Lanoue ("History," 6–7) reads conspicuous resemblances between the prologue and Revelation. Laurence De Looze notes the generally apocalyptic flavor of *JRN* ("Masquage et démasquage de l'auteur dans les *Jugements* de Guillaume de Machaut," in *Masques et déguisements dans la littérature médiévale*. Ed. Marie-Louise Ollier. Montréal: Presses de l'Université de Montréal, 1988. 206–7).

20. Lanoue ("History," 9) notes the special attention injustice receives in the prologue.

Comment par conseil de taverne	How by barroom counsel
Li mondes par tout se gouverne;	the world is everywhere ruled,
Comment justice et verité	how justice and truth
Sont mortes par l'iniquité	were killed by the iniquity
D'Advarice qui en maint regne	of Avarice who in so many places
Com dame souvereinne regne.	reigns as sovereign lady.
(vv. 39–44)	

In response to human iniquity, Machaut's narrator shows us God deciding to unleash his own justice:

Quant Dieus vit de sa mansion	When God saw from his dwelling
Dou monde la corruption	the corruption of the world
Qui tout partout estoit si grans,	which everywhere was so great,
N'est merveilles s'il fu engrans	it's no wonder if he wanted
De penre crueuse vengence	to take harsh vengeance
De ceste grant desordenance;	for this awful disorder;
Si que tantost, sans plus attendre,	and so, without waiting any longer,
Pour justice et vengence prendre,	for the sake of vengeance and justice,
Fist la mort issir de sa cage.	he sprang Death from her cage.
(vv. 347–55)	

Et par tout le munde couroit,	And [Death] ran across the world,
Tout tuoit et tout acouroit	killing and destroying all,
Quanqu'il li venoit a l'encontre	whomsoever she met.
N'on ne pooit resister contre.	Nor could anyone resist her.
(vv. 363–66)	

The good judgment of Machaut's late patrons is swept away with their passing, yielding to a darkened universe in which any stable concept of justice or truth has likewise perished. The corruption of humanity requires a final intervention from on high; accordingly, the narrator represents the plague not merely as an instance of divine retribution in the here and now, but as the beginning of the Judgment Day itself, which God will put off no longer ("sans plus attendre," v. 353).

In *JRB*, the low and comical position of Machaut's narrator in the bush afforded him a vantage point from which he could observe the disputing knight and lady and help bring their case to Jean de Luxembourg. In *JRN*'s prologue, the narrator adopts a much loftier perspective, one that claims special knowledge of divine judgment. Although in his little room, he seems to see from God's dwelling (*mansion*), looking out at the entire world as it is cut down by Death for its sins. No longer merely the humble court functionary he was in *JRB*,[21] the narrator now casts himself as a fearful judge to replace his deceased patrons. Most notoriously, he indicts the Jews of Europe, who were accused during those years of having caused the plague by poisoning water sources.[22] The image here is an explicitly visual one, highlighting the omniscient divine gaze that the narrator-poet claims to share:

Mais cils qui haut siet et long voit,	But He who is seated on high and sees far,
Qui tout gouverne et tout pourvoit,	who governs all and provides all,
Ceste traïson plus celer	no longer wished this treason
Ne volt, eins la fist reveler	to remain hidden, so he revealed it
Et si generaument savoir	and made it so well known
Qu'il perdirent corps et avoir.	that [the Jews] lost their lives and goods.
(vv. 229–34)	

Along with strange movements of the stars, earthquakes, war, heresy and pestilence, alleged Jewish conspiracies against Christians were considered by some to be a sign of the Apocalypse, and the subsequent retaliation against Jews was understood as one with heaven's righteous anger.[23]

While this cannot excuse Machaut's apparent anti-Semitic bias in today's court of reader opinion, the poem's entire treatment of historical events was highly conventional. Critics, beginning with Alfred Coville, have noted similarities between *JRN*'s prologue and contemporary plague chronicles; Coville even labeled the beginning of *JRN* a "chronique en vers."[24] As potential sources for the prologue, we might cite, for example, the chronicles of Machaut's close contemporary Jean le Bel,[25] or Gabriele

---

21. Earp (*A Guide to Research*, 8–9) notes that Machaut himself was employed as the secretary or notary of Jean de Luxembourg.

22. Notably, René Girard has made much of Machaut's anti-Semitic discourse, using it to introduce his seminal work on the scapegoat (*Le bouc-émissaire*. Paris: Grasset, 1982. 7–21).

23. See Delumeau, *La peur en Occident*, 213.

24. Alfred Coville, "Poèmes historiques de l'avènement de Philippe VI de Valois au Traité de Calais, 1328–1360," in *Histoire littéraire de la France*. 43 vols. Paris: Imprimerie Nationale, 1865–2005. XXXVIII: 329. Coville (XXXVIII: 328–31) discusses Machaut's historiography more generally. See also Palmer, ed., *The Judgment of the King of Navarre*, 215 n; Stephen M. Taylor, "Portraits of Pestilence: The Plague in the Work of Machaut and Boccaccio." *Allegorica* 5.1 (1980 Summer): 105–18. Taylor (105) cites similarities with the work of Simon de Covino and Guy de Chauliac, although without arguing that Machaut was influenced by them.

25. Jean le Bel, *Chronique de Jean le Bel*. Ed. Jules Viard, Eugène Déprez. 2 vols. Paris: Renouard, 1904–5. Lanoue ("History," 3) notes similarities to the account of Jean le Bel.

de Mussis's *Historia de Morbo* (c. 1348), which, like *JRN*'s prologue, mixes imagery from Revelation with astrological portents and blames the corruption of the air.[26] But Machaut seems to have been borrowing quite broadly from the chronicle tradition, making it a futile endeavor to trace *JRN*'s prologue to a single ur-source.[27] The major elements of Machaut's account are found in any number of contemporary chronicles: war, bad weather and earthquakes as signs of the apocalypse (vv. 89–90, vv. 95–98, vv. 172–80, vv. 189–211, vv. 265–306), the accusation of Jews for well-poisoning and divinely-authorized retaliation by Christians (vv. 212–40), the appearance of flagellant heretics from the Rhineland (vv. 241–56), the foul air (vv. 27–30, vv. 307–20), strange movements of the stars (vv. 151–71), the plague's disturbing pathology (vv. 321–46), the universality of its affliction (v. 321, v. 332, vv. 347–430), the abandonment of friends and family members for fear of contagion (vv. 329–40), the decimation of rural populations and of the agricultural economy (vv. 407–30).[28] Shared with most contemporary accounts is the hypothesis of divine retribution for the world's sins.[29] The universality of human guilt and the correspondingly universal nature of the plague's affliction were arguably the master themes of all fourteenth-century plague accounts,[30] and Machaut's prologue likewise insists on the general culpability of mankind.

Although innovative for its transposition of events from the chronicles into verse, *JRN*'s prologue reads like a veritable anthology of plague his-

---

26. See de Mussis's text in John Aberth, *The Black Death: The Great Mortality of 1348–1350: A Brief History with Documents*. Boston: Palgrave Macmillan, 2005. 98–100. Another important source for the plague, especially the astrological influence and the resulting contagion of the air, would have been the 1348 *Compendium* published as a tract by the University of Paris medical faculty. On the *Compendium*, see Sylvie Bazin-Tacchela, "Rupture et continuité du discours médical à travers les écrits sur la peste de 1348," in *Air, miasmes et contagion: les épidémies dans l'Antiquité et au Moyen Âge*. Ed. Sylvie Bazin-Tacchela, Danielle Quéruel, Évelyne Samama. Langres: Dominique Guéniot, 2001. 108–11.

27. In his edition of *JRN* (215 n), Palmer suggests that Machaut would have been following one such source closely but does not propose a specific text.

28. For a general discussion of medieval plague chronicles, see Ann G. Carmichael, "1 Universal and Particular: The Language of Plague, 1348–1500." *Medical History Supplement* 27 (2008): 17–52; Gabriele Zanella, "Italia, Francia e Germania: una storiografia a confronto," in *La peste nera: dati di una realtà ed elementi di una interpretazione, atti del xxx convegno storico internazionale; Todi, 10–13 ottobre 1993*. Spoleto: Centro Italiano di Studi sull Alto Medieovo, 1994. 44–135. For specific discussion of the topoi of meteorological and astrological phenomena, see Laura A. Smoller, "Of Earthquakes, Hail, Frogs and Geography: Plague and the Investigation of the Apocalypse in the Later Middle Ages," in *Last Things: Death and Apocalypse in the Middle Ages*. Ed. Caroline Walker Bynum, Paul H. Freedman. Philadelphia: University of Pennsylvania Press, 2000. 156–87.

29. See Zanella, "Italia, Francia e Germania," 88.

30. See Carmichael, "1 Universal and Particular." See also Nicole Chareyron, *Jean le Bel: le maître de Froissart, grand imagier de la guerre de Cent Ans*. Brussels: De Boeck Larcier, 1996. 192–95; Lanoue, "History," 5.

tories, compressing most of that tradition's major topoi into a little over four hundred lines. While Machaut was likely an eyewitness to the plague's horrors while at Reims or elsewhere, there is virtually no detail in *JRN*'s account that could not have been found in a handful of other sources, both Latin and vernacular. What I believe may be inferred from the very borrowed discourse of the prologue is a certain ironic awareness of its limitations. Machaut's narrator's tirade is anything but an instance of perfect divine judgment; rather, it is an all too human attempt, which quickly falls flat, to see through the eyes of God. In this, the initial section of *JRN* corresponds to Claudia Rattazzi Papka's term "fiction of judgment," defined as "a work that claims access to divine revelation while acknowledging its status as a human artifact, and in which visions of order and meaning are presented by the author as if from a divine perspective."[31] But compared with Dante's *Commedia* and Langland's *Piers Plowman*—Papka's chief examples—Machaut's fiction of judgment is much more transparently a fiction, its failure to produce definitive revelation deliberately highlighted. For this is not the End but a beginning—a prologue—and the narrator's apocalyptic voice fades as suddenly as it appears.

First, Machaut contrasts the narrator's claims to share in divine revelation with his lack of awareness while the plague was actually happening. Having repeatedly affirmed his special revelation of the final end of humanity, the narrator then reminds readers that he had been shut up in his room and thus knew very little about what was going on outside:[32]

Si qu'en doubtance et en cremeur	So in dread and terror
Dedens ma maison m'enfermay	I shut myself up in my house
Et en ma pensée fermay	and locked myself in my thoughts
Fermement que n'en partiroie	so tightly that I would not leave
Jusques a tant que je saroie	until I knew to what end
A quel fin ce porroit venir;	this all would come;
Si laisoie Dieu couvenir.	I would leave all to God's will.
Si que lonc temps, se Dieus me voie,	So for a long time, God help me,
Fui einsi que petit savoie	I stayed there with little knowledge
De ce qu'on faisoit en la ville,	about what was going on in the city,

---

31. Claudia Rattazzi Papka, "The Limits of Apocalypse: Eschatology, Epistemology, and Textuality in the *Commedia* and *Piers Plowman*," in Bynum and Freedman, eds., *Last Things*. 233. For a lively discussion of how Machaut's vision diverges from that of the divine, see Jacqueline Cerquiglini, "'Le clerc et le louche': Sociology of an Esthetic." Trans. Monique Briand-Walker. *Poetics Today: Medieval and Renaissance Representation: New Reflections* 5.3 (1984): 479–91—especially 488–89.

32. On how the narrator's admissions of weakness and fear contribute to Machaut's poetic persona, see Taylor, "Portraits of Pestilence," 108–9.

> Et s'en morut plus de .xx. mille,   and more than 10,000 died,
> Cependant que je ne sceus mie.   of which I learned nothing.
> (vv. 442–53)

In fact, Machaut's narrator admits a *willful* ignorance of the events transpiring around him, which he attributes to his vain desire not to become personally touched by loss:

> Car riens n'en voloie savoir,   For I wanted to know nothing,
> Pour meins de pensées avoir,   in order to have fewer worries,
> Comment qu'asses de mes amis   although many of my friends
> Fussent mors et en terre mis.   had died and been buried.
> (vv. 455–58)

The juxtaposition between the narrator's enlightened doom prophecy and his blind terror is a sharp one, and it serves to remind us that the author is not in fact God, that any judgments he makes are subject to immediate question.

At the same time, the narrator's move away from the Apocalypse privileges the particular judgment, as Machaut's narrator turns the accusation on himself and confesses:

> Je ne fui mie si hardis   I wasn't nearly so brave that
> Que moult ne fusse acouardis.   I wasn't cut down to a coward's size.
> Car tuit li plus hardi trambloient   For all the bravest men trembled
> De päour de mort qu'il avoient.   from their fear of death.
> Si que trés bien me confessai   So I confessed myself fully
> De tous les pechiez que fais ay   of all the sins I've committed
> Et me mis en estat de grace   and put myself into a state of grace,
> Pour recevoir mort en la place,   ready to die then and there
> S'il pleüst a Nostre Signeur.   should it have pleased the Lord.
> (vv. 433–41)

No longer the judge of humanity, the narrator loses his self-righteous posture of omniscience and is left to account for himself before the Almighty. But the judgment of the narrator's soul doesn't happen either, any more than the collective day of wrath. While it signals an important change of tone, a personalization of the eschatological, the narrator passes quickly over his confession; he certainly doesn't confess anything to readers, other than the fact that he has confessed.

And once the threat of imminent death is removed, Machaut's narrator also seems to find it difficult to maintain a penitential, introspective heart. Hearing sounds of celebration, he throws open his window; he is then told by a friend that the plague is over and that it is safe to come out (vv. 465–75). Immediately, he forgets about the end of the world and his sins, leaving his room to breathe the fresh air. As if overnight, spring has returned to the earth (vv. 482–86). The world outside is filled once again with sweet breezes and birdsong (v. 483, vv. 526–29). After the poem's apocalyptic verses, this scene symbolically reopens *JRN* by evoking the beginning of *JRB*, where the carefree narrator had likewise reveled in the beauty of the new season before his encounter with the quarreling knight and lady.[33] After the devastation of the plague, spring triumphs in an inevitable return, and Machaut's narrator is given new life. From the brink of certain death, he has been reborn into the "temps pascour" of the author's earlier poem, the moment of a less serious, courtly judgment.[34]

Most of all, the rebirth of the Easter season represents the activity of the poet himself, the work of writing and rewriting. As it suddenly interrupts the bleak voice of the prologue, this scene reattaches *JRN* to the most traditional opening of courtly poetry, the *reverdie* (literally "re-greening"), in which the return of spring both catalyzes and symbolizes the poet's work.[35] The dramatic departure of Machaut's narrator from his room into a landscape of budding flowers and warbling songbirds suggests that for him, the Judgment can be put aside as the adventure of poetic creation becomes possible again.

As it turns out, this is something of a false assumption for Machaut's narrator. Since the world will not end after all, he decides to spend the day blithely coursing hares. For readers, however, there is something decidedly too easy about the disappearance of the Apocalypse and the reappearance of spring, the return to the untroubled day of judgment in *JRB*. While Machaut's oblivious narrator puts the end of the world out of mind immediately to delight his senses, the effect on the audience is quite different: in the abrupt juxtaposition of *JRN*'s two opening scenes—Apocalypse and *reverdie*—it is difficult not to feel the lingering presence of death and

---

33. See Calin, *A Poet at the Fountain*, 128.
34. Sarah Kay has suggested that this may be a rewriting of the allegorical birth of Deguileville's pilgrim in *Pèlerinage de vie humaine* (*The Place of Thought: The Complexity of One in Late Medieval French Didactic Poetry*. Philadelphia: University of Pennsylvania Press, 2007. 98). Escaping the plague for the delights of courtly literature also evokes the *Decameron* of Machaut's contemporary Boccaccio. On correspondences, see Butterfield, "Pastoral and the Politics of Plague."
35. See Poirion, *Le poète et le prince*, 115, 488; Michel Zink, *Nature et poésie au Moyen Âge*. Paris: Fayard, 2006. 176.

judgment behind the surface of this bright spring day, and to recall the narrator's hell-fire condemnation of man's iniquity to man. Our generic expectations for an apocalyptic text are partly frustrated, and yet we continue to anticipate a Judgment of some kind.

This is especially the case in that the narrator's springtime frolicking appears as an episode of spiritual laxity, following his momentary repentance in the face of death. Hunting hares was a common medieval figure for vain sensual pursuits, and particularly for sexual conquest.[36] The implication thus seems to be that the narrator has quickly fallen back into sin after his panicked moments of self-accusation during the plague. Although he claims to have made a thorough confession in anticipation of his judgment (v. 437–38), he seems now to have forgotten that penitential introspection is to be practiced constantly throughout life and not only *in extremis.*

It is into this context that Dame Bonneurté emerges to demand a reckoning which the narrator seems never to have foreseen, even as he imagined himself before the throne of God. While the narrator is hunting, Bonneurté sends a messenger to summon him to her. When he arrives before this mysterious lady, she calls him by his name, Guillaume, for the first time and accuses him of having defamed women in *JRB*. Although Guillaume's meeting with Bonneurté parallels his encounter with the knight and the lady in *JRB*[37] and occasions a second, opposing judgment, Bonneurté does not simply continue the trial begun in the first *Jugement* by overturning its decision. Rather, Bonneurté's judgment may be read as a means of fulfilling the eschatological expectation prompted by *JRN*'s prologue, albeit in a rather different form. Bonneurté's accusation breaks through the lyric veneer of the *reverdie* to remind Guillaume that his writing is constantly subject to both the judgment of God and the judgment of the reader.

Bonneurté's interruption of Guillaume's hare-hunting is, in fact, evocative of a common medieval eschatological motif—the theme of an abrupt warning, delivered from the world beyond, to repent of one's sins before it is too late. In texts of the *memento mori* genre, the hunt appears as the most exemplary of vain pursuits, whose participants are suddenly reminded of their eventual death and their immanent judgment. For example, in the widespread medieval legend of the Trois Morts et les Trois Vifs (The Three Living and Three Dead), a group of hunting noblemen are met by their own decomposing corpses, come from the future to warn them to repent.[38]

---

36. See Calin (*A Poet at the Fountain,* 121) on the significance of the hare-hunting scene.
37. See De Looze, *Pseudo-Autobiography,* 71.
38. Anne Rooney discusses resemblances to the *memento mori* tradition in Chaucer's *Book of the Duchess,* but only makes passing mention to this scene in *JRN,* which would have been Chaucer's

As the hunt is cut short, man's pretensions to mastery over the forces of nature are quickly overturned. In much the same vein, Bonneurté's appearance suddenly jars the narrator from his insouciance with a reminder of his ongoing judgment. Her accusation recalls the divine judgment that the narrator has put out of mind, by demanding that he repent for what he has written.

And while Bonneurté is radiantly beautiful, not a rotting cadaver, she may well represent the dead come to warn the narrator, as in the Trois Morts legend. Bonneurté is an enigmatic figure who performs a number of important metamorphoses in the course of *JRN*. Perhaps the most striking aspect of her identity, however, is her resemblance in name to Bonne de Luxembourg, under whose patronage Machaut had likely begun *JRN* and who had died in the autumn of the year the poem begins, 1349. Whether or not one accepts Ernest Hœpffner's theory that *JRN* was written to appease actual members of Machaut's female readership offended by the verdict of *JRB*, it is clear from Bonneurté's accusation that she is an incensed reader, and a reader intimately familiar with Machaut's work.[39] For this reason especially, it seems plausible that she is meant to suggest the poet's late patroness.

Although it is generally accepted that Bonne died in the same plague outbreak that forms the backdrop for *JRN*'s prologue, rumors reported in the chronicle of Machaut's contemporary Jean le Bel tell a different story: many believed that she had been deliberately killed.[40] If so, it may have been under the orders of her husband Jean, duke of Normandy (soon thereafter Jean II, king of France) as a result of suspicions that she had committed adultery with Raoul de Brienne, constable of France.[41] In any case, the constable was himself summarily beheaded by Jean II the following year, upon his return from English captivity, possibly because letters Jean

---

most immediate source ("*The Book of the Dutchess:* Hunting and the 'Ubi Sunt' Tradition." *The Review of English Studies* 151.38 [1987]: 299). On the Trois Morts legend, see Pierroberto Scaramella, "L'Italia dei trionfi e dei contrasti," in *Humana fragilitas: i temi della morte in Europa tra duecento e settecento.* Ed. Alberto Tenenti. Clusone: Ferrari Editrice, 2000. 26–31. Scaramella explains the recurrence of the hunting detail in the legend by tracing it to an illumination in the late thirteenth-century manuscript *De arte venandi*, written by Emperor Frederick II. Calin (*A Poet at the Fountain*, 123) notes that the encounter with Bonneurté recalls traditional romance entrances into the Arthurian otherworld.

39. *Œuvres de Guillaume de Machaut.* Ed. Ernest Hœpffner. 3 vols. Paris: Firmin, 1908–21. I: lxix. On the identity of Bonneurté as Bonne, see Calin, *A Poet at the Fountain*, 40–41; Cerquiglini, '*Un engin si soutil,*' 61; Root, '*Space to Speke,*' 121.

40. Jean le Bel, *Chronique de Jean le Bel*, ch. 84 (ed. Viard and Déprez, II: 183).

41. See Earp, *A Guide to Research*, 24.

received inculpated Raoul in double-dealing with the English, but also possibly due to the same rumors of adultery that may have led to Bonne's death.[42] Having executed Raoul, Jean conferred the title of constable on the widely unpopular Charles d'Espagne, who was rumored to be the king's lover, and who was also made count of Angoulême in short order. The countship, however, was a hereditary title already claimed by the infuriated Charles de Navarre, who responded by having the other Charles assassinated in 1353.

As for Machaut, the poet had thus far spent his entire career closely tied to the House of France and to those who, like Jean de Luxembourg and his daughter, were allied with that house. Yet after Bonne's death, there is little evidence that Machaut directly entered the service of her husband the king, which would have been the more predictable career choice.[43] Instead, he swiftly aligned himself with Charles de Navarre and the House of Évreux, Jean II's bitter and bloody rivals.[44] That decisive move is reflected explicitly in *JRN,* which announces Machaut's new allegiance through the nomination of the young Charles de Navarre as patron-judge, in parallel to Jean de Luxembourg in *JRB.* What is more, the lamentation of iniquity in *JRN*'s prologue may constitute an implicit critique of Jean II's actions, particularly since Jean le Bel's chronicle—a likely source for the prologue—states that the execution of Raoul de Brienne was "sans loy et sans jugement."[45]

At least one scholar, Lawrence Earp, has suggested that the violent court intrigue of 1349–50 may have been a motivating factor in Machaut's departure from the House of France.[46] The poet would not have been alone in reacting this way, since Raoul de Brienne's execution without trial sparked a wave of anger among the constable's friends and allies in the Norman nobility, many of whom became partisans of Charles de Navarre as a result.[47] In

---

42. Jean le Bel, *Chronique de Jean le Bel,* ch. 87 (ed. Viard and Déprez, II: 198–200).
43. See Raymond Cazèlles, *Société politique, noblesse et couronne sous Jean le Bon et Charles V.* Geneva: Droz, 1982. 88; Claude Gauvard, "Portrait du prince d'après l'œuvre de Guillaume de Machaut: étude sur les idées politiques du poète," in *Guillaume de Machaut, poète et compositeur: colloque-table ronde, organisé par l'Université de Reims, 19–22 avril 1978.* Ed. Jacques Chailley, et al. Paris: Klincksieck, 1982. 23–29.
44. See Palmer's introduction to his edition of *JRN,* xiv–xv. Machaut did not definitively cut himself off from the House of France, however, as he later enjoyed the patronage of Jean Duke of Berry, who was the son of Bonne and Jean II, and in whose service Machaut portrays himself in his *Fonteinne amoureuse* (1360). See the editions of *Fonteinne* by Palmer and Cerquiglini-Toulet (New York: Garland, 1993 and Paris: Stock, 1993).
45. Jean le Bel, *Chronique de Jean le Bel,* ch. 87 (ed. Viard and Déprez, II: 200).
46. Earp, *A Guide to Research,* 25.
47. See Cazèlles, *Société politique,* 88.

any event, it hardly seems a coincidence that the central matter for judgment in *JRN*, as in *JRB*, is an aristocratic love affair ending in death, and that the sequel, beginning with its disturbing prologue, gives the problem of human mortality an even stronger presence.[48] During *JRN*'s trial scene, for instance, the disputants consider the exemplum of an unfaithful stork killed by her mate when he discovers her infidelity (vv. 1671–862). Perhaps even more telling are the words Bonneurté uses as she details her accusation to Guillaume. Comparing the knight's suffering to the lady's in *JRB*, she says that the love affair that ended in death torments her personally:

Mais ce n'est pas chose pareille	But [the knight's pain] is not a comparable thing
Au fait d'amours qui me remort,	to the love affair that torments me,
Qui se defenist par la mort.	which was undone by death.
(vv. 1006–8)	

The word *remort* could also be translated as "causes regret," leading one to wonder if Bonneurté/Bonne herself had not assumed the place of the grieving lady in *JRB*. But whether Bonneurté is tormented because she is one of the principal actors in this lethal love affair, or only because she is upset about the judgment the lady received in *JRB*, it is hard to deny that a debate poem about love and death would have hit much closer to home for Machaut's audience in 1349–50 than in the early 1330s.

Come, perhaps from the grave, to admonish Guillaume to regard himself more critically, Bonneurté transforms the spectral other of the *memento mori* into an imagined, idealized reader, the patron whose memory lives on and who demands that Machaut do her justice. As can be seen through a close analysis of her accusations, Bonneurté's mysterious appearance serves to shift the otherworldly expectation of the prologue away from an imminent future beyond time and toward the everyday practice of reading and writing. The emergence (or resurrection) of the disapproving patroness signals not so much a departure from the poem's mood of eschatological anticipation, as an acknowledgement that the Judgment is always already happening through human relationships, including that of poet and reader. In the legal and eschatological *procès* that takes place between author and audience, Machaut is called upon to defend his authority, and to speak for a corpus to which he is forever bound.

---

48. See Lanoue, "History," especially 10–11; Calin, *A Poet at the Fountain*, 127.

III. Bonneurté's Case and Guillaume's *Livres*

When the narrator arrives before Bonneurté, she scolds him for having ignored her presence (vv. 760–68), rebuking him for his lack of awareness, as one might expect of an apparition from the other world. Then, once Bonneurté has Guillaume's attention, she moves on to the matter that prompted her to summon him in the first place: his sins. Similar to the way that hunter becomes hunted in the *memento mori* tradition, Bonneurté turns the tables on Guillaume by making him an object of pursuit, in the full judicial sense.[49] She exhorts Guillaume to judge himself in the here and now. At first, she refuses to specify her accusation and insists that he find the answer for himself, examining his own "livres":

Guillaume, sachies, orendroit	Guillaume, know right from the start
N'en arez plus de ma partie.	that you'll have no more from me.
Car la chose est einsi partie:	For the affair is underway:
Se je le say, vous le savez,	If I know it, you know it.
Car le fait devers vous avez	Your offense is something
En l'un de vos livres escript,	you've written in one of your books,
Bien devisié et bien descript:	thoroughly laid out and well described.
Si resgardes dedens vos livres,	Look then into your books;
Bien say que vous n'estes pas ivres	I'm sure you aren't drunk
Quant vos fais amoureus ditez.	when you compose your tales of love,
Dont bien savez de vos dittez,	so you must know of your poems
Quant vous les faites et parfaites,	when you make and perfect them,
Se vous faites bien ou forfaites,	whether you do well or ill,
Dès qu'il sont fait de sanc assis	since you put your will into them
Autant a un mot comme a sis.	as much in one word as in six.
S'il vous plaist, vous y garderez,	Please, look there for the answer,
Qu'autre chose n'en porterez	for you'll get nothing more from me,
De moy, quant a l'eure presente.	at least not for the moment.
Solez certeins que c'est m'entente.	You can be sure that that is my intention.
(vv. 862–80)	

Despite the narrator's earlier claim to have thoroughly confessed his sins (v. 438), Bonneurté indicates that there is unfinished business left for his soul, that Guillaume's introspection is not yet complete. Given her insistence that Guillaume look inward to discover the nature of his own fault,

---

49. Calin (*A Poet at the Fountain,* 122) has noted this role reversal, although without reference to the *memento mori* tradition.

Bonneurté's choice of words ("livres," v. 869) strongly recalls the proverbial Book of Conscience.

Like the "ouvrages" for which Guillaume de Deguileville must respond in his *Pèlerinage de l'âme*, the most immediate context for Guillaume's *livres* is literary, since Bonneurté means that she is offended by the judgment pronounced in Machaut's *JRB*. In response to Bonneurté's accusation, Guillaume claims that he cannot recall having committed such a sin in his writing (vv. 881–98). So Bonneurté spells it out for him; she takes issue with the judgment of *JRB* that the lady whose lover died feels less pain than the jilted knight:

Vous avez dit et devisié	You have said and laid out
Et jugié de fait avisié	and judged from knowledge of the facts
Par diffinitif jugement	by definitive judgment
Que cils a trop plus malement,	that he has much more
Grieté, tourment, mal, et souffraite	grief, torment, pain and suffering
Qui trueve sa dame forfaite	who finds his lady unfaithful
Contre lui en fausse maniere,	to him and false,
Que la trés douce dame chiere	than that very gentle dear lady
Qui avera son dous amy	who has her sweet lover
Conjoint a son cuer, sans demy,	joined fully to her heart,
Par amours, sans autre moien,	by love and no other force,
Puis le savera en loien	then learns that he is in the bonds
De la mort ou il demourra,	of death and so will remain,
Si que jamais ne le verra.	so that she will never see him again.
(vv. 1013–26)	

According to Bonneurte's wording (vv. 1013–14), the role of judge has passed from the late King of Bohemia—in whose mouth Machaut had placed the first judgment—to the poet himself. Although the narrator has no judicial agency in *JRB*, appearing merely as Jean de Luxembourg's notary or secretary, Bonneurté's indictment confers upon Guillaume the responsibility for having made the judgment, not just for having written it down.[50] Bonneurté regards Guillaume as fundamentally guilty for having neglected to see the validity of the woman's position, the extent of her pain.

With her accusation, Bonneurté insists upon the real ethical importance of the judgments made in poetry. The debate tradition upon which

---

50. See Root, '*Space to Speke*,' 122; De Looze, *Pseudo-Autobiography*, 71–72. R. Barton Palmer, "Transtextuality and the Producing-I in Guillaume de Machaut's Judgment Series." *Exemplaria* 5.2 (1993): 300.

Machaut's *Jugement* poems are partly modeled already contains a distinct ethical quality, in that it systematically questions the minutiae of proper conduct for lovers.[51] Bonneurté's accusation, however, focuses not on the finer points of courtly behavior, but rather upon the ethics of writing itself.

Her accusation is also a means of calling greater attention to Machaut's authorship. Guillaume's failure to find in his *livres* the sin to which Bonneurté alludes highlights the extensive nature of Machaut's corpus at the time of *JRN*'s composition. Guillaume says that he has no idea what specific part of his work she finds objectionable, nor should he reasonably be expected to know, considering his vast poetic output:

Dame, qu'est ce que dit avez?	Lady, just what do you mean?
Selonc le bien que vous savez,	You know very well
Trop mieus savez que vous ne dites:	that you know more than you are saying.
J'ay bien de besongnes escriptes	I have so many written works
Devers moy, de pluseurs manieres,	before me, in many styles,
De moult de diverses matieres,	on many diverse topics,
Dont l'une l'autre ne ressamble.	each having no resemblance to the others.
Consideré toutes ensamble,	When considered all together,
Et chascune bien mise a point,	and each work examined thoroughly,
D'ordre en ordre et de point en point,	section by section and line by line,
Dès le premier commencement	from the very beginning
Jusques au darrein finement,	until the very end,
Se tout voloie regarder	even if I wished to look through it all
—Dont je me vorrai bien garder—	—and that's certainly not the case—
Trop longuement y metteroie;	it would take me too long.
Et d'autre part, je ne porroie	Besides the fact that I couldn't find
Trouver ce que vous demandez	what you refer to
S'a vos paroles n'amendez.	unless you tell me more.
(vv. 881–98)	

Guillaume's protest is on one level a comic instance of self-promotion: how can he possibly recall everything that he has written throughout such a long and productive career? Taken as a reflection of Machaut's own evolv-

---

51. Literary critic and legal historian Peter Goodrich considers that the courts of love constitute an ethically serious "minor jurisprudence" inseparable from the prehistory of modern law and existing somewhere between literary and legal culture. Goodrich argues that the courts of love privilege fluidity over closure, creating an interminable *procès* which constantly rewrites the law and which is tied to the particular jurisprudence of women (*Law in the Courts of Love: Literature and Other Minor Jurisprudences*. London: Routledge, 1996. 178–81). Bonneurté's judgment, as I argue here, should be read similarly.

ing corpus, Guillaume's description of his work is quite accurate. At the time of *JRN*'s composition, Machaut's body of work comprised as many as five narrative *dits*, including the innovative lyric-narrative hybrid *Remede de Fortune*, as well as a substantial amount of lyric pieces and music.[52]

Does Guillaume's description of Machaut's poetry, deeply heterogeneous but also assembled together in front of him as a whole ("devers moy," v. 885; "consideré toutes ensamble," v. 888), imply its compilation? The earliest extent "complete-works" Machaut manuscript is the celebrated MS. *C* (BNF fr. 1586), whose most reliable dating ranges from 1350 to 1356.[53] The traditional and widely accepted dating of *JRN* is 1349–50, but this is entirely due to the historical details presented in the prologue, so that it can only be placed with any certainty as being written in 1349 or later.[54] It is thus well within the realm of possibility that *JRN* is contemporaneous with *C* or even postdates it, especially since *C* contains *JRB* and the *Dit de l'alerion*, but not *JRN*.

Although it is not entirely clear whether the *livres* of which Bonneurté and Guillaume speak may also refer to such a bound codex, it is nevertheless striking that Guillaume displays an awareness of his sundry poetry as constituting a textual whole that he might put in front of himself to reexamine, like the personal Book of Conscience. Machaut uses Bonneurté's accusation, and Guillaume's response to it, to call attention to what the poet has already written, and to strengthen Machaut's resemblance to his poetic persona.

Much like Deguileville, Machaut saw important stakes in the ability of his compiled texts to present a coherent version of the author, which is why Bonneurté's command that Guillaume consult his *livres* is so closely modeled on discourses of personal introspection. As Kevin Brownlee and Sylvia Huot have both shown, Machaut's manuscripts represent a pioneering instance of vernacular poetry compilations in which "the personality of the author is deemed central enough to inspire the conjoining of texts that would not ordinarily be associated."[55] Through careful control over

---

52. On the chronology of the narrative poems, see Earp, *A Guide to Research*, 189–94; on the chronology of the music, see Ibid., 273–74.

53. See François Avril, "Les manuscrits enluminés de Guillaume de Machaut: essai de chronologie," in Chailley, et al, eds., *Guillaume de Machaut, poète et compositeur*, 119, 124; Earp, *A Guide to Research*, 192. Both Avril and Earp lean toward the latter part of this range of dates. Earp (*A Guide to Research*, 26–27) speculates, however, that the manuscript may have been started, like *JRN* itself, for Bonne de Luxembourg, who died in 1349, while Avril (71 n17) acknowledges some evidence that *C* already existed as early as 1353.

54. See Earp, *A Guide to Research*, 190–92.

55. Huot, *From Song to Book*, 234. Huot considers that, before Machaut, only Adam de la Halle's manuscripts represent "an author corpus treated as a small book unto itself, with generic division, yet

the ordering of his manuscripts, Machaut sought to define himself as a corpus-author, tying his identity and authority as a poet to the coming together of separate compositions into a bound whole.[56] Whether or not Guillaume's initial dialog with Bonneurté implies that a complete-works compilation already existed at the time of *JRN*'s composition, Guillaume's response to her accusation simultaneously demonstrates the size and diversity of his work and establishes its unity as the extension of a particular human being.[57] Guillaume's protest to Bonneurté is an assertion of authorship, and specifically of the author as the generator of a corpus (if not yet a book) whose unity reflects to some degree the ontological coherence of its maker.

At the same time, Guillaume's response to Bonneurté also betrays a paradoxical facet of Machaut's self-representation as a poet. That is, Machaut's unique status as an author is in no small way guaranteed by the extent to which his corpus can display formal diversity while still referring to its origin in the same human being. The poet's virtuosity is tested and affirmed by an overarching narrative that has his narrator-persona performing a variety of poetic roles over time.[58] Accordingly, in his retort to Bonneurté, Guillaume simultaneously acknowledges his identity as a book-writer and his present distance from what has come before in his body of work: how can he possibly remember all of it?

In response to Guillaume's protest, Bonneurté reverses her earlier refusal to explain the charges and carefully specifies her accusation (vv. 1013–26). Guillaume's knowledge of his wrongdoing does not come from within, then, as Bonneurté originally demands. It is Bonneurté the reader who, after the fact, makes Guillaume responsible for the ruling of Jean de Luxembourg, through an interpretive judgment on his writing. It is the reader

---

also as a self-contained whole subject to poetic organization and provided with an explicit" (*From Song to Book*, 235). Brownlee likewise shows that "Machaut's concept of the vernacular *poète* involves the explicit unification of a generically and linguistically diverse corpus of first-person poems into a single œuvre" (*Poetic Identity*, 14–15). Brownlee further argues that Machaut represents himself as both poet and compiler in *JRN* as well as in the *Voir dit* (*Poetic Identity*, 15). For more on Machaut's manuscripts, see Deborah McGrady, *Controlling Readers: Guillaume de Machaut and his Late Medieval Audience*. Toronto: University of Toronto Press, 2006.

56. See Brownlee, *Poetic Identity*, 25; Huot, *From Song to Book*, 235.

57. See Deborah McGrady, "Guillaume de Machaut," in *The Cambridge Companion to Medieval French Literature*. Ed. Simon Gaunt, Sarah Kay. Cambridge: Cambridge University Press, 2008. 114. De Looze argues that the *Jugement* poems constitute a "mini *corpus poetae*" (*Pseudo-Autobiography*, 70) and represent "the first sketch by Guillaume de Machaut of the relationship between the poet's life and the book that re-creates it" (Ibid., 71), thus anticipating the full-blown meta-textual phenomenon that is Machaut's *Voir dit*.

58. See, again, Brownlee, *Poetic Identity*, 14–15.

who bestows upon Guillaume his identity as a maker of books and of judgments, confirming his authority even as she attacks him for his moral shortcomings and demands that he abandon his earlier opinion. Significantly, then, it is also Bonneurté the reader who gives the narrator his name, calling him "Guillaumes de Machaut" for the first time when she summons him before her.[59] In much the same way, Guillaume de Deguileville uses the evidence against him—in the form of Grace Dieu's acrostic letter—to provide a colorful signature for his *Pèlerinage de l'âme*.[60] Accusation and advertisement come together naturally in the reader's judgment: any publicity is good publicity. But like the charges facing Deguileville's pilgrim, Bonneurté's complaint from beyond the grave retains a solemn aspect. Her accusation stresses that writing is an ethical act whose diverse and unpredictable effects on readers must somehow be taken into account.

Bonneurté's allegation, again, also implies that Guillaume's previous turn to introspection, the self-judgment of the confessional (v. 437–38) was not sufficient. Since Guillaume cannot understand what has so upset Bonneurté—since he cannot find the offending portion of his *livres*—she must explain it to him. In this sense, the confessional attempt to provide a conclusive record of the individual is as flawed as the narrator's efforts in the prologue to impose a last word on human history.[61] Instead, Bonneurté suggests that, to be ethical and authoritative, the poet must constantly submit himself to the judgments of readers; it is not enough simply to accuse himself. Machaut's textual self, his *corpus*, represented by his hapless narrator, must respond to the summons of that other who always lies just beyond his grasp, and whose reading continually transforms both author and text.

Having clarified her accusation about *JRB*, Bonneurté calls upon Guillaume to overturn his earlier judgment (vv. 1027–33). But Guillaume will have none of it; twice he stands firm and refuses to reverse *JRB*'s verdict or to write a new one:

---

59. In the first instance, this occurs through the mouth of Bonneurté's messenger (v. 573). On the importance of this act of naming, see De Looze, *Pseudo-Autobiography*, 72; De Looze, "Masquage," 205. Brownlee points out that this is the only instance in Machaut's corpus where the poet is named "within the context of the *dit* itself" (*Poetic Identity*, 21).

60. See above, Chapter 2, 65.

61. R. Barton Palmer considers that the narrator's new responsibility, assigned to him by Bonneurté, goes against the historical mode of writing: "The passivity of the historical subject (who must suffer what God ordains) gives way to the activity of the poet, who is responsible for the meaning of his poems even as he continues to write, in important senses, what tradition demands" ("The Metafictional Machaut: Reflexivity in the Judgment Poems," in Palmer, ed., *Chaucer's French Contemporaries*, 86).

Dès que mes jugemens outrez	As soon as a judgment is uttered
Est de moy, je le soustenray,	by me, I will uphold it,
Tant com soustenir le porray.	just as long as I am able.
(vv. 1044–46)	

Car ce seroit a ma grant honte,	For it would be to my great shame
Selonc vostre meïsme conte,	according to your own account,
S'endroit de moy contredisoie	if I contradicted myself
Le fait que jugié averoie.	concerning the case I judged.
(vv. 1065–68)	

Guillaume's position here is confusing. Shortly before (vv. 881–98), he had asserted that his body of work was too large and too varied for him to be closely attached to any single piece of it. Now, however, his categorical refusal to modify any judgments he has made affirms his corpus as representing a stable, unified identity. While Guillaume acknowledges—or indeed, boasts of—the formal diversity of his corpus, he is much more reluctant to extend a similarly privileged status to diversity of opinion.

Guillaume explains his refusal to reverse his judgment by saying that if he contradicted himself he would be shamed or dishonored ("Car ce seroit a ma grant honte," v. 1065). In this case, honor carries political significance, since by switching his stance Guillaume would also risk undermining the reputation of the late Jean de Luxembourg, for whom Machaut reserved an uncommon affection throughout his career. The change in Machaut's political allegiance, symbolized by the reversal of judgments between *JRB* and *JRN*, is a difficult point for the poet's authority. It is a development that threatens the historical coherence of Machaut's evolving corpus, since the poet must revise his opinions concerning his allegiance to the House of France as well as the relative emotional experience of men and women.

Nothing is more emblematic of this potentially awkward revision than *JRN*'s place in manuscripts. Reading through the narrative poems in Machaut's complete-works codices, one may trace the poet's life in broad strokes, since the poems are arranged in a progression that mirrors their order of composition, constructing an implied master-narrative of Machaut's career.[62] *JRN* is the glaring exception to this chronological order, as it is only found in manuscripts immediately after *JRB*, when it was written rather later and refers to a later point in the poet's career.[63] Since Machaut is

---

62. On the chronology of the narrative *dits*, see, again, Earp, *A Guide to Research*, 189–94; De Looze, *Pseudo-Autobiography*, 67.

63. That is, *JRB* was most likely produced in the mid-1330s (Earp, *A Guide to Research*, 207),

generally thought to have had a relatively strong role in the ordering of his manuscripts, the disruption of an otherwise tidy pseudo-autobiographical narrative points to a certain self-consciousness on the poet's part concerning the way his ties to the House of France had been suddenly thrown into uncertainty.[64]

The same problem about the coherence of an historical, textual self confronts Machaut's narrator during his dialog with Bonneurté. In response to her accusation, Guillaume holds fast to his faith in objective and definitive truth. He is thus still attached, despite himself, to a certain kind of judgment already symbolized by *JRN*'s apocalyptic prologue. Although the narrator's meditation on the Judgment fails to yield conclusive meaning, it continues to color his attitude toward his own judgments, which he refuses, on principle, to revise. Guillaume's obsession with certainty also informs his expectations of how the trial against Bonneurté will go. He initially sees the proceedings as an opportunity to prove himself correct once and for all and to preserve his honor:

Dame, fait avez .i. devis	Lady, what you've proposed
Ou ma grant deshonneur moustrez,	suggests my great dishonor,
Mais li procès n'est pas outrez,	but the trial has not yet begun,
Ne mis en fourme justement.	nor been put into proper form.
Pour faire certein jugement,	To reach a certain judgment,
Vous me deüssiez dire en quoy	you must tell me how
J'ay forfait, et tout le pourquoy	I have done wrong, and bring
Amener a conclusion.	everything to a conclusion.
(vv. 840–47)	

It is Guillaume, not the plaintiff Bonneurté, who insists upon a proper trial, brought to a lawful "conclusion" (v. 847), and a "certein jugement"

---

while due to the historical account given in *JRN*'s prologue, the earliest possible date for that poem's completion is 1349. Machaut's *Remede de fortune, Dit du lyon* and *Dit de l'alerion* were almost certainly composed between *JRB* and *JRN* but appear consistently after the latter in manuscripts (See Earp, *A Guide to Research*, 77–97, 191). The celebrated General Prologue to Machaut's works represents a different kind of exception to this chronology: although it was written late in the poet's career and placed before the rest of the poems, it claims to recount the beginning of Machaut's vocation, while *JRN* makes no such artificial concession to narrative order. (For the General Prologue, see Hoepffner, ed., *Œuvres de Guillaume de Machaut*, I: 1–12.)

64. On Machaut's possible role in the production of his manuscripts, see Sarah Jane Williams, "An Author's Role in Fourteenth-Century Book Production: Guillaume de Machaut's *Livre ou je mets toutes mes choses*." *Romania* 90 (1969): 433–54; Brownlee, *Poetic Identity;* Huot, *From Song to Book*, 232–38, 242–301; McGrady, *Controlling Readers*. For a more cautious view of Machaut's role in manuscript production, see William W. Kibler and James I. Wimsatt, "Machaut's Text and the Question of his Personal Supervision," in Palmer, ed., *Chaucer's French Contemporaries*, 103–9.

(v. 844)—a *sententia diffinitiva* in medieval legal terminology.[65] Guillaume holds fast to his faith, first expressed in his chronicler's Apocalypse, that some kind of definitive ruling might be possible.

Even more than exoneration, then, Guillaume wants closure in the affair, but he won't get it from Bonneurté. Her conception of justice seems diametrically opposed to his—based on movement and change rather than stability and consistency. In their initial dialog, for instance, Bonneurté tells Guillaume that he should be able to make the opposite judgment just as easily as he made the first judgment:

Guillaume, se vous tant valez,	Guillaume, if you are worthy enough
Vous le pouez bien einsi faire	you could easily act to
Par soustenir tout le contraire.	uphold precisely the contrary opinion.
Car li contraires, c'est li drois	For what is contrary is correct
En tous bons amoureus endrois.	in all questions of love.
(vv. 1034–38)	

This statement, loaded with ambiguity, is difficult to translate. On the surface, Bonneurté's claim is simply that Guillaume should be morally and intellectually competent to realize which judgment is correct, namely that a woman whose lover has died necessarily feels more heartache than a man whose lady has left him. Her apparent insistence that there is a right and a wrong side to the issue will later be underlined when the parties in the dispute assemble for trial and Bonneurté presents Guillaume to the court of Charles de Navarre as an incorrigible sophist who doesn't much care what side he's on (vv. 1499–504).

However, there is another, opposing sense to Bonneurté's statement in vv. 1034–38. "Guillaume, se vous tant valez, / Vous le pouez bien einsi faire / Par soustenir tout le contraire" could also mean that if Guillaume is worth his salt as a poet, he should be capable of arguing both sides, changing his judgment not for the sake of moral rectitude, but for the sake of changing judgments. Likewise, Bonneurté's "Car li contraires, c'est li drois / En tous bons amoureus endrois" could mean something like "the specific contrary of your earlier judgment is always the right one ("li drois") in matters of love, and so the correct and just position to take is that the lady's suffering is greater." On the other hand, these verses could just as easily be read to express that the contrary position, whatever it might be, is always the right one in matters of love, that contrariety itself is the defining criterion or law ("li drois") of good judgment in this domain, since love

---

65. See Brundage, *Medieval Origins*, 161.

is founded on the coming together of opposites, the encounter of the self with others.

In much the same way, the narrator of Jean de Meun's *Roman de la Rose* learns in his quest for knowledge about love that truth cannot be apprehended except by navigating the interplay of contraries: "Ainsi va des contraires choses: / Les unes sont des autres gloses" ("So it is with contrary things / Each is the other's gloss," vv. 21577–78). Dependent upon the theoretical convergence of contrary qualities, erotic love provides a fertile space for dialectics, which is why it supplied such abundant matter for debate poetry in the Middle Ages, and why Machaut used it to transfer the dialectical play of that tradition to the meta-narrative of the individual author and his corpus. Machaut was not the first to use debate poetry to stage the fragmented self; indeed, some of the oldest examples of the genre already suggest this, particularly the many versions of debates between the Body and Soul, such as Deguileville would later incorporate into his *Pèlerinage de l'âme* (*PA*, vv. 4052–352). Rather, one of Machaut's greatest contributions to the debate tradition was in making the conflicting judgments of the divided self a model of literary self-creation. In the *Jugement* poems, the contradictory nature of the poetic subject is shown not as a function of the dualistic tension between matter and spirit, but rather in terms of the necessary textual changes which must occur in an author's work over time, in response to his own changing opinions and those of his readers.[66]

Taken in light of the dialectical/debate poetry tradition, Bonneurté's statement about contrariety seems to suggest that, to do justice to the truth, the poet must cultivate, rather than discourage multiple perspectives throughout his corpus. In this, mysterious Lady Happiness embodies the author's difficult labor, the endless but necessary task of rewriting. Her accusation puts into question not only the judgment of *JRB* but also the narrator's belief in a coherent, trans-historical self represented in and by the text. Although it replaces an apocalyptic judgment with a reader's incrimination, Bonneurté's accusation is no less ethically rigorous: it promises that there will be no end to the author's responsibility to his audience.

By the time the trial commences in Charles de Navarre's court, then, two irreconcilable expectations for justice have been proposed. Following the Doomsday scenario of his prologue, Guillaume looks forward to an ending—a "certein jugement"—that will exonerate him or at least put the issue to rest once and for all. Bonneurté, however, begins to suggest that

---

66. Catherine Attwood has argued that Machaut initiated a trend toward the greater internalization of dialogic forms (*Dynamic Dichotomy: The Poetic 'I' in Fourteenth- and Fifteenth-Century French Lyric Poetry*. Amsterdam: Rodopi, 1998. 200).

the author must constantly revise his opinions, rather than aiming for the establishment of absolute truths. If only loosely adapted from the *memento mori* trope, Bonneurté's judgment remains eschatological in an important sense: it transfers the apocalyptic anxiety of the poem's prologue to the ongoing process of literature, showing how the work of writing is inscribed within the poet's responsibility to heaven. In the next section, I consider *JRN*'s trial scene in some detail, in order to demonstrate how it serves as a counterpoint to the Last Judgment scene of the prologue. Rather than simply highlighting the imperfection of human judgment already decried in the Apocalypse section, the narrator's absurd trial in the court of Charles de Navarre places literature under an alternative model of divine scrutiny.

IV. Judgment in the Court of Charles de Navarre

While Guillaume had nominated the late King of Bohemia as judge in *JRB*, he now seems at a loss to find a good man to preside over the appeal; he therefore defers the choice to Bonneurté, who immediately proposes Charles de Navarre. In doing so, she employs laudatory rhetoric similar to that which the narrator himself had used to describe Jean de Luxembourg in *JRB*.[67] This is perhaps a sly political statement on Machaut's part; if we are to infer Bonneurté's resemblance to Bonne, we have by implication Jean de Luxembourg's daughter and Jean le Bon's wife (or her vengeful ghost) endorsing Machaut's move to the ranks of the rival house.

Once the two disputants have agreed upon Charles as arbiter, they make their way to the new patron's castle. Having arrived there, as in the corresponding scene of *JRB*, Guillaume finds a lively court full of personified virtues to assist in the operation of judgment, though it is a different court, whose members seem to resemble the virtues of Aristotle's *Nichomachean Ethics*, in which happiness (Bonneurté, or *eudaimonia* [εὐδαιμονία]) is the highest end, the *telos*, of virtue.[68] Bonneurté is warmly received and attended by her court of personifications, who help her prepare the case against Guillaume. The personification Raison holds for Bonneurté a set of scales, designated as both a "balance" and a "livre":

---

67. Compare *JRB*, vv, 1291–348 and *JRN*, vv. 1089–114.
68. See Kay, *The Place of Thought*, 101–13; Margaret J. Ehrhart, "Guillaume de Machaut's *Jugement dou roy de Navarre* and Medieval Treatments of the Virtues." *Annuale Medievale* 19 (1979): 46–67. Confusingly, the virtues appear alternately as the component parts of Bonneurté, her entourage, and her clothing.

Et aussi la juste balance	And moreover the just balance
Li demoustroit signefiance	showed her the meaning—
Qu'elle devoit en tous cas vivre	that she must in every way live
Aussi justement com la livre	as justly as the *livre*
Ou on ne puet, par nulle voie,	which one cannot in any way add to
Mettre n'oster, qu'on ne le voie.	or take from such that the change isn't seen.
(vv. 1187–92)	

Livre translates to "book" when it is masculine, while here the feminine definite article gives the word the immediate sense of "scales." But the pun is evident: like the scales, judicial and eschatological symbol *par excellence*, the particular justice of the book is in the way it testifies to what is added and removed, bearing witness to changes of opinion in the course of an author's life without allowing past judgments to be expunged from the record. Although the scales are an instrument of justice, they do not themselves pass judgment, but leave that task to the reader, whose interpretative work is likewise a never-ending effort to achieve balance among divergent points of view. The set of scales held by Justice in Guillaume de Deguileville's later *Pèlerinage de l'âme* also reflects the dual literary and judicial identity of the *livre,* and like Deguileville, Machaut suggests that continually adding to the book is a necessary ethical process for the author.[69]

As Bonneurté's accusation implies, the act of revision must come in response to the reader's judgment, in order to be truly ethical. The new patron-judge, Charles de Navarre, adopts this principle for judgment when he tells Bonneurté and the virtues that they must not only convince him of Guillaume's wrongdoing in order for their side to win, but that they must also persuade the defendant (vv. 1626–28).[70] That Guillaume must freely admit his own guilt suggests that the narrator is to become other to himself as he is tried, seeing himself and his work from the perspectives of readers. As a stand-in for the author, Guillaume must come to an understanding that the meaning of his work is dependent upon the person who encounters it from moment to moment.

As it unfolds, *JRN*'s lengthy trial scene makes this point especially in the way it considers evidence. The bulk of the trial section is composed of

---

69. See above, Chapter 2, 96.

70. Charles's requirement is also a reference to the conventions of scholastic *disputatio*—a strong influence on medieval debate poetry and a required exercise for university students, including law students, which required that one party in the debate convince his opponent in order to win. The practice is closely tied to the definition of dialectic as found, for example, in John of Salisbury's *Metalogicon* (Ed. J. B. Hall, K. S. B. Keats-Rohan. Turnhout: Brepols, 1991. 3.2).

exempla from a wide variety of sources, including natural history, mythology and romance, which Guillaume and the virtues both cite at length in order to support their cases. The exempla are but tenuously connected to the initial object of debate, since the text of *JRB* does not enter directly into the proceedings, and since the exempla themselves are totally inconclusive. Guillaume, for his part, tells the story (vv. 2215–314) of a certain clerk of Orléans who, upon receiving letters to the effect that his lady has married another man, goes mad from heartbreak. He then exhorts the court to judge the exemplum as evidence that men suffer more from women's inconstancy (vv. 2308–14). On the other hand, the personification Foy (Faith) carefully reminds the court of the details of Guillaume's exemplum, and concedes to her adversary that the story itself is likely factual in these points (vv. 2315–52). However, according to Foy, since the content of the letters the clerk received cannot be known any more than the identity of the person who sent them, the story is inconclusive, and judgment on it must be deferred to God:

Car Diex en ce siecle terrestre	For God has in this mortal world
A main jugemens si enclose	enclosed so many judgments
Qu'estre ne porroient esclos	that could never be revealed
D'omme mortel par sa science.	by the ways of men.
(vv. 2358–61)	

Meeting such hermeneutic barriers at every step, the proceedings turn away from their expressed end just as the law undermines itself in the figure of the clerk of Orléans, who begins as a prudent and well-read jurist (v. 2219) but is quickly reduced to sleeping on dung heaps (v. 2293) by the movements of love and fortune.[71] As Guillaume develops his arguments, his own exemplum of the clerk grows out of proportion to itself, taking him further and further afield from his original position, in the very effort to defend that position. Ostensibly in order to bring out the meaning of the story of the Clerk of Orléans, the two sides produce a plethora of divergent tales which succeed only in complicating the discussion by multiplying the possibilities for interpretive disagreement. The personification Charité, for her part, follows the story of the clerk with a tale of a rich man, his orchard and its most beloved tree (vv. 2434–532), while Guillaume attempts to elucidate his own point through an anecdote about a mad dog with a worm

---

71. That the clerk is from Orléans also serves to play up his legal learning, since by the late thirteenth century the city had become the most important center for law in France, even rivaling Bologna. See Brundage, *Medieval Origins*, 232–33.

in its tongue (vv. 2656–92). Franchise then moves with little transition to an enumeration of Greek myths (vv. 2707–822).

The purported links between these diverse exempla are as tangential as they sound, and for that reason I will not attempt to explain them in terms of a coherent trial process. Instead, what is much more interesting is how these loosely connected pieces of evidence illustrate judgment as a constantly evolving creative act. Rather than making a rigorous examination of each exemplum based on its content, the disputants form the bulk of their interpretations around entirely different narratives. Testimony is multiplied ad infinitum but does not add up to a convincing case for either side. [72]

In addition to the potentially endless digressions, the original issue brought before Charles de Navarre is quickly abandoned, as a secondary dispute arises as to whether men or women are more loyal in love. Judgment breaks down into judgments, into an ongoing creative process quite different from the apocalyptic historiography of *JRN*'s prologue, which had insisted on verifiable certainty, on the last word. It is equally significant, therefore, that calls to judgment in the trial scene come as often in reference to the examination of particular pieces of evidence than to the ultimate verdict to be rendered. Guillaume, for example, urges the court not to "mesjugier" when interpreting the exemplum of the clerk of Orléans (v. 2314). On the other side, Attemprance recounts the story of a lovelorn girl, who eventually dies of her heartbreak (vv. 1863–2012). As the girl lies in bed, physicians unsuccessfully examine her urine for diagnostic clues, and their actions are twice referred to by a form of the verb "jugier" in as many lines (vv. 1913–14). Such instances of inconclusive judgment given as evidence serve to show the collapse of any claims by Guillaume or his opponents to a stable model of deliberation. Instead of pushing toward a *telos* of justice through the historical synthesis of lesser observations and lesser narratives, the trial demonstrates that even the smallest of details may prevent interpretive closure and thus demand the poet's constant vigilance as he faces his audience.

The comically impossible nature of the trial is clear to readers, but that does not stop both sides from declaring that sufficient evidence has been produced for Charles to come to a definitive ruling. Guillaume makes this claim in order to bolster his own rhetoric (vv. 2903–4). As it attempts to

---

72. See Jean-Louis Picherit, "Les exemples dans le *Jugement dou roy de Navarre* de Guillaume de Machaut." *Les lettres romanes* 36.2 (May 1982): 109. Picherit holds that Machaut uses exempla incorrectly whereas his adversaries are well-versed in classical mythology and win for that reason. More important, in my view, is how both sides use exempla in a way that is, strictly speaking, not exemplary. McGrady (*Controlling Readers*, 66) points to a similar strategy in Machaut's *Voir dit*.

push on toward its closing arguments, the prosecution also pretends that the fragmentation of judgment is not happening, and affirms that justice has been done through an objective and universal examination of the facts in the case. The personification Mesure, for one, asserts that the virtues have successfully proved their case without being distracted by particulars ("Sans rien d'especïal jugier," v. 3572), when in fact nothing could be further from the truth. Despite the chaotic turn taken by their arguments, the disputants still appear fixated on the "certein jugement" demanded by Guillaume and first imagined in his apocalyptic vision. In this spirit, Raison speaks up to demand a decision:

Sire juges, certeinnement	Your honor, certainly
Chose n'a sous le firmament	there is nothing under the heavens
Qui ne tende a conclusion:	that doesn't seek its end:
Les unes a perfection	some tend toward perfection
Pour pluseurs cas de leur droit tendent;	according to their own laws,
Et si a autres qui descendent	while others descend
De haut ou elles ont esté	from on high where they have been,
En declinant d'un temps d'esté	falling from the summertime
En l'iver qu'on dit anientir.	into the winter of destruction.
Dont cils plais desire a sentir	Likewise this trial wishes to reach
De droit conclusions hastive	by law a swift conclusion
Par sentence diffinitive,	and a definitive sentence,
Pour ce qui est bien pris parfaire	in order to perfect what is good
Et ce qui est mal pris deffaire.	and undo what is wicked.
(vv. 3735–48)	

Like *JRN*'s prologue, Raison's speech is ironic—it reaffirms an ideal of definitive judgment which is not to take place, at least not in Charles de Navarre's court. Raison's conclusion is just as premature as Guillaume's imagined day of wrath. Because judgment must be a composite of many separate observations, and because the singular judgments of that composite have each proved inconclusive, the disputants can only rely on a series of tautologies to argue their cases.[73] In William Calin's words, "the fourteenth-century public could not help but recognize the absurdity of trying to prove universal psychological and moral judgments based upon a few contemporary or historical anecdotes."[74]

---

73. See Calin, *A Poet at the Fountain*, 113.
74. Ibid., 120.

However, the problem with this trial is more involved than a disconnect between supposedly inappropriate particular examples and the universal truths about men and women they are intended to prove. The collapse of *JRN*'s prologue has already begun to suggest the problems inherent in an objective, universal and "certain jugement." As Sarah Kay has shown, the trial scene which symbolically replaces the Judgment ultimately serves to put universality itself into question as against its composite particulars.[75] Avoiding the judgment of particulars appears in the trial as an impossible ideal of jurisprudence, since for final judgments to be produced, preliminary and necessarily subjective judgments must go into them.

Eventually, Charles de Navarre assents to Raison's request and passes judgment. Yet his way of doing so is the farthest thing from the "sentence diffinitive" that Raison clamors for or the "certein jugement" that Guillaume demands. Indeed, the patron-judge's pronouncement marks the end of any pretense toward finality in judgment. Charles finds Guillaume guilty, but then—laughing—sentences him to write three lyric pieces: a *lay*, a *chanson* and a *ballade* (vv. 4173–94). This is a decision that Guillaume seems only too happy to accept. Just as Deguileville uses his soul's term in purgatory as an occasion for more writing, Guillaume's sentence represents a new commission for Machaut, which he partially fulfills by writing in the voice of the grieving lady in his "Lay de plour."[76] The poet is ever changing as he shifts the position from which interpretive judgments are made, taking on even the voice of his opponent, even the voice of a woman.[77]

A large part of Guillaume's argument during the trial is that the emotional experience of women is weaker because it is more inconstant.[78] But by bringing Guillaume to justice, Bonneurté ultimately makes a virtue of the supposedly feminine vice of fickleness. By staging her trial in the court of Machaut's new patron, Bonneurté proves to the court that for Guillaume to be an authoritative poet he must embrace rather than scorn the vagaries of fortune, challenging his opinions often.[79] Differing from himself,

---

75. Kay, *The Place of Thought*, 95–122.

76. The irony of a court poet being "punished" by having to write more poetry has not escaped critical attention. See especially Palmer, "Transtextuality and the Producing-I," 298; Kay, *The Place of Thought*, 98. On resemblances between Machaut's sentence and the prologue of Chaucer's *The Legend of Good Women*, see above in this chapter, n3.

77. See De Looze, *Pseudo-Autobiography*, 77; Palmer, "Transtextuality and the Producing-I," 294.

78. See, especially, *JRN*, vv. 3019–46.

79. This is a crucial reversal of the position voiced by Boethius's Lady Philosophy, to whom Bonneurté bears considerable resemblance. Sarah Kay has noted that such a positive reevaluation of fortune is one of the most important elements of later medieval rewritings of Boethius, including in Machaut's own *Remede de Fortune* ("Touching Singularity: Consolation, Philosophy, and Poetry in the French *Dit*," in *The Erotics of Consolation: Desire and Distance in the Late Middle Ages*. Ed. Catherine E. Léglu, Stephen J. Milner. New York: Palgrave Macmillan, 2008. 34).

Guillaume has been led into the very position of female inconstancy that he has denounced. Like the feminine advocacy portrayed in the Marian devotional tradition, Bonneurté's victory suggests that the judgment of women—the hard-to-please readership of vernacular courtly poetry—may be a positive model of creative power for the poet as he is forced to reinvent himself over time.

As Doubtance tells Guillaume sarcastically during the trial, he has been to the "school of change":

Mon biau sire, se Diex me gart,	God help me, good sir,
Moult avez estrange regart,	but you look quite strange
Et s'avez diverse parole;	and your words are divergent.
Et s'avez esté a l'escole,	You have been to the school of change,
Si com je croy, d'aler en change.	or so it seems to me.
(vv. 3109–13)	

Doubtance's statement is meant to expose Guillaume's deceitful rhetoric before the court, but it really serves as a testimony to his mistress, Dame Bonneurté, who has indeed taught him the literary and ethical merit of changing his opinions, by putting him through a trial that enacts the perpetual renegotiation of textual meaning. From this perspective, we may also reread the original charge that Dame Bonneurté brought against Guillaume, that he spoke falsely about women "par diffinitif jugement" (v. 1015). Given the way that judgment itself shifts in the course of *JRN*, we might conclude that the fault Bonneurté finds with the King of Bohemia's initial ruling has less to do with its content than with its *definitive* nature— that her demand that Guillaume revise his judgment likewise has more to do with the act of revision, than with the new opinion itself.[80]

Calling for more writing and thus for more judgments to be made by eventual readers, Charles's sentence does not end the trial, even if the patron-judge, too, speaks of a "conclusion" (v. 4194). Because it immediately signals its own open-endedness, the new decision does not really reverse the verdict of *JRB* in the fashion of an appeal to a higher court, but only adds a particular judgment to Machaut's corpus in juxtaposition. In the same way, Charles de Navarre's judicial authority is not presented as better or worse than that of Jean de Luxembourg, but only different, the product of divergent opinion newly embraced by the poet, who has finally

---

80. Similarly, Bonneurté's initial demand that Guillaume "rappelez" his earlier judgment (v. 1033) suggests that it is being recalled in both senses of the word, brought back up in the text that claims to overturn it.

been forced to admit that differing from himself over time may be as much an artistic and ethical virtue as a political one. The two judgments of *JRB* and *JRN* stand side by side in manuscripts and bear witness to the way that the poet has become other to his own textual past without, however, undoing it.[81]

Bonneurté's call to embrace the conflicting perspectives of readers suggests an alternative not only to the Last Judgment of the prologue, but also to the narrator's confession which follows it (vv. 437–38). Through Bonneurté's intervention, the ideal of definitive repentance is replaced by the subject's experience of constant metamorphosis.[82] As Bonneurté tells Guillaume shortly before the trial begins,

Levez vous, car il plaist a nous	We'd like you to stand up, please,
Que plus ne parlez a genous.	and no longer speak on your knees.
(vv. 1394–95)	

One way of interpreting this statement is that Guillaume should be open to amending his past but should avoid adopting a penitential discursive posture—speaking on his knees—as he does momentarily in *JRN*'s prologue. With the need to lay claim to a diverse body of work, penitence is no longer a fitting gesture for the author, because old judgments must be upheld even as new ones are produced. More than the thirteenth-century *poésie pénitentielle* of a Guillaume le Clerc or a Rutebeuf, and more even than the divine rhetoric of Deguileville, Machaut's self-defense affirms that the poet's ability to transform his personal book must rely on a continual process of questioning and rewriting. Rather than an idealized trajectory toward spiritual perfection, in which the work of art is seen through the optic of God's eternal judgment, the conception of poetic judgment which triumphs in *JRN* redescribes the poet's ethical obligation to rewrite as the inherent result of shifting opinions over time. There can be no final act of contrition, no definitive, trans-historical judgment on the self, but only acts of revision in response to the largely unforeseeable reactions of readers and to the changing opinions of the author himself. If Bonneurté is a reference to Aristotle's *telos* of happiness, she also represents the poet's nagging impulse to keep amending what he has already

---

81. For this reason, *JRN* is also not a palinode in the strict sense, since it does not actually effect a retraction. See Didier Lechat, *'Dire par fiction': métamorphoses du 'je' chez Guillaume de Machaut, Jean Froissart et Christine de Pizan*. Paris: Champion, 2005. 81–82.

82. In his discussion of Montaigne's *Essais,* Patrick Riley describes a similar process of continual "micro-conversions" of the subject (*Character and Conversion in Autobiography: Augustine, Montaigne, Descartes, Rousseau, and Sartre*. Charlottesville: University of Virginia Press, 2004. 21).

composed, chasing after an elusive satisfaction in his work. Bonneurté calls the writer to submit his poetry to the challenge of new perspectives, in view of a process of self-perfection that may never be complete, at least not until the Last Judgment.

We have come a long way from the prologue and its vision of human society slipping headlong toward a terrible reckoning. Yet we cannot forget that Bonneurté's appearance is meant to shatter the narrator's spiritual negligence, bringing him back to an awareness of the Judgment that is forever taking place through the relationship of author and audience. Bonneurté's insistence on the considerable ethical duty of the poet fulfills the eschatological expectation of the prologue in a surprising way, just as Bonneurté herself unexpectedly fulfills the role of *memento mori* apparition. Thus, even in the midst of Charles's anarchic court, the narrator's anticipation of his examination before God does not disappear. Instead, *JRN* redefines the poet's supreme ethical burden as a vigilant flexibility, rather than a dissemination of singular truths. Guillaume's rhetoric in *JRN* is not particularly divine—far from it, the narrator's attempts at self-defense are clumsy and comically unsuccessful, even buffoonish. But only in the very act of responding to the audience, only in the poet's crushing responsibility, can the literary subject emerge, for his authority begins in the reader's judgment and the way it shapes the corpus. Moreover, Bonneurté's privileging of endless revision, expressed through slippery legal pleading, is not without recalling how divine rhetoricians beginning with the lawyerly Virgin championed the power of the rewritten text.

The eschatological significance of revising the corpus emerges most explicitly of all in the "Lay de plour," which is often appended to *JRN* as the fulfillment of Guillaume's prescribed penance. At the end of this sad poem, the mourning female voice prays that she and her dead lover might have eternal life together "in the book":

Ta mort tant me contralie	Your death tortures me so
Et tant de maus me repart,	and gives me so much pain,
Amis, que li cuers me part;	my lover, that my very heart leaves me;
Mais einsois que je devie,	but before I do depart this life,
Humblement mes cuers supplie	my heart humbly pleads with
Au vray Dieu qu'il nous regart	the true God that he look on us
De si amoureus regart	with such a loving gaze
Qu'en livre soiens de vie.	that in the Book we might have life.
(vv. 203–10) [83]	

---

[83]. Palmer's edition of *JRN* numbers the verses of "Lay de plour" separately from the rest of the text.

Laurence De Looze has rightly interpreted these verses as a reference to both the *Liber vitae* and to Machaut's own evolving corpus: "Certainly the Book of the Lord is a common topos, and every good Christian hopes to have his name inscribed there. But there is also a more immediate and more appropriate referent, namely, the profane book Guillaume de Machaut is writing and in which the lovers achieve a kind of eternal life."[84] The ending figure of the book thus "concludes" Machaut's *Jugement* poems with yet another transformation of traditional eschatological imagery. The *Liber vitae*, momentarily recalling the apocalyptic declarations of the prologue, is the ultimate closed book: it objectively reflects the actions of each individual in life, and after death what has been written in this book cannot be added to. Its opening at the end of time can only provide a revelation of history, never an instance of its emendation.

Machaut's book, however, does not claim to encompass a timeless reality; rather, it is the product of an interminable labor of revision, always frustrating attempts to impose a last word.[85] The book not only gives life, it is alive, dependent upon processes of negotiation between author and reader. This is where eschatological reckoning and poetic regeneration (*reverdie*)—the two juxtaposed opening leitmotifs of *JRN*—are finally united, as ethical literary judgment is redefined as a process of generating new meaning rather than establishing absolute, trans-historical truth.[86] After *JRN*'s prologue, judgment is no longer apocalyptic, but post-apocalyptic; it has moved beyond certainty and into the world of the still living (and in Bonneurté's case, perhaps the recently dead), for whom judgment is still a work in progress. In *JRN* the transformation of the eschatological into a continuous trial becomes a master metaphor for the work of the author, whose personal and literary identity is likewise transformed with each act of judgment, rather than merely revealed or reiterated.

The reversal of opinion in *JRN* and the female impersonation of the "Lay de plour" were far from the last metamorphoses Machaut the author performed. In *Confort d'ami* (1357), for example, Machaut returned directly to the juxtaposed judgments of his two most famous patrons, and to the turmoil of fourteenth-century French politics; in this poem, in the genre

---

84. De Looze, *Pseudo-Autobiography*, 76.

85. As De Looze puts it, "The insistence on bookmaking militates against the sequential, temporal view of one verdict giving way to another. Rather, the two verdicts will remain in dialectic as texts in the codex" (*Pseudo-Autobiography*, 77).

86. De Looze ("Masquage," 208) notes the general association of "procréation et création littéraire" in *JRN* and calls the "Lay de plour" a sign of "survie textuelle" ("Masquage," 206). See also the Introduction to this book (19–21), where I discuss Genius's sermon on the Judgment Day in Jean de Meun's *Rose*.

of consolation, Machaut again addresses Charles de Navarre. At the time of composition, Charles was imprisoned for the murder of his political rival Charles d'Espagne—part of the fallout of the same scandal which seems to haunt *JRN*.[87] Although Machaut's tone is indeed mostly consolatory, *Confort* also displays a distinct note of frustration on the part of the poet, who implicitly scolds Charles for his rash behavior, and advises him to take a lesson in good governance from the late Jean de Luxembourg. Effectively, then, *Confort* might be considered as a third text in the *Jugement* series, once again reversing the central authority figure.

Machaut's corpus is even more famous for its generic diversity than for its sustained play of judgments. For example, in Machaut's last poem, *La prise d'Alexandrie* (c. 1369–71),[88] the poet tried his hand again at the historical chronicle genre in which he had dabbled in *JRN*'s prologue. Machaut's most celebrated achievement, though, is probably the pioneering blend of narrative and lyric forms in *dits* like *Remede de Fortune* (c. 1340s) and *Fonteinne amoureuse* (1360).[89] In Machaut's masterpiece, *Le livre du voir dit* (c. 1361–65), the poet experimented still further with generic hybridization, combining not only narrative and lyric forms, but also prose epistles.[90] *Voir dit* carries echoes of *JRN*, since it is constructed largely as a dialog between the aged poet and an elite female reader. This is a young lady named Toute-Belle with whom the first-person narrator of this *voir dit*, or "true story," has a brief and ill-fated love affair. As Machaut's narrator and Toute-Belle exchange letters and poems, and as the reader's judgment shapes the poet's work, Machaut allows us a supremely intimate view into the collaborative process of the *œuvre*.[91]

This brief sampling of the rest of the Machauldian corpus is not to mention the musical compositions for which the poet is often better remembered. In particular, Machaut's motets and especially his mass were among the most influential early polyphonic pieces—a fact that should not be forgotten when gauging this poet's taste for texts inhabited by a multitude of disputing voices.

---

87. See, again, Palmer's edition of *Confort d'ami*. For discussion of the scandal, see above in this chapter, 118–20.

88. See the edition of *La prise d'Alexandrie* by R. Barton Palmer. New York: Routledge, 2002.

89. See Machaut, *Le jugement du roy de Behaigne; and, Remede de Fortune*. Ed. and trans. James I. Wimsatt, William W. Kibler. Athens: University of Georgia Press, 1988; *The Fountain of Love/La fonteinne amoureuse, and Two Other Love Vision Poems*. Ed. R. Barton Palmer. New York: Garland, 1993.

90. See the edition of *Le livre du voir dit* by Paul Imbs and Jacqueline Cerquiglini-Toulet. Paris: Librairie Générale Française, 1999.

91. See, among other studies of the *Voir dit*, McGrady, *Controlling Readers*.

Playing a variety of roles over time, and trying on a variety of characters and genres, Machaut was exploring the borders of the compiled corpus and of the poetic persona represented there. Machaut is an essential figure in the development of single-author compilation, and thus also in the history of poetic authority as a concept. The lingering Judgment of *JRN* brings to a crisis point several problems with much wider implications for the field of later medieval vernacular poetry. Among the most important of these problems is the question of how the author's historical existence can be reconciled with the fictionalized contours of the corpus, a document that asks to be taken seriously as a kind of Book of Conscience even as it purposefully blurs the lines between person and persona. Within the bound pages of the book, the ability of the author to stretch his poetic limits and to challenge previous versions of himself is the hallmark of authority, even as it threatens to destabilize the identity of the writing subject and to undermine the historical or aesthetic coherence of the compiled object.

From this perspective, the vacillation between courtly frolic and apocalypse in *JRN* is one of many register changes made with ease by this virtuosic poet. At the same time, however, this jarring movement also marks an important stage in Machaut's own narrative of poetic development. For here, eschatological discourse does not simply bump up against the precious confines of courtly poetry; rather, it spills over into them, forever complicating the poet's work with the awareness of its exposure to the Judge's unblinking gaze. Here, Machaut narrates not only his change in political affilation, but his initiation into a new consciousness of the corpus itself as a document which gives shape to the author despite—and because of—his many contradictions. And this awareness is inseparable from the knowledge that it is the reader who occupies the throne of Judgment, sharing only with God the necessary perspective from which to judge the writing subject, in all of his disorder and incongruity, as a singular and authoritative being. As for Machaut's narrator Guillaume, the author can only exist fully once he is named, and, like Dante and Deguileville, he can only be named as the object of accusation, by the reader whose interpretive work binds him to the text. The author can only be named in accusation, and this is not simply because of the vain indecency of naming oneself.[92] Rather, it speaks to the *impossibility* of naming oneself, independently of the other's judgment.

A poet whose concerns are often regarded as primarily secular and courtly, Machaut has the capacity to surprise us with such spiritually

---

92. Dante, for example, takes pains to note that his name's appearance at the beginning of Beatrice's accusation is of pure necessity (*Purgatorio* 30.63).

charged explorations into the nature of literary authority. And indeed, although Machaut was a churchman, a devotional poet, and a liturgical composer as well as a courtly entertainer, his vision of *auctoritas* does claim a secular aspect foreign to the likes of Deguileville and reliant, above all, on the poet's justification by wealthy patrons outside of the Church. But Machaut's skillful manipulation of the eschatological scene shows that the eschatological tenor of fourteenth-century literary anxiety was in no way confined to didactic texts like the *Pèlerinage* cycle, or to a pastoral conception of the poet's relationship to his audience. Rather, Machaut's (post)-apocalypticism suggests a strong commonality between the rollicking world of fourteenth-century courtly poetry and more traditional modes of Christian writing. In both spheres, vernacular poets found themselves having to confront a Judgment unlike any other—the thoroughly messy, inherently emotional, and insistently ethical *procès* of reception.

•

The genius of Machaut's book lies not only in the extent to which it rewrites itself as the author becomes other, but also in the way it invites rewriting by authors who are absolutely other—the way that, following the terminology of Roland Barthes, it constitutes a *texte scriptible* ("writable text").[93] In this sense, the final judgment scene of *JRN* extends the multivalence and ambiguity of the text well beyond the author's physical death. Machaut's literary afterlife was to be far-reaching in both time and space, but his most immediate successor and reinterpreter in the French tradition was Jean Froissart, the subject of the next chapter. As I show, Froissart reversed Machaut's eschatological exposition by ending, rather than beginning, his *Joli buisson de Jonece* (c. 1373) from the perspective of the Last Judgment, which he used to symbolically reject erotic poetry and to overturn a judgment he himself had made in an earlier poem, *L'espinette amoureuse* (c. 1369). Nevertheless, like his master Machaut, Froissart also introduced uncertainty into this supposedly final judgment, using the eschatological scene—and readers' expectations for it—to stage the continual reinterpretation of poetry in the encounter of the author with his demanding audience.

---

93. The term is introduced in and used by Barthes throughout *S/Z* (Paris: Seuil, 1970). Attwood (*Dynamic Dichotomy*, 16) discusses both Machaut and Froissart in terms of Barthes's conception of the *texte scriptible*. De Looze ("Masquage," 208) notes that the survival of textual legacy in *JRN* depends upon the reader.

CHAPTER 4

The Judgment of Jupiter
Froissart's *Joli buisson de Jonece*

I. Introduction

Jean Froissart (c. 1337–1405) is today best known for his *Chroniques,* a massive work of French prose documenting the events of the first half of the Hundred Years War, based largely on the author's personal reporting and interviews with eye-witnesses. Before becoming the most important historian of the Middle Ages, however, Froissart was already famous among the courts of Europe as a poet. Froissart the versifier's debt to Guillaume de Machaut is widely acknowledged by scholars, particularly in regard to the later poet's tendency to mix lyric and narrative forms in his *dits,* inspired by such Machauldian works as *Remede de Fortune* and the *Voir dit.*[1] Froissart's *L'espinette amoureuse* (*The Hawthorn Bush of Love,* c. 1369) and its sequel, *Le joli buisson de Jonece* (*The Fair Bush of Youth,* 1372–73) are two such lyric-narrative *dits,* blending a strong first-person narrative with inset lyrics whose composition is performed in the text itself by the author's narrator/poetic persona.

---

1. For example, see Huot, *From Song to Book,* 302–9; De Looze, *Pseudo-Autobiography,* 105–6; Lechat, '*Dire Par Fiction,*' 267, 295–304, 321; Philip E. Bennett, "The Mirage of Fiction: Narration, Narrator, and Narratee in Froissart's Lyrico-Narrative *Dits.*" *MLR* 86.2 (April 1991): 286. The two poets also traveled in many of the same circles, as both enjoyed the patronage of the houses of Luxembourg and Bohemia. On this point, see Nigel Wilkins, "A Pattern of Patronage: Machaut, Froissart and the Houses of Luxembourg and Bohemia in the Fourteenth Century." *French Studies* 37.3 (July 1983): 257–84.

Like Machaut's body of work, Froissart's *dits* are arranged in single-author manuscripts to construct a poetic corpus that is also a meta-narrative of the poet's career.[2] In *L'espinette amoureuse*, Froissart's narrator portrays himself as a foolish, twelve-year-old lover and a novice love poet whose efforts to win the heart of a certain young lady go awry time and time again. This proto-*künstlerroman* provides the frame for a number of inset lyric poems which the narrator offers, without much success, to the young lady. Although he is consistently rejected by the object of his desire, Froissart's inexperienced narrator is blinded by love and thus fails to understand that she has no feelings for him.

In the sequel, *Le joli buisson de Jonece,* Froissart's narrator is now thirty-five and has seemingly, like the author at the time, entered the priesthood. Although he is disenchanted with love, the narrator travels back to the days of *Espinette* in a long dream vision, in which he relives his adolescent courtship of the young lady, with much the same results as the first time around: he writes poetry for her, and she does not share his affection. Finally, he wakes up and realizes that the return to youth has all been merely a deceptive dream. Renouncing love and love poetry once and for all, he asserts his unwavering allegiance to God and the Virgin Mary in a final lyric composition entitled the "Lay de Nostre Dame."

Espinette and *Buisson,* which as a set I take the liberty of referring to as the *Bush* poems, are among Froissart's works most evocative of Machaut.[3] For example, in *Espinette* as in Machaut's *JRB,* the action begins when the narrator crawls beneath a bush on a beautiful spring day. And while Machaut's narrator symbolically travels back in time to the Easter season of *JRB* from the apocalyptic November scene which opens its sequel, the dream vision of Froissart's *Buisson* begins on a dismal November night as the narrator is suddenly transported back to the bright springtime of his own earlier poem, *Espinette.*

---

2. On Froissart's poetic manuscripts as examples of single-author compilation, see Huot, *From Song to Book,* 302–27.

3. In this chapter, I cite from the editions of both poems by Anthime Fourrier: *L'Espinette amoureuse.* Paris: Klincksieck, 1963; *Le Joli buisson de Jonece.* Geneva: Droz, 1975. On correspondences with *Voir dit,* see for example, Huot, *From Song to Book,* 317; Picherit, "Le rôle des éléments mythologiques," 499. On *Fonteinne,* see Claire Nouvet, "La fragmentation du système poetico-lyrique de Jean Froissart." Diss. Princeton University, 1981. 163, 185; De Looze (*Pseudo-Autobiography,* 105–6) discusses resemblances between *Espinette* and Machaut's *Remede de Fortune, Dit dou lyon, Fonteinne amoureuse* and *Confort d'ami.* On Froissart's debt to Machaut's Judgment of Paris scene in *Fonteinne,* which I discuss later in this chapter, see Fourrier, ed., *Espinette,* 34; Lechat, *'Dire par fiction,'* 295; Margaret J. Ehrhart, *The Judgment of the Trojan Prince Paris in Medieval Literature.* Philadelphia: University of Pennsylvania Press, 1987. 146.

Correspondences like these abound, but Froissart's *Bush* poems display their strongest point of structural resemblance with *JRB* and *JRN* in that the overarching narrative of the two texts is organized around a series of opposing judgments.[4] At the beginning of *Espinette,* the narrator embarks on his career as a love poet by repeating the mythological Judgment of Paris and choosing Venus as the fairest of the goddesses, over Juno and Pallas. In turn, the narrator's judgment in favor of Venus becomes the pattern for a whole series of bad judgments throughout *Espinette* as, rendered foolish by the goddess of love, he misinterprets the words and actions of the young lady and continues to pursue her after she has repeatedly told him she is not interested.

In *Buisson,* the chronic bad judgment shown by the narrator after repeating the Judgment of Paris is remedied as he assumes a new and more pious perspective on his life and work. In his November dream vision, the narrator meets Venus once again, and she leads him back in time to the titular bush of *Espinette,* the hawthorn under which he had judged in her favor twenty-three years earlier. He finds that the bush has grown to immeasurable size, but within it he is able to relive the events of *Espinette* as if they were happening all over again. Aside from repeating his old mistakes and being rejected one more time by the young lady, he also learns an important lesson from the personified figure who guides him through the bush, Jonece (Youth). Outlining a version of Ptolemy's theory of the seven ages of man,[5] Jonece explains to the narrator that once a man has attained the astrological age of Jupiter, his judgments grow clearer; under Jupiter's influence, a man finally turns his thoughts to God and learns to reflect clearly on the state of his soul. In this identification of the Jovian age with piety and worldly renunciation, Froissart follows the common late medieval tendency to allegorize Jupiter as the Christian God, as in the early fourteenth-century *Ovide moralisé,* a key source of myth material for both Machaut and Froissart.[6]

While the Judgment of Paris begins the narrator's service to Venus in *Espinette,* his initiation into the age of Jupiter is made official in *Buisson* as

---

4. This particular structural resemblance has been pointed out by Sarah Kay, "'Le moment de conclure': Initiation as Retrospection in Froissart's *Dits Amoureux,*" in *Rites of Passage: Cultures of Transition in the Fourteenth Century.* Ed. Nicola F. McDonald, W. M. Ormrod. Rochester, NY: York Medieval Press, 2004. 155.

5. Although Froissart would not have known Ptolemy in the original Greek, the philosopher's seminal work on astrology, the *Tetrabiblos* (Latin *Quadripartitum*), was circulated widely in the West beginning with Plato of Tivoli's 1138 translation from Arabic to Latin.

6. On both poets' use of the Judgment of Paris from the *Ovide moralisé,* see Ehrhart, *The Judgment of the Trojan Prince Paris,* 133.

he becomes painfully aware of the divine judgment to which he is subject. Awakening from his dream, he concludes that the pursuit of erotic love and love poetry are vanities ("wiseuses," v. 5160) and will be condemned by God when it is time for the soul to account for its actions:

Car ce sont painnes et nuiseuses	For these things are harmful
Pour l'ame, qui noient n'i pense	for the soul, which doesn't think about them, but
Et qui il faut, en fin de cense,	for which it is necessary at the end of its tenure
Rendre compte de tous fourfais	to give an accounting of all the bad things
Que li corps ara dis et fais,	that the body will have said and done—
Qui n'est que cendre et poureture.	the body which is but ashes and decay.
(vv. 5161–66)	

This epiphany leads Froissart's narrator to abandon *eros* for the Virgin, as expressed in his "Lay de Nostre Dame" (vv. 5198–442). Faced with eternal condemnation for serving Venus, the narrator can only pray that Mary will speak for him, acting as an "advocate" (v. 5186) on his behalf. Only in this way might he find a positive answer to the *Dies irae* hymn's chilling question, "Quid sum miser tunc dicturus?":

Que diras,	What will you say
Quant veras	when you meet
Ton Signour	your Lord
Au darrain jour?	on the Last Day?
(vv. 5333–36)	

For the narrator, the question of what can be said in his defense weighs heavily, since it is his own use of language—his poetry—which comes under the most scrutiny in this imagined day of reckoning. As for Guillaume le Clerc in the thirteenth century, Froissart uses the Judgment as a dramatic backdrop against which to perform the renunciation of earlier, vain writing.[7]

Espinette and *Buisson* show Froissart at his most pseudo-autobiographical,[8] and the second poem's Last Judgment on love poetry has usually been understood as part of a larger reflection made by Froissart on his own

---

7. On Guillaume le Clerc, see above, Introduction, 17–18.
8. See De Looze, *Pseudo-Autobiography,* 102–28, for a discussion of *Espinette* and *Prison amoureuse.* On De Looze's conception of the pseudo-autobiographical as it applies to Froissart, see also Nicole Lassahn, "Pseudo-Autobiography and the Role of the Poet in Jean Froissart's *Joli buisson de Jonece.*" Essays in Medieval Studies 15 (1998): 123–28.

career. At the time of *Buisson*'s composition in 1373, Froissart had recently been ordained as a priest and been granted the benefice of Estinnes-au-Mont (in the present-day Belgian province of Hainaut), a position secured for him by his patron, Wenceslas I.⁹ Froissart's new status as a man of the cloth is announced in *Buisson*'s prologue with the narrator's mention of his "ordenance nouvelle":

> Or voi je cangié mon afaire
> En aultre ordenance nouvelle.
> (vv. 458–59)

> Now I see my situation changed
> into another, new way of life.

After *Buisson*, the author would turn his attention increasingly away from love poetry and *dits* to the writing of his *Chroniques* and his more obscure Arthurian romance *Meliador*, of which no completed copy exists. Citing this turning point in the poet's career, Michelle Freeman has iconically labeled *Buisson* Froissart's "farewell to poetry."¹⁰ Most scholars have likewise affirmed that the poem articulates a kind of palinode, or dramatic recantation, of the first half of Froissart's body of work. Peter Dembowski and then William Kibler, for instance, have referred to *Buisson* as a Dantesque "mid-life crisis" in which Froissart's poet-narrator performs the author's own change of direction.¹¹ This decisive moment is also reflected in the way Froissart's works are compiled, as the earlier poetic works are not found together with *Meliador* or the *Chroniques*.¹²

---

9. See Laurence De Looze, ed., *Prison amoureuse*. New York: Garland, 1994. xii. Wenceslas was the son of Jean de Luxembourg, Machaut's most exalted patron.

10. Michelle Freeman, "Froissart's *Le joli buisson de Jonece*: A Farewell to Poetry?" in *Machaut's World: Science and Art in the Fourteenth Century*. Ed. Madeleine Pelner Cosman, Bruce Chandler. New York: New York Academy of Sciences, 1978. 235–47. Kay (*The Place of Thought*, 124) notes how the rubrics, indexes and explicits of Froissart's poetic manuscripts also reinforce this reading.

11. Peter Dembowski, *Jean Froissart and his* Meliador: *Context, Craft and Sense*. Lexington, KY: French Forum, 1983. 36–41; William Kibler, "*Le joli buisson de Jonece*: Froissart's Midlife Crisis," in *Froissart Across the Genres*. Ed. Donald Maddox, Sara Sturm-Maddox. Gainesville: University Press of Florida, 1998. 63–80. Lassahn also notes the similarity with Dante's narrator at his "mezzo del cammin" ("Pseudo-Autobiography and the Role of the Poet," 127 n3). Sylvia Huot has articulated the following, more nuanced account of Froissart's gesture in *Buisson*, which is closer to my own argument in this chapter: "Froissart's 'farewell to poetry' in no sense entails a loss of respect for the poetic arts, nor does it imply that Froissart's own abilities are waning. It implies simply that the themes of lyricism and 'courtly love' no longer serve Froissart's needs, and he turns to a different sort of literature. Indeed, as Froissart passes in review the French lyrico-narrative tradition and his own participation therein, one senses that he is not so much turning away from poetry as he is transposing poetic process into a new register" (*From Song to Book*, 316). Claire Nouvet's unpublished dissertation ("La fragmentation du système poetico-lyrique de Jean Froissart," Diss. Princeton University, 1981) is probably the most ambitious attempt to account for Froissart's "farewell" in terms of his larger corpus and career.

12. On Froissart's poetics of compilation, see Huot, *From Song to Book*, 302–27.

Given the way it puts Froissart's career into perspective, it is not my intention to question the "farewell" gesture of *Buisson*. One thing about the poem, however, cannot be overemphasized: that it represents a spectacularly poetic farewell, more self-celebration, homage to the poet's influences, and elaborate thank-you to his adoring fans, than searing self-judgment. Like *Espinette, Buisson* provides a fantastic narrative frame for Froissart's love lyrics even as it distances the author from erotic poetry in time and mentality. *Buisson* is also a celebration of the great and wealthy courts whose generous patronage Froissart enjoyed. The poet draws attention to his financial success in *Buisson* by spending nearly 150 verses (vv. 230–373) cataloging the various gifts and sums of cash he has received from his many loyal patrons.

Froissart's humorous treatment of money is by no means unique to *Buisson*.[13] In this poem, as elsewhere, it reflects the author's awareness of his status as a literary figure, and of his texts as literary commodities, if among a relatively small and intimate readership. Froissart's poetic works seem never to have achieved the wide circulation of his *Chroniques* and are preserved today in only two manuscripts.[14] Nevertheless, the author expressed a distinct concern with his own textual coherence, more explicitly so even than Machaut, whose manuscripts enjoyed greater popularity and richer workmanship.[15] As Jacqueline Cerquiglini puts it, "Froissart's essential activity is that of collecting."[16] The nature of the collection is the author-book, the compiled corpus, which was for Froissart more overtly than for Machaut an object of economic exchange with a distinct value in the marketplace. Because he was so conscious of his public literary status and of his participation in a wider economy of book production, Froissart could not be content to simply write off any part of his work. Accompanying the critical perspective on love poetry in *Buisson*, then, there is also a strong impulse to recuperate past writing, to defend its place in the literary record. Like Machaut's *JRN*, this sequel is not simply a point of rupture with an earlier version of the writing subject, but a conjunction of past and future poetry which emphasizes the importance of both.

---

13. See especially the *Dit dou florin* (1389, in Jean Froissart, *'Dits' et 'Débats.'* Ed. Anthime Fourrier. Geneva: Droz, 1979. 175–190. On *Florin*, see also Michel Zink, "Le temps, c'est de l'argent: remarques sur le *Dit du florin* de Jean Froissart," in *Et c'est la fin pour quoy nous sommes ensemble: hommage à Jean Dufournet: littérature, histoire et langue du Moyen Âge*. 3 vols. Paris: Champion, 1993. III: 1455–64.
14. BNF fr. 830 and BNF fr. 831.
15. See Lechat, *'Dire par fiction,'* 265.
16. Jacqueline Cerquiglini, "Fullness and Emptiness: Shortages and Storehouses of Lyric Treasure in the Fourteenth and Fifteenth Centuries." Trans. Christine Cano. *Yale French Studies Special Issue: Contexts: Style and Values in Medieval Art and Literature* (1991): 230.

As I show in this chapter, Froissart's will toward re-collection is surprisingly evident in *Buisson*'s meditation on the Last Judgment, which serves not only to mark renunciation, but also to reaffirm and validate the past. In that it both abjures and defends the poet's youthful poetry, Froissart's Last Judgment corresponds closely to the way that Gisèle Mathieu-Castellani has defined her concept of *la scène judiciaire de l'autobiographie:* "La scène judiciaire se met en place dans un double geste de répudiation et de rappel" ("The judicial scene [of autobiography] takes place through a double gesture of repudiation and recollection").[17] Deguileville's *PA* and Machaut's *JRN* have already provided two examples of this *double geste*, in which earlier writing is spotlighted as it is indicted, advertised as it is accused. In Froissart's *Buisson*, even as the judgment of God blames the subject for having written vain poetry, so too does it celebrate his literary past.

For Froissart, the need for a complete poetic record is not only because, as Saint Bernard put it, what has been written on the parchment of the soul can never be scratched out, can never be hidden from the eyes of an omniscient God.[18] This is certainly an important part of the impulse to remembering the past in *Buisson*, and the poem is even framed as a literary testament in which Froissart's pseudo-autobiographical narrator will give a sincere and thorough accounting of his life before he dies (vv. 1–10). Yet Froissart suggests that the responsibility he feels toward his readers also makes it necessary for him to reaffirm the value of past poetry. Not only may the author be guilty for having endangered readers' souls with vain entertainment, but, quite apart from that, he is indebted to audiences for the generous financial support they provided for his more youthful works. As it concludes what is perhaps the most overtly humorous of all the texts I consider in this book, Froissart's scene of Last Judgment expresses a distinct ethical seriousness about literature which is further complicated—and not only enlivened—by the capitalistic relationship of a writer and his aristocratic and princely consumers. If the more literal account book of author-patron transactions is to be squared with the great Book of judgment, how does the poet define the nature of his responsibilities to the reader? Specifically, is the now repentant author guilty of having brought into the world poetry he himself has characterized as vain? Have well-paying readers been left with a worthless, or even a harmful product?

As a *double geste*, I believe Froissart's use of the divine judgment motif in *Buisson* may be read as a symbolic attempt to reconcile the two great

---

17. Mathieu-Castellani, *La scène judiciaire*, 97.
18. See above, Introduction, 15–16.

judges of his life—God and the Patron. In this chapter, working my way back to Froissart's closing meditation on the Judgment, I show how this eschatological meditation constitutes both a repudiation and a reendorsement of the author's love poetry, and of the larger courtly tradition into which it is inscribed.

Following the most conventional reading of *Buisson,* I begin with repudiation. In the first section of this chapter, I consider how Froissart's imagined Judgment works to enact the "farewell to poetry" spoken of by Freeman.[19] Examining the *Bush* poems as a continuous narrative, I show how Froissart employed the imagined scene of eschatological judgment at the end of *Buisson*—the allegorical judgment of Jupiter—as a counterpoint to the uncertainty of the judgments his pseudo-autobiographical narrator had exhibited while in the service of Venus. What I add to prior scholarly discussion of Froissart's "farewell" and his "mid-life crisis" is a more nuanced picture of the ways in which the poet used judgment motifs to weigh the ethics of his own writing and to narrate the difficult *procès* of acquiring both moral and poetic authority.

In the second part of the chapter, I turn to the aspect of *rappel* and to the way that the ethical relationship of author and reader comes to depend on Froissart's defense and revalorization of his earlier poetry as much as on its renunciation. Needing to respond to his expectant readers as well as to God, Froissart calls earlier writing back to mind in order to justify its presence as part of the author's corpus, his complete works. The Last Judgment of *Buisson* suggests a symbolic means of uniting past, present and future, as it does not in fact condemn Froissart's erotic works outright. Instead, it argues for a new interpretation of the poet's past, enabling him to defend his authority to God and the Patron at once.

II. Froissart's Judgment of Paris, or a Portrait of the Artist as a Young Machaut

To work back toward Froissart's meditation on the Judgment Day as it functions in the larger narrative of the *Bush* poems, the best place to begin is another scene of judgment with cosmic proportions, this one near the beginning of *Espinette amoureuse.* This first judgment scene represents the start of the poet's vocation, and not coincidentally, it is more than a little

---

19. Freeman, "A Farewell to Poetry?" 238.

inspired by Guillaume de Machaut's *Jugements*.[20] At the beginning of *Espinette*, in the "joli mois de may" (v. 351), while he sits beneath a hawthorn bush, Froissart's twelve-year-old narrator is suddenly confronted by four mysterious figures embroiled in a dispute. As he too had lain in a bush in the springtime, the narrator of Machaut's *JRB* had encountered a knight, a lady, her lady-in-waiting and a small dog. In Froissart's *Espinette*, the group of four assumes more grandiose proportions: they are the god Mercury and the goddesses Juno, Venus and Pallas; but just like Machaut's group, the goddesses are fighting amongst themselves and seek a judgment to resolve their dispute.

Addressing the narrator, Mercury claims that he has been quietly watching over him for four years. He then refers to the Judgment of Paris legend to explain why he and the goddesses have come to visit the young man so unexpectedly. The legend's details, which Mercury largely skips over, go like this: at the wedding feast of Peleus and Thetis, all the deities of Olympia are in attendance and having a good time, when suddenly Eris—Discord—crashes the party. Attempting to provoke a quarrel among Juno, Pallas and Venus, Eris places a golden apple before them, inscribed with the words "For the Fairest." Naturally, all three goddesses claim the apple for themselves, leading them to seek arbitration from Jupiter. Jupiter does not wish to incur the wrath of the other goddesses (including his badtempered wife Juno) by favoring one of them, so he recuses himself from the judgment and delegates the shepherd Paris for the task instead. Mercury leads the three goddesses to Mount Ida, where Paris tends his flock, and the goddesses plead their cases and offer various bribes to the bemused young man. In the end, Paris awards the apple to Venus because her offer proves more seductive. In return, the goddess gives him the love of Helen, putting into motion the Trojan War.

Speaking to the twelve-year-old narrator in Froissart's bucolic scene of judgment, Mercury explains that Pallas and Juno are still enraged by Paris's decision, and that they have demanded the judgment be resubmitted to another authority, none other than the narrator himself. Claiming that since he is young and innocent he ought to be able to make a more clear-headed choice than Paris (vv. 474–82), Mercury asks the narrator which goddess *he* thinks the fairest. When the narrator admits his ignorance, Mercury is more than willing to lend an opinion; he explains in no uncertain terms that Paris made a disastrous judgment in awarding

---

20. See Fourrier, ed., *Espinette*, 34; Ehrhart, *The Judgment of the Trojan Prince Paris*, 146; Bennett, "The Mirage of Fiction," 286–87; Lechat, *'Dire par fiction,'* 296–304.

the apple to Venus, as among other things, this caused the Trojan War (vv. 440–66). Mercury thus offers the narrator a chance to right Paris's decision by strongly suggesting that he not choose the goddess of love this time. But the narrator just has to learn the hard way and disregards Mercury's advice. With little hesitation, he repeats the judgment of Paris and opts for Venus (vv. 483–524). This does not surprise Mercury; with a sigh, the god says only that he thought as much: all lovers make the same decision ("Tout li amant vont celle voie," v. 524). Mercury then disappears into thin air, leaving the narrator in the hands of the goddess of love. The narrator's judgment for Venus signifies the choice of erotic love and love poetry as his vocation, as against the military career represented by Pallas and the life of material wealth by Juno. Venus is overjoyed by the narrator's decision, and she promises that she will reward him by accepting him into her service (vv. 605–8).

As things turn out, this does not seem like much of a reward. Although it does not bring about a second Trojan War, the narrator's judgment has catastrophic results for him personally. The momentary choice of a particular life—the service of Venus, the vocation of love poetry—determines the narrator's interpretation of reality thereafter. Namely, love and its poetry blind him to the fact that the object of his desire does not return his sentiments.[21] As in Machaut's *Jugement* poems, then, *Espinette* exploits the semantic ambiguity between *jugement* as an official pronouncement and *jugement* as an individual mental faculty used at each moment of life to interpret the world. The tragicomic series of events following the judgment for Venus, recounted with irony by Froissart's more mature narrator, deserves to be summarized here in some detail, since it helps to show how bad judgment is portrayed in *Espinette* as a symptom of erotic desire, and of courtly poetry.

After Venus promises to reward the narrator, she disappears and he meets a young lady reading Adenet le Roi's thirteenth-century romance *Cléomades* (v. 696).[22] The two read together for a time; afterward, the young lady asks him to lend her another good book. Smitten, he writes her a ballad (vv. 927–44) declaring his love and folds it into the volume he lends her,

---

21. See Ehrhart, *The Judgment of the Trojan Prince Paris*, 141–42.

22. The young lady remains effectively anonymous throughout the *Bush* poems, although at the end of *Espinette* (vv. 4179–85), Froissart's narrator claims that her name is hidden in a previous passage (vv. 3386–89) along with his own. Based on v. 3389 ("Violettes et margerites") the young lady has usually been identified as "Margerite," but William Kibler has suggested that her name could also be "Violette" ("Self-Deception in Froissart's *Espinette amoureuse*." *Romania* 97 [1976]: 80–81). Because of this uncertainty and the fact that she is never directly named in the text, I call her simply the "young lady."

Mahieu le Poirier's *Baillieu d'Amours*, a seminal text of the medieval love debate tradition.[23] Upon receiving the book back from the young lady, the narrator is dismayed to find that his literally-inserted lyric is right where he put it, as if she chose to ignore it. And indeed, although she clearly likes to read, the young lady does not care for any of the narrator's poems. He, however, is blinded by Venus and burns with desire, remaining oblivious to the disinterest of his audience.

Over time, the narrator composes a substantial amount of fixed-form lyric poetry for the young lady, which Froissart inserts into his own text. In these lyrics and in the narrative that frames them, the gulf between the young lady's feelings of annoyance toward the narrator and his ability to judge those feelings grows ever wider. Sometime later, for instance, the narrator offers the young lady a rose, which she tries politely to decline (vv. 994–1004). He, however, misconstrues her refusal as false modesty, insisting that she take the gift. After another negative response to his pleas (v. 1120), he writes the young lady a ballad demanding her love, to which she replies in exasperation, "He's really asking a lot!" ("Ce qu'il demande, c'est grant cose!" v. 1296). But against his better judgment, the narrator still does not lose hope. When he learns that the young lady is to be married, his first reaction is to vow to kill her husband (vv. 1435–36), but soon thoughts of the impending union propel him into a long state of fever, during which he writes a new batch of unwanted poetry for her (vv. 1556–2355). He seems to lose his grip on reality entirely as he is possessed by the heat of desire; at one point hallucinating the young lady's presence in a mirror she has given him, he convinces himself that she has sent him a poem of comfort (vv. 2617–996).[24] Later in *Espinette*, the young lady resigns herself to tolerating the narrator's continued intrusions into her life, although she dismisses the poetry he writes for her as emotionally feigned (vv. 3583–85), an insult that he does not register. Soon thereafter, she breaks off their relationship, giving the excuse of malicious rumors told about them (vv. 3751–58). At the end of *Espinette*, the narrator attempts to enter back into contact with the young lady and asks her to sit beside him: "Les moi venes chi douce

---

23. Froissart cites the title of the book as the "*Baillieu d'Amours*" (v. 871), which Fourrier (ed., *Espinette*, 176 n871) has identified as Mahieu Le Poirier's *Court d'Amours*. See the edition of this poem by Terence Scully, *Le* Court d'Amours *de Mahieu le Poirier et la suite anonyme de* La court d'amours. Waterloo, ON: Wilfrid Laurier University Press, 1976.

24. This scene is another good example of Froissart's frequent gestures of homage toward Machaut, since it bears a close resemblance to the intervention of Venus that follows the Judgment of Paris in Machaut's *Fonteinne amoureuse*, as well as to scenes in his *Remede de Fortune* and *Voir dit*. De Looze (*Pseudo-Autobiography*, 110) notes similarities in the mirror episodes in both authors, as does Picherit ("Le rôle des éléments mythologiques," 499).

amie" ("Come here beside me, sweet friend," v. 3781). She responds with the perfectly unambiguous words, "point d'amie chi pour vous!" ("There's no friend for you here!" v. 3783). When she sees that she has still not gotten her point across, she vents her frustration by violently tearing a handful of hair from his scalp (vv. 3789–92). The narrator, however, is only momentarily deterred, and finally decides to interpret this gesture as a definitive token of her affection (vv. 3817–33), which he composes a closing ballad and lay to celebrate (vv. 3834–4146).[25] He is not simply stubborn or ignorant, but suffers from chronic self-deception, perhaps, as he himself muses in retrospect, as the result of having been too young for love (vv. 133–36).[26]

So does one bad judgment—the fatefully repeated choice of Paris—cause the narrator's entire deliberative faculty to be knocked askew in its interpretation of the world and of the reactions of his very first reader, the anonymous young lady.[27] Although religious themes are not as explicit in *Espinette* as in *Buisson,* already in the earlier poem the narrator's choice for Venus and its repercussions can be traced directly to later medieval Christian beliefs about the faculty of judgment. As Margaret Ehrhart has shown in her study of the Judgment of Paris legend, the decision of Froissart's narrator to bestow the golden apple on Venus follows the traditional medieval reading of the legend, which was based on the allegorical interpretation given to it by the Church Father Fulgentius (c. 460–c. 530).[28] For Fulgentius, Jupiter's deferral of judgment to Paris represented God's endowment of man with free will and the ability to choose for himself a life of contemplation, of activity, or of pleasure-seeking.[29] In the early fourteenth century, the *Ovide moralisé* had effected the myth's translation into popular Christian allegory by identifying the golden apple with the forbidden fruit of Eden and Paris's choice with the moment of the Fall.[30]

In her account, Ehrhart demonstrates how this basic pattern of Christian allegoresis was applied to the Judgment of Paris legend throughout the Middle Ages and in Froissart's poem.[31] As the emblem of judgments made

---

25. Kibler analyzes this scene in detail ("Self-Deception," 94–95).
26. See Ibid.
27. On the young lady as a reader, and on Froissart's women in general, see Philip E. Bennett, "Female Readers in Froissart: Implied, Fictive and Other," in *Women, the Book and the Godly/ Women, the Book and the Worldly: Selected Proceedings of the St. Hilda's Conference, 1993.* Ed. Lesley Smith, Jane H. M. Taylor. 2 vols. Woodbridge, Suffolk, UK: D. S. Brewer, 1995. II: 13–23.
28. Ehrhart, *The Judgment of the Trojan Prince Paris.*
29. Ibid., 76, 84.
30. Ibid., 85–93. Ehrhart (90) notes that the *Ovide moralisé* is the first text to interpret the Judgment of Paris in the light of salvation history.
31. Ibid., 141–51.

in the state of blindness incurred by original sin and by his own adolescent sexuality, the narrator's inevitable repetition of Paris's judgment is the catalyst for his inability to judge the words and actions of the young lady. That the narrator's perceptions are distorted by overheated sexual desire shows how one bad judgment reproduces itself endlessly on the level of the individual poet, much as the faulty judgment made by Adam and Eve reproduces itself in the human lineage as a whole and will do so until the Last Judgment puts things right.[32]

While the narrator's poor judgment is everyone's judgment after the Fall and the judgment of all lovers ("Tout li amant," v. 524), it is also the judgment of Guillaume de Machaut. Not only does Froissart's Judgment of Paris recall the bushy beginning of Machaut's *Jugement dou roy de Behaingne*, it conflates that scene with the climactic episode of one of Machaut's most famous *dits*, *La fonteinne amoureuse* (1360),[33] an episode which is Machaut's own version of the Judgment of Paris.[34] In *Fonteinne*, Machaut's narrator-poet meets a certain lovelorn prince—identifiable with Machaut's then patron, Jean duc de Berry, who is weary with heartache because he has to leave France, and the woman he loves, to become a hostage in England. After talking at length and collaborating on some poetry, poet and prince fall asleep together beside a fountain. In a shared dream, Venus comes to them and recounts the judgment of Paris from her own perspective (vv. 1633–2144). She tells them how Paris chose her and how she gave him Helen in return, conveniently omitting to mention what happened afterward between the Greeks and the Trojans. Boasting of her magical power over lovers, Venus then proves her point by making the prince's lady appear to him in the dream and console him (vv. 2207–526). As a result, the prince is saved from a heartache too cruel to endure and declares that he is converted to the cult of Venus, promising to build the goddess a temple and make sacrifices to her (vv. 2543–60). In his account of the Judgment of Paris, Machaut lends a relatively sympathetic portrait to Venus. Most of all, she proves a benevolent influence in permitting the beloved to transmit herself to the lover over great distances through the medium of poetry.[35] For the poet, the prince's double in *Fonteinne*, the choice of Venus

---

32. As Ehrhart points out, "The author of the *Ovide moralisé* sees in the Judgment not the fall of Adam and Eve but the fall of Everyman, the individual reenactment of our first parents' sin" (*The Judgment of the Trojan Prince Paris*, 92).

33. I cite the edition of *La fonteinne amoureuse* by Cerquiglini-Toulet (Paris: Stock, 1993).

34. See Ehrhart, *The Judgment of the Trojan Prince Paris*, 130–41.

35. And, as R. Barton Palmer (ed., *Fonteinne*, lxii) argues, Machaut's version "connects the young man's choice (viewed as sinful in the *Ovide moralisé*) with a morally worthy dedication to the different aspects of the aristocratic life."

likewise suggests that the goddess is a desirable force in the composition of good verse. As a servant of Venus, Machaut's narrator gives expression to his patron's longing, which makes it possible for the lover who is absent to become present.[36]

Putting him beneath the bush, and at the center of the Judgment of Paris, Froissart casts his narrator as a young Machaut, identifying the posture he himself had adopted as a writer of lyrics and *dits* with that of his most important influence. For the younger Froissart, the choice for Venus is something of a non-choice, as it represents both a state of sin—carnal desire—into which all people are born, and a poetic over-determination: who else but Machaut could Froissart have imitated? Who else but Venus could he have served in writing poetry? By redescribing the service of Venus as the poet's vocation, Froissart parodies his younger attraction to Machauldian courtly poetry even as he continues to pay homage to Machaut.[37]

In particular, Froissart's conflation of the bush scene from *JRB* with the Judgment of Paris scene from *Fonteinne amoureuse* serves to reference the way that Machaut had used shifting judgments as a plot device throughout his body of work, including in the *Jugement* poems. *Espinette* evokes Machaut's mastery of that spirit of controlled chaos, of constantly fluctuating opinions, which Thomas L. Reed has labeled the "aesthetics of irresolution," characteristic of much medieval debate poetry.[38] But Froissart's Judgment of Paris, in comparison with Machaut's, is more unequivocally the depiction of a foolish decision, a rewriting which also serves to characterize Machauldian courtly poetry in terms of dubious judgment.

---

36. In *Fonteinne,* these powers are also associated with the God Morpheus, the poem's alternate title being the *Livre du Morpheüs.* The exaltation of Venus is not without its ironies; Margaret Ehrhart has argued that Machaut's is a moralizing interpretation of the Judgment of Paris legend directed at Jean duc de Berry, who at the time of the poem's composition was about to leave his new bride Jeanne d'Armagnac to become a hostage in England, where he would remain for the next seven years. According to Ehrhart, Machaut would have used the choice of Venus by both Paris and the fictionalized patron as a negative exemplum of how the pursuit of *eros* leads to folly (*The Judgment of the Trojan Prince Paris,* 130–41). This interpretation of Machaut's poem has its merits, since it was Jean de Berry's obligation at the time of the poem to reject Venus for Pallas, the goddess of war.

37. Lechat (*'Dire par fiction,'* 298) argues that through his own interpretation, Froissart reads Machaut's Judgment of Paris as a reference to the poet's vocation.

38. Thomas L. Reed, Jr. uses this expression specifically in regard to medieval English debate poetry (*Middle English Debate Poetry and the Aesthetics of Irresolution.* Columbia: University of Missouri Press, 1990). Machaut's *Voir dit* provides another good example of the author's fascination with uncertain judgments, as the dreaming narrator asks "Le Roi qui ne ment" for advice on love, but this supposed authority figure only laughs at him (see Imbs and Cerquiglini-Toulet, eds., *Le livre du voir dit,* vv. 5244–733). The game of the "roi qui ne ment" is also referenced in Froissart's *Espinette* (v. 220) as part of the narrator's long litany of childhood pursuits, and then replayed in the dream world of *Buisson* (v. 4427).

Appearing four years after *Espinette*, *Buisson* is an attempt to strike down the Judgment of Paris once and for all and to move beyond the unstable judgments of venereal verse. The emblem of the narrator's newfound sobriety is the planet and deity Jupiter, whose importance is revealed to him by Jonece when he first revisits the bush. The narrator, amazed by the boundless green shrub all around him, asks Jonece to explain its meaning. Jonece tells his charge that, according to the astronomy lessons he received some time ago, the bush's seven branches correspond to the seven planets that influence man throughout life, in seven neatly demarcated periods of astrological influence (vv. 1554–707) extending from the Moon at birth to Saturn at man's decline and death.

Jonece's understanding of the planets corresponds to the schema of the seven ages of man as found in the fourth book of Ptolemy's *Tetrabiblos*.[39] According to Jonece, the Moon nourishes the child for the first four years of its life (vv. 1616–26). Mercury, who looks after the child for the next ten years, teaches it to speak and move (vv. 1626–36), before relinquishing control to Venus for the following decade:

Puis vient Venus, qui le reprent	Then comes Venus who takes him
Et qui .X. ans apriés en songne.	and teaches him for ten years with care,
Vous devés savoir de quel songne:	and you should know with what goal:
D'ignorance le leve et monde,	from ignorance she raises and purifies him,
Et li fait congnoistre le monde	and introduces him to the world
Et sentir que c'est de delis,	and makes him feel what pleasure is,
Tant de viandes com de lis,	in the bedroom and at the table,
Et le fait gai, joli et cointe	and makes him happy, handsome and wise
Et de tous esbanois l'acointe.	and knowledgeable of all sorts of fun.
(vv. 1637–45)	

Although Mercury did hand the young narrator over to Venus after his judgment in *Espinette*, Jonece's vision of celestial influence does not perfectly describe the narrator's own experiences with the goddess of love. He was twelve, not fourteen, when he entered Venus's service, and this after

---

39. See J. A. Burrow's discussion of the Ptolemaic schema, which acknowledges its influence on Froissart (*The Ages of Man: A Study in Medieval Writing and Thought*. Oxford: Clarendon, 1986. 37–42, 179–80). The association of Jupiter with justice is not particularly Ptolemaic, but the planet is nevertheless identified in the *Tetrabiblios* with "the renunciation of manual labor, toil, turmoil and dangerous activity" and the assumption of "decorum, foresight, retirement, together with all-embracing deliberation, admonition and consolation" (*Tetrabiblios* 4.10, trans. F. E. Robbins [Cambridge, MA: 1940], cited in Burrow's appendix, *The Ages of Man*, 198). In *Paradiso* (cantos 18–20), Dante places the just in the sphere of Jupiter.

only four years in Mercury's care, not ten.⁴⁰ Moreover, Jonece's description of the goddess's power is surprisingly positive, casting her as a teacher who frees man of ignorance and acquaints him with the great sensual pleasures of life. Jonece's explanation does not account for the foolish things that the narrator did under Venus's service or the considerable pain she caused him. Jonece's description therefore seems an ironic touch on Froissart's part, since the reader of *Buisson* who has also read *Espinette* is well aware of the havoc Venus has wreaked, and since the original Ptolemaic model likewise presents the goddess in a rather negative light:

> Venus, taking in charge the third age, that of youth, for the next eight years, corresponding in number to her own period, begins, as is natural, to inspire, at their maturity, an activity of the seminal passages and to implant an impulse toward the embrace of love. At this time particularly a kind of frenzy enters the soul, incontinence, desire for any chance sexual gratification, burning passion, guile, and the blindness of the impetuous lover.⁴¹

This list of physical and psychological symptoms more accurately describes Froissart's twelve-year-old narrator after his judgment under the hawthorn bush.⁴² He too had been hormonally blinded to the reality of his situation, engulfed by the flames of passion.

Once he has returned to the hawthorn, the narrator of *Buisson* is just as distracted as he had been in his youth, so he pays little attention to Jonece's answer to his question. He confesses that he just cannot concentrate on this astrology lesson, since he wants only to think about love, springtime, music and dancing (vv. 1709–55). Although Froissart's newly reenchanted narrator gives no thought to it for the time being, however, Jonece's vision of the seven ages foreshadows his literal and figurative awakening at the end of *Buisson*—his sudden awareness of the Last Judgment—in that this model describes the path the narrator will take from Venus to Jupiter. After Venus, says Jonece, the next ten years of a man's life belong to the Sun, when his desires move from love to the acquisition of honor and fortune (vv. 1646–51). Next, Mars begins a twelve-year term similarly devoted to the pursuit of wealth and power, but with more sinister connotations of

---

40. As the narrator admits in *Espinette* (vv. 133–36), he may have been too young for Venus.
41. *Tetrabiblios* 4.10 (in Burrow, *The Ages of Man*, 198).
42. Although it does not rely on theories of astrological influence, Philippe de Novare's *Quatre ages de l'homme* (first half of the thirteenth century) notes that "les jones genz ont faus jugement en aus" because of excessive sexual desire (*Les quatre ages de l'homme*. Ed. M. de Fréville. Paris: Société des Anciens Textes Français, 1888. 2.49).

greed and material acquisition through violence (vv. 1652–67). Following Mars, says Jonece, Jupiter at last directs a man's attention to the welfare of his immortal soul, for twelve years or more, prior to the age of Saturn, the time of his death. As Jonece explains, it is Jupiter who teaches man to think upon his end and thus to live correctly:

Puis vient Jupiter tout le cours,	Then the time of Jupiter comes around,
Qui a l'omme fet grant secours,	which brings great help to a man, for
Car d'outrages et de folies	from presumptuous and silly acts
Et de pluiseurs merancolies,	and prolonged bouts of melancholy,
Ou jadis il s'est embatus	in which he had long been sunk,
Et dont il a esté batus	and by which he had been beaten,
Tant par li com par l'autrui ire,	as much by himself as by others' anger,
Compains, vous poés moult bien dire	friend, you can truly say
Que la planette l'en delivre	that the planet delivers him at last
Et plus seür estat li livre,	and brings him a more certain state of mind,
Qu'on doit prisier et honnourer,	that we all should value and honor,
Car elle li fait savourer	for it allows us to feel
Pais de corps et repos pour l'ame,	peace in the body and in the soul,
Ordener sepulture et lame,	to prepare our sepulcher and stone,
Amer l'Eglise et Dieu cremir,	to love the Church and fear God,
Recongnoistre et de ce fremir	to recognize and tremble at the thought
Que chils mondes n'est q'uns trespass.	that this world is only passing.
Ceste planette ne lait pas	This planet never abandons the man,
L'omme, anchois l'estoie et yverne	but lights his way summer and winter,
Et .XII. ans ou plus le gouverne.	and directs him for twelve years or more.
(vv. 1668–87)	

Since "presumptuous and silly acts" and "prolonged bouts of melancholy" (vv. 1670–71) are exactly what the love-struck narrator had experienced in *Espinette*, Jupiter seems particularly effective in ridding his subjects of the bad judgments of Venus, who has now returned to tempt the middle-aged dreamer by leading him back to the great *buisson*.

Chronologically, it may be true that Froissart's narrator is not yet at the right moment in his life to fall under the sway of Jupiter. According to Jonece's model, at thirty-five he should have just left the Sun and be under Mars. But as the *telos* and not simply the end of a Christian life, Jupiter is more than just a step along the way at a prescribed period of time; rather, by the conclusion of the poem the planet comes to represent the narrator pulled out of time altogether and into the eternal present of God's judgment, the *nunc stans,* as he is finally saved from the pain of temporal existence and the frailty of human perception. Jupiter's is the perfected age, which prepares man for the dark days of Saturn, his decline and death.[43] Not strictly chronological, but eschatological, Jupiter signifies man come to terms with his end, his soul readied for the final Judgment.

With Jupiter and Venus vying for control over the narrator, the intervention of the other planets remains largely in the background. However, the desire for material acquisition, characteristic of both the Sun and Mars, is also important. In a passage near the beginning of *Buisson*, the narrator confesses that he has sinned against his nature by unsuccessfully trying his hand at commerce (vv. 94–97).[44] It is not long afterward that he lists the various sums he has been given for his writing by Froissart's many patrons (vv. 230–373). One may well infer that Jupiter's age, the time when a man's thoughts draw toward the ultimate reward, moves the subject away from the vain pursuit of riches as well as from the vanity of erotic desire and erotic poetry.

As I see it, the purpose of Jonece's discussion of the seven ages within the larger narrative of the *Bush* poems is two-fold. In the first place, it lends further emphasis to the changing judgments of the pseudo-autobiographical narrator-poet as a function of his existence in time. Like the reversals of opinion in Machaut's *Jugement* poems, the Ptolemaic model depicts the poet as a creature of differing opinions in the course of a career. The influences of the heavenly bodies represent not only various ways of being, but ways of seeing the world based on divergent desires, different value judgments that shape one's interpretation of reality. While Venus represents the younger narrator's careless practice of love poetry, and the Sun and Mars stand in for the narrator writing for money and honor, Jupiter corresponds to the author turning his rhetorical gifts to pastoral ends, to the more serious endeavor of prose historiography in a time of horrific warfare, and to non-erotic themes in general. By portraying the ages of life as a tumultuous course of competing celestial influences, Jonece's schema of the seven ages amplifies the representation of the author's own career and corpus as being subject to inevitable shifts in judgment during twenty-three years of poetry.

---

43. Sarah Kay ("Le moment de conclure," 156) notes that the "Lay de Nostre Dame" signifies the Age of Jupiter. Freeman ("A Farewell to Poetry," 242) and Kibler ("Froissart's Midlife Crisis," 66) both note, in my opinion, incorrectly, that Mars is responsible for governing judgment and reward in *Buisson*, while Kelly (*Medieval Imagination*, 179) considers that the narrator's "rude awakening" to a "world of age, care and sin" corresponds to the sign of the Sun.

44. "Si me mis en le marcandise" (v. 94). It is not clear to me whether Froissart is referring to actual commerce or to the idea of writing for financial gain.

In the second place, Jonece's exposition of the psychological life-cycle serves to naturalize these shifts in judgment, by making them a regular part of the human developmental pattern, as much as they are stages in a narrative of Christian spiritual growth.[45] This naturalization works to suggest that the poet's errors in judgment are relatively excusable, since they are appropriate to the moment in which they took place. As the narrator puts it in *Buisson*, "leurs saisons ont toutes coses" ("all things have their season," v. 1735), and by extension, all things have their place in the evolving corpus. Already in *Espinette*, Froissart's older narrator had forgiven his younger self because of the natural inclinations of his age:[46]

Mais tant qu'au fait, j'escuse mieux	But all the same I forgive more readily
Assés les jones que les vieux,	the young than the old,
Car jonece ne voelt qu'esbas.	for youth wants nothing but fun.
(vv. 17–19)	

But as there is a time for *esbas*, there is also a time for repentance and preparation for the Judgment, as Jonece makes clear in his description of Jupiter's age. Unlike Machaut's conflicting *Jugement*s, then, Jonece's theory of planetary influence fits the fragmentation of the self over time and throughout a body of work into an overall narrative progression with a beginning and, especially, an End. Rewriting Machaut's *JRB* and *JRN* in his own diptych of contradictory judgments, Froissart affirms and even amplifies the depiction of the poet and his corpus as fragmented by divergences of opinion, all of which have their time and place. But Froissart transforms his narrator-persona's changes of opinion and sentiment into a narrative of moral perfection and, finally, repentance in the face of divine judgment.

In this process of self-transformation, which is also a quest for moral and poetic authority, Froissart performs a systematic replacement of the kind of "aesthetics of irresolution"[47] typical of later medieval debate poetry. If the young poet's limited worldview is identifiable with the fluid and uncertain judgments of the love debate works he reads—symbolized especially by the narrator's copy of the *Baillieu d'Amours* and by his abundant

---

45. See Burrow, *The Ages of Man*, 42, 179.
46. In a similar way, Dante explains that his *Convivio* is not necessarily to be thought an improvement on his previous work, *La vita nuova*; rather, *Convivio* reflects a different point in the author's life, which calls for different themes. See *Il convivio*. Ed. Gian Carlo Garfagnini. Rome: Salerno, 1997. 1.16.
47. See, again, Reed, *Middle English Debate Poetry*.

references to Machaut—Jupiter replaces these typically courtly judgments with a faith in the lasting certainty of Christian truth.

This substitution is represented most dramatically near the end of the dream vision of *Buisson*, where a classically courtly trial scene takes place. The young lady assumes the role of the narrator's judge as she reads his poetry. The personification Desir acts as the narrator's "advocas" (v. 4348) by bringing the young lady a ballad (vv. 3996–4013) which the narrator had written for her, and which is described as "witnessing" to his suffering and "representing him" (vv. 3887–88). A *virelay* is then entered into evidence (vv. 4048–69), various personifications make speeches, and finally, the narrator himself pleads directly to the young lady for a verdict of mercy, claiming his long suffering:

> Merchi vous pri a jointes mains,   With folded hands I pray you for mercy,
> Que vos frans coers me soit humains.   that your noble heart be human to me.
> (vv. 4483–84)

The principal question to be judged here is an old one, oft-repeated in courtly texts and used by Brunetto Latini in his *Rettorica* as a means of transferring legal rhetoric to vernacular love poetry: does the lover's suffering entitle him to mercy?[48] Does the beloved have an ethical obligation, if not to return his feelings, then at least to take pity and reward his love service with like affection? When he asks for the young lady's judgment, the narrator hopes to hear her pronounce the compassionate sentence "Je te retieng pour mon servant" ("I retain you as my servant," v. 4546); but instead, she says only this:

> Fols est qui sert qui son tamps pert,   He's a fool who serves and wastes his time,
> Mes services fais loyaument   but service performed loyally
> A personne d'entendement   for a person of understanding
> Ne fu onques mors ne peris   never was dead or wasted
> Qu'en le fin ne soit remeris.   so that it was not rewarded in the end.
> (vv. 4556–60)

---

48. See above, Chapter 1, 39–40. Bloch (*Medieval French Literature and Law*, 184–88) discusses this pseudo-juridical question as it occurs in the work of the Occitan troubadours, from whom Latini's account of the legal posture is ultimately drawn. In the *Baillieu* or *Court d'amours*—the book the narrator lends the young lady and into which he inserts his first poem to her—the question of *merci* is also brought up for judgment. See Mahieu Le Poirier, *Le* Court d'Amours *de Mahieu le Poirier*, ed. Scully, vv. 2010–79.

It is not at all clear whether the young lady is designating the narrator as one still wasting his time in useless service after twenty-three years, or one who will be rewarded in the end. Even if the latter case is true, it is not yet apparent when that end might come.[49]

Before the narrator and the young lady can speak further to clarify these points, her boisterous court of personifications interrupts them. The personifications—Plaisance, Desir, Humilité, Jonece, Maniere, Pité, Douls Samblant and Francise—begin a lyric poetry competition. All of them compose *souhetz*, wish-poems that evoke courtly themes, especially the desire for eternal love and springtime (vv. 4639–991). As they are recited, the *souhetz* are dutifully recorded by the narrator-poet and inserted into Froissart's own text. In order to determine whose *souhet* is the best, the competitors agree to submit their compositions to the judgment of the Dieu d'Amours (v. 5044). In the dream, steeped in courtly preciosity, this *nominatio iudicis* would seem to refer to Cupid, or Eros, Venus's son and one of the most traditional arbiters of love debate poetry.[50]

But this judgment is also interrupted. Before the Dieu d'Amours can be consulted, the dream ends and the narrator-poet suddenly wakes up. After thinking about his dream, he rejects Venus and her poetry, fearful of the Judgment to come; clearly, the true Dieu d'Amours is now Christ, to whom all of the narrator's actions—but especially his poetry—are to be submitted. Likewise, the burning desire the narrator had felt for the young lady becomes the eternal fire ("ardant painne," v. 5202) into which unrepentant sinners will be cast. Venus's influence is rejected for the pious and circumspect age of Jupiter, and the wish poems of the dream and the narrator's own love poems to the young lady are transformed into prayers to the Virgin. The end (*fin*) when all faithful servants will be rewarded with mercy no longer refers to the ambiguous terms of the young lady's judgment, but to the Judgment itself. Likewise, the narrator's service to Venus and his request that the young lady grant him *merchi* and accept him into her service are replaced by the service he will now undertake to the Church and the clemency he hopes the Virgin's advocacy will win for him:

---

49. In a similar vein, in *Espinette* the narrator says that he has been "mortelement jugiés" ("sentenced to death," v. 3742) by the personification Male Bouche and the young lady.

50. See, for example, *Les débats du clerc et du chevalier: étude historique et littéraire suivie de l'édition critique des textes*. Ed. Charles Oulmont. Paris, 1911. Repr. Geneva: Slatkine, 1974. In the *Baillieu d'Amours*, the text which the narrator lends the young lady, cases are presented to the baillif of the God of Love. See *Le Court d'Amours de Mahieu le Poirier*, ed. Scully. In this edition, Scully (xvi n13, n14; xvii n15) also points to the depiction of the court of the God of Love in *Li fablel dou Dieu d'amours*, in *De Venus la deesse d'amour*, and in Guillaume de Lorris's *Rose* (vv. 863–70).

Humlement je me voel retraire	Humbly I wish to retire myself
Viers le Mere dou Roi celestre,	toward the Mother of God in heaven,
Et li prie qu'elle voelle estre	and pray that she agree to act
Pour moi advocate et moiienne	as my advocate and intermediary
A son Fil, qui tout amoiienne,	with her Son, who mediates everything
Et qui est vrais feus habondans,	and who is the true living fire,
Caritables et redondans,	merciful and abundant,
Pour coers enflamer et esprendre.	that sets every heart ablaze.
(vv. 5183–90)	

And now that he is cognizant of his own soul's peril, the narrator does not hesitate to exhort his readers to repentance as well:

Dont, entroes	So while
Que bien tu te poes	you still can
Et as loisir dou retourner,	and have time to turn back,
Si t'esmoes	rouse yourself
Et ton coer promoes	and press your heart
Au justement considerer	to consider carefully
Quel conquoes	all the ways that
Li Viels ou li Noes	the Old and the New
Testamens te puet pourfiter.	Testaments can profit you.
(vv. 5354–62)	

For the narrator, the movement toward Jupiter represents a new and superior ethics of writing. Placing his work in the perspective of the Last Judgment, he understands that the real purpose of revisiting his younger days as a love poet in the bush has been his salvation through a very public repentance, providing closure to his past and turning his talents toward devotional and evangelical ends. In the process, the intentionally disjointed judgments of Machaut and of the broader courtly tradition become the object of parody and critique.

But while this gesture of worldly renunciation is dramatically announced by the narrator, it is only half of the overall effect of the *Bush* poems and their juxtaposition of judgments. To concentrate exclusively on Froissart's renunciation in *Buisson* is to overlook the various ways that the author expresses a debt to his readers, not only to the uncaring young lady for whom he first began to write, but also to the more appreciative audiences Froissart had found among the various courts of Europe. As Froissart suggests, his material and ethical obligation to patrons demands that he defend and revalorize the poetry he had written for them, even as he claims to move beyond it.

I have now shown how Froissart positioned his Jovian Last Judgment as a counterpoint to love poetry and its disorderly judgments. It remains to see how the ultimate judgment scene of *Buisson* also serves to reaffirm the poet's connection to the courtly tradition and to his own past writing. Thus I now move from *répudiation* to *rappel*, examining in more detail how Froissart recalls his earlier poetry just as he distances himself from it, and how the need to re-collect past writing becomes for the author an ethical impulse just as important as the need to recant.

III. God's Capital, Venus's Gifts, and the Judgment of the Patron

As he sits down to compose *Buisson*'s prologue, Froissart's narrator seems already to have undergone the spiritual transformation related at the end of the poem, when he awakens from his dream fantasy of young love and realizes that he is not young but middle-aged, that it is not May but November, and that with each passing day he draws closer to his death and Judgment. When he introduces *Buisson*, then, the narrator is already under the sign of Jupiter. As he begins the poem, the now spiritually mature narrator frames his dream vision of the bush as part of a literary testament, in which he will make a thorough moral inventory of the past before he dies:[51]

Des aventures me souvient	I remember the adventures
Dou temps passé. Or me couvient,	of times past. Now it is necessary,
Entroes que j'ai sens et memore,	while I still have sense and memory,
Encre et papier et escriptore,	ink, paper and a place to write,
Kanivet et penne taillie,	a knife and sharpened quill,
Et volenté apparellie	and a readied will
Qui m'amonneste et me remort,	which warns and exhorts me
Que je remonstre avant me mort	to tell before I die
Comment ou Buisson de Jonece	how in the Bush of Youth

---

51. Freeman ("A Farewell to Poetry?" 243) has noted the testamentary style of *Buisson*'s opening lines (vv. 1–10). Although Freeman identifies Mars as the governing planet for judgment and reward, these verses seem to fulfill Jonece's claim that the age of Jupiter prompts one to get one's last affairs in order ("Ordener sepulture et lame," v. 1681). On Froissart's place in the tradition of testamentary literature, see Lechat, *'Dire par fiction,'* 260. Lechat argues that the testamentary opening and the ending prayer of *Buisson* "signifient tous deux sans equivoque le renoncement à la poésie amoureuse" (*'Dire par fiction,'* 319).

Fui jadis, et par quel adrece.	I once was, and how I got there.
(vv. 1–10)	

In that *Buisson* is also a re-vision of *Espinette,* itself a satirical portrait of Froissart's younger days as a writer of love lyrics, the testament promises closure on the poet's life and work, prior to his death ("avant me mort," v. 8). Paired with the Last Judgment at the end of *Buisson,* the testamentary opening fashions a retrospective and penitential narrative, a final putting-to-rights of the author's accounts which is also a symbolic *dénouement* of Froissart's poetic corpus.[52]

But the narrator's project of personal accounting is made more difficult from the beginning by the seemingly divergent ethical claims that God and the readership place on his soul. Readings of *Buisson* as a conversion narrative ("farewell to poetry," "mid-life crisis") risk oversimplifying what is in fact a highly complex tale of personal change and inner conflict, in which the narrator's judgments are constantly shifting. It is especially important to remember that, even well *before* his transformative dream and his meditation on the Last Judgment, Froissart's narrator clearly expresses his desire to repent for serving Venus and for wasting his time with vain love poetry. The first thing that *Buisson*'s narrator recounts as he makes out his testament is an episode from his more recent past when, in middle age, he was visited by a version of Boethius's classic character Lady Philosophy. Froissart's "Dame Philozophie"—actually more of a voice in the narrator's head than a fully fleshed-out Boethian personification[53]—accuses the narrator of offending Nature by giving up writing (vv. 102–94). As Philozophie contends, Froissart's narrator is exceptionally gifted in poetry, and it would be a grave sin indeed to hide his light under a bushel:[54]

Tu ne dois pas escarciier	You must not be greedy with
Ce qui te poet agratiier;	that which can give you a good name;

---

52. See Lechat, '*Dire par fiction,*' 319.

53. Contrary to much of the Boethian tradition, Froissart does not recount Philozophie's appearance with any detail, and does not even treat her as a separate character until over a hundred verses after she has begun to speak (vv. 59–191). Before Philozophie is named, her voice is identified simply as "Pensees" (v. 102), seemingly internal to the narrator.

54. Freeman notes that Philozophie's argument reflects "the clerkly topos that one must not hide one's light under a bushel" ("A Farewell to Poetry?" 237–38). That Philozophie, like Machaut's equally Boethian Bonneurté, may be read as giving voice to eschatological accusation, provides something of a counterpoint to Michael Cherniss's view of the medieval Boethian tradition as a secularization of the apocalyptic (*Boethian Apocalypse: Studies in Middle English Vision Poetry.* Norman, OK: Pilgrim Books, 1987).

> Se tu ies ables et propisses
> D'aucun art et celi guerpisses,
> Enviers ta nature mesprens.
> (vv. 139–43)

> if you are skillfull and apt
> at some art but abandon it,
> you sin against your very nature.

As a voice in the narrator's head, Philozophie gives expression to readers, imagining what they would say if they knew he was calling it quits. Philozophie's "accusation" is worth quoting at length, both because it is funny, and because it expresses the specific duties of those whom God, or Nature, has endowed with the gifts of poetry.

> Neis, que diroient li signeur
> Dont tu as tant eü dou leur,
> Li roi, li duch et li bon conte,
> Des quels tu ne sces pas le compte,
> Les dames et li chevalier?
> Foi que je doi a saint Valier,
> A mal emploiiet le tenroient
> Et aultres fois il retenroient
> Leurs grans largeces et leurs dons.
> Et de droit ossi li pardons
> Ne t'en deveroit estre fes,
> Quant tu ies nouris et parfés,
> Et si as discretion d'omme,
> Et le science qui se nomme,
> Entre les amoureuses gens
> Et les nobles, li mestiers gens,
> Car tous coers amoureus esgaie,
> Tant en est li oïe gaie.
> Et tu le voes mettre hors voie,
> Si que jamais nuls ne le voie?
> Il ne fait mie a consentir.
> Bien t'en poroies repentir!
> (vv. 147–68)

> And what, indeed, would the lords say
> who gave you so much of what was theirs,
> the kings, the dukes and the good counts,
> whose number you can't even figure,
> the ladies and the knights?
> By the faith I owe Saint Vallier,
> they'd consider it a waste
> and another time would refuse you
> their liberal payments and their gifts.
> And they'd be right, too,
> not to pardon you,
> since you are well brought-up and made,
> and you have the good sense of a man,
> and the knowledge that is called
> among lovers
> and among aristocrats, 'the noble profession,'
> for it makes every amorous heart rejoice,
> such is its hearing gay.
> And you want to push it to the side,
> so that no one can ever know it?
> This is not right at all.
> You could well repent of it!

In much the same way that Deguileville and Machaut use their literary guilt as a clever occasion for new poetry, Froissart imagines himself facing the accusations of readers in order to insist that he be allowed to keep writing. But compared with the texts I have considered by Deguileville and Machaut, Froissart's wittiest riff on the trope of reader accusation is that his poet-narrator is judged first and foremost for ceasing to write, not for the questionable things he has written; surely, he has lots more great poetry to offer the world!

In his humble retirement, the repentant narrator wants nothing of the return to poetry, and much less to the pain and burning desire of young love. The first time that Philozophie suggests he begin writing again, he tells her in no uncertain terms that he is not interested:[55]

Pour Dieu, laissiés moi reposer!	For God's sake, leave me in peace!
Vous dittes que bons jours m'ajourne	You wish me good day
Et qu'en grant aise je sejourne:	and that I be in great comfort.
Je le vous acorde. Atant, pes!	Okay, you've got it. Now enough, be quiet!
(vv. 218–21)	

Nevertheless, Philozophie persists and continues to argue that poetry is the narrator's true purpose as a created being:

Se Diex vosist, il t'euïst fet	Had God wanted, he would have made you
Un laboureur grant et parfet	a great and powerful laborer
A une contenance estragne	with a strange face
Ou un bateur en une gragne	or a thresher in a granary
Un maçon ou un aultre ouvrier	or a mason or another such manual worker,
Je na'i cure quel manouvrier.	I don't care what kind.
Et il t'a donné le science	He gave you the know-how
De quoi tu poes par conscience	through which you can in good conscience
Loer Dieu et servir le monde.	praise God and serve the world.
(vv. 179–87)	

In its emphasis on the poet as a specific member of the estates with specific duties to perform unto God and man, Philozophie's diatribe evokes Guillaume le Clerc's thirteenth-century poem *Le besant de Dieu,* discussed in the introduction.[56] In *Besant,* the poet affirms that his rhetorical talents have a God-given purpose which he must fulfill—the saving of souls—and that he must repent for the "vaine matire" (*Besant,* v. 82) of his past, namely his "romanz, / fablels e contes" (*Besant,* vv. 80–81) with no spiritual value.

---

55. Freeman ("A Farewell to Poetry?" 237) does note that the narrator is reluctant to return to love poetry, but in my view does not adequately address how this starting point complicates the "farewell" gesture at the end of the poem.

56. See above, 17–18.

Once again, however, Philozophie's is an accusation that weighs more on the author's failure to continue writing than on sins committed in his earlier work. Not only, claims Philozophie, have (vernacular) poets been necessary to record the gallant deeds of heroes like Tristan, Perceval and Arthur (vv. 405–13), but the narrator is not all that different from the Doctors and Evangelists whose writings founded the Church itself (vv. 414–21). Philozophie is remarkably irreverent in that, while she affirms the narrator may be able to "loer Dieu et servir le monde" (v. 187) with poetry, she seems to disregard any traditional distinction between moralizing verse and the sort of "vaine matire" of which Guillaume le Clerc repents to begin his *Besant*.[57] Philozophie moves without pause between the writers of romance and the Fathers of the Church. Are praising God and serving the world united for the narrator, then, as they might be in the ministry of a parish priest, or are they two separate and contradictory activities? Does the world (*monde*) refer to the readership of worldly poetry, or perhaps to the flock of souls for whom Froissart is now personally responsible? If Machaut's corpus is distinguished by diversity of form and opinion, Philozophie seems to suggest that Froissart's narrator should not be afraid of founding his own authority on a body of work in which erotic and religious compositions are freely mixed.

To an even greater degree than in Philozophie's treatment of the estates, Froissart recalls Guillaume le Clerc's *Besant de Dieu* in his repeated use of monetary language.[58] Guillaume's eponymous *besant* is the coin, or *talent*, of Matthew 25, the specific spiritual capital that God has given to each human being to invest, and of which God will make a thorough accounting at the Judgment. Like Guillaume, Froissart is clear that his own spiritual capital is the ability to write well. But, as is one of the poet's trademarks, Froissart makes his accounting much more about the literal money he received for writing, and the responsibilities it entails. Philozophie demands that the narrator recite the names of those who supported his work over the years. He obliges, and, in a lengthy passage (vv. 230–373), enumerates Froissart's many real-life benefactors, including Philippa de Hainaut, Blanche of Lancaster, King Charles V of France and King David II of Scotland, as well as Froissart's beloved patron and sometime

---

57. On the irreverence of this version of Dame Philozophie, see Douglas Kelly, "Imitation, Metamorphosis, and Froissart's Use of the Exemplary *Modus tractandi*," in Maddox and Sturm-Maddox, eds., *Froissart Across the Genres*. 112.

58. Likewise, he recalls *La repentance Rutebeuf* by struggling with the problem of receiving financial gains for vain writing. See above, Introduction, 19.

poetic collaborator Wenceslas I,[59] who had recently helped to secure the poet's new benefice at Estinnes-au-Mont. The list of patrons reads like a ledger book in which the narrator notes the specific sums he received for his work: among other entries, one hundred florins from King Edward III of England (v. 261), "chevaus et florins sans compte" (v. 275) from Lord Edouard Spencer, fistfuls of florins more from Enguerrand VII, "li bons sire de Couchi" (vv. 279–81), twenty gold florins from the Count of Savoy (v. 343), and forty ducats from Lord Tiercelés de le Bare (vv. 360–62).

Accusing the converted narrator of ingratitude for the generous support shown his writing, Philozophie insists that these literal sums of money have their ethical weight just as much as the parabolic capital he received from God. The narrator is thus in a bind: if his previous work is sinful and to be left in the past without further explanation, as he wishes, is he not guilty for bilking his readers, giving them poetry that is not only valueless but perhaps spiritually destructive? On the other hand, if this is not the case, as Philozophie suggests, then isn't the poet's silence an affront to God, Nature and the Reader alike? Inserted into Froissart's literary testament, the financial relationship of poet and patron threatens to frustrate the narrator's desire for a quiet retirement during which he can concentrate on the betterment of his soul. In this way, Mars and the Sun—both emblematic of money—are not fully eclipsed by Jupiter, but also contained within the Jovian perspective. If Froissart is to make it up to God and claim a new spiritual authority, he must remain aware of what he owes human beings.

Froissart further underlines the need to reconcile the demands of his generous audience with the demands of religion when, at the beginning of his litany of patrons, his narrator refers to the late Philippa of Hainaut, Queen of England, as having "made and created him" ("Car elle me fist et crea," v. 237). This statement implicitly conflates the generous gifts of the patron and her crucial role in literary creation with the poetic abilities Froissart received from the ultimate Creator, insisting on the problem of divided loyalties: to whom is the poet most immediately accountable for his talents, and how can he possibly do justice to both God and the reader? In a similar way to Machaut's *Jugement* poems, then, *Buisson* and the *Bush* poems in general are about the author's need to resolve the conflicting judgments of various patrons over time and throughout the evolving corpus. The difference is that Froissart's newest patrons are God, the Church and the Virgin Mary, not the infamous Charles de Navarre. But like Machaut's *JRN*,

---

59. In *Prison amoureuse*, a number of lyric poems may have been written by Wenceslas, while lyrics appended to Froissart's *Meliador* are explicitly attributed to him.

Buisson does not suggest an easy answer to the conflict. Even when Froissart's narrator thinks he has achieved a more perfect perspective, renouncing his vain works for a pious self-judgment, the voice of the readership and the presence of his earlier writing continue to haunt him.

As he recites the long list of patrons—some of whom are registered as deceased—the narrator is moved to reflect on the fleeting nature of human life ("Mes temps s'en fuit ensi qu'uns ombres," v. 376) and again asks Philozophie to just leave him alone so that he can think about more important matters than love poetry:

Si vous suppli, tres chiere dame,	So I beg you, very dear lady,
Laissiés moi dont penser pour l'ame.	just let me be to think upon my soul.
J'ai eü moult de vainne glore,	I have had much vainglory.
S'est bien heure de che tamps clore	Now it is truly time to put an end to this age
Et de criier a Dieu merchi,	and to ask the forgiveness of God,
Qui m'a amené jusqu'a chi.	who has brought me thus far.
(vv. 385–90)	

In a sense, Philozophie's visitation of the narrator is a reversal of the more traditional narrative of sudden eschatological awareness (*memento mori*): it does not interrupt the pursuit of vanity with thoughts of man's last end, but rather interrupts the narrator's attempts to think about his last end with the "accusation" on behalf of those for whom the narrator had written worldly poetry, which he now dismisses as "vainne glore" (v. 387). The effect of this reversal cannot simply be reduced to parody, because Philozophie's glib accusation nevertheless emphasizes the reality of the author's debts to the audience. Retiring from the world is too easy a solution, in that it neglects the extent to which the author's responsibility to other human beings is also his responsibility to God. In a similar way to the unexpected entrance of Dame Bonneurté in Machaut's *JRN*, the voice of Philozophie complicates the eschatological judgment by demanding that the audience be given its due. As in *JRN*, God emerges as the *tiers* between author and patron, summoning him to trial just when he least expects it.

Little by little, the reluctant narrator is won over by the entreaties of Philozophie, the imagined, collective voice of the readership. But since he is now an older man removed from the passions of youth and beginning his life as a priest, he fails to see what more he can possibly write. He asks Philozophie "Que porai je de nouvel dire?" ("What new can I say?" v. 433) and, in order to protest that he is *no longer* the same person famous among the great courts of Europe for his exercise of "li mestiers gens" ("the noble profession," v. 160), he proceeds to recite the titles of Froissart's *dits,* as well as the lyric forms he had once excelled in:

Voirs est q'un livret fis jadis	It's true that once I wrote a book
Qu'on dist *l'Amoureus Paradis*	they call *Le paradis amoureux*
Et ossi celi del *Orloge,*	and also *L'orloge amoureuse,*
Ou grant part del art d'Amours loge;	which contains much of the art of love;
Apriés, *l'Espinette amoureuse,*	after that, *L'espinette amoureuse,*
Qui n'est pas al oÿr ireuse;	which is not so rough on the ear;
Et puis *l'Amoureuse Prison,*	and then *La prison amoureuse,*
Qu'en pluiseurs places bien prise on,	that people in many places really like,
Rondiaus, balades, virelais,	also *rondeaux, balades, virelais,*
Grant fuison de dis et de lais;	and a whole lot of *dits* and *lais*;
Mais j'estoie lors pour le tamps	but then, because of the time,
Toutes nouveletés sentans	I felt completely fresh and new,
Et avoie prest a le main	and I had ready to hand
A toute heure, au soir et au main,	at every moment, day and night,
Matere pour ce dire et faire.	the material to do and say such things.
Or voi je cangié mon afaire	Now I see my business changed
En aultre ordenance nouvelle.	into a new order of things.
(vv. 443–59)	

Now that he has remembered his earlier patrons, it is only right that the narrator recall and honor the poems he wrote in exchange for their money, gifts and hospitality. Froissart's is a literary testament in the fullest sense: not only does it make public the private spiritual accounting of the moribund person, it also gives a thorough accounting of the compiled corpus, to which *Buisson* itself is added. As in Guillaume's protest to Bonneurté in *JRN,* this work of re-collection is at once a gesture of distancing and a gesture of recuperation that insists upon the value of past poems for their audiences.

In response to the narrator's protests of irreversible writer's block, Philozophie encourages him to look back on his earlier writing to find inspiration and continuity with the present:

Et adonques me renouvelle	And thus Philozophie brought back to me
Philozophie un haut penser	a sublime thought,
Et dist, 'Il te couvient penser	and said, 'You must think

Au temps passé et a tes oevres	about the time past and about your works—
Et voel que sus cesti tu oeuvres.'	this is what I want you to work on.'
(vv. 460–64)	

Philozophie's words here recall Bonneurté's accusation in Machaut's *JRN* ("Si resgardes dedens vos livres," *JRN*, v. 869) as well as Saint Michael's pronouncement that Deguileville's pilgrim should respond for his *ouvrages* (*PA*, v. 1121). For Philozophie, as for Bonneurté and Saint Michael, the poet's body of work ("tes oevres," v. 463) also happens to constitute the weightiest body of evidence for or against his soul. The corpus requires the author's continued answerability to God and man, which makes rewriting his most important and difficult labor ("tu oeuvres," v. 464).

To inspire the narrator, Philozophie asks him to take out of storage a portrait he had once commissioned of his "droite dame" (v. 485), the young lady of *Espinette*. The narrator retrieves the beautifully rendered image from the box in which he had kept it hidden for many years and, immediately upon seeing the young lady's face, he is taken back to vivid memories of the time over two decades earlier when he first wrote for her. Then, he is inspired to compose the first lyric insertion of *Buisson*, a *virelay* (vv. 563–91). As the narrator puts it, the spark was reignited in him (vv. 620–24), enrapturing him once again with young love and its poetry.

After she has convinced the narrator to reread his corpus, Philozophie vanishes. Again, the narrator oscillates between his desire to return to the past and his desire to renounce that past. In fact, it is at this point that he makes a first, lengthy meditation on the Last Judgment, just as terrifyingly vivid as the imagined eschatological scene at the end of *Buisson*:

La n'i ara nullui couvert	There no one shall be covered
De kamoukas ne de velus;	with fine silk or velour;
Sains Jehans, sains Mars et sains Lus	Saint John, Saint Mark, Saint Luke
Et sains Mahieus droit la seront,	and Saint Matthew will be right there
Qui leurs buisines sonneront	and will sound their trumpets
Dont ressusciteront li mort.	which will cause the dead to rise up.
Vechi pour nous .I. grant remort,	Let this be for us a great warning,
Car cascuns rara sa char propre.	for each will have his own flesh again.
La n'ara pité nul opprobre	There will be no pity for sin,
Ne signourie point d'arroi,	nor will rank have any meaning,
Mes vera on le puissant Roi	but we will see the great Lord
Rendre sa crueuse sentense:	render his frightening sentence:

Je tramble tous quant bien g'i pense.	I shake all over when I think about it.
(vv. 805–17)[60]	

It is unclear whether this is the voice of the fully mature (Jovian) narrator speaking from after his dream as he writes his testament or the voice of the still-hesitating narrator speaking before the dream.[61] In either case, the sudden interruption of the Judgment into an episode of nostalgia for youthful love further accentuates the oscillation of renunciation and writing, between the judgment of the reader and the judgment of God. Froissart continues to build a mood of eschatological expectation into his text, all the while conflating the immanence of divine judgment with the voice of a dissatisfied audience demanding its money's worth.

After his dialog with Philozophie, the narrator's internal conflict is heightened as his dream vision begins and another of the poet's benefactors returns to visit the narrator and accuse him of ingratitude. This is none other than Venus, the goddess whose service the narrator entered long ago when he judged in her favor beneath the hawthorn bush. Seeing Venus again, he is moved to praise her for giving him "very precious gifts" ("don moult riche," v. 890); the goddess, then, is also an important patron. But the narrator's gratitude soon fades, and he proceeds to complain at length about the rejection and pain he experienced in Venus's employ, finally blurting out his long-suppressed anger at the goddess and her ilk:

Siques je di que tout vo sort	So that I say about all your kind,
Ne me sont que confusions	that they are nothing but trouble to me
Et tres grandes abusions.	and are very great delusions.
(vv. 921–23)[62]	

In response, Venus scolds the narrator for blaming her unfairly and for being ungrateful (vv. 924–48). Then, like Philozophie, she encourages him to look back on his past, borrowing from the language of penitential introspection:

Te souvient il de le saison	Do you remember the time
Pour quoi a laidengier m'acoelles?	for which you now begin to badmouth me?

---

60. This is an excerpt of the full passage (vv. 802–37).
61. On the temporal ambiguity of this passage, see Kay, "'Le moment de conclure,'" 164–65.
62. This outburst might be compared to Deguileville's pilgrim's rejection of Venus in *PVH2* (vv. 8765–66). See above, Chapter 2, 79.

Je t'en pri que tu le recoelles	I pray that you recollect it
Et ton coer bien en examines	and that you examine your heart thoroughly
Et jusques au droit fons le mines.	and search it to its very core.
(vv. 949–53)	

Also like Philozophie, Venus complicates the narrator's initial repentance by suggesting that he is in error for rejecting love poetry out of hand. In order to prove her point, she leads the narrator to the giant hawthorn bush of the poem's title, where he meets Jonece. In the bush, the narrator replays his disastrous attempts to woo the young lady and, awakening from his dream some four thousand verses later, realizes that the return to spring and youth was an illusion, another bad judgment caused by reading too much love poetry. This sudden shock of mortality causes the narrator to reflect on his impending Judgment and, once again, to reject Venus—seemingly for good this time. Thinking about his dream, the narrator even returns to his concern with economic motifs, by designating sin as a merciless money-lender:

Pour ce me vodrai retrenchier	So I wish to renounce
Que d'acroire a un tel crenchier	borrowing from such a creditor
Que pechiés est, qui tout poet perdre:	as sin, who can make me lose everything:
Je ne m'i doi ne voel aherdre.	I should not, nor do I, wish to attach myself to it. |//
(vv. 5174–77)	

With the Judgment hanging over his head, the narrator reconsiders his personal book of accounts, attempting to declare his worldly debts null and void so that he can repay his supreme creditor.

But as dramatic as it is, the Last Judgment that Froissart's narrator makes on his poetry is only one part of a much more complex internal struggle between the narrator's perceived duties to readers (and Venus) and his perceived duties to God. That it serves to close *Buisson*, and to end Froissart's career as a writer of *dits*, should not blind us to the fact that this Last Judgment reveals Froissart's double ethical impulse, in which the author's debt to his audience is acknowledged as much as his debt to God—or, indeed, as an inalienable part of his debt to God, which must somehow be squared with the imperative to put away childish things now that he has reached the Jovian age. As I show in the next section, Froissart used the closing lay of *Buisson* in order to reclaim earlier writing for the benefit of audiences, finally reconciling his duty to indulgent readers—and his debt to Venus—with his duty to God.

IV. Recollection and Redemption in Froissart's "Lay de Nostre Dame"

In Chapter 1, I considered how Marian poets called upon the lawyerly Virgin (Advocata Nostra) to represent human subjects in a new light, a trope Guillaume de Deguileville (Chapter 2) then transferred to the author's defense of his earlier poetry and his ability to rewrite himself at will. Froissart owed much to French Marian poetry. In particular, the *souhetz* composed by the personifications at the end of *Buisson*'s dream vision are evocative of the confraternal tradition of devotion made famous by the *puys* of northern France. Froissart, in fact, competed successfully at the *puys* of Abbeville, Lille, Valenciennes and probably Tournai; his master Machaut had been involved in the same circuit of competitions.[63] Even before the sobering conclusion of the narrator's dream in *JBJ*, some of the *souhetz* already resemble the prayer-poems of the confraternal feasts, as their desire drifts away from earthly love and continuous springtime—the illusory universe of courtly poetry—and toward the Christian promise of eternal life. The personification Douls Samblant, for example, makes reference to the Judgment as he composes his wish for ever-lasting youth, love and poetry, just before the personifications ask the narrator to present their *souhetz* to the Dieu d'Amours for judgment:

En cel estat, non pas .I. an entier,	In this state, not one year only,
Mais jusqu'a dont que Diex pour nous jugier	but until that time when God, to judge us,
Vorra cha jus ses signes envoieer,	will send his signs down into this world.
Peüissons nous ensi soalsciier	May we thus rejoice
En l'eage que nous ariens plus chier!	in the age that we all hold dearest!
(vv. 4921–25)	

Even as he expresses the desire that young love last forever, Douls Samblant acknowledges its impermanence, and his awareness of the Judgment to be made on all poetry by the true God of Love. In turn, this nod to the devotional tradition signals a change in Froissart's conception of authority—it marks a transition from the rhetoric of earthly love to the divine rhetoric of prayer that has become the poet's highest calling.

---

63. See Gros, *Le poème du puy marial*, 84–97. See also Cerquiglini-Toulet, *La couleur de la mélancholie*, 10–11. Freeman ("A Farewell to Poetry?" 242) notes that the *souhetz* evoke the poetry of the *confréries*. Froissart wrote in Picard French, the original language of the *puys*.

In his devotional turn, Froissart also drew inspiration directly from Machaut, whose large corpus of lyrics to the Virgin had helped to define much of the preceding tradition of fixed-form poetry in French, and whose polyphonic *Messe de Nostre Dame* (c. 1365) had changed the shape of the liturgy itself.[64] In *Buisson*, Froissart's narrator appears to reference Machaut's devotional side at the very moment when he himself turns to Mary: it is a certain "motet nouviel" from Reims (vv. 5075–76) that *Buisson*'s narrator sings in the very last moments of his dream, on his way to present his poem to the judgment of the Dieu d'Amours, who begins as Cupid but becomes Christ after the narrator has awakened. Ending the dream, this allusion to the Marian motets of Guillaume de Machaut, canon at Reims, provides Froissart with a kind of symbolic transition point between human and divine judgment, and profane and religious expressions of love, in which he can situate his literal and figurative awakening to a higher authority on poetry.[65] Thus, just as he had identified his earlier self with Machaut's chaotic judgments and his praise of Venus, so does Froissart's narrator identify his awakened, Jovian self with Machaut's more spiritually mature compositions. In this way, Froissart makes a stronger Machauldian homage than ever, by suggesting that Machaut's own ability to surpass earthly poetry for celestial subjects had inspired his own.

By requesting the Virgin's advocacy at the Judgment, like so many of his predecessors, Froissart was also signaling the traditional role of Advocata Nostra as a proponent of creative interpretation, whose ability to transform personal narratives and texts was closely tied to her capacity for obtaining mercy. As in *Pierre le changeur* or Deguileville's *Pèlerinage de l'âme,* the appeal of Froissart's narrator to the lawyerly Virgin stages the reinterpretation, and thus revalorization, of his own personal narrative, and by implication, of Froissart's own corpus.

The "Lay de Nostre Dame," the closing eschatological meditation and Marian prayer of *Buisson,* serves to reevaluate and ultimately redeem Froissart's earlier poetry as part of a Christian narrative. In the lay, references to earlier moments in the *Bush* poems are frequent. For example, while in both *Espinette* and in *Buisson*'s dream vision the narrator suffers from the intense burning of erotic desire, the lay transforms this sensation into the

---

64. See Daniel Leech-Wilkinson, *Machaut's Mass: An Introduction.* Oxford: Clarendon, 1990.

65. See Sylvia Huot, "Reading Across Genres: Froissart's *Joli buisson de Jonece* and Machaut's Motets." *French Studies* 57.1 (2003): 1–10. Huot argues that the motet, "a hybrid genre juxtaposing erotic and devotional registers, has a dramatic effect on the denouement of Froissart's last *dit amoureux*" (2) and marks "the point at which erotic fantasies give way to penitential meditation" (9). On the motet from Reims, see also Lechat, *'Dire par fiction,'* 321.

torments of hell ("ardant painne," v. 5202) from which only the Virgin's intercessory power can save sinners; the lover's fire also becomes the holy flame ("ce saint feu," v. 5191; "li feus plaisans," v. 5408) that Christ ignites in the hearts of the faithful. Similarly, the narrator's identification in *Espinette* of erotic love as the root ("rachine," v. 83) of goodness becomes instead "la rachine jesse" (v. 5396), which is to say the Virgin as announced in Old Testament prophecy. The ever-expanding *buisson*, too, undergoes one last metamorphosis; it is no longer the site of nostalgia for young love or even Ptolemy's cosmos, but now the burning bush ("Buissons resplendissans," v. 5402) that spoke to Moses, which the narrator cites as yet another Old Testament prefiguration of the Virgin (vv. 5374–77, vv. 5402-6).[66]

The images of the root of Jesse and the burning bush are particularly good examples of a textual continuum between erotic and spiritual desire, rather than a rupture between them, because these images suggest that the bush of *Espinette* figuratively grows into the *Buisson* and ultimately into the burning bush of the lay. While Froissart gestures toward the poet's teleological ascent to divine truth, he also reasserts the presence of the root which cannot be cut out without killing the mature being—the corpus and the Christian subject. The original judgment of the hawthorn bush, the choice of Venus, is revalidated in the narrator's Last Judgment. Venus finally proves that she is not to blame after all, but rather has been an important step in the narrator's development—a teacher, just as Jonece claimed her to be in his description of the ages of man (vv. 1637–45). Likewise, the young lady's ambiguous judgment near the end of the dream, that loyal service is always rewarded in the end (vv. 4556–60), comes to fruition: the end transforms and authorizes what has come before it and justifies the poet-lover's tribulation, which has not in the last accounting come to nothing. Not only has the narrator not wasted his youth with unrequited longing, damned himself, or squandered his master's capital, but he will be rewarded, because his desire to serve God was there all along—for those who know how to interpret his earlier poetry.

In Christian understanding, the Last Judgment is not only the time for revealing individual moral worth, but also for finally unveiling the full significance of Scripture to all mankind. For Froissart's narrator, the imagined Last Judgment is likewise as much a spiritual fulfillment of the author's youthful writing as a pronouncement of his guilt or innocence. As Alice Planche has noted, the ultimate model for the work that the "Lay de

---

66. On this motif, see Mâle, *L'art religieux du XIIIe siècle en France,* 148; Huot, *From Song to Book,* 321. Kelly ("Imitation, Metamorphosis," 113) uses the example of the burning bush to highlight *Buisson*'s emphasis on the poet's transformative powers.

Nostre Dame" performs on Froissart's profane poetry is scriptural allegoresis, which reinterprets the narrator's earthly desire as the beginning of his ascent toward higher things, and as a foretelling of his new calling:

> À en croire la fin, les brûlures de l'amour et l'image de la Dame sont répudiées et exorcisés. Pourtant elles apparaissent au lecteur comme d'obscures annonces, comme des essais et des promesses: un avant, et un Avent [. . .] On accepte mal que les aspects sensuels en soient récusés, sans cicatrice et sans nostalgie, dans un mouvement manichéïste.[67]

> To believe the end [of *Buisson*], the flames of love and the image of the Lady are rejected and exorcised. And yet they appear to the reader as obscure portents, as a past time [*avant*] that is also an Advent [. . .] One accepts with difficulty that the sensual aspects are banished [from the text], without scars and without nostalgia, in a Manichean movement.

As Planche's description suggests, Froissart drew close parallels between his own work and Scripture. Throughout the "Lay de Nostre Dame," the narrator insists upon the way Old Testament prophecy announces the Virgin and the birth of Christ:

Anchiennement	Long ago
Par mainte gent	by many people
Et justement	and justly
Selonc l'Anchiien Testament,	according to the Old Testament,
Estoit prophetisiet et dit	had been prophecied and announced
L'avenement	the coming
Dou saint Advent.	of Christ's holy birth.
(vv. 5230–36)	

Et ceste oevre auctorisie	And this authorized work
Estoit un grant temps devant	was, a great time before
Apparant,	made clear,
Demonstree et prononchie	demonstrated and pronounced
Par Ysaïe,	by Isaiah,
Et Jheremie,	by Jeremiah,
Par David et par Helie.	by David and by Elijah.
(vv. 5252–58)	

---

67. Alice Planche, "Du *Joli buisson de Jeunesse* au *buisson ardent*: le Lai de Notre Dame dans le *dit* de Froissart," in *La prière au Moyen Âge: littérature et civilisation*. Paris: Champion, 1981. 411.

The narrator symbolically associates his youthful poetry of profane love with the prophecy of the Old Testament and with its typological events, now fulfilled in Froissart's new "testament," the symbolic last accounting of *Buisson*. Cleverly, Froissart suggests that the verses he wrote while in Venus's service also contain higher truth which should not be left out of his corpus, since they prepared him for Christian devotion, and since they prefigure that devotion for readers of Froissart's complete poetic works.

In this sense, the lay also appears to fulfill Philozophie's earlier affirmation in *Buisson*, that the narrator might become a participant in the same spiritual work as the Evangelists and Doctors, even through his worldly poetry.[68] As Philozophie puts it in her accusation, he can "Loer Dieu et servir le monde" (v. 187) all at the same time. Through its insistence on allegorical reading and creative reinterpretation, Froissart's "Lay de Nostre Dame" not only defends Froissart's earlier poetry but upholds its value for readers. By reevaluating the texts into which they have invested time and money as newly worthy of Christian contemplation, *Buisson*'s Last Judgment asserts that the audience may turn back to the author's earlier work without being scandalized or feeling cheated.

By instructing his audience on just how to interpret his writing, Froissart the priest also makes the ethics of reading part of his evangelical message. Curiously, in the "Lay de Nostre Dame," the narrator directly addresses the "Jewish law" (and later simply "Jew" ["Juïs," v. 5380]) in the second person singular; it is this hearer whom he exhorts to repent before it is too late:

Par virtu noble et divine,	By noble and divine power,
Lois juïse, or adevine	oh Jewish Law, now think
Comment et par quel doctrine	how and by what teaching
Chils qui le monde enlumine,	he who illuminates the world,
Couchiés ou monument digne,	couched in his worthy monument,
Ressuscita dou tombiel.	rose again from the tomb.
(vv. 5302–7)	

Given his repeated insistence on the allegorical sense of Scripture and, by extension, of his own past poetry, it is my belief that Froissart's addressee should likewise not be understood only in the literal or historical sense, as the Israelites and their descendants.[69] Instead, the apostrophe to the Jewish

---

68. Planche ("*Buisson ardent*," 397) notes Froissart's self-comparison to the Doctors of the Church.

69. This sense, whereby "Jewish law" signifies simply "the Jews," has been the traditional reading of the passage beginning with Auguste Scheler: "*Lois juïse* (vocatif) doit se traduire par: 'peuple

law may be taken in the typological sense in which it represents a pharisaical adherence to the strict letter of the text. In my discussions of the Devil's Rights tradition and Deguileville's *Pèlerinage de l'âme*, I have suggested how this sort of literalism, characterized as both Hebraic and Satanic in representations of eschatological judgment, could also be used to depict certain bad readers of poetic texts, those unable to correctly interpret allegory or to accept the author's ability to rewrite himself. Sternly placing the same sort of undesirable audience member before the seat of Judgment, Froissart's narrator suggests that the ethics of literature are reciprocal—that while the author has a duty not to mislead or swindle readers, they in turn must be careful not to misjudge his good intentions (even if the author himself was unaware of them at the time). Accordingly, the two halves of Froissart's poetic personality should be read together as complements, just as the Old and New Testaments complement each other in Christian teaching:

Dont, entroes	So while
Que bien tu te poes	you still can
Et as loisir dou retourner,	and have time to turn back,
Si t'esmoes	rouse yourself
Et ton coer promoes	and press your heart
Au justement considerer	to consider carefully
Quel conquoes	all the ways that
Li Viels ou li Noes	the Old and the New
Testamens te puet pourfiter.	Testaments can profit you.
(vv. 5354–62)	

Taken as an exegetical model to be applied to Froissart's own erotic poetry, the insistence on the essential complementarity of the historical and figurative senses of Scripture demands that the palinode be read, like the advent of the New Law, as both transformation and fulfillment. In this gesture, however, the historical reality of past events is also upheld. Just as it is necessary for Moses's encounter with the burning bush to be both a literal occurrence and a prefiguration of Mary, so too is it necessary for Froissart's erotic longing to have really existed, and to be preserved in the record of the corpus, in order for its allegorical sense to be fulfilled.[70]

qui vis sous la loi judaïque'" (Jean Froissart, *Œuvres de Froissart: poésies. Ed. Auguste Scheler*. 3 vols. Brusells: V. Devaux et cie, 1870–72. II: n157). The interpretation is echoed by Fourrier in his edition of *Buisson* (264 n) and by Marylène Possamai-Perez in her modern French edition (*Le joli buisson de Jeunesse. Ed. and trans. Marylène Possamai-Perez*. Traductions des Classiques Français du Moyen Âge 57. Paris: Champion, 1995. 122 n184).

70. In Erich Auerbach's understanding of the terms, Froissart's scriptural poetics would be less allegorical as such and closer to Auerbach's conception of *figura*, which he considered the domi-

In this creative mode of interpretive judgment, even Jupiter—Froissart's astrological emblem of divine certainty in judgment—is subject to more than one meaning. For Ovid and Petrarch, the god had represented the very inconstancy of the lover's identity as he underwent the metamorphoses of desire.[71] Even in the *Ovide moralisé*, which Froissart knew well, Jupiter is not only allegorized as the Christian God, but also left intact as the lascivious pagan deity who is always changing his shape in order to effect sexual conquest. In a similar way, the narrator's own belonging to the age of Jupiter can and should be read as double—for it includes both a continued attachment to sexual desire and a higher judgment which transforms that desire, retroactively, into a prefiguration. The past stays where it is in the corpus, as allegorical portent and real presence.[72]

---

nant exegetical mode of the Middle Ages: something real and historical that announces something else real and historical and whose reality does not diminish when the thing it announces comes to fruition (Auerbach, "Figura," in *Scenes from the Drama of European Literature*. Trans. Ralph Manheim. Gloucester, MA: Peter Smith, 1973. 11–76). See also Jesse M. Gellrich, "*Figura*, Allegory, and the Question of History," in *Literary History and the Challenge of Philology: The Legacy of Erich Auerbach*. Ed. Seth Lerer. Stanford, CA: Stanford University Press, 1996. 107–23; Minnis, *Medieval Theory of Authorship*, 88.

71. Froissart's Ovidian poetics have been much discussed, including Froissart's tendency to radically rewrite Ovid, or to simply invent pseudo-Ovidian material, and his tendency, like Petrarch, to use Ovid's metamorphoses as a means of figuring his own transformations as an author and a poetic subject. On these points, see Douglas Kelly, "Les inventions ovidiennes de Froissart: réflexions intertextuelles comme imagination." *Littérature* 41 (February 1981): 82–92; Kelly, "Imitation, Metamorphosis"; Kelly, *Medieval Imagination*, 156–59; Audrey Graham, "Froissart's Use of Classical Allusion in His Poems." *Medium Aevum* 32 (1963): 24–33; Picherit, "Le rôle des éléments mythologiques"; Huot, *From Song to Book*, 319–22; Kevin Brownlee, "Ovide et le moi poétique à la fin du Moyen Âge français: Jean Froissart et Christine de Pizan," in *Modernité au Moyen Âge: le défi du passé*. Ed. Brigitte Cazelles, Charles Méla. Geneva: Droz, 1990. 153–73; Bernard Ribémont, "Froissart, le mythe et la marguerite." *Revue des langues romanes* 94.1 (1990): 129–37; Ribémont, "Froissart et le myth de Daphné." *Revue des langues romanes* 98.1 (1994): 189–99; Sarah Kay, "Mémoire et imagination dans le *Joli buisson de Jonece* de Jean Froissart: fiction, philosophie et poétique." *Francofonia* 23.45 (2003 Autumn): 177–95; Geri L. Smith, "Froissart's Téléphe: A Revealing Link Between Ovidian Invention, the 'Pastourelles,' and the Poet's Persona." *Fifteenth Century Studies* 29 (2004): 200–9; Lechat, '*Dire par fiction*,' 262–64, 340–43; Bennett, "The Mirage of Fiction," 296. Patricia Berrahou Phillippy argues that Petrarch's palinode rewrites the conversion scenario of Augustine's *Confessions*, in which the subject makes a definitive break with a sinful past of erotic desire. Instead of such a singular, Augustinian turning point, as Phillippy puts it, Petrarch privileges a model of "Ovidian conversion" which charts the subject's existence through a potentially endless series of metamorphoses (*Love's Remedies: Recantation and Renaissance Lyric Poetry*. Lewisburg, PA: Bucknell University Press, 1995. 62, 72). On Petrarch's use of Jupiter, see also Sturm-Maddox, "*La pianta più gradita in cielo*: Petrarch's Laurel and Jove," in *Dante, Petrarch, Boccaccio: Studies in the Italian Trecento in Honor of Charles S. Singleton*. Ed. Aldo S. Bernardo, Anthony L. Pellegrini. Binghamton, NY: Medieval and Renaissance Texts and Studies, 1983. 255–71, especially 259–61. On Froissart's probable familiarity with Petrarch, see Huot, *From Song to Book*, 309; Huot, "The Daisy and the Laurel: Myths of Desire and Creativity in the Poetry of Jean Froissart." *Yale French Studies Special Edition: Contexts: Style and Values in Medieval Art and Literature* (1991): 245; De Looze, ed., *Prison amoureuse*, xiii.

72. See, again, Auerbach, "Figura" and above in this chapter, n70.

At least, such is the judgment that the narrator seeks in his request that Mary, his ultimate reader and patron, defend him—in the heavenly court on the Last Day, and in the court of reader opinion. As in so much Marian poetry, Froissart's Virgin signals the triumph of the New Law, and its power to both rewrite and fulfill the Old:

Sains Jehans au doi	What does Saint John
Nous enseigne quoi?	point to for our instruction?
Ton Fil, qui pour nous volt morir,	That your Son, who wished to die for us,
No Nouvelle Loi	confirmed by his death
Confrema par soi,	our New Law
Quant homs mortels volt devenir.	when he agreed to become man.
(vv. 5224–29)	

Directing readers toward a new understanding of Froissart's earlier poetry, the closing palinode of *Buisson* is more optimistic than it initially seems in regard to the possibility that more language will serve in the poet's defense. In *Buisson*'s Judgment scene, the poem's central question, which the narrator asks Philozophie before his dream—"Que porai je de nouvel dire?" (v. 433)—is transformed into the troubling question of the "Lay de Nostre Dame," borrowed by Froissart from the *Dies irae* hymn: "Que diras?" (v. 5333). But the poet's greatest hope—that something new really can be said in his cause—is fulfilled precisely as he completes a rewriting of his past.

Froissart's rewriting is not only a response to the new imperative to impart spiritual truth to readers, but also to the audience's demand for enjoyment—our desire to get our money's worth, as expressed before the narrator's dream vision by Dame Philozophie.[73] Froissart's Last Judgment on himself authorizes our appreciation of the play of meanings in his poetry, the contradictory desires of the subject over the course of time. It thus symbolically holds the poetic corpus together as a complete package, unifying the writing subject as a moral being and his book as a discrete unit of economic exchange which, like the Old and New Testaments, should be read as a whole. A good Christian reader might well take a lesson from the narrator's renunciation of inordinate sexual desire; but as a reader one is also invited by the same palinodic gesture to begin all over again, to return like Froissart's narrator to earlier poetry and to the pangs and thrills of young love, to enjoy the intimately human spectacle of an individual

---

73. On the author's and reader's enjoyment of the text, see Schira Schwam-Baird, "Sweet Dreams: The Pursuit of Youthful Love in Jean Froissart's *Joli buisson de Jonece* and René d'Anjou's *Livre du cuer d'amours espris.*" *Moyen Français* 38 (1996): 56.

struggling with conflicting judgments over time, and the dramatic evolution of a great artist in the course of his career.[74]

Significantly, both of Froissart's extant poetic manuscripts end not with *Buisson*, but with the short *Plaidoirie de la rose et de la violette*, a legal debate between two flowers—the Rose and the Violet—about which of the two is more beloved.[75] After the flowers' respective advocates have pleaded their cases before Imagination, they agree to submit them to the judgment of the Fleur de Lis, who resides in the "noble royaume de France" (v. 306). It would be difficult to find a more light-hearted, typically courtly, and even Machauldian representation of judgment as this.[76] While Froissart never wrote another *dit* after *Buisson*, he did not completely abandon the jovial and uncertain judgments of courtly debate poetry, which he had both lampooned and celebrated in *Espinette* and *Buisson*.

Like the prologue to Machaut's *Jugement dou roy de Navarre*, then, Froissart's "Lay de Nostre Dame" hardly represents a final judgment. Instead, it evokes a much less definitive kind of eschatological trial—the continuous ordeal to which the poet is subject as, in the face of a dissatisfied audience, he recognizes the presence of the divine judge. Like Machaut, Froissart used an eschatological *mise en scène* not to bolster his claims to absolute truth, but to suggest that the poet's judgment must be constantly answerable to the perspectives of the readership. It is this answerability which, even in the rarified air of the Jovian perspective, guarantees that the poet will never be finished reinventing himself. But it is this answerability which, tying the author to his work, also founds his authority.

While *Buisson* makes an eloquent plea for regarding Froissart's courtly and religious sides as part of the same whole, it is important to remember that, unlike Machaut's corpus, Froissart's body of work was physically fragmented, since *Meliador* and the *Chroniques* are compiled separately from each other and from the lyric poetry and *dits*. This apparent disunity is actually a testament to the strength and variety of Froissart's output, since

---

74. This *double geste* is similar to Petrarch's Marian palinode in *Rime sparse* 366, which Froissart may have known (see above, n71). On the double nature of Petrarch's palinode, see Phillippy, *Love's Remedies: Recantation and Renaissance Lyric Poetry*, 61–91.

75. See Scheler's edition, in *Œuvres de Froissart: poésies*, II: 235–45. In ms. BNF fr. 830, *Buisson* is followed by *Le dit dou florin* and then *La plaidoirie*. In BNF fr. 831, *Buisson* is followed directly by *La plaidoirie*. It bears noting that *Buisson* does not follow directly upon *Espinette* in either manuscript. In BNF fr. 830 the two poems are separated by the collections of *ballades*, *virelais* and *rondeaux*. In BNF fr. 831, the same intervening poems are present, as well as *La prison amoureuse*, the *lais amoureus*, the *pastourelles*, and the *chançons royaus amoureuses et serventoys de Nostre Dame*.

76. Anthime Fourrier (ed., *'Dits' et 'Débats,'* 67–68) has pointed to Machaut's *Dit de la fleur de lis et de la marguerite* as a likely source for this poem.

the three sections of his work are too large to realistically be contained within a single codex. Yet the conflict between courtly and religious registers in *Buisson* also refers, less directly, to the generic break represented by *Meliador* and especially the *Chroniques*. The decision to leave off writing love poetry was not, after all, followed by a sustained burst of religious composition. Rather, the turn toward historical writing was far more consequential for Froissart's career and legacy, and this new direction is also referenced, however obliquely, by the same apocalyptic crisis which puts the earlier love poetry into question.

Although I have focused here primarily on the tension between the courtly and the devotional in Froissart's verse, it is interesting to note that, as in Machaut's *JRN*, we also see Froissart in *Buisson* at the crossroads of the courtly and historical modes. And like Machaut, we see Froissart struggling with the problem of how to reconcile the poet's historical existence with that of the pseudo-autobiographical persona constructed through first-person narrative and single-author compilation. In the end, Froissart seems to have solved this problem in a different way than his master: in the *Chroniques*, Froissart transformed the historical genre itself into a highly subjective medium told through the first-person reporting of the author.[77] This subject, no longer a poetic persona but a prose documentarian, switches the central focus of his narrative from the collaborative production of verse to the collaborative production of historical meaning. Instead of travelling the land to dash off lyric compositions for rich patrons and disdainful young ladies, Froissart the chronicler now shows himself travelling the land to gather and weigh testimony from a wide variety of interlocutors.[78] This becomes the raw material for the author who uses his faculties of judgment to reshape it into his own version of history. It is thus, of course, a heavily biased version of history, and one particularly favorable to the England of Froissart's beloved patroness Philippa de Hainaut and her husband King Edward III. Yet, unlike *JRN*'s prologue (partly inspired by Froissart's most important chronicle source, Jean le Bel), there is no pretense to a Last Judgment or a last word on history here. Rather, as in the *Bush* poems, the *œuvre* reveals itself as an endless renegotiation of truth by the author, his sources, and his audiences. This work does not establish an objective version of events—no more than Machaut's trial before Charles de Navarre results in a "certein jugement." Instead, it

---

77. This tendency is particularly evident beginning with Book 3 of Froissart's *Chroniques*. See Sarah Kay, Terence Cave, and Malcolm Bowie, *A Short History of French Literature*. Oxford: Oxford University Press, 2003. 81.

78. See Ibid., 81, for a similar comparison of the *dit* form to Froissart's *Chroniques*.

constantly gestures toward its own subjectivity, insisting on the ethical primacy of the particular judgments made by individual subjects at individual moments in time.[79]

In the generation after Machaut, Froissart the poet and historian is indicative of an increasingly bold expression of vernacular literary authority throughout Europe, and of the increasingly sophisticated practices of patronage and compilation upon which that authority depends. As a later fourteenth-century example of the poet facing Judgment, Froissart's work is especially representative of the growing prominence of single-author compilation—still a novelty in Machaut's day—and, more generally, of the book as a consumer object in high demand.

Yet if Froissart belonged to a moment in time that allowed him to claim his authority with greater confidence, the later fourteenth century also posed a different kind of ethical challenge for the author, relative to his involvement in new systems of economic exchange. In the wake of the Black Death—Machaut's moment of crisis in *JRN*—a large-scale trend of urban reconcentration was under way, bringing with it a greater circulation of capital. While Machaut always depicts himself writing in the service of patrons, the monetary compensation he received from them is rarely, if ever, shown in the text. In contrast, although Froissart represents his favorite readers as a relatively small and elite group, the poet's fascination with a monetized economy speaks to his awareness that his audience was growing, and that he himself had become a kind of commodity on the marketplace. What is more, although money is integrated into the patron-poet relationship, in Froissart's work it also threatens to destabilize that relationship, by shattering its feudal foundations and replacing them with a much wider system of circulation in which any reader might participate on equal terms. As the issue of monetary gain is reflected in the poet's scene of Judgment, it shows to what extent the later fourteenth-century author's value was no longer simply a function of his skillful use of spiritual capital—like Guillaume le Clerc's *besant*—but tied to an increasingly specialized conception of professional authorship with its own distinct problems to work out.

In the next and final chapter, I conclude by suggesting that, in the generations after Froissart, such changing ideas of poetic vocation and poetic authority eventually distanced later poets from the kind of eschatological *mise en scène* that I have described as a feature of fourteenth-century

---

79. Paul J. Archambault has argued that the subjective, ever-shifting perspective of the *Chroniques* may have been influenced by Froissart's encounters with Ockhamist thought ("Froissart and the Ockhamist Movement: Philosophy and its Impact on Historiography." *Symposium* 28.3 [Fall 1974]: 197–211).

French poetry. In particular, the fifteenth and sixteenth centuries would see a new emphasis on the primacy of individual expertise, and on the subjective judgment of the author, as against the objection of critical readers or the voice of prior authority. This development, heralded in part by deeply self-reflective authors like Froissart, drew fifteenth- and sixteenth-century poets away from the anxious ethical dialog of the fourteenth-century *scène judiciaire*. Instead of a deferential and at times self-abasing model of apologetics, later poets would come to privilege a different kind of legal scene, in which their authority to make judgments—and not the audience's—sits in closest proximity to the divine.

CONCLUSION

In Lieu of a Last Judgment
Beyond the Fourteenth Century

In the thirteenth century, vernacular poets began to shape detailed poetic personae around an acute awareness of the Judgment, evoking the great and terrible reckoning in order to mark the renunciation of earlier poetry and to call audiences to repentance. At the same time, some of these poets blended vernacular composition, legal rhetoric, and prayer into a new model of poetic authority and subjectivity. Devotional poets began to suggest that their rhetorical work made them special subjects in regard to divine judgment: within the larger process of intercession, their lyric pleas could have an exceptional effect, moving the heavenly court to mercy and, perhaps, to a new interpretation of the facts weighing for and against human beings.

With the fourteenth century came an unprecedented rise to prominence of vernacular authors, and a new set of anxieties regarding the nature of literary authority, the ethical responsibilities of the writer, and the transmission of texts. More than their thirteenth-century forerunners, fourteenth-century poets used the obligatory eschatological meditation of the period to explore the uncharted territory of vernacular literary fame, and the problems inherent to writing in the first person and releasing texts into circulation as a unitary corpus. These authors made themselves answerable to a readerly God and a divine Reader, highlighting the infinite responsibility of their calling, but also using the singular forum of the Judgment to participate in dialog with the readership, to speak in self-defense and to advocate for a continual renegotiation of meaning. They created a unique expression of that master-trope described by Mathieu-Castellani as "la scène judiciaire de l'autobiographie," in which God is the invisible Third Party (*tiers*) between the poet and his public.[1]

This use of the Judgment as a site of ethical encounter between author and audience surpassed any neat distinction between religious and secular poetry. While the spiritual allegorist Guillaume de Deguileville put himself into the defendant's seat of the heavenly court in order to make a sharp rejoinder to his ecclesiastical critics, Guillaume de Machaut suggested that the same overlap between divine and human judgment of the literary work could extend to the poetry of courtly love, and to the otherwise worldly relationship of author and patron. As he depicted his own crisis of conscience, Machaut's disciple Jean Froissart continued to blur the boundaries between the poet's duties to God and to man; in so doing, he created new reflections on the nascent capitalistic structures of poetic production and the ethical problems of writing for earthly gain.

Furthermore, all three of the major fourteenth-century authors I have considered represented divine judgment as an ongoing *procès* rather than a singular and definitive event. One risks overlooking much that is properly "eschatological" in medieval representation if one limits the term to judgments after death. To understand medieval eschatology in general, it is essential to remember that divine judgment was perceived not only as one of the "Last Things" in a chronological sense, but as the immediate scrutiny facing the sinner through his dealings with others. The terrible awareness of this Judgment effectively brought the sinner beyond time, to the *eschatos* (last or furthermost point) even as he continued to live. If, in the later Middle Ages, God's judgment was no longer made explicitly manifest through judicial ordeals,[2] its presence continued to be felt in the most mundane of settings, including in the sphere of literary production and the interpretive work carried out together by author and reader. Even Guillaume de Deguileville, enacting a traditional scene of the post-mortem judgment of the soul, strongly reminded readers that the trial we are to experience upon departing this life has already begun. For Machaut and Froissart, likewise,

---

1. Mathieu-Castellani, *La scène judiciaire*, 60–61.
2. Judicial ordeals were effectively abolished in 1215, when the Fourth Lateran Council forbade clerical participation in them. However, as Esther Cohen argues, their spirit lived on in the very same legal system that replaced them: "Just as human prowess was evidence of the truth in the duel, human verbal dexterity was an audible proof of the same. The abolition of ordeals in no way excluded supernatural justice from human courts, for even an honest mistake could carry the same meanings and consequences as the loss of a trial by battle" (*The Crossroads of Justice*, 67).

the Last Judgment is but a culmination of the ongoing trials of human relationships. This is why it bears repeating that the eschatological *scène judiciaire* does not stand in allegorically for the continual dialog of author and audience, but rather exposes itself as the logical extension of that dialog.

As they echoed contemporary theological and devotional emphases on the immanence of Judgment, fourteenth-century poets also showed an awareness of the unending task of reinterpretation and rewriting to which they were summoned by the readership. For Deguileville, Machaut and Froissart, this *procès* could only be performed ethically if the poet resisted the impulse to deal in absolute truths. In the tumultuous later medieval environment of material book production, violent politics, competing legal systems, religious and social conflict, and changing tastes, the poet could not reasonably hope to found his authority on the Last Word. Instead, the eschatologically expectant labor of rewriting one's personal book of accounts (*correctio*)[3] was a necessity at once spiritual, ethical, and artistic. As for Machaut in his *Jugements,* the act of the author changing his mind became less an occasional poetics of repentance (what J. C. Payen has called a "poésie personnelle de la conversion et de la pénitence"[4]) as a recognition that literature must entail a continual transformation of the writing subject, through his answerability to the reading Other. For all three of the major poets I have considered, divine judgment symbolically enacts this submission to the inscrutable opinions of the audience, acknowledging the reader's seminal collaborative role in literary creation.

In using eschatological motifs to frame acts of reading and writing, authors like Deguileville, Machaut and Froissart thus also produced important meditations on the complex and varying nature of human judgment. One must be careful, nevertheless, not to overstate the value which fourteenth-century authors placed on human judgment per se. If the reader could stand in for God, it was not because he or she shared in divine powers of discernment, but because his or her reception of the literary work—as flawed or as unpredictable as it might be—entailed ethical consequences for its author in the next world. The instability of human judgment complicated the imagined scene of divine reckoning immeasurably without, however, proclaiming the autonomy of reader reception. As Deguileville in particular reminds us, the reader has his own responsibilities, with their own immediate consequences in the next world.[5]

---

3. On the allegorical aspect of *correctio,* see above, Introduction, 21–22; and see, again, Huot, "The Writer's Mirror;" Shimomura, *Odd Bodies,* 39–84.

4. Payen, *Le Motif du Repentir,* 589.

5. See above, Chapter 2, especially 80–84, 97–98.

While fourteenth-century readers were not shown making judgments in complete independence from God, fourteenth-century authors assigned themselves still less autonomy in their own judgments. If the readership assumed an aspect of the godly, it was precisely because it was understood as wholly other, an unpredictable and at times spectral entity whose judgments called the author outside of himself, putting his very existence into question. The abject and apologetic posture of the accused relies on his deferral of authority to somebody else, the one who summons him to respond for what he has written and determines his guilt or innocence. In that the judgments of the audience are responsible for making the author an author and the book a book, the writing subject cannot exist outside of the reception—favorable or unfavorable—of his work. It is for this reason that authors as different as Dante, Deguileville and Machaut all name themselves for the first time in their texts as they recount readers' accusations against them. Standing trial is a necessary undertaking for the poet, who cannot be entered into the *Liber vitae* until the audience has given its consent. While he makes judgments, then, the fourteenth-century author is not primarily a judge, but most of all a defendant compelled to represent himself. It is in the very act of standing trial—rather than through any conclusive judgment produced by that trial—that the fourteenth-century poet assumes his authority and his identity as a subject.

Although I would like to avoid strict periodizations, I have focused especially on the French fourteenth century because it offers an especially rich viewpoint on a unique convergence of phenomena, namely the concomitant development of a strong, pseudo-autobiographical *poésie personnelle* and of a culture saturated with a sense of eschatological immanence. Together, these factors helped to produce an expression of authorial subjectivity and divine judgment which was unique to its time and place.

Fifteenth-century French literature does include texts which use eschatological meditations to frame the persona of the author, such as Jean Regnier's *Fortunes et adversitez* (c. 1430s),[6] the *Temps perdu* and *Temps retrouvé* of Pierre Chastellain (mid-1400s),[7] and especially François Villon's *Lais* (1456) and *Testament* (1461–62).[8] But in the course of the fifteenth

---

6. Jean Regnier, *Les fortunes et adversitez de Jean Régnier.* Ed. Eugénie Droz. Paris: Champion, 1923.

7. Pierre Chastellain, *Les Œuvres de Pierre Chastellain et de Vaillant, poètes du XVe siècle.* Ed. Robert Deschaux. Geneva: Droz, 1982.

8. In François Villon, *Poésies complètes.* Ed. Claude Thiry. Paris: Librairie Générale Française, 1991. 59–253. The most comprehensive work on conscience and judgment in Villon is Odette Petit-Morphy, *François Villon et la scolastique.* 2 vols. Diss. Université de Lille III, 1977. Paris: Champion, 1977. On divine judgment in Villon, see also Eglal Doss-Quinby, "La composition numérique du *Testament* de Villon ou la symbolique du jugement." *Fifteenth-Century Studies* 12 (1987): 131–44.

and sixteenth centuries, the portrayal of human judgment underwent a sea change. Thinkers and artists increasingly privileged reason, subjective opinion, and their own personal experience, in the gradual elaboration of humanism in its broadest possible sense. It is with the beginnings of this turn toward individual human deliberation that my study reaches its end. For while the roots of modern literary subjectivity can be situated, in part, in the pseudo-autobiographical poetics of the later Middle Ages, the cultivation of a more strictly autobiographical perspective coincided with the turn toward individual reasoning justly regarded as a distinguishing feature of the early modern period. And while humanist and enlightenment thought did not banish the divine presence from literature or empty literary ethics of their Judeo-Christian heritage, they nevertheless treated human judgment as an increasingly free-standing category deserving of its own attention. The growing emphasis on, and valorization of, human judgment had a profound impact on literary subjectivity. No longer was the posture of the author—especially the vernacular author—quite so tied to the rhetoric of self-defense.[9] No longer was judgment on the author's work endlessly deferred to an imperious readership who assumed qualities of the divine. Instead, the author's own judgments began to take priority.

A supreme fifteenth-century example of this early humanist trend can be found in Christine de Pizan (1364–c. 1430), whose prolific and erudite body of work included political and philosophical writings, lyric poetry, prose narratives, and *dits* in the vein of Machaut and Froissart. Venetian born, Christine came to Paris with her father, Thomas de Pizan, the court doctor and astrologer of Charles V. In the 1390s, following the deaths of her father and husband, Christine made the decision—bold for someone in her late twenties and almost unthinkable for a medieval woman—to reinvent herself as an author. She succeeded, gaining important royal patronage and becoming one of the first truly professional writers in the European vernacular—a status born of the do-or-die economic necessity in which she found herself as a widow.

As Douglas Kelly has demonstrated, Christine represents "a new emphasis in late medieval French literature" on human opinion and its formation through personal, autobiographical experience.[10] In one of Christine's most enduring works, the prose *Livre de la cité des dames* (1405), this difference

---

9. For another important instance of self-defense used to justify first-person vernacular poetics, see Dante, *Convivio* 1.2.

10. Douglas Kelly, *Christine de Pizan's Changing Opinion: A Quest for Certainty in the Midst of Chaos*. Cambridge: D. S. Brewer, 2007. vii. On Christine's privileging of personal experience, see also Mary Anne C. Case, "Christine de Pizan and the Authority of Experience," in *Christine de Pizan and the Categories of Difference*. Ed. Marilynn Desmond. Minneapolis: University of Minnesota Press, 1998. 71–87.

can be clearly seen through a distinct new take on the scene of eschatological judgment.[11] As *Cité* begins, Christine despairs of the countless negative judgments made against women by male authors over the centuries. Crying out to heaven, she pleads to know how it can be that women, created by God, are as imperfect as alleged:

> Ne formas tu toy mesmes tres singulierement femme et dés lors lui donnas toutes teles inclinacions qu'il te plaisoit qu'elle eust? Et comment pourroit ce estre que tu y eusses en riens failli? Et toutevoys voycy tant de si grandes accusacions, voire toute jugees, determinees et concluses contre elles. Je ne scay entendre ceste repugnance. (1.1)

> Did you not yourself create woman quite uniquely and from the moment of her creation give her all of the tendencies that it pleased you for her to have? And how could it be that you failed in any respect? Yet here are such heavy accusations, or rather judgments which have now been completely determined and concluded against her. I cannot understand this contradiction.

Christine's very Jobian demand for an explanation is quickly answered as God sends three messengers to her—the virtues Raison, Droitture (Rectitude) and Justice. As Raison explains, Christine is able to communicate directly with these celestial forces because of her exceptional dedication to the truth:

> Car quoyque nous ne soyons pas communes en plusieurs lieux et que nostre congnoissance ne viengne a toutes gens, neantmoins toy, pour la grant amour que tu as a l'inquisicion de choses vrayes par lonc et continuel estude [. . .] tu as desservi et dessers estre de nous (1.3)

> For although we are not common in many places and although knowledge of us does not come to everybody, you nevertheless, for the great love that you have for the uncovering of true things through long and diligent study [. . .], have deserved and continue to deserve to be one of us.

According to Raison, "la providence de Dieu" established the three virtues in the world "affin de mettre en ordre et tenir en equité les establissemens fais par nous mesmes selon le vouloir de Dieu en divers offices" ("to put

---

11. I cite from the edition of *Le livre de la cité des dames* by Eric Hicks and Thérèse Moreau. Série Moyen Age. Paris: Stock, 1986.

into order and keep in equity what we have established here in diverse [human] offices, according to the will of God," 1.3).[12] Among the "divers offices" to which Raison refers is that of the author, fulfilled by Christine, who makes judgments in the confidence that her opinion is well-formed. She is not God, but she operates on the special authority he has given her to decide difficult ethical matters.[13]

Because Christine's deliberative faculty has attained a divine standard of truth, the virtues tell her that she must not fear the deafening majority opinion of venerable authors like Matheolus, Ovid, Cecco d'Ascoli, Cato of Utica, and Jean de Meun, who have all spoken ill of her fellow women. Instead, she must trust her own judgment and what she knows from experience in order to determine the moral worth of women and to defend their reputation. This she does by constructing the *Livre* itself, from whose pages rises a brand new *Cité* filled with the virtuous women of history. It is an eschatological city, since it is based directly on the Augustinian *Civitas Dei,* the same destination that Guillaume de Deguileville has in view in his *Pèlerinages*. By using her own God-given reasoning to determine exactly who among women deserves to inhabit the heavenly metropolis, Christine assumes a privileged knowledge of divine judgment. Similarly to Augustine, for whom the earthly and divine cities "are mixed together and confused in this world until the Last Judgment will separate them,"[14] the task that Christine assigns herself is making the heavenly city appear as clearly as possible *now,* before the End, separating it from the visible world which has obscured it for so long.[15] Nevertheless, Christine implicitly includes Augustine in the large group of male authors whom she defies, by fundamentally transforming his monumental vision of heaven, which had contained precious few women.[16]

12. This rhetoric of the poet's divine connection is quite prevalent in *Cité*. For example, Droiture characterizes herself as Christine's "advocate ou ciel" (1.5).

13. As Kelly points out (*Changing Opinion,* 1–2), Christine distinguished among different kinds of certainty available to human beings, differentiating opinion, the province of literature, from religious faith and *certainne science.* Nevertheless, as the character Dame Oppinion teaches Christine in *Le livre de l'advision Cristine* (1405), opinion is the mother of all human knowledge apart from that revealed directly through Scripture, and is thus an essential force in the world. Indeed, it has helped Christine to attain the same level of understanding as "clercs ou religieux" (*Le livre de l'advision Cristine.* Ed. Christine Reno, Liliane Dulac. Paris: Champion, 2001. 2.22.27).

14. *De civitate Dei* 1.35.

15. For Augustine, as for Christine, this included the task of unveiling the sacred from the lies of poetry (*De civitate Dei* 2.10).

16. As Mary Agnes Edsall writes, "Just as the universal 'he' and 'men' excludes women, so Christine's use of women to epitomize the city of God excludes men. This exclusion is also a critique; for if women constitute the city of God, the corresponding city of men—in this case all men—is in the rule of the devil" ("Like Wise Master Builders: Jean Gerson's Ecclesiology, *Lectio Divina,* and

Much like Deguileville, Christine thus used a traditional *mise en scène* of eschatological judgment—the city of God—in order to address an ethical problem of literature, namely, the endless library of misogynistic texts unjustly weighing on the proverbial left side of the scales against womankind. And as for Deguileville, rewriting such a traditional eschatological scene was for Christine an act of defensive rhetoric—on behalf of women everywhere, and on behalf of her own outspoken audacity as a female writer.[17] But this *scène judiciaire* is quite unlike the anxious self-defenses of Christine's fourteenth-century counterparts, because it highlights the artist's own sovereign authority in making judgments, her independence from outside opinion.

Christine's self-assuredness is precisely what makes her such a striking herald of Renaissance sensibilities. In contrast to her precursors, Christine does not plead for her soul before either God or the reader, but shows herself making eloquent and radical judgments against thousands of years of established precedent. She is less *rhetor divinus* than *iudex divinus*. Indeed, the narrative of *Cité* is best understood as the author's journey to divine truth, as it proceeds from the vicious self-doubt expressed during Christine's initial lamentation (1.1) to the confident application of her God-given powers of discernment.

The fifteenth century was, of course, hardly devoid of social anxiety, and was marked more deeply by religious uncertainties than the preceding centuries. The Papal Schism (1378–1418) divided the western Church among two, and then three, popes. The Hussite movement, which only intensified after Jan Hus's execution for heresy in 1415, openly challenged ecclesiastical authority, laying the groundwork for the Protestant Reformation. The Hussites, and before them the Wycliffites, brought controversial questions about vernacular authority and reader participation to a new kind of text entirely—the translated Bible.

The increased focus on personal opinion-formation has partly to do with such tendencies toward reform, but it can also be ascribed to efforts by those within the Church to calm the chaos of a fragmented Christianity. Jean Gerson, the Chancellor of the University of Paris and a collaborator with Christine de Pizan in her polemic against the *Roman de la Rose*, was particularly concerned with the problem of the Schism, and with the unnecessary scruples suffered by the millions of Christians who could not

---

Christine de Pizan's *Livre de la cité des dames*." *Medievalia et Humanistica* 27 [2000]: 40). One notable exception to Augustine's heavy reliance on male figures is the sibyl Erythrea (*De civitate Dei* 14.23), whom Christine also places in her *Cité* (2.2).

17. See Edsall, "Like Wise Master Builders," 46.

determine with absolute certainty which pope held pontifical authority.[18] To relieve such excess scrupulosity, as Rudolf Schüssler has shown, Gerson developed a new category of moral certainty (*certitudo moralis*) designed to lessen the burden on individuals making judgments in ethical situations without a clear solution.[19] While for Gerson supernatural certainty is infallible and natural certainty based on mathematical proof, moral certainty does not admit of such absolute truth; instead, it leaves more latitude to the individual subject's ability to discern the ethical from the unethical using reason and experience rather than received authority.

Christine's own vision of human judgment presents striking parallels with Gerson's. Christine consistently opposed human opinion to both "certainne science" and religious faith, which she often called *loy*.[20] This division of certainties corresponds closely to Gerson's separation of supernatural, natural (mathematical) and moral certainties. And as for Gerson's *certitudo moralis*, Christine set aside specific ethical domains in which the exercise of opinion is best suited because of the unavailability of absolute certainty. As is clear from *Cité*, which opposes one woman's judgment to centuries of misogynistic opinion, literature is one such place where individual opinion must be cultivated instead of received authority.[21] But while it does not allow for supernatural certainty, Christine nevertheless shows literature to be supernatural, by revealing the Judgment already at work behind the ethical *procès* of author and audience, in a similar way to Machaut, Deguileville, and Froissart. The difference, once again, is that prior to the final Judgment and the certainty it provides, it is the author herself—and not the readership—who is best suited to fill the place of divine proxy.

---

18. See, again, McWebb, ed., *Debating the Roman de la Rose*. For more on Gerson, see Hobbins, *Authorship and Publicity Before Print;* Brian Patrick McGuire, *Jean Gerson and the Last Medieval Reformation*. University Park, PA: Penn State University Press, 2005. Gerson's influence on Christine has been a major focus of criticism. See, for example, Edsall, "Like Wise Master Builders"; Lori J. Walters, "Gerson and Christine, Poets," in *Poetry, Knowledge and Community in Late Medieval France*. Ed. Rebecca Dixon, Finn E. Sinclair, with Adrian Armstrong, Sylvia Huot, Sarah Kay. Woodbridge, Suffolk, UK: DS Brewer, 2008. 69–81; Earl Jeffrey Richards, "Christine de Pizan and Jean Gerson: An Intellectual Friendship," in *Christine de Pizan 2000: Studies on Christine de Pizan in Honour of Angus J. Kennedy*. Ed. John Campbell, Nadia Margolis. Amsterdam: Rodopi, 2000. 197–208.

19. Rudolf Schüssler, "Jean Gerson, Moral Certainty and the Renaissance of Ancient Scepticism." *Renaissance Studies* 23.4 (2009): 445–62.

20. Kelly, *Changing Opinion*, 1–2. Kelly (*Changing Opinion*, 1, 31–32) notes that Christine uses the word opinion much more than her opponents in the *Rose* debate and that only she uses it positively.

21. To take another example, in *L'advision Cristine*, the personification Oppinion lays claim to all poetic invention, including Christine's own work (2.4.5-6, 2.21.25-29).

After Christine's work, as Kelly rightly notes, no French text is more emblematic of the growing emphasis on individual experience and subjective opinion than Montaigne's *Essais* (c. 1570–1592), themselves shaped by the deep uncertainties of the French Wars of Religion.[22] The jurisconsult Montaigne never stopped putting his own judgments into question,[23] but he used his constantly shifting perspective as a new approach for investigating reality and ethics. In "Du Repentir," one of the most revealing of the *Essais,* Montaigne describes his book as consubstantial with himself, a fluid portrait of individual life in which author and text are one and the same object of readers' judgment:[24] "Icy, nous allons conformément et tout d'un trein, mon livre et moy. Ailleurs, on peut recommander et accuser l'ouvrage à part de l'ouvrier; icy, non: qui touche l'un, touche l'autre. Celuy qui en jugera sans le connoistre, se fera plus de tort qu'à moy; celui qui l'aura conneu, m'a du tout satisfaict."[25] ("Here we go hand in hand together, my book and I. Elsewhere, one may praise or accuse the work separately from the worker; here, it is not so: he who touches one, touches the other. He who will judge the work without knowing the worker, will do to himself more injustice than to me; he who will have known the worker, will have satisfied me in every way.")

In Montaigne's book can be found traces of the fourteenth-century idea of the corpus, which, modeled upon the *Liber vitae,* provides a precise moral and ontological record of the individual author. For Montaigne, as for Machaut and Froissart, repentance loses most of its relevance because the subject is bound to judge and act according to the circumstances in which he finds himself at each moment in life, in each part of the book: "Lors que je consulte des deportements de ma jeunesse avec ma vieillesse, je trouve que je les ay communement conduits avec ordre, selon moy; c'est

---

22. Kelly, *Changing Opinion,* 170. Kelly goes on to contrast Christine with Montaigne by emphasizing that her use of personal experience and opinion are always balanced by faith ("She may have doubts, but she is not a sceptic" [Ibid., 170]). See also Kelly's comparisons of Christine to Rabelais (Ibid., 4) and to Rousseau (Ibid., 179). In a similar vein, Reno and Dulac (eds., *Advision,* xvi–xvii) have compared Christine's treatment of opinion to Erasmus's *In Praise of Folly.*

23. On Montaigne's relationship to the law, see, for example Richard L. Regosin, "Rusing with the Law: Montaigne and the Ethics of Uncertainty." *L'ésprit créateur* 46.1 (Spring 2006): 51–63; André Tournon, "Justice and the Law: On the Reverse Side of the *Essays,*" in *The Cambridge Companion to Montaigne.* Ed. Ullrich Langer. Cambridge: Cambridge University Press, 2005. 96–117; Ian Maclean, "The Place of Interpretation: Montaigne and Humanist Jurists on Words, Intention and Meaning," in *Neo-Latin and Vernacular in Renaissance France.* Ed. Graham Castor, Terence Cave. Oxford: Clarendon, 1984. 252–72.

24. "Du Repentir," in Michel de Montaigne, *Essais.* Ed. Pierre Villey, Verdun L. Saulnier. Paris: Quadrige-Presses Universitaires de France, 2004. 804–17. See also Riley, *Character and Conversion,* 21, 61–73.

25. Montaigne, *Essais,* ed. Villey-Saulnier, 806.

tout ce que peut ma resistance. Je ne me flatte pas: à circonstances pareilles, je seroy tousjours tel."[26] ("When I compare the deeds of my youth with my old age, I find that I have done them both with order, according to me; that is all my resistance is capable of. I do not flatter myself: in similar circumstances, I would always be the same.") Montaigne's *Essais,* much like Deguileville's *Pèlerinages,* Machaut's book, or Froissart's poetic corpus, embrace the change of opinions over time as ethically and creatively necessary. Yet the catalyst for change comes increasingly from within the subject, because the judgment of the other—God and the Readership—does not cast such a long shadow. The reader is asked to judge the work carefully, following the same model of subjective reasoning furnished by the author, who constantly expresses doubts about what he knows. Nevertheless, Montaigne's most important trial is much more internal than the great *scènes judiciaires* of the fourteenth century: it takes place according to his laws and in his courtroom: "J'ay mes loix et ma court pour juger de moy, et m'y adresse plus qu'ailleurs." ("I have my own laws and my own court to judge myself, and I speak to them more than to elsewhere.")[27]

Much later, in the eighteenth century, Jean-Jacques Rousseau's imagined eschatological scene, at the beginning of his *Confessions,* expresses even more dramatically the autonomy of the authorial subject in making judgments and creating art.[28] Using the same trope employed by Deguileville in his *Pèlerinage de l'âme* and by Peire Cardenal in his "Sirventes novel,"[29] Rousseau imagines himself standing before the throne of God with his text in hand, defending his life and work; but he shows considerably less anxiety about how he and his writing will be judged. Instead, he suggests that the book itself, the product of his own judgments and sentiments, and the record of his singular existence in time, is already his salvation. Even if it contains certain gaps and "ornements," the book is holy because it is wholly *his*—the unadulterated reflection of an individual consciousness claiming liberation from outside influence. Rousseau's version of the classic eschatological scene of literature vividly affirms the independence of the author in his exercise of moral reasoning and aesthetic judgment. As such, the scene stands as a powerful emblem of Enlightenment and pre-Romantic sensibilities of literary selfhood. Now the accusatory reader—Rousseau's Voltaire—is still present in the courtroom, but he no longer exerts an unbending ethical power over the author.

---

26. Ibid., 813.
27. Ibid., 807.
28. See above, Introduction, 1–3.
29. On Peire Cardenal's *sirventes,* see above, Chapter 1, 36–37.

As it announces itself, the literary evolution of the "humanist" or "Cartesian" writing subject might thus be described partly as a lessening of anxiety, in which the subject no longer stakes his claim to authority primarily on the outcome of another's judgment, but rather as a product of his own individually cultivated faculty of reason. However, as Rousseau somewhat ironically shows, and as Mathieu-Castellani's work suggests, the eschatological imagination has only continued to color authorial self-representation; as a literary motif, the Judgment has been as inescapable for the author as it is for the sinner in Christian theology. And even in Rousseau's judicial scene, a certain measure of unease betrays itself behind the subject's claims to self-sufficiency; the inevitable reappearance of the heavenly court reminds us that the roots of the modern, secular subject are solidly anchored to the outward- and upward-looking angst of the earlier tradition.

And as much as we may take for granted the modernity of an autobiographical, autonomous subject, the pseudo-autobiographical, dependent subject of medieval poetry is in many ways strikingly *post*modern. The last century and a half of philosophy has increasingly stressed the concept of alterity, with the result that subjectivity has undergone what can be termed an antihumanist deconstruction. Instead of a preexisting, natural unity, the subject has become an effect of the Other, whether as an ideological construct or as an inherent result of the structures of consciousness. In particular, thinkers like Foucault, Derrida, Lacan, Bourdieu, and Althusser have provided a blueprint for literary understandings of the subject as a response to the perceived authority of others.[30] Althusser's concept of "interpellation" or "hailing," for instance, recalls the fourteenth-century *scène judiciaire,* in that it defines the subject as the one who hears the policeman call, "Hey, you there!" and then turns around.[31] For Althusser, it is only in the gesture of turning around that the subject is born, as it assumes the role that has been assigned to it by intractable forces of social and political ideology. In a similar way, it is the response to readers' accusations that creates the author of fourteenth-century poetry. In both cases, self-representation is a deferral of authority to somebody else, a recognition that subjectivity begins beyond, and prior to, the self.

---

30. See, for example, Sarah Kay's *Subjectivity in Troubadour Poetry,* which approaches the twelfth-century lyric subject from a Lacanian perspective.

31. "Ideology and Ideological State Apparatuses," in *Lenin and Philosophy.* Trans. B. Brewster. New Left Books, 1971. Extracts reprinted in *Literary Theory: An Anthology.* Rev. Edition. Ed. Julie Rivkin, Michael Ryan. Malden, MA: Blackwell, 2001. 294–304. 301.

While Althusser's account of subject-formation is based on various insidious mechanisms of state control, postmodern thought has not completely abandoned the idea that the *I* comes into being as it faces the judgment of heaven. In the work of Emmanuel Levinas (1906–1995), the model of subjectivity as a response to accusation is understood more in terms of metaphysical reality than ideological construct. For Levinas, the "eschatological" refers not to a privileged term in a dichotomy between earthly and heavenly judgment, but to a kind of deliberation which is divine and yet performed through the judgments of human beings, in the ethical *procès* continually taking place between self and Other. My experience of the Other is eschatological in that the Other interrupts my sense of time, calling me to a cataclysmic judgment *now*, at each moment:[32] "Ce n'est pas le jugement dernier qui importe, mais le jugement de tous les instants dans le temps où l'on juge les vivants."[33] ("It is not the Last Judgment which matters, but the judgment of every moment in time when we judge the living.")[34] Levinas's everyday eschatology is not merely analogous to divine judgment or a preliminary apprehension of it. Rather, it is only through the judgment of the human Other that I become the object of divine judgment; it is only through the face of the Other that we may come into proximity with the deity:

> Il ne peut y avoir, séparée de la relation avec les hommes, aucune 'connaissance' de Dieu. Autrui est le lieu même de la vérité métaphysique et indispensable à mon rapport avec Dieu. Il ne joue point le rôle de médiateur.[35]

> There cannot be, separate from human relationships, any 'knowledge' of God. The Other [Autrui] is the very site of metaphysical truth and indispensable to my relationship with God. He does not play the part of mediator.

For Levinas, my responsibility to the Other precedes my own being and being itself; ethics precede ontology. Accordingly, eschatological judgment is not the process of determining the subject's preexisting moral value; the Other's judgment is the very thing through which the subject has any

---

32. On the time of the other as eschatological rather than ontological, see Travis T. Anderson, "Eschatology and Textuality in Levinas." *Literature and Belief* 28.1 (2008): 41–53.
33. *Totalité et infini* (henceforth *TI*), 8.
34. Or "when the living are judged." The impersonal subject *on* creates some difficulty in translation.
35. *TI*, 77.

meaning at all, for it is only in response to accusation that he may speak. The true eschatological judgment is that meeting with the Other in which I defend myself and thus constantly become myself:

> Être jugé ainsi, ne consiste pas à entendre un verdict, s'énonçant impersonnellement et implacablement à partir de principes universels. Une telle voix interromprait le discours direct de l'être soumis au jugement, ferait taire l'apologie, alors que le jugement où se fait entendre la défense, devrait confirmer en vérité la singularité de la volonté qu'il juge.[36]

> To be judged in this way does not consist in hearing a verdict, pronouncing itself impersonally and implacably from universal principles. Such a voice would interrupt the direct speech of the being submitted to judgment, would silence that being's apology,[37] while the judgment where the defense is heard would have to confirm in truth the singularity of the will [of the individual being] that it judges.

Specifically, it is the emergence of the *tiers* (Third Party) in the face of the Other that makes divine judgment manifest and confirms the subject's being: "La présence du visage—l'infini de l'Autre—est dénuement, présence du tiers (c'est-à-dire de toute l'humanité qui nous regarde)"[38] ("The presence of the face—the infinitude of the Other—is an unveiling, the presence of the Third Party, which is to say of all humanity watching us"). While *Autrui* for Levinas is the singular Other who calls me to account—such as the poor and the prisoner—the face of *Autrui* also makes me aware of the *tiers,* or all others in their infinitude of being. The *tiers* deeply complicates the duality of the "I-Thou" relationship in that it clashes with my perceived duties to *Autrui* and reminds me that my responsibility can never be completely assumed, since the Other is infinite. As the subject encounters other Others, judgment never stops, constantly remaking both the law and the subject.

Predicated on radical alterity, eschatological justice does not promise a singular Judgment more perfect than all others, but rather insists on the autonomy of individual judgments made at particular moments in time, by particular subjects. The eschatological is what ends history, but not as

---

36. *TI,* 273. See also Ibid., 276: "Ce jugement de Dieu qui me juge, à la fois me confirme."
37. Levinas's *apologie* should be understood in the fullest sense of the term, as both an act of defense and as a humiliation or abjection before the Other.
38. *TI,* 234.

a *telos* or end-point of human events.³⁹ The final judgment of history—for Levinas, the archetypal Last Judgment—is spoken through a universalizing, impersonal voice, "la troisième personne,"⁴⁰ which negates the subject's interiority.⁴¹ The truly eschatological judgment, however, causes a rupture in the fabric of the historical, in which the Other's summons prompts the subject to speak in its defense *à la première personne,* assuming its particularity: "L'idée eschatologique du jugement [. . .] implique que les êtres ont une identité 'avant' l'éternité, avant l'achèvement de l'histoire, avant que les temps soient révolus, pendant qu'il en est encore temps"⁴² ("The idea of eschatological judgment [. . .] implies that beings have identities 'before' eternity, before the end of history, before the ages [of the world] have all passed, while there is still time"). Thus, the *eschatos* of Levinas's thought refers not to a future point at the end of a universal history, but to the infinite ethical relationship which lies beyond being and time, as revealed now in the Other's accusation.

The insistence on a plurality of judgments, rather than a totalizing Judgment, does not constitute an instance of moral relativism, or of an "indulgence," "which would indicate a flaw in judgment."⁴³ That is because the nature of the trial ensures that the subject's responsibility can never decrease, but only grow:

> L'exaltation de la singularité dans le jugement se produit précisément dans la responsabilité infinie de la volonté que le jugement suscite. Le jugement se porte sur moi dans la mesure où il me somme de répondre. La vérité se fait dans cette réponse à la sommation. La sommation exalte la singularité précisément parce qu'elle s'adresse à une responsabilité infinie. L'infini de la responsabilité ne traduit pas son immensité actuelle, mais un accroissement de la responsabilité, au fur et à mesure qu'elle s'assume; les devoirs s'élargissent au fur et à mesure qu'ils s'accomplissent. Mieux j'accomplis mon devoir, moins j'ai de droits; plus je suis juste et plus je suis coupable.⁴⁴

---

39. On eschatology versus teleology in Levinas, see Graham Ward, "On Time and Salvation: The Eschatology of Emmanuel Levinas," in *Facing the Other: The Ethics of Emmanuel Levinas.* Ed. Seán Hand. Curzon Jewish Philosophy ser. Richmond, Surrey, UK: Curzon, 1996. 153–72, especially 162.
40. *TI,* 271. The *troisième personne* is not to be confused with the *tiers.*
41. Ibid., 272–73.
42. Ibid., 8.
43. "ce qui indiquerait une faille dans le jugement" (Ibid., 273).
44. Ibid., 73–74. See also *Autrement qu'être,* 26–27: "Au fur et à mesure que les responsabilités sont prises, elles se multiplient. [. . .] La dette s'accroît dans la mesure où elle s'acquitte."

The exaltation of singularity in judgment takes place precisely in the infinite responsibility of the individual will that the judgment brings into being. The judgment is brought to bear on me in the measure that it summons me to respond. Truth is produced in this response to the summons. The summons exalts singularity precisely because it addresses itself to an infinite responsibility. The infinitude of this responsibility does not refer to its actual size, but to a constant growth of responsibility, just as it is assumed; duties grow at the very same time as they are fulfilled. The better I accomplish my duty, the fewer rights I have; the more just I am, the guiltier I become.

Because it is not one, but many Others before whom I stand in judgment, my burden grows with each response I make. This impossible situation does not express the futility of the human condition, but rather the necessary striving toward justice which offers the only chance of approaching the divine.

For Levinas, eschatological justice is carried out by means of language, which alone permits the emergence of the *tiers*, transcending[45] the "I-Thou" relationship to include all eventual others and their judgments on the subject: "Le langage, comme présence du visage, n'invite pas à la complicité avec l'être préféré, au 'je-tu' se suffisant et oublieux de l'univers; [. . .] Le tiers me regarde dans les yeux d'autrui—le langage est justice."[46] ("Language, as presence of the face, does not encourage complicity with a favorite being, or with the 'I-thou' relationship, self-sufficient and forgetful of the universe; [. . .] the Third Party watches me in eyes of the Other—language is justice"). Language allows the presence of all others to be glimpsed, calling me to a duty which can never be fulfilled because it is always expanding and changing. The instability of language is thus not a hindrance to justice in Levinas's thought, but rather sets out the infinite parameters toward which justice must strive, ensuring that there can be no end to responsibility in the face of the other.[47]

For Levinas, language is also justice because it allows the subject to speak in self-defense, taking shape as a first-person voice exclusively in its response to the other's accusation: "Il faut que le jugement soit porté sur une volonté qui puisse se défendre dans le jugement et, par son apologie,

---

45. Or, typically for Levinas, *ex*-cending. This lexical particularity allows the philosopher to describe in more precise terms his concept of a departure from ontology.
46. *TI*, 234.
47. On the infinite nature of the subject's responsibility, see especially Ibid., 73–74 and *Autrement qu'être*, 26–27.

être présente à son procès"[48] ("Judgment must be brought to bear on a willing subject who can defend itself in judgment, and through its apology, be present at its trial"). The centrality of language to eschatological judgment in Levinas's thought pertains to writing as well as to speech. This is because, as Ann W. Astell and Justin A. Jackson assert, literature is an ethical endeavor dependent upon "the intersubjective space of the community."[49] The infinite presence of those others who will read the text ensures that its meaning can never be reduced to a "written synthesis—a kind of *nunc stans* from which the whole can be systematically regarded."[50] Instead, writing becomes a perpetual labor of reevaluation and reinterpretation, in which the present act of saying (*le Dire*) incessantly destabilizes what has already been said (*le Dit*).[51]

This redefinition of the eschatological applies particularly well, I think, to the judgment of the readership as it is represented in fourteenth-century scenes of divine judgment. For both Levinas and fourteenth-century poets, the "eschatological" judgment may be characterized not as an event to take place at the end of time, but as a process continually unfolding through all human interactions. As it reveals the presence of an infinite third-party (God, *toute l'humanité*, the shadowy audience of poetry), the accusation of *Autrui* (the poor, the prisoner, the singular reader) also makes the subject aware of himself through the realization of a responsibility he can never completely assume. For the author, this is the duty of responding justly to criticism of his work. As readers and their judgments change over time, so too do the perspectives poets take on their own texts, which they must revise in an interminable process of self-defense and correction. For Deguileville, Machaut and Froissart, as for Levinas, the Last Judgment appears as too simple a solution, because it does not take into account the infinite nature of the responsibility which a community of readers places on the author.

As in the prologue to the *Jugement dou roy de Navarre*, the Last Judgment is revealed to be the work of an impersonal voice which unsuccessfully attempts to impose on human history a definitive "verdict, s'énonçant

---

48. *TI*, 272.
49. Astell and Jackson, eds., in their introduction to *Levinas and Medieval Literature*, 4. Here, the editors are referring specifically to the Bible as its reading was understood by Levinas and medieval thinkers, both Jewish and Christian.
50. Adriaan Peperzak, *To the Other: An Introduction to the Philosophy of Emmanuel Levinas*. West Lafayette, IN: Purdue University Press, 1993. 218.
51. The relationship of the Dit and the Dire is explained in particular detail in *Autrement qu'être*. See also Bernard Waldenfels, "Levinas on the Saying and the Said," in *Addressing Levinas*. Ed. Eric Sean Nelson, Antje Kapust, Kent Still. Evanston, IL: Northwestern University Press, 2005. 86–97.

impersonnellement et implacablement à partir de principes universels."[52] The failure of this conclusive revelation to take place reflects the author's awareness of a different kind of ethical standard, just as for Froissart, the poet's effort to think about his last end is continually frustrated by readers' demands for new writing. Likewise, Deguileville's dream of the particular judgment and his vision of the writer's purgatory stand in stark opposition to the *grans assises* to be held at the end of time. For these three great fourteenth-century authors, at least, it was not the Last Judgment that counted, but "le jugement de tous les instants dans le temps où l'on juge les vivants."[53] Although compilations of their work were conceived in parallel to the comprehensive spiritual accounting of the *Liber vitae*, they did not claim to reflect the changelessness of the eternal book—"a kind of *nunc stans* from which the whole can be systematically regarded."[54] Rather, the fourteenth-century author's corpus was a living book. It was, in the Levinasian sense, a volatile kind of saying (a *Dire* composed of *dits*), not primarily because of a latent culture of orality or a more or less unstable milieu of manuscript transmission, but, more fundamentally, according to a conception of literature as an endless ethical dialog between its producers and its consumers.

At first glance, this vision of the later medieval text might seem contrary to the significant efforts made by all the authors I have studied to exert some degree of control over the production, circulation, and reception of their manuscripts. In Deborah McGrady's formulation, for instance, Machaut's manuscripts are designed precisely for the purpose of "controlling readers," that is, for shaping the reading practices of new lay audiences by instructing them in how to find deeper meaning in secular texts, and in how to regard the authority of the vernacular poet.[55] But for all the authors I have studied, the obsession with complete power over the work is manifestly an impossible desire. Compilation practices and the rhetoric of vernacular authority can only help to persuade the readership to favorable judgment, and they constitute only one half of the *œuvre* as such. The other half is the author's deference to the reader's authority—his fretful submission of the work to a trial process that alone can confirm its value and significance, and which always remains partly inaccessible to him, as if behind the great curtain that separates Deguileville's narrator from his otherworldly opponents and judges.

---

52. *TI*, 273.
53. Ibid., 8.
54. Peperzak, *To the Other*, 218.
55. See, again, McGrady, *Controlling Readers*.

Later medieval authors staged their encounters with the audience as encounters with otherness itself, with the unapprehendable Third Party who is at once God and the reading public. As for Levinas, the imposing *tiers* of fourteenth-century poetry renders justice through language, which simultaneously accuses the subject before all humanity and provides him with the means to defend himself as an individual. In all of its potential for ambiguity and uncertainty, language assures that the author's duty to the infinity of potential readers will never be complete. Language, and in particular, vernacular language, was the root of later medieval poets' palpable anxiety, which is why, for authors like Deguileville, Machaut and Froissart, the Other's command to write more was an onerous penance, or a purgatory, as much as an endorsement of poetic prowess or a generous commission. But as for the devotional poets of northern France who emulated Advocata Nostra, language was also the miraculous instrument of divine judgment in its capacity for mercy—it allowed the medieval literary subject to defend himself and thus constantly to remake himself in response to the summons of the Other. For the medieval author as for Levinas, this was the inherent bind of subjectivity and authority: it is only through its *apologie* to the Other that the subject can be "present at its trial,"[56] only as an uneasy response to what is outside of and prior to itself that the first person takes shape.

---

56. *TI*, 272.

BIBLIOGRAPHY

Editions of Primary Texts

Adam de la Halle, *Œuvres complètes*. Ed. Pierre-Yves Badel. Paris: Livre de Poche, 1995.

Augustine. *Confessiones*. Eds. John Gibb and William Montgomery. New York: Arno, 1979.

———. *De civitate Dei*. Eds. Bernard Dombert and Alphonse Kalb. 2 vols. Stuttgart: Teubner, 1993.

———. *La doctrine chrétienne/De doctrina christiana* (Latin and French). Trans. Madeleine Moreau. Notes by Isabelle Bochet and Goulven Madec. Paris: Institut d'Études Augustiniennes, 1997.

Beaumanoir, Philippe de. *Coutumes de Beauvaisis: Texte critique publié avec une introduction, un glossaire et une table analytique*. Ed. Admédée Salmon. 3 vols. Paris, 1899–1900. Repr. Paris: Picard, 1970–74.

Bernard de Clairvaux. *De conversione ad clericos* (French and Latin). Eds. J. Leclercq, H. Rochais, and Ch. H. Talbot. Introduction, translation, and notes by Françoise Callerot, Jürgen Miethke, Christiane Jaquinod. Paris: Cerf, 2000.

Biblia Sacra juxta vulgatam versionem. Ed. R. Weber, et al. 2nd ed. Stuttgart: Deutsche Bibelgesellschaft, 1983.

Boccaccio, Giovanni. *Decameron*. Ed. Cesare Segre, with commentary by Maria Segre Consigli. Milan: Mursia, 1966.

Cardenal, Pierre. *Poésies complètes du troubadour Peire Cardenal (1180–1278): Texte, traduction, commentaire, analyse des travaux antérieurs, lexique*. Ed. and trans. René Lavaud. Toulouse: Privat, 1957.

Chastellain, Pierre, and Pierre de Vaillant. *Les Œuvres de Pierre Chastellain et de Vaillant, poètes du XVe siècle*. Ed. Robert Deschaux. Geneva: Droz, 1982.

Chaucer, Geoffrey. *Canterbury Tales*. Ed. A. C. Cawley, with an introduction by Derek Pearsall. Everyman's Library. New York: Alfred A. Knopf, 1992.

---. *The Legend of Good Women*. Eds. Janet Cowen and George Kane. East Lansing, MI: Colleagues Press, 1995.

Christine de Pizan. *Debating the Roman de la Rose: A Critical Anthology.* Ed. Christine McWebb. Introduction and Latin translations by Earl Jeffrey Richards. New York: Routledge, 2007.

---. *La città delle dame* (*Le livre de la cité des dames,* French and Italian). Eds. and trans. Patrizia Caraffi and Earl Jeffrey Richards. Biblioteca Medievale 2. Milan: Luni Editrice, 1997.

---. *Le livre de la cité des dames*. Eds. and trans. Eric Hicks and Thérèse Moreau. Série Moyen Age. Paris: Stock, 1986.

---. *Le livre de l'advision Cristine*. Eds. Christine Reno and Liliane Dulac. Paris: Champion, 2001.

---. "The *Livre de la cité des dames* of Christine de Pizan: A Critical Edition." Ed. Maureen Cheney Curnow. 2 vols. Diss. Vanderbilt University, 1975.

---. *The Love Debate Poems of Christine de Pizan*. Ed. Barbara K. Altmann. Gainesville: University Press of Florida, 1998.

Cicero, M. Tullius. *De inventione/De l'invention* (Latin and French). Ed. and trans. Guy Achard. Collection des Universités de France, Série Latine 320. Paris: Les Belles Lettres, 1994.

[*Conflictus inter Deum et Diabolum*]. "An Edition and Study of the *Conflictus inter Deum et Diabolum.*" Ed. C. W. Marx. *Medium Ævum* 59.1 (1990): 16–40.

Dante Alighieri. *De vulgari eloquentia* (Latin and English). Ed and trans. Steven Botterill. Cambridge Medieval Classics 5. New York: Cambridge University Press, 1996.

---. *The Divine Comedy* (*La divina commedia,* Italian and English). Ed. Charles S. Singleton. 3 vols. Rev. ed. Bollingen Ser. 80. Princeton, NJ: Princeton University Press, 1977.

---. *Il convivio*. Ed. Gian Carlo Garfagnini. Rome: Salerno, 1997.

Le débat sur le Roman de la Rose. Ed. Eric Hicks. Paris: Champion, 1977.

Les débats du clerc et du chevalier: Étude historique et littéraire suivie de l'édition critique des textes. Ed. Charles Oulmont. Paris, 1911. Repr. Geneva: Slatkine, 1974.

Deguileville, Guillaume de. *Le pèlerinage de l'âme*. Ed. J. J. Stürzinger. London: Nichols, 1895.

---. *Le pèlerinage de vie humaine*. Ed. J. J. Stürzinger. London: Nichols, 1893.

---. *Le pèlerinage Jhesucrist*. Ed. J. J. Stürzinger. London : Nichols, 1897.

---. "Un roman inédit de Guillaume de Digulleville: *Le roman de la fleur de lis.*" Ed. Arthur Piaget. *Romania* 62 (1936): 317–58.

Étienne de Bourbon. *Anecdotes historiques, légendes et apologues tirés du recueil inédit d'Étienne de Bourbon*. Ed. Richard Albert Lecoy de la Marche. Paris: Renouard, 1877.

[*Everyman*]. *A Mirror of Everyman's Salvation: A Prose Translation of the Original* Everyman *Accompanied by* Elckerlijc *and the English* Everyman *Along with Notes*. Eds. and trans. John Conley, Guido de Baere, H. J. C. Schaap, W. H. Toppen. Amsterdam: Rodopi, 1985.

Froissart, Jean. *Chroniques*. Eds. Siméon Luce and Gaston Raynaud, Léon Mirot. 13 vols. Paris: Renouard, 1869–1919.

---. *'Dits' et 'débats.'* Ed. Anthime Fourrier. Textes Littéraires Français 274. Geneva: Droz, 1979.

---. *La prison amoureuse/The Prison of Love* (Middle French and English). Ed. and trans. Laurence De Looze. Garland Library of Medieval Literature 96. New York: Garland, 1994.

———. *L'espinette amoureuse.* Ed. Anthime Fourrier. Paris: Klincksieck, 1963.

———. *Le joli buisson de Jeunesse* (Modern French). Ed. and trans. Marylène Possamai-Perez. Traductions des Classiques Français du Moyen Âge 57. Paris: Champion, 1995.

———. *Le joli buisson de Jonece.* Ed. Anthime Fourrier. Geneva: Droz, 1975.

———. *Le paradis d'amour and L'orloge amoureus.* Ed. Peter F. Dembowski. Geneva: Droz, 1986.

———. *Œuvres de Froissart: poésies.* Ed. Auguste Scheler. 3 vols. Bruxelles: V. Devaux et cie, 1870–72.

Gerson, Jean. *Œuvres complètes.* Ed. Palémon Glorieux. 10 vols. Paris: Desclée, 1960–73.

Guillaume d'Auvergne (William of Auvergne). *Rhetorica divina, seu ars oratoria eloquentiae divinae.* Ed. Roland J. Teske. Leuven: Peeters, 2013.

Guillaume de Lorris, and Jean de Meun. *Le roman de la Rose.* Ed. Armand Strubel. Paris: Librairie Générale Française, 1992.

Guillaume le Clerc de Normandie. *Le besant de Dieu.* Ed. Pierre Ruelle. Brussels: Éditions de L'Université de Bruxelles, 1973.

Hughes de Saint-Victor. *Hugonis de Sancto Victore De sacramentis christiane fidei.* Ed. Rainer Berndt. Aschendorff, Germany: Monasterii Westfalorum, 2008.

Jacques de Vitry. *The Exempla or Illustrative Stories from the Sermons of Jacques de Vitry* (*Exempla ex sermonibus vulgaribus*). Ed. Thomas Frederick Crane. London: D. Nutt, 1890.

Jean de Meun. *Le testament Maistre Jehan de Meun: Un caso letterario.* Ed. Silvia Buzzetti Gallarati. Alessandria: Edizioni dell'Orso, 1989.

Jean le Bel. *Chronique de Jean le Bel.* Eds. Jules Viard and Eugène Déprez. 2 vols. Paris: Renouard, 1904–5.

Jerome. *Sancti Eusebii Hieronymi epistulae.* Ed. Isidorus Hilberg. 4 vols. Corpus Scriptorum Ecclesiasticorum Latinorum 54–56. Vienna: Austrian Academy of Sciences, 1996.

John of Salisbury. *Metalogicon.* Eds. J. B. Hall and K. S. B. Keats-Rohan. Corpus Christianorum-Continuatio Medievalis 98. Turnhout: Brepols, 1991.

[*L'advocacie Nostre Dame*]. *Our Lady's Lawsuits in L'advocacie Nostre Dame (Our Lady's Advocacy) and La chapelerie Nostre Dame de Baiex (The Benefice of Our Lady's Chapel in Bayeux)* (Anglo-Norman and English). Eds. and trans. Judith M. Davis, F. R. P. Akehurst. Based on the text edited by Gérard Gros. Tempe: Arizona Center for Medieval and Renaissance Studies, 2011.

Latini, Brunetto. *Li livres dou tresor.* Ed. Francis J. Carmody. Berkeley: University of California Press, 1948.

———. *La rettorica.* Ed. Francesco Maggini. Florence: Felice le Monnier, 1968.

Laurent d'Orléans. *La somme le roi.* Eds. Édith Brayer and Anne-Françoise Leurquin-Labie. Paris: Société des Anciens Textes Français, 2008.

Le Fèvre, Jean. *Le respit de la mort.* Ed. Geneviève Hasenohr-Esnos. Paris: Picard, 1969.

Le Jugement Dernier/Lo Jutgamen General: Drame provençal du XVe siècle (Occitan and French). Ed. and trans. Moshe Lazar. Bibliothèque Française et Romane, série B: Éditions Critiques de Textes 10. Paris: Klincksieck, 1971.

Le mystère du Jour du Jugement: Texte original du XIVe siècle. Eds. Jean-Pierre Perrot and Jean-Jacques Nonot. Besançon: Éditions Comp'Act, 2000.

Le Poirier, Mahieu. *Le* Court d'Amours *de Mahieu le Poirier et la suite anonyme de* La court d'amours. Ed. Terence Scully. Waterloo, ON: Wilfrid Laurier University Press, 1976.

Lombard, Peter. *Magistri Petri Lombardi Parisiensis episcopi Sententiae in IV libris distinctae.* 2 vols. 3rd ed. Grottaferrata: Editiones Collegii S. Bonaventurae ad Claras Aquas, 1971–81.

Lothario dei Segni. *De miseria conditionis humane* (Latin and English). Ed. and trans. Robert E. Lewis. Athens, GA: University of Georgia Press, 1978.

Lydgate, John. *The Fall of Princes.* Ed. Henry Bergen. 4 vols. London: Early English Text Society, 1924.

Machaut, Guillaume de. *La prise d'Alexandrie/The Taking of Alexandria* (Middle French and English). Ed. and trans. R. Barton Palmer. New York: Routledge, 2002.

———. *Le confort d'ami/Comfort for a Friend* (Middle French and English). Ed. and trans. R. Barton Palmer. Garland Library of Medieval Literature 67. New York: Garland, 1992.

———. *Le jugement du roy de Behaigne; and, Remede de Fortune.* Eds. and trans. James I. Wimsatt and William W. Kibler. Athens, GA: University of Georgia Press, 1988.

———. *Le livre de la fontaine amoureuse* (Middle French and Modern French). Ed. and trans. Jacqueline Cerquiglini-Toulet. Série Moyen Âge. Paris: Stock, 1993.

———. *Le livre du voir dit* (Middle French and Modern French). Eds. and trans. Paul Imbs and Jacqueline Cerquiglini-Toulet. Paris: Librairie Générale Française, 1999.

———. *The Fountain of Love/La fonteinne amoureuse, and Two Other Love Vision Poems* (Middle French and English). Ed. and trans. R. Barton Palmer. Garland Library of Medieval Literature 54. New York: Garland, 1993.

———. *The Judgment of the King of Bohemia/Le jugement dou roy de Behaingne* (Middle French and English). Ed. and trans. R. Barton Palmer. Garland Library of Medieval Literature 9. New York: Garland, 1984.

———. *The Judgment of the King of Navarre/Le jugement dou roy de Navarre* (Middle French and English). Ed. and trans. R. Barton Palmer. Garland Library of Medieval Literature 45. New York: Garland, 1988.

———. *Œuvres de Guillaume de Machaut.* Ed. Ernest Hœpffner. 3 vols. Paris: Firmin, 1908-21.

Miracles de Nostre Dame par personnages. Eds. Gaston Paris, Ulysse Robert, and François Bonnardot. 8 vols. Paris: Firmin Didot & Cie, 1881.

Missale romanum anno 1962 promulgatum. Eds. Cuthbert Johnson and Anthony Ward. Subsidia, Instrumenta Liturgica, supp. 2. Bibliotheca Ephemerides Liturgicae. Rome: CLV-Edizioni Liturgica, 1994.

Molinier, Guilhem. *Las leys d'amors, manuscrit de l'Académie des Jeux Floraux.* Ed. Joseph Anglade. 4 vols. Toulouse: Privat, 1919–20.

Montaigne, Michel de. *Les essais.* Eds. Pierre Villey and Verdun L. Saulnier. Paris: Quadrige-Presses Universitaires de France, 2004.

Nouveau recueil complet des Fabliaux. Eds. Willem Nommen and Nico van den Boogaard. 10 vols. Assen, NL: Van Gorcum, 1983-98.

Novare, Philippe de. *Les quatre ages de l'homme.* Ed. M. de Fréville. Paris: Société des Anciens Textes Français, 1888.

Ovid. *Ibis.* Ed. Robinson Ellis. Exeter, UK: Bristol Phoenix Press, 2008.

———. *Tristia.* Ed. John Barrie Hall. Bibliotheca Scriptorum Graecorum et Romanorum Teubneriana. Stuttgart: Teubner, 1995.

Ovide moralisé: Poème du commencement du quatorzième siècle. Ed. Cornelius De Boer, et al. In *Verhandelingen der Koninklijke Akademie van Wetenschapen te Amsterdam: Afdeeling Letterkunde.* Nieuwe Reeks ser. 15, 21, 30, 37, 43. Amsterdam: 1915–1938.

Petrarca, Francesco. *Petrarch's Songbook: Rerum Vulgarium Fragmenta* (Italian and English). Ed. Gianfranco Contini. Trans. James Wyatt Cook. Introduction by Germaine Warkentin. Binghamton, NY: Medieval and Renaissance Texts and Studies 15, 1995.

Regnier (Régnier), Jean. *Les fortunes et adversitez de Jean Régnier.* Ed. Eugénie Droz. Paris: Champion, 1923.

Rhetorica ad Herrenium/Rhétorique à Hérennius (Latin and French). Ed. and trans. Guy Achard. Collection des Universités de France. Paris: Les Belles Lettres, 2003.

Rousseau, Jean-Jacques. *Les confessions.* Eds. Bernard Gagnebin and Marcel Raymond. Preface by J.-B. Pontalis. Notes by Catherine Kœnig. Paris: Gallimard, 1973.

Rutebeuf. *Œuvres complètes.* Ed. Michel Zink. Lettres Gothiques-Classiques Garnier. Paris: Livre de Poche, 2001.

Thomas Aquinas. *Abrégé de théologie, ou bref résumé de théologie pour le frère Raynald (Compendium theologiae,* Latin and French). Ed. Jean-Pierre Torrell. Paris: Cerf, 2007.

———. *Aquinas's Shorter Summa: St. Thomas Aquinas's own Concise Version of his Summa theologica (Compendium theologiae,* English). Manchester, NH: Sophia Institute Press, 2002.

———. *Summa theologica.* Blackfriars edition (Latin and English). 61 vols. New York: McGraw-Hill, 1964–81.

Villon, François. *Poésies complètes.* Ed. Claude Thiry. Paris: Librairie Générale Française, 1991.

Voltaire. *Œuvres complètes.* 52 vols. Paris: Garnier Frères, 1877–85.

Modern Critical, Philosophical, and Reference Works

Aberth, John. *The Black Death: The Great Mortality of 1348–1350: A Brief History with Documents.* Boston: Palgrave Macmillan, 2005.

Akehurst, F. R. P., and Judith M. Davis, eds. *A Handbook of the Troubadours.* Berkeley: University of California Press, 1995.

Althusser, Louis. "Ideology and Ideological State Apparatuses." In *Lenin and Philosophy.* Trans. B. Brewster. New Left Books, 1971. Extracts reprinted in *Literary Theory: An Anthology.* rev. edition, eds. Julie Rivkin and Michael Ryan, 294–304. Malden, MA: Blackwell, 2001.

Anderson, Travis T. "Eschatology and Textuality in Levinas." *Literature and Belief* 28.1 (2008): 41–53.

The Anglo-Norman Dictionary Online. Aberystwyth University, Swansea University. Eds. David Trotter and William Rothwell, et al. <http://www.anglo-norman.net>.

Archambault, Paul J. "Froissart and the Ockhamist Movement: Philosophy and Its Impact on Historiography." *Symposium* 28.3 (Fall 1974): 197–211.

Ariès, Philippe. *L'homme devant la mort.* Paris: Seuil, 1977.

Ascoli, Albert Russell. *Dante and the Making of a Modern Author.* Cambridge: Cambridge University Press, 2008.

Astell, Ann W., and Justin A. Jackson, eds. *Levinas and Medieval Literature: The 'Difficult Reading' of English and Rabbinic Texts.* Pittsburgh: Duquesne University Press, 2009.

Attwood, Catherine. *Dynamic Dichotomy: The Poetic 'I' in Fourteenth- and Fifteenth-Century French Lyric Poetry.* Amsterdam: Rodopi, 1998.

Auerbach, Erich. *Scenes from the Drama of European Literature.* Trans. Ralph Manheim. Gloucester, MA: Peter Smith, 1973.

Avril, François. "Les manuscrits enluminés de Guillaume de Machaut: Essai de chronologie." In *Guillaume de Machaut, poète et compositeur: Colloque-table ronde organisé par l'Université de Reims, 19–22 avril 1978,* eds. Jacques Chailley, et al., 117–33. Actes et Colloques 23. Paris: Klincksieck, 1982.

Badel, Pierre-Yves. *Le Roman de la Rose au XIVe siècle: Étude de la réception de l'œuvre.* Geneva: Droz, 1980.

Bakhtin, Mikhail Mikhailovich. *Art and Answerability: Early Philosophical Essays.* Eds. Michael Holquist and Vadim Liapunov. Trans. and notes Vadim Liapunov, supplement trans. Kenneth Brostrom. University of Texas Slavic Studies 9. Austin: University of Texas Press, 1990.

Barolini, Teodolinda. *The Undivine Comedy: Detheologizing Dante.* Princeton, NJ: Princeton University Press, 1992.

Barthes, Roland. *S/Z.* Paris: Seuil, 1970.

Baschet, Jérôme. "Jugement de l'âme, Jugement dernier: Contradiction, compléméntarité, chevauchement?" *Revue Mabillon* 6 (1995): 159–203.

Batiouchkof, Théodor. "Le débat de l'âme et du corps." *Romania* 20 (1891): 1–55, 513–78.

Bauckham, Richard. *The Fate of the Dead: Studies on the Jewish and Christian Apocalypses.* Leiden: Brill, 1998.

Bazin-Tacchela, Sylvie. "Rupture et continuité du discours médical à travers les écrits sur la peste de 1348." In *Air, miasmes et contagion: Les épidémies dans l'Antiquité et au Moyen Âge,* eds. Sylvie Bazin-Tacchela, Danielle Quéruel, and Évelyne Samama, 105–56. Langres: Dominique Guéniot, 2001.

Bennett, Philip E. "Female Readers in Froissart: Implied, Fictive and Other." In *Women, the Book and the Godly/Women, the Book and the Worldly: Selected Proceedings of the St. Hilda's Conference, 1993,* eds. Lesley Smith and Jane H. M. Taylor, 2:13–23. Woodbridge, Suffolk, UK: D. S. Brewer, 1995.

———. "The Mirage of Fiction: Narration, Narrator, and Narratee in Froissart's Lyrico-Narrative *Dits.*" *MLR* 86.2 (April 1991): 285–97.

Bériou, Nicole. "L'intercession dans les sermons de la Toussaint." In *L'intercession du Moyen Âge à l'époque moderne: Autour d'une pratique sociale,* ed. Jean-Marie Moeglin, 127–56. Hautes Études Médiévales et Modernes 87. Geneva: Droz, 2004.

Bevington, David, ed. *Homo, Memento Finis: The Iconography of Just Judgment in Medieval Art and Drama.* Kalamazoo: Medieval Institute Publications, Western Michigan University, 1985.

Bloch, R. Howard. *Medieval French Literature and Law.* Berkeley: University of California Press, 1977.

Boss, Sarah Jane. *Empress and Handmaid: On Nature and Gender in the Cult of the Virgin Mary.* New York: Cassell, 2000.

Boyle, Leonard E. "The Fourth Lateran Council and Manuals of Popular Theology." In *The Popular Literature of Medieval England,* ed. Thomas J. Heffernan, 30–43. Tennessee Studies in Literature 28. Knoxville: University of Tennessee Press, 1985.

Brandon, Samuel George Frederick. *The Judgment of the Dead: The Idea of Life after Death in the Major Religions*. New York: Scribner, 1967.

Braswell, Mary Flowers. *The Medieval Sinner: Characterization and Confession in the Literature of the English Middle Ages*. East Brunswick, NJ: Associated University Presses, 1983.

Briscoe, Marianne J., and Barbara H. Jaye. *Artes praedicandi/ Artes orandi*. Turnhout: Brepols, 1992.

Brown, Peter. *The Cult of the Saints: Its Rise and Function in Latin Christianity*. Chicago: University of Chicago Press, 1981.

Brownlee, Kevin. "Ovide et le moi poétique à la fin du Moyen Âge français: Jean Froissart et Christine de Pizan." In *Modernité au Moyen Âge: Le défi du passé*, eds. Brigitte Cazelles and Charles Méla, 153–73. Geneva: Droz, 1990.

———. *Poetic Identity in Guillaume de Machaut*. Madison: University of Wisconsin Press, 1984.

Brundage, James A. *The Medieval Origins of the Legal Profession: Canonists, Civilians, and Courts*. Chicago: University of Chicago Press, 2008.

Burrow, John Anthony. *The Ages of Man: A Study in Medieval Writing and Thought*. Oxford: Clarendon, 1986.

Butterfield, Ardis. "Pastoral and the Politics of Plague in Machaut and Chaucer." *Studies in the Age of Chaucer* 16 (1994): 3–27.

Bynum, Caroline Walker, and Paul Freedman, eds. *Last Things: Death and the Apocalypse in the Middle Ages*. Philadelphia: University of Pennsylvania Press, 2000.

Calin, William. *A Poet at the Fountain: Essays on the Narrative Verse of Guillaume de Machaut*. Lexington: University of Kentucky Press, 1974.

Camille, Michael. "The Devil's Writing: Diabolic Literacy in Medieval Art." In *World Art: Themes of Unity in Diversity: Acts of the XXVIth International Congress of the History of Art*, ed. Irving Lavin, 2:355–60. University Park: University of Pennsylvania Press, 1989.

———. "The Illustrated Manuscripts of Guillaume de Deguileville's *Pèlerinages*, 1330–1426." 2 vols. Diss. Cambridge University, 1985.

Carmichael, Ann G. "1 Universal and Particular: The Language of Plague, 1348–1500." *Medical History Supplement* 27 (2008): 17–52.

Carruthers, Mary. *The Book of Memory: A Study of Memory in Medieval Culture*. 2nd ed. Cambridge: Cambridge University Press, 2008.

Case, Mary Anne C. "Christine de Pizan and the Authority of Experience." In *Christine de Pizan and the Categories of Difference*, ed. Marilynn Desmond, 71–87. Minneapolis: University of Minnesota Press, 1998.

Cazèlles, Raymond. *Société politique, noblesse et couronne sous Jean le Bon et Charles V*. Geneva: Droz, 1982.

Cerquiglini, Jacqueline (Jacqueline Cerquiglini-Toulet). *La couleur de la mélancholie: La fréquentation des livres au XIVe siècle, 1300–1415*. Paris: Hatier, 1993.

———. "Fullness and Emptiness: Shortages and Storehouses of Lyric Treasure in the Fourteenth and Fifteenth Centuries." Trans. Christine Cano. *Yale French Studies Special Issue: Contexts: Style and Values in Medieval Art and Literature* (1991): 224–39.

———. "Le Clerc et l'écriture: Le *Voir dit* de Guillaume de Machaut et la définition du dit." In *Literatur in der Gesellschaft des Spätmittelalters*, ed. Hans Ulrich Gumbrecht, with Ursula

Link-Heer and Peter M. Spangenberg, 151–68. Grundriss der romanischen Literatur des Mittelalters, Begleitreihe, vol. 1. Heidelberg: Carl Winter, 1980.

———. "'Le clerc et le louche': Sociology of an Esthetic." Trans. Monique Briand-Walker. *Poetics Today: Medieval and Renaissance Representation: New Reflections* 5.3 (1984): 479–91.

———. *'Un engin si soutil': Guillaume de Machaut et l'écriture au XIVe siècle.* Geneva: Slatkine, 1985.

Chailley, Jacques, Paul Imbs, and Daniel Poirion, eds. *Guillaume de Machaut, poète et compositeur: colloque-table ronde, organisé par l'Université de Reims, 19–22 avril 1978.* Actes et Colloques 23. Paris: Klincksieck, 1982.

Chareyron, Nicole. *Jean le Bel: Le maître de Froissart, grand imagier de la guerre de Cent Ans.* Brussels: De Boeck Larcier, 1996.

Chenu, Marie-Dominique. *L'éveil de la conscience dans la civilisation médiévale.* Montréal: Institut d'Études Médiévales, 1969.

Cherniss, Michael D. *Boethian Apocalypse: Studies in Middle English Vision Poetry.* Norman, OK: Pilgrim Books, 1987.

Cheyette, Frédéric L. "Custom, Case Law, and Medieval 'Constitutionalism': A Reconsideration." *Political Science Quarterly* 78.3 (1963): 362–90.

Chiffoleau, Jacques. *La comptabilité de l'au-delà: Les hommes, la mort et la religion dans la région d'Avignon à la fin du Moyen Âge (vers 1320–vers 1480).* Rome: École Française de Rome, 1980.

Cohen, Esther. *The Crossroads of Justice: Law and Culture in Late Medieval France.* New York: Brill, 1993.

Coville, Alfred. "Poèmes historiques de l'avènement de Philippe VI de Valois au Traité de Calais, 1328–1360." In *Histoire littéraire de la France*, 38:259–333. Paris: Imprimerie Nationale, 1865–2005.

Cox, Virginia. "Ciceronian Rhetoric in Italy, 1260–1350." *Rhetorica* 17.3 (Summer 1999): 239–88.

Dagenais, John. *The Ethics of Reading in Manuscript Culture: Glossing the* Libro de buen amor. Princeton, NJ: Princeton University Press, 1994.

De Looze, Laurence. "Masquage et démasquage de l'auteur dans les *Jugements* de Guillaume de Machaut." In *Masques et déguisements dans la littérature médiévale*, ed. Marie-Louise Ollier, 203–9. Montréal: Presses de l'Université de Montréal, 1988.

———. *Pseudo-Autobiography in the Fourteenth Century: Juan Ruiz, Guillaume de Machaut, Jean Froissart, and Geoffrey Chaucer.* Gainesville: University Press of Florida, 1997.

Delumeau, Jean. *Le péché et la peur: La culpabilisation en Occident, XIIIe–XVIIIe siècles.* Paris: Fayard, 1983.

———. *La peur en occident: XIVe–XVIIIe siècles: Une cité assiégée.* Paris: Fayard, 1978.

Dembowski, Peter F. *Jean Froissart and his* Meliador: *Context, Craft and Sense.* Lexington, KY: French Forum, 1983.

———. "La position de Froissart-poète dans l'histoire littéraire: Bilan provisoire." *Travaux de linguistique et de littérature* 16.1 (1978): 131–47.

Desmond, Marilynn, ed. *Christine de Pizan and the Categories of Difference.* Minneapolis: University of Minnesota Press, 1988.

DMF: Dictionnaire du Moyen Français, version 2010. ATILF-CNRS & Nancy Université. <http://www.atilf.fr/dmf>.

Doss-Quinby, Eglal. "La composition numérique du *Testament* de Villon ou la symbolique du jugement." *Fifteenth-Century Studies* 12 (1987): 131–44.

Dufournet, Jean. "Deux poètes du Moyen Âge en face de la mort: Rutebeuf et Villon." In *Dies Illa: Death in the Middle Ages: Proceedings of the 1983 Manchester Colloquium*, ed. Jane H. M. Taylor, 155–75. Trowbridge, Wiltshire, UK: Francis Cairns, 1984.

Duval, Frédéric, and Fabienne Pomel, eds. *Guillaume de Digulleville: Les* Pèlerinages *allégoriques*. Rennes: Presses Universitaires de Rennes, 2008.

Duval, Yvette. "Les saints protecteurs ici-bas et dans l'au-delà: L'intercession dans l'Antiquité chrétienne." In *L'intercession du Moyen Âge à l'époque moderne: Autour d'une pratique sociale*, ed. Jean-Marie Moeglin, 17–39. Geneva: Droz, 2004.

Earp, Lawrence. *Guillaume de Machaut: A Guide to Research*. Garland Composer Research Manuals 36, Garland Reference Library of the Humanities 996. New York: Garland, 1995.

Easting, Robert. "Personal Apocalypses: Judgement in Some Other-World Visions." In *Prophecy, Apocalypse and the Day of Doom: Proceedings of the 2000 Harlaxton Symposium*, ed. Nigel Morgan, 68–85. Donington, UK: Shaun Tyas, 2004.

Edsall, Mary Agnes. "Like Wise Master Builders: Jean Gerson's Ecclesiology, *Lectio Divina*, and Christine de Pizan's *Livre de la cité des dames*." *Medievalia et Humanistica* 27 (2000): 33–56.

Edwards, Graham Robert. "Making Sense of Deguileville's Autobiographical Project: The Evidence of Paris, Bibliothèque nationale de France MS Latin 14845." In *The* Pèlerinage *Allegories of Guillaume de Deguileville: Tradition, Authority and Influence*, eds. Marco Nievergelt and Stephanie A. Viereck Gibbs Kamath, 129–50. Cambridge: D. S. Brewer, 2013.

Ehrhart, Margaret J. "Guillaume de Machaut's *Jugement dou roy de Navarre* and Medieval Treatments of the Virtues." *Annuale Medievale* 19 (1979): 46–67.

———. *The Judgment of the Trojan Prince Paris in Medieval Literature*. Philadelphia: University of Pennsylvania Press, 1987.

Ellington, Donna Spivey. *From Sacred Body to Angelic Soul: Understanding Mary in Late Medieval and Early Modern Europe*. Washington, DC: The Catholic University of America Press, 2001.

Emmerson, Richard K, and Bernard McGinn, eds. *The Apocalypse in the Middle Ages*. Ithaca, NY: Cornell University Press, 1992.

Enders, Jody. *Rhetoric and the Origins of Medieval Drama*. Ithaca, NY: Cornell University Press, 1992.

Evans, Gillian-Rosemary. *Law and Theology in the Middle Ages*. London: Routledge, 2002.

Faes de Mottoni, Barbara. "Quelques aspects de la doctrine de l'intercession dans la théologie de Bonaventure et de Thomas d'Aquin." In *L'intercession du Moyen Âge à l'époque moderne: Autour d'une pratique sociale*, ed. Jean-Marie Moeglin, 105–26. Hautes Études Médiévales et Modernes 87. Geneva: Droz, 2004.

Fagan, Patricia C. "El Mal Rey y la Ley: The Devil as Lawyer in the Divine Court of the *CSM*." *Romance Review* 5.1 (Spring 1995): 47–53.

Faral, Edmond. "Guillaume de Digulleville: Moine de Chaalis." In *Histoire littéraire de la France*, 39:1–132. Paris: Imprimerie Nationale, 1865–2005.

Fenster, Thelma. "'*Perdre son latin*': Christine de Pizan and Vernacular Humanism." In *Christine de Pizan and the Categories of Difference*, ed. Marilynn Desmond, 91–107. Minneapolis: University of Minnesota Press, 1988.

Fiddes, Paul S. *The Promised End: Eschatology in Theology and Literature*. Challenges in Contemporary Theology. Oxford: Blackwell, 2000.

Fin des temps et temps de la fin dans l'univers médiéval. Sénéfiance 33. Aix: Centre Universitaire d'Études et de Recherches Médiévales d'Aix (C. U. E. R. M. A.), 1993.

Fleming, John. "The Moral Reputation of the *Roman de la Rose* before 1400." *Romance Philology* 18.4 (May 1965): 430–35.

Foucault, Michel. *Histoire de la sexualité*. 3 vols. Paris: Gallimard, 1976–84.

———. *Surveiller et punir: naissance de la prison*. Paris: Gallimard, 1975.

Freeman, Michelle. "Froissart's *Le joli buisson de Jonece*: A Farewell to Poetry?" In *Machaut's World: Science and Art in the Fourteenth Century*, eds. Madeleine Pelner Cosman and Bruce Chandler, 235–47. New York: New York Academy of Sciences, 1978.

Galpin, Stanley Leman. "Notes on the Sources of Deguileville's *Pèlerinage de l'âme*." *MLN* 28.1 (1913 January): 8–10.

———. "On the Sources of Guillaume de Deguileville's *Pèlerinage de l'âme*." *PMLA* 25.2 (1910): 275–308.

Gardiner, Eileen. *Visions of Heaven and Hell before Dante*. New York: Italica, 1989.

Gaunt, Simon, and Sarah Kay, eds. *The Cambridge Companion to Medieval French Literature*. Cambridge: Cambridge University Press, 2008.

———. *The Troubadours: An Introduction*. Cambridge: Cambridge University Press, 1999.

———. *Troubadours and Irony*. Cambridge: Cambridge University Press, 1989.

Gauvard, Claude. "Portrait du prince d'après l'œuvre de Guillaume de Machaut: Étude sur les idées politiques du poète." In *Guillaume de Machaut, poète et compositeur: Colloque-table ronde, organisé par l'Université de Reims, 19–22 avril 1978*, ed. Jacques Chailley, et al., 23–29. Actes et Colloques 23. Paris: Klincksieck, 1982.

Gellrich, Jesse M. "*Figura*, Allegory, and the Question of History." In *Literary History and the Challenge of Philology: The Legacy of Erich Auerbach*, ed. Seth Lerer, 107–23. Stanford, CA: Stanford University Press, 1996.

———. *The Idea of the Book in the Middle Ages: Language Theory, Mythology and Fiction*. Ithaca, NY: Cornell University Press, 1985.

Ghil, Eliza M. "Imagery and Vocabulary." In *A Handbook of the Troubadours*, eds. F. R. P. Akehurst and Judith M. Davis, 421–46. Berkeley: University of California Press, 1995.

Girard, René. *Le bouc-émissaire*. Paris: Grasset, 1982.

Goodrich, Peter. "Gay Science and Law." In *Rhetoric and Law in Early Modern Europe*, eds. Victoria Kahn and Lorna Hutson, 95–124. New Haven, CT: Yale University Press, 2001.

———. *Law in the Courts of Love: Literature and Other Minor Jurisprudences*. London: Routledge, 1996.

Graham, Audrey. "Froissart's Use of Classical Allusion in his Poems." *Medium Ævum* 32 (1963): 24–33.

Green, Richard Firth. *A Crisis of Truth: Literature and Law in Ricardian England*. The Middle Ages Series. Philadelphia: University of Pennsylvania Press, 1999.

Gros, Gérard. *Ave Vierge Marie: Étude sur les prières mariales en vers français, XIIe–XVe siècles*. Lyon: Presses Universitaires de Lyon, 2004.

———. *Le poème du puy marial: Étude sur le serventois et le chant royal du XIVe siècle à la Renaissance*. Paris: Klincksieck, 1996.

———. *Le poète, la Vierge et le prince du puy: Étude sur les puys marials de la France du nord du XIVe siècle à la Renaissance.* Paris: Klincksieck, 1992.

———. *Le poète, la Vierge et le prince: Étude sur la poésie mariale en milieu de cour aux XIVe et XVe siècles.* Saint-Étienne: Publications de l'Université de Saint-Étienne, 1994.

———. "'Que feray je se n'ay argent?': Une étude sur le Testament de Jean Régnier (*Fortunes et adversitez,* vers 3577–3774)." In *Fin des temps et temps de la fin dans l'univers médiéval,* 211–24. Sénéfiance 33. Aix: Centre Universitaire d'Études et de Recherches Médiévales d'Aix (C. U. E. R. M. A.), 1993.

Gunn, Alan Murray Finlay. *The Mirror of Love: A Reinterpretation of* The Romance of the Rose. 2nd ed. Lubbock: Texas Tech Press, 1952.

Guyon, G. D. "La justice pénale dans le théâtre religieux du XIVe siècle: Les *Miracles de Notre Dame par personnages.*" *Revue historique de droit français et étranger* 69.4 (1991): 465–86.

Gybbon-Monypenny, G. B. "Guillaume de Machaut's Erotic 'Autobiography': Precedents for the Form of the *Voir dit.*" In *Studies in Medieval Literature and Languages in Memory of Frederick Whitehead,* ed. W. Rothwell, et al., 133–52. Manchester: Manchester University Press, 1973.

Heffernan, Thomas J., ed. *The Popular Literature of Medieval England.* Tennessee Studies in Literature 28. Knoxville: University of Tennessee Press, 1985.

Herzman, Ronald B. "'Let us Seek Him Also': Tropological Judgment in Twelfth-Century Art and Drama." In *Homo, Memento Finis: The Iconography of Just Judgment in Medieval Art and Drama,* ed. David Bevington, 59–88. Kalamazoo: Medieval Institute Publications, Western Michigan University, 1985.

Hobbins, Daniel. *Authorship and Publicity Before Print: Jean Gerson and the Transformation of Late Medieval Learning.* Philadelphia: University of Pennsylvania Press, 2009.

Hogan, Linda. *Confronting the Truth: Conscience in the Catholic Tradition.* Mahwah, NJ: Paulist Press, 2000.

Hollander, Robert. "Dante's Book of the Dead: A Note on *Inferno* XXIX, 57." *Studi Danteschi* 54 (1982): 31–51.

Holmes, Olivia. *Assembling the Lyric Self: Authorship from Troubadour Song to Italian Poetry Book.* Medieval Cultures vol. 21. Minneapolis: University of Minnesota Press, 2000.

Hüe, Denis. "L'apprentissage de la louange: Pour une typologie de la prière dans les *Pèlerinages* de Guillaume de Digulleville." In *Guillaume de Digulleville: Les* Pèlerinages *allégoriques,* eds. Frédéric Duval and Fabienne Pomel, 159–84. Rennes: Presses Universitaires de Rennes, 2008.

———. *La poésie palinodique à Rouen, 1486–1550.* Bibliothèque Littéraire de la Renaissance Série 3, t. 44. Paris: Champion, 2002.

Huot, Sylvia. "The Daisy and the Laurel: Myths of Desire and Creativity in the Poetry of Jean Froissart." *Yale French Studies Special Edition: Contexts: Style and Values in Medieval Art and Literature* (1991): 240–51.

———. *From Song to Book: The Poetics of Writing in Old French Lyric and Lyrical Narrative Poetry.* Ithaca, NY: Cornell University Press, 1987.

———. "Reading Across Genres: Froissart's *Joli buisson de Jonece* and Machaut's Motets." *French Studies* 57.1 (2003): 1–10.

———. *The* Romance of the Rose *and its Medieval Readers: Interpretation, Reception, Manuscript Transmission.* Cambridge Studies in Medieval Literature 16. Cambridge: Cambridge University Press, 1993.

———. "The Writer's Mirror: Watriquet de Couvin and the Development of the Author-Centered Book." In *Across Boundaries: The Book in Culture and Commerce,* eds. Bill Bell, Philip Bennett, and Jonquil Bevan, 29–46. New Castle, DE: Oak Knoll, 2000.

Jennings, Margaret. "The Preacher's Rhetoric: The *Ars componendi sermones* of Ranulph Higden." In *Medieval Eloquence: Studies in the Theory and Practice of Medieval Rhetoric,* ed. James J. Murphy, 112–26. Berkeley: University of California Press, 1978.

Kamath, Stephanie A. Viereck Gibbs. "Naming the Pilgrim: Authorship and Allegory in Guillaume de Deguileville's *Pèlerinage de la vie humaine.*" *Studies in the Age of Chaucer* 32 (2010): 179–213.

———. "Unveiling the 'I': Allegory and Authorship in the Franco-English Tradition, 1270–1450." Diss. University of Pennsylvania, 2006.

Karpik, Lucien. *Les avocats entre l'état, le public et le marché, XIIIe–XXe siècles.* Paris: Gallimard, 1995.

Kay, Sarah. "'Le moment de conclure': Initiation as Retrospection in Froissart's *Dits Amoureux.*" In *Rites of Passage: Cultures of Transition in the Fourteenth Century,* eds. Nicola F. McDonald and W. M. Ormrod, 153–71. Rochester, NY: York Medieval Press, 2004.

———. "Mémoire et imagination dans le *Joli buisson de Jonece* de Jean Froissart: Fiction, philosophie et poétique." *Francofonia* 23.45 (2003 Autumn): 177–95.

———. *The Place of Thought: The Complexity of One in Late Medieval French Didactic Poetry.* Philadelphia: University of Pennsylvania Press, 2007.

———. *Subjectivity in Troubadour Poetry.* Cambridge Studies in French. Cambridge: Cambridge University Press, 1990.

———. "Touching Singularity: Consolation, Philosophy, and Poetry in the French *Dit.*" In *The Erotics of Consolation: Desire and Distance in the Late Middle Ages,* eds. Catherine E. Léglu and Stephen J. Milner, 21–38. New York: Palgrave Macmillan, 2008.

Kay, Sarah, Terence Cave, and Malcolm Bowie. *A Short History of French Literature.* Oxford: Oxford University Press, 2003.

Keiser, George R. "The Middle English *Planctus Mariae* and the Rhetoric of Pathos." In *The Popular Literature of Medieval England,* ed. Thomas J. Heffernan, 167–93. Tennessee Studies in Literature 28. Knoxville: University of Tennessee Press, 1985.

Kelly, Douglas. *Christine de Pizan's Changing Opinion: A Quest for Certainty in the Midst of Chaos.* Cambridge: D. S. Brewer, 2007.

———. "The Genius of the Patron: The Prince, the Poet, and Fourteenth-Century Invention." In *Chaucer's French Contemporaries: The Poetry/Poetics of Self and Tradition,* ed. R. Barton Palmer, 1–27. New York: AMS, 1999.

———. "Imitation, Metamorphosis, and Froissart's Use of the Exemplary *Modus tractandi.*" In *Froissart Across the Genres,* eds. Donald Maddox and Sarah Sturm-Maddox, 101–18. Gainesville: University Press of Florida, 1998.

———. "Les inventions ovidiennes de Froissart: Réflexions intertextuelles comme imagination." *Littérature* 41 (February 1981): 82–92.

———. *Medieval Imagination: Rhetoric and the Poetry of Courtly Love.* Madison: University of Wisconsin Press, 1978.

———. "Topical Invention in Medieval French Literature." In *Medieval Eloquence: Studies in the Theory and Practice of Medieval Rhetoric,* ed. James J. Murphy, 231–51. Berkeley: University of California Press, 1978.

Kermode, Frank. *The Sense of an Ending: Studies in the Theory of Fiction*. Rev. ed. Oxford: Oxford University Press, 2000.

Kibler, William W., and James I. Wimsatt. "*Le joli buisson de Jonece:* Froissart's Midlife Crisis." In *Froissart Across the Genres*, eds. Donald Maddox and Sara Sturm-Maddox, 63–80. Gainesville: University Press of Florida, 1998.

———. "Machaut's Text and the Question of his Personal Supervision." In *Chaucer's French Contemporaries: The Poetry/Poetics of Self and Tradition*, ed. R. Barton Palmer, 103–9. New York: AMS Press, 1999.

———. "Self-Deception in Froissart's *Espinette amoureuse*." *Romania* 97 (1976): 77–98.

Kinne, Elizabeth. "Rhetorical Reasoning, Authority, and the Impossible Interlocutor in *Le vilain qui conquist paradis par plait*." In *The Old French Fabliaux: Essays on Comedy and Context*, ed. Kristin L Burr, et al., 55–68. Jefferson, NC: McFarland, 2007.

Lanoue, D. G. "History as Apocalypse: The 'Prologue' of Machaut's *Jugement dou roy de Navarre*." *Philological Quarterly* 60.1 (Winter 1981): 1–12.

Lassahn, Nicole. "Pseudo-Autobiography and the Role of the Poet in Jean Froissart's *Joli buisson de Jonece*." *Essays in Medieval Studies* 15 (1998): 123–28.

Lauwers, Michel. *La mémoire des ancêtres, le souci des morts: Morts, rites et société au Moyen Âge: Diocèse de Liège, XI–XIIIe siècles*. Paris: Beauchesne, 1997.

Le Bouteiller, Agnès. "Le Procès de Paradis du *Pèlerinage de Jésus-Christ*: Un débat allégorique, juridique et théologique porté au seuil de la dramatisation." In *Guillaume de Digulleville: les Pèlerinages allégoriques*, eds. Frédéric Duval and Fabienne Pomel, 131–58. Rennes: Presses Universitaires de Rennes, 2008.

Lechat, Didier. *'Dire par fiction': Métamorphoses du 'je' chez Guillaume de Machaut, Jean Froissart et Christine de Pizan*. Paris: Champion, 2005.

Leech-Wilkinson, Daniel. *Machaut's Mass: An Introduction*. Oxford: Clarendon, 1990.

Leff, Michael C. "Boethius' *De differentiis topicis*, Book IV." In *Medieval Eloquence: Studies in the Theory and Practice of Medieval Rhetoric*, ed. James J. Murphy, 3–24. Berkeley: University of California Press, 1978.

Léglu, Catherine. "Defamation in the Troubadour *Sirventes*: Legislation and Lyric Poetry." *Medium Ævum* 66.1 (1997): 28–41.

———. "Languages in Conflict in Toulouse: *Las leys d'amor*." *Modern Language Review* 103.2 (April 2008): 383–96.

———. "Moral and Satirical Poetry." In *The Troubadours: An Introduction*, eds. Simon Gaunt and Sarah Kay, 47–65. Cambridge: Cambridge University Press, 1999.

Le Goff, Jacques, and René Remond. *Histoire de la France Religieuse*. 4 vols. Paris: Seuil, 1988–92.

———. *La civilisation de l'Occident médiévale*. Paris: Arthaud, 1964.

———. *La naissance du Purgatoire*. Paris: Gallimard, 1981.

Levinas, Emmanuel. *Autrement qu'être ou au-delà de l'essence*. The Hague: Martinus Nijhoff, 1978. Repr. Paris: Kluwer Academic, 1991.

———. *Totalité et infini: Essai sur l'extériorité*. The Hague: Martinus Nijhoff, 1971. Repr. Paris: Kluwer Academic, 2008.

Little, Katherine C. *Confession and Resistance: Defining the Self in Late Medieval England*. Notre Dame, IN: University of Notre Dame Press, 2006.

Lowe, Jeremy. *Desiring Truth: The Process of Judgment in Fourteenth-Century Art and Literature.* Studies in Medieval History and Culture 30. New York: Routledge, 2005.

Maclean, Ian. "The Place of Interpretation: Montaigne and Humanist Jurists on Words, Intention and Meaning." In *Neo-Latin and Vernacular in Renaissance France,* eds. Graham Castor and Terence Cave, 252–72. Oxford: Clarendon, 1984.

Maddox, Donald, and Sara Sturm-Maddox, eds. *Froissart Across the Genres.* Gainesville: University Press of Florida, 1998.

———. *Parisian Confraternity Drama of the Fourteenth Century: The Miracles de Nostre Dame par personages.* Medieval Texts and Cultures of Northern Europe 22. Turnhout: Brepols, 2008.

Mâle, Émile. *L'art religieux du XIIIe siècle en France.* 7th ed. Paris: Armand Colin, 1931.

Marchesi, Simone. "Distilling Ovid: Dante's Exile and Some Metamorphic Nomenclature in Hell." In *Writers Reading Writers: Intercultural Studies in Medieval and Early Modern Literature in Honor of Robert Hollander,* 21–39. Newark, DE: University of Delaware Press, 2007.

Marx, C. W. *The Devil's Rights and the Redemption in the Literature of Medieval England.* Rochester, NY: D. S. Brewer, 1995.

Mathieu-Castellani, Gisèle. *La scène judiciaire de l'autobiographie.* Paris: Presses Universitaires de France, 1996.

Maupeu, Philippe. "*Bivium*: l'écrivain nattier et le *Roman de la Rose.*" In *Guillaume de Digulleville: Les* Pèlerinages *allégoriques,* eds. Frédéric Duval and Fabienne Pomel, 21–41. Rennes: Presses Universitaires de Rennes, 2008.

———. "La tentation autobiographique dans le songe allégorique édifiant de Guillaume de Deguileville: *Le pèlerinage de vie humaine.*" In *Songes et songeurs (XIIIe–XVIIIe siècle),* eds. Nathalie Dauvois and Jean-Philippe Grosperrin, 49–67. Québec: Les Presses de l'Université Laval, 2003.

———. *Pèlerins de vie humaine: Autobiographie et allégorie narrative, de Guillaume de Deguileville à Octovien de Saint-Gelais.* Paris: Champion, 2009.

McGerr, Rosemarie P. *Chaucer's Open Books: Resistance to Closure in Medieval Discourse.* Gainesville: University Press of Florida, 1998.

McGrady, Deborah. *Controlling Readers: Guillaume de Machaut and His Late Medieval Audience.* Toronto: University of Toronto Press, 2006.

———. "Guillaume de Machaut." In *The Cambridge Companion to Medieval French Literature,* eds. Simon Gaunt and Sarah Kay, 109–22. Cambridge: Cambridge University Press, 2008.

McGuire, Brian Patrick. *Jean Gerson and the Last Medieval Reformation.* University Park, PA: Penn State University Press, 2005.

McLaughlin, Megan. *Consorting with Saints: Prayer for the Dead in Early Medieval France.* Ithaca, NY: Cornell University Press, 1994.

Minnis, Alastair. *Magister Amoris: The* Roman de la Rose *and Vernacular Hermeneutics.* Oxford: Oxford University Press, 2001.

———. *Medieval Theory of Authorship: Scholastic Literary Attitudes in the Later Middle Ages.* London: Scolar Press, 1984.

Moeglin, Jean-Marie, ed. *L'intercession du Moyen Âge à l'époque moderne: Autour d'une pratique sociale.* Hautes Études Médiévales et Modernes 87. Geneva: Droz, 2004.

Moreau, John. "'*Ce mauvais tabellion*': Satanic and Marian Textuality in Deguileville's *Pèlerinage de l'âme.* In *The* Pèlerinage *Allegories of Guillaume de Deguileville: Tradition, Authority and Influence,* eds. Marco Nievergelt and Stephanie A. Viereck Gibbs Kamath, 113–28. Cambridge: D. S. Brewer, 2013.

Morris, Colin. *The Discovery of the Individual, 1050–1200.* 2nd ed. Toronto: University of Toronto Press, 1987.

Murphy, James J., ed. *Medieval Eloquence: Studies in the Theory and Practice of Medieval Rhetoric.* Berkeley: University of California Press, 1978.

———. *Rhetoric in the Middle Ages: A History of Rhetorical Theory from Saint Augustine to the Renaissance.* Berkeley: University of California Press, 1974.

Nievergelt, Marco, and Stephanie A. Viereck Gibbs Kamath, eds. *The* Pèlerinage *Allegories of Guillaume de Deguileville: Tradition, Authority and Influence.* Cambridge: D. S. Brewer, 2013.

Nouvet, Claire. "La fragmentation du système poetico-lyrique de Jean Froissart." Diss. Princeton University, 1981.

Oakes, Catherine. *Ora Pro Nobis: The Virgin as Intercessor in Medieval Art and Devotion.* London: Harvey Miller, 2008.

———. "The Scales: An Iconographic Motif of Justice, Redemption and Intercession." *Maria* 1 (2000): 11–36.

Ourliac, Paul. "Troubadours et juristes." *Cahiers de civilisation médiévale* 8 (January–March 1965): 159–77.

Palmer, R. Barton, ed. *Chaucer's French Contemporaries: The Poetry/Poetics of Self and Tradition.* New York: AMS, 1999.

———. "The Metafictional Machaut: Reflexivity in the Judgment Poems." In *Chaucer's French Contemporaries: The Poetry/Poetics of Self and Tradition,* ed. R. Barton Palmer, 71–92. New York: AMS, 1999.

———. "Transtextuality and the Producing-I in Guillaume de Machaut's Judgment Series." *Exemplaria* 5.2 (1993): 283–304.

Papka, Claudia Rattazzi. "The Limits of Apocalypse: Eschatology, Epistemology, and Textuality in the *Commedia* and *Piers Plowman.*" In *Last Things: Death and the Apocalypse in the Middle Ages,* eds. Caroline Walker Bynum and Paul Freedman, 233–56. Philadelphia: University of Pennsylvania Press, 2000.

Paterson, Linda. *Troubadours and Eloquence.* Oxford: Clarendon Press, 1975.

Payen, Jean-Charles. *Le motif du repentir dans la littérature française médiévale, des origines à 1230.* Publications Romanes et Françaises 98. Geneva: Droz, 1967.

Peperzak, Adriaan. *To the Other: An Introduction to the Philosophy of Emmanuel Levinas.* West Lafayette, IN: Purdue University Press, 1993.

Peters, Ursula, and Andreas Kablitz. "The *Pèlerinage* Corpus: A Tradition of Textual Transformation Across Western Europe." In *The* Pèlerinage *Allegories of Guillaume de Deguileville: Tradition, Authority and Influence.* eds. Marco Nievergelt and Stephanie A. Viereck Gibbs Kamath, 25–46. Cambridge: D. S. Brewer, 2013.

Petit-Morphy, Odette. *François Villon et la Scolastique.* 2 vols. Diss. Université de Lille III, 1977. Paris: Champion, 1977.

Phillippy, Patricia Berrahou. *Love's Remedies: Recantation and Renaissance Lyric Poetry.* Lewisburg, PA: Bucknell University Press, 1995.

Phillips, Helen. "Chaucer and Deguileville: The ABC in Context." *Medium Ævum* 62.1 (Spring 1993): 1–19.

Picherit, Jean-Louis. "Le rôle des éléments mythologiques dans le *Joli buisson de Jonece* de Jean Froissart." *Neophilologus* 63 (1979): 498–508.

———. "Les exemples dans le *Jugement dou roy de Navarre* de Guillaume de Machaut." *Les lettres romanes* 36.2 (May 1982): 103–16.

Planche, Alice. "Du *Joli buisson de Jeunesse* au *buisson ardent*: Le Lai de Notre Dame dans le *dit* de Froissart." In *La prière au Moyen Âge: Littérature et civilisation*, 395–413. Paris: Champion, 1981.

Poirion, Daniel. *Le poète et le prince: L'évolution du lyrisme courtois de Guillaume de Machaut à Charles d'Orléans*. Paris: Presses Universitaires de France, 1965.

Pomel, Fabienne. "Enjeux d'un travail de réécriture: Les *incipits* du *Pèlerinage de vie humaine* de Guillaume de Digulleville et leurs remaniements ultérieurs." *Le Moyen Âge* 109.3–4 (2003): 457–71.

———. "Le *Roman de la Rose* comme voie de paradis: Transposition, parodie et moralisation de Guillaume de Lorris à Jean Molinet." In *De la Rose: Texte, image, fortune*, eds. Catherine Bel and Herman Braet, 355–76. Dudley, MA: Peeters, 2006.

———. "Les écrits pérégrins ou les voies de l'autorité chez Guillaume de Deguileville: Le modèle épistolaire et juridique." In *The* Pèlerinage *Allegories of Guillaume de Deguileville: Tradition, Authority and Influence*, eds. Marco Nievergelt and Stephanie A. Viereck Gibbs Kamath, 91–111. Cambridge: D. S. Brewer, 2013.

———. *Les voies de l'au-delà et l'essor de l'allégorie au Moyen Âge*. Paris: Champion, 2001.

Purkart, Josef. "Boncompagno of Signa and the Rhetoric of Love." In *Medieval Eloquence: Studies in the Theory and Practice of Medieval Rhetoric*, ed. James J. Murphy, 319–31. Berkeley: University of California Press, 1978.

Rebillard, Éric. *In hora mortis: Évolution de la pastorale chrétienne de la mort aux IVe et Ve siècles dans l'Occident latin*. Rome: École Française de Rome, 1994.

Reed, Thomas L., Jr. *Middle English Debate Poetry and the Aesthetics of Irresolution*. Columbia: University of Missouri Press, 1990.

Regosin, Richard L. "Rusing with the Law: Montaigne and the Ethics of Uncertainty." *L'ésprit créateur* 46.1 (Spring 2006): 51–63.

Ribémont. Bernard. "Froissart et le mythe de Daphné." *Revue des langues romanes* 98.1 (1994): 189–99.

———. "Froissart, le mythe et la marguerite." *Revue des langues romanes* 94.1 (1990): 129–37.

Richards, Earl Jeffrey. "Christine de Pizan and Jean Gerson: An Intellectual Friendship." In *Christine de Pizan 2000: Studies on Christine de Pizan in Honour of Angus J. Kennedy*, eds. John Campbell and Nadia Margolis, 197–208. Amsterdam: Rodopi, 2000.

Riley, Patrick. *Character and Conversion in Autobiography: Augustine, Montaigne, Descartes, Rousseau, and Sartre*. Charlottesville: University of Virginia Press, 2004.

Rooney, Anne. "*The Book of the Duchess*: Hunting and the 'Ubi Sunt' Tradition." *The Review of English Studies* 151.38 (1987): 299–314.

Root, Jerry. *'Space to Speke': The Confessional Subject in Medieval Literature*. New York: Peter Lang, 1997.

Santi, Francesco. "Guglielmo D'Auvergne e l'Ordine dei Domenicani tra Filosofia Naturale e Tradizione Magica." In *Autour de Guillaume d'Auvergne (†1249)*, eds. Franco Morenzoni and Jean-Yves Tilliette, 137–53. Turnhout, Brepols, 2005.

Scaramella, Pierroberto. "L'Italia dei trionfi e dei contrasti." In *Humana fragilitas: I temi della morte in Europa tra duecento e settecento,* ed. Alberto Tenenti, 25–98. Clusone: Ferrari Editrice, 2000.

Schüssler, Rudolf. "Jean Gerson, Moral Certainty and the Renaissance of Ancient Scepticism." *Renaissance Studies* 23.4 (2009): 445–62.

Schwam-Baird, Schira. "Sweet Dreams: The Pursuit of Youthful Love in Jean Froissart's *Joli buisson de Jonece* and René d'Anjou's *Livre du cuer d'amours espris.*" *Moyen Français* 38 (1996): 45–60.

Senior, Matthew. *In the Grip of Minos: Confessional Discourse in Dante, Corneille, and Racine.* Columbus: The Ohio State University Press, 1994.

Sheingorn, Pamela. "'For God is Such a Doomsman': Origins and Development of the Theme of Last Judgment." In *Homo, Memento Finis: The Iconography of Just Judgment in Medieval Art and Drama,* ed. David Bevington, 15–58. Kalamazoo: Medieval Institute Publications, Western Michigan University, 1985.

Shimomura, Sachi. *Odd Bodies and Visible Ends in Medieval Literature.* The New Middle Ages. New York: Palgrave MacMillan, 2006.

Smith, Geri L. "Froissart's Télèphe: A Revealing Link Between Ovidian Invention, the 'Pastourelles,' and the Poet's Persona."*Fifteenth Century Studies* 29 (2004): 200–9.

Smith, Nathaniel B. "Rhetoric." In *A Handbook of the Troubadours,* eds. F. R. P. Akehurst and Judith M. Davis, 400–20. Berkeley: University of California Press, 1995.

Smith, William, and John Lockwood. *Chambers Murray Latin-English Dictionary.* Edinburgh: Chambers-Murray, 2004.

Smoller, Laura A. "Of Earthquakes, Hail, Frogs and Geography: Plague and the Investigation of the Apocalypse in the Later Middle Ages." In *Last Things: Death and Apocalypse in the Middle Ages,* eds. Caroline Walker Bynum and Paul H. Freedman, 156–87. Philadelphia: University of Pennsylvania Press, 2000.

Solère, Jean-Luc. "De l'orateur à l'orant: La 'rhétorique divine' dans la culture chrétienne occidentale." *Revue de l'histoire des religions* 211.2 (1994): 187–224.

Spence, Sarah. "Rhetoric and Hermeneutics." In *The Troubadours: An Introduction,* eds. Simon Gaunt and Sarah Kay, 164–80. Cambridge: Cambridge University Press, 1999.

Sturm-Maddox, Sara. "*La pianta più gradita in cielo*: Petrarch's Laurel and Jove." In *Dante, Petrarch, Boccaccio: Studies in the Italian Trecento in Honor of Charles S. Singleton,* eds. Aldo S. Bernardo and Anthony L. Pellegrini, 255–71. Medieval and Renaissance Texts and Studies 22. Binghamton, NY: Medieval and Renaissance Texts and Studies, 1983.

Symes, Carol. *A Common Stage: Theater and Public Life in Medieval Arras.* Ithaca, NY: Cornell University Press, 2007.

Szittya, Penn. "Domesday Bokes: The Apocalypse in Medieval English Literary Culture." In *The Apocalypse in the Middle Ages,* eds. Richard K. Emmerson and Bernard McGinn, 374–97. Ithaca, NY: Cornell University Press, 1992.

Taylor, Jane H. M., ed. *Dies Illa: Death in the Middle Ages.* Proceedings of the 1983 Eugene Vinaver International Colloquium, Manchester. Liverpool: Francis Cairns, 1984.

Taylor, Scott L. "Reason, Rhetoric, and Redemption: The Teaching of Law and the *Planctus Mariae* in the Late Middle Ages." In *Medieval Education,* eds. Ronald B. Begley and Joseph W. Koterski, 68–79. New York: Fordham University Press, 2005.

Taylor, Stephen M. "Portraits of Pestilence: The Plague in the Work of Machaut and Boccaccio." *Allegorica* 5.1 (Summer 1980): 105–18.

Tilliette, Jean-Yves. "Oraison et art oratoire: Les sources et les propos de la *Rhetorica divina.*" In *Autour de Guillaume d'Auvergne (†1249),* eds. Franco Morenzoni and Jean-Yves Tilliette, 203–215. Turnhout: Brepols, 2005.

Tournon, André. "Justice and the Law: On the Reverse Side of the *Essays.*" In *The Cambridge Companion to Montaigne,* ed. Ullrich Langer, 96–117. Cambridge: Cambridge University Press, 2005.

Veysseyre, Géraldine, Julia Drobinsky, and Émilie Fréger. "Liste des manuscrits des trois *Pèlerinages.*" In *Guillaume de Digulleville: Les* Pèlerinages *allégoriques,* eds. Fréderic Duval and Fabienne Pomel, 425–53. Rennes: Presses Universitaires de Rennes, 2008.

Waldenfels, Bernard. "Levinas on the Saying and the Said." In *Addressing Levinas,* eds. Eric Sean Nelson, Antje Kapust, and Kent Still, 86–97. Evanston, IL: Northwestern University Press, 2005.

Walters, Lori J. "Gerson and Christine, Poets." In *Poetry, Knowledge and Community in Late Medieval France,* eds. Rebecca Dixon, Finn E. Sinclair, with Adrian Armstrong, Sylvia Huot, and Sarah Kay, 69–81. Woodbridge, Suffolk, UK: D. S. Brewer, 2008.

Ward, Graham. "On Time and Salvation: The Eschatology of Emmanuel Levinas." In *Facing the Other: The Ethics of Emmanuel Levinas,* ed. Seán Hand, 153–72. Curzon Jewish Philosophy ser. Richmond, Surrey, UK: Curzon, 1996.

Ward, John O. *Ciceronian Rhetoric in Treatise, Scholion and Commentary.* Turnhout: Brepols, 1995.

———. "The Commentator's Rhetoric: From Antiquity to the Renaissance: Glosses and Commentaries on Cicero's *Rhetorica.*" In *Medieval Eloquence: Studies in the Theory and Practice of Medieval Rhetoric,* ed. James J. Murphy, 25–67. Berkeley: University of California Press, 1978.

Wilkins, Nigel. "A Pattern of Patronage: Machaut, Froissart and the Houses of Luxembourg and Bohemia in the Fourteenth Century." *French Studies* 37.3 (July 1983): 257–84.

Williams, Sarah Jane. "An Author's Role in Fourteenth-Century Book Production: Guillaume de Machaut's *Livre ou je mets toutes mes choses.*" *Romania* 90 (1969): 433–54.

Wright, Steven. "Deguileville's *Pèlerinage de vie humaine* as 'contrepartie édifiante' of the *Roman de la Rose.*" *Philological Quarterly* 68.4 (1989): 399–422.

Yalom, Marilyn. *A History of the Breast.* New York: Alfred A. Knopf-Random House, 1997.

Zaleski, Carol. *Otherworldly Journeys: Accounts of Near-Death Experience in Medieval and Modern Times.* New York: Oxford University Press, 1987.

Zanella, Gabriele. "Italia, Francia e Germania: una storiografia a confronto." In *La peste nera: Dati di una realtà ed elementi di una interpretazione, atti del xxx convegno storico internazionale; Todi, 10–13 ottobre 1993,* 44–135. Spoleto: Centro Italiano di Studi sull Alto Medioevo, 1994.

Zink, Michel. *Froissart et le temps.* Paris: Presses Universitaires de France, 1998.

———. "L'amour en fuite: *L'espinette amoureuse* et *Le joli buisson de Jeunesse* de Froissart ou la poésie comme histoire sans objet." In *Musique naturele: Interpretationen zur französischen Lyrik des Spätmittelatters,* ed. Wolf-Dieter Stempel, 195–209. Munich: Wilhelm Fink Verlag, 1995.

———. *La subjectivité littéraire: Autour du siècle de saint Louis.* Paris: Presses Universitaires de France, 1985.

———. "Le temps, c'est de l'argent: Remarques sur le *Dit du florin* de Jean Froissart." In *Et c'est la fin pour quoy nous sommes ensemble: Hommage à Jean Dufournet: Littérature, histoire et langue du Moyen Âge,* 3:1, 455–64. Paris: Champion, 1993.

———. *Nature et poésie au Moyen Âge.* Paris: Fayard, 2006.

Zumthor, Paul. *Essai de poétique médiévale.* Paris: Seuil, 1972.

INDEX

Abbeville, *puy* of, 177

Abelard, Pierre, *Historia calamitatum*, 68n18, 86

acrostics, 65, 84, 87, 126. *See also* signatures and naming

Acteon, use of myth by Deguileville, 85, 86n55

actio, in rhetoric, 47, 50n39, 55

Adam and Eve, 44, 46, 94, 156. *See also* original sin

Adam de la Halle, 12, 14, 60, 124n55. *See also jongleurs* of Arras

Adenet le Roi, *Cléomades*, 153

Advocacie Nostre Dame, 45–49; and Deguileville's *Pèlerinage de l'âme*, 63, 67, 94

Advocata Nostra, adoration of the Virgin Mary as, 30, 44–52, 53–54; and confraternal poets, 56; and Deguileville, 67, 93; and Froissart, 177–78, 207; and Machaut, 139

ages of man, Ptolemaic trope in Froissart, 146, 158–62, 180. *See also* Ptolemy

Alain de Lille: *liber experientiae*, 68n18; *De planctu naturae*, 19n43

Alighieri, Dante, 10, 29; contrast with French poets, 43–44; *Convivio*, 42, 162n46, 193n9; and Deguileville, 42, 43–44, 62, 65n9, 86n55, 96n77, 97, 142, 192; *Divina commedia*, 9, 22n49, 40–42, 56n54; and Machaut, 114, 142, 192; and Froissart, 148, 158n39, 162n46; *Vita nuova*, 42, 162n46; *De vulgari eloquentia*, 40

allegory, 7–8, 191; and Deguileville, 62, 69, 70, 71, 72, 74n27, 76, 77, 78, 79, 80n45, 83, 93, 95, 99, 116n34; and eschatological record-books, 16–23, 31; and Froissart, 32, 146, 151, 155–56, 180–183; and Guillaume d'Auvergne, 56, 95; as a problem for medieval poets, 9, 14; in *Vilain qui conquist paradis par plait*, 36n6

Althusser, Louis, 200

angels, 50, 52n41, 64, 97. *See also* Cherubin; Michael, Saint

Anne of Bohemia, patron of Chaucer, 104n3

apologetic discourse, 10n20, 12, 20, 80, 84, 188, 192, 202, 204–5, 207. *See also* confessional discourse; repentance; rhetoric

Aquinas, Thomas, 6n9, 34n2, 52–53, 97n80

Ariès, Philippe, 8n14, 9n18, 16, 26n59

Aristotle, 53, 131, 138

228

Arras, 22n49, 57–58, 59. See also *jongleurs* of Arras

ars poetica, 43. *See also* second rhetoric

Ascoli, Albert Russell, 40–41

Astell, Ann W., 205

auctoritas. See authority, poetic

Auerbach, Erich, concept of *figura*, 182n70, 183n72

Augustine, Saint, 3; *De civitate Dei*, 52n43, 195; *Confessiones*, 183n71; *De praedestinatione sanctorum*, 53n44

authority, poetic, 4, 5, 10, 12, 14, 22, 23, 24, 28, 29, 33, 43, 62, 188, 189, 191, 192, 196, 200, 206, 207; and Christine de Pizan, 195–96; and Dante, 41; and Deguileville, 96, 97, 99, 100; and Froissart, 151, 152, 162, 170, 171, 177, 178, 179, 185, 187; and Machaut, 101, 120, 125–27, 136, 139, 142–43, 206; and; Marian poets, 43–44, 57–58, 60; and Rousseau, 199–200. *See also* first-person voice; persona; subjectivity

autobiography, 4n8, 10, 193, 200; *See also* pseudo-autobiography, *scène judiciaire de l'autobiographie*

Badel, Pierre-Yves, 60n68, 73n25, 75n30, 75nn32–33, 77n34, 77nn37–38, 78, 80n43, 93n66

Barthes, Roland, concept of the *texte scriptible*, 143

Basoche, legal organization, 59n65

Beatrice, character in Dante, 41–42, 65n9, 142n92

Benedictus Deus, papal bull, 9n17, 64n4, 65

Bernard de Clairvaux, 8n15, 15–16, 95

Black Death, 110–16, 187

Blanche of Lancaster, patron of Froissart, 170

Boccaccio, Giovanni, 10; *Decameron*, 54n47, 116n34

Bodel, Jean, 12

Boethius, *Consolation of Philosophy*, 136n79, 168

Bologna, center of legal learning, 42, 49, 133n71

Bonaventure, 52–53

Bonne de Luxembourg, patron of Machaut, 31, 104n3, 110, 118–20, 125n53

Bonneurté, character in Machaut, 31, 103, 105–8, 110, 117–32, 136–40, 167n54, 172, 173, 174

Book of Conscience, 15–16, 22, 61, 88, 90–91, 107, 122, 124, 142. See also *Liber vitae*

Book of Life. See *Liber vitae*

book trade, 14

Bourdieu, Pierre, 200

Brownlee, Kevin, 101n83, 124–25, 126n59, 128n64

burning bush, image in Froissart, 179, 182

Calin, William, 109n10, 110n16, 116n33, 117n36, 118nn38–39, 120n48, 121n49, 135

Camille, Michael, 48–49, 49n36, 64n3, 65n6, 76n34, 77n39, 92n63

Cantigas de Santa Maria, 52n41, 58n62

capital, 17, 150, 170–71, 187, 190; as spiritual metaphor, 17–18, 37, 170–71, 180

Cardenal, Peire, 36–37, 38, 199

Carité de Notre Dame des Ardents. See *jongleurs* of Arras

Castille, influence of northern French confraternal poetry on, 58

Cato of Utica, judged by Christine de Pizan, 195

Cecco d'Ascoli, judged by Christine de Pizan, 195

Cerquiglini, Jacqueline, 29n68, 60n69, 110n16, 114n31, 118n39, 119n44, 141n90, 149, 156n33, 157n38, 177n63

certitudo moralis, in Jean Gerson and Christine de Pizan, 197

Chaalis, abbey of, 63, 73n26, 74n27, 75, 76, 85–87, 97, 98

Charles V (king of France), 170, 193

Charles de Navarre, 31, 103–4, 105, 106, 107, 119, 129, 130, 131–32, 134, 135, 136, 137, 141, 171, 186

Charles d'Espagne (Charles de la Cerda), 119, 141

Chartier, Alain, 10

Chastellain, Pierre, 192

Chaucer, Geoffrey, 10; *Book of the Duchess,* 117n38, *Canterbury Tales,* 11n25, 12, 23, 29; and Deguileville, 67n11; *Legend of Good Women,* 29n67, 103n3, 136n76; and Machaut, 103n3, 136n76

Cherubin (angel), 98

Christine de Pizan, 10, 33, 193–97; compared with later authors, 198n22; and Jean Gerson's *certitudo moralis,* 197; *Livre de la cité des dames,* 193–96; *Livre de l'advision Cristine,* 195n13; Querelle de la Rose, 21n47, 77n37, 196

chronique, genre in Machaut, 129, 141. *See also* Froissart, Jean; Gabriele de Mussis; Jean le Bel

Cicero, rhetoric of, 39–41, 42, 44, 51, 55–56

Cistercian order, 63, 66, 67, 77, 86, 95, 96n79

city of God, 70, 72, 74, 76, 77, 88, 195–96. *See also* Augustine, Saint

civil law, 6, 24, 35, 42, 46, 59

civitas Dei. See city of God; *for the text, see* Augustine, Saint

compilation. *See* manuscripts, compilation of

complete-works codices. *See* manuscripts, compilation of

confession, sacrament, 8, 12, 16, 23, 54n47, 55, 115, 117, 126, 138. *See also* repentance

confessional discourse, 8, 12–13, 26, 55, 96, 138. *See also* apologetic discourse; repentance

confessional manuals, 35

Conflictus inter Deum et Diabolum, 44–45

confraternities, 32, 43–44, 56–60, 177. *See also jongleurs* of Arras

conscience, 8, 12, 15, 17n38, 32, 35, 64, 90–92, 93, 169, 190, 192n8. *See also* Book of Conscience

copyists, 21, 48, 61, 86, 92–93, 94–95

corpus of the author, 14, 16, 18, 23, 28, 31, 61–62, 189, 206; and Deguileville, 23, 62, 68–69, 81n46, 84, 88–89, 99, 101; and Froissart, 23, 32, 145, 148n11, 149, 151, 161, 162, 167, 170, 171, 173–74, 178–79, 181–87; and Guillaume le Clerc, 17–18; and Jean de Meun, 19–21; and Machaut, 23, 32, 101, 102, 106, 108, 120, 123–25, 126–27, 130, 137, 139, 140–42, 170, 171; and Montaigne, 198–99; and Rutebeuf, 18–19. *See also* manuscripts, compilation of; *œuvre*

correctio, spiritual metaphor, 22n49, 191

courtly poetry, 10, 31–32, 41, 101, 102, 107, 109–10, 116, 137, 142–43, 148n11, 151, 153, 157, 163, 164, 165, 166, 177, 185, 186, 190

courts of love, 123n51. *See also* debate poetry; Le Poirier, Mahieu

Coville, Alfred, 112

Daniel, Book of, 15

Dante. *See* Alighieri, Dante

debate poetry, 6, 109, 120, 122–23, 130, 132n70, 154, 157, 162, 164, 185; body and soul debates, 98, 130; *jeux-partis,* 109. *See also* courts of love; *Débats du clerc et du chevalier;* Le Poirier, Mahieu

Débats du clerc et du chevalier, 164n50

Deguileville, Guillaume de, 4n8, 5, 6, 14, 23, 29, 42, 60–62, 63–101, 104, 106, 107, 124, 138, 142, 143, 168, 177, 191, 192, 195, 196, 197, 199, 205, 207; *Pèlerinage de l'âme,* 30–31, 32, 63–70, 88–101, 122, 126, 130, 132, 136, 150, 174, 178, 182, 190, 199, 206; *Pèlerinage de vie humaine,* 68–88, 89–96, 98, 175n62; *Pèlerinage Jhesucrist,* 68–99; *Roman de la fleur de lis,* 68n16

De Looze, Laurence, 6n12, 7n13, 11, 14, 68n18, 110n19, 117n37, 122n50, 125n57, 126n59, 127n62, 136n77, 140, 143n93.

See also Gybbon-Monypenny, G. B.; pseudo-autobiography

Dembowski, Peter, 148

Derrida, Jacques, 200

Deschamps, Eustache, 10; *Art de dictier,* 43

Devil. *See* Satan

Devil's Rights, 44–52, 55, 56, 61, 62, 63, 64, 65–66, 67, 88, 93–94, 98, 100, 182

devotional poetry, 5, 6, 24, 30–31, 32, 38, 43–52, 56–61, 67, 102, 137, 143, 165, 177, 181, 186, 189, 191, 207. *See also* confraternities; *jongleurs* of Arras; *Leys d'amors;* prayer

dialectic, 130, 132n70, 140

dialog: between authors and readers, 13, 25, 69, 100, 101, 188, 189–90, 191, 206; and Deguileville, 79; and Froissart, 175; between God and man, 6, 13, 28, 55n53, 56; and the *jongleurs* of Arras, 57; and Machaut, 125, 128, 129, 141; between priest and penitent, 13

Dies irae, hymn, 34–35, 147, 184

Dieu d'Amours. *See* God of Love

dit (genre), 29–30, 91–92, 100, 102, 124, 127n62, 141, 144–45, 148, 156, 157, 173, 176, 185, 186n78, 193, 206

Domesday Boke, 15n31

dreams, in poetry, 32, 63, 67n12, 70, 71, 73, 74n27, 76, 77

Durbui, court of Jean de Luxembourg at, 108–9

Earp, Lawrence, 103n3, 110n13, 110n17, 112n21, 118n41, 119, 124n52, 127nn62–63

Edward III (king of England), 171, 186

Ehrhart, Margaret J., 131n68, 145n3, 146n6, 152n20, 153n21, 155, 156n32, 156n34, 157n36

England, 10, 12n28, 15n21, 58, 186

episcopal courts, 35

eschatological, definition of, 25–28, 190–91, 201–6

Estinnes-au-Mont, Froissart's benefice at, 148, 171

ethics: judicial, 49; in Levinas, 201, 203, 205, 206; literary, 5, 7, 8, 9, 11–12, 13–14, 16, 23, 25, 26–28, 31, 32, 33, 60, 62, 69, 79, 84, 92–93, 98, 99–100, 105, 106, 107, 108, 122–23, 126, 130, 132, 137, 138, 139, 140, 143, 150, 151, 163, 165–66, 167, 171, 176, 181–82, 187, 188, 189, 190, 191, 193, 195, 196, 197, 198, 199, 205, 206. *See also* responsibility

Étienne de Bourbon, 35

evangelical responsibility. *See* ethics; pastoral duty of the poet; responsibility

Everyman (morality play), 16

Exodus, Book of, 15

exordium, in rhetoric, 51, 55

Fastoul, Baude, 12

female readers and audience members, 76, 105, 118, 141, 153–55, 163–64. *See also* Anne of Bohemia; Bonne de Luxembourg; patronage; Philippa de Hainaut

fiction, moral suspicions about, 78

figura. See Auerbach, Erich

first-person voice, 10, 14, 21n46, 27–28, 29, 30, 40, 67, 69, 70, 73, 74n27, 77, 88, 91, 92, 100, 124n55, 141, 144, 186, 204–5. *See also* persona; subjectivity

fixed-form poetry. *See* lyric composition

Florence: and Brunetto Latini, 39; center of legal learning, 42; and Dante, 42, 86n55

Foucault, Michel, 8, 200

Freeman, Michelle, 148, 151, 161n43, 166n51, 167n54, 169n55, 177n63

free will, 72, 75, 155

Froissart, Jean, 5, 10, 14, 23, 29, 60, 67, 91, 100, 101, 144–87, 190–91, 193, 197, 198–99, 205, 206, 207; *Chroniques,* 144, 148, 149, 185–87; *Dit dou florin,* 149n13, 185n75; *Espinette amoureuse,* 32, 143, 144–47, 149, 151–58, 159, 160, 162, 167, 173, 179, 185; *Joli buisson de Jonece,* 32,

143, 144–51, 155, 158–86; "Lay de Nostre Dame," 145, 147, 161n43, 178–84, 185; lyric forms, 173, 174, 185n75; *Meliador*, 148, 185–86; *Orloge amoureuse*, 173; *Paradis amoureux*, 173; *Plaidoirie de la rose et de la violette*, 185; *Prison amoureuse*, 173

Fulgentius, 155

Gabriele de Mussis, *Historia de morbo*, 112–13

General judgment. See Last Judgment

Genesis, Book of, 46–47, 61

Genet, Jean, 3

Genius, character in *Roman de la Rose*, 19–21

Gerson, Jean, 10n19, 21n47, 77n37, 196–97

God of Love (Dieu d'Amours), 19, 104n3, 164, 177, 178

Gower, John, 10

grace, divine, 18, 37, 49, 52, 56, 66, 75, 78, 95, 115

Grace Dieu, character in Deguileville, 65, 70, 72, 73, 78, 81, 83, 88, 89, 126

Gratian, 47n32

Gros, Gérard, 16n36, 45n30, 58, 60n69, 177n63

Guillaume d'Auvergne, *Rhetorica divina*, 43, 54–56, 59, 60, 95

Guillaume de Lorris, *Roman de la Rose*, 19, 20, 77, 79, 80n45, 164n50. See also Jean de Meun

Guillaume le Clerc, *Besant de Dieu*, 12, 17–18, 20, 21, 24, 61, 138, 147, 169, 170, 187

Gybbon-Monypenny, G. B., 11. See also pseudo-autobiography; De Looze, Laurence

Hainaut (Belgian province), 148

heavenly court, 2, 6–7, 12, 15, 30, 36, 40, 41, 42, 43, 45, 47, 50, 52, 56, 57, 61, 62, 63–64, 66, 69, 70, 87, 92, 95, 96, 100–101, 184, 189, 190, 200

hell, 13, 19–20, 35, 36, 41, 63, 66, 97, 99, 179

Hœpffner, Ernest, 118, 128n63

Hostiensis, *Summa*, 35n5

Hughes de Saint-Victor, *De sacramentis christiane fidei*, 8n15

humanism, 193

Hundred Years War, 144, 161

hunting: and Deguileville, 85, 86n55; and Machaut's use of *memento mori*, 103, 117–18, 121. See also Acteon; *memento mori*; Trois Morts et les Trois Vifs

Huot, Sylvia, 14n30, 21–22, 22nn49–51, 29n68, 60n68, 77n38, 80n35, 101n38, 124–25, 128n64, 144n1, 145nn2–3, 148n11, 178n65, 179n66, 183n71, 191n3, 197n18

Hussite movement, 196

intercession of the saints, 6, 24, 43, 52–54, 56, 58, 59, 67, 179, 189

Isaiah, Book of, 15, 180

Italy: poets of, 10, 29; legal and rhetorical learning in, 39, 42. See also Alighieri, Dante; Bologna; Florence; Latini, Brunetto

Jackson, Justin A., 205

Jacques de Vitry, *Exempla*, 35

Jean II (king of France), 118–19

Jean de Luxembourg (king of Bohemia), patron of Machaut, 103, 106, 108–9, 110, 111, 112n21, 119, 122, 125, 127, 131, 137, 141, 148n9

Jean de Meun, 61, 195; *Roman de la Rose*, 19–21, 24, 77–78, 79, 82–83, 86, 91n62, 130; *Testament*, 21, 24, 91n62

Jean duc de Berry, patron of Machaut, 119n44, 156, 157n36

Jean le Bel, *Chronique*, 112, 118–19, 186
Jerusalem, heavenly. *See* city of God
Jewish law, and Froissart, 181–82. *See also* Old and New Laws
Jews, accusations against in Machaut's *Jugement dou roy de Navarre*, 112–13
Job, Book of, 6, 67, 194
John of Fribourg, *Summa confessorum*, 35n5
Jonece, character in Froissart, 146, 158–62, 164, 166n51, 176, 179
jongleurs of Arras, 22n49, 57–59. *See also* confraternities; devotional poetry
Judgment Day. *See* Last Judgment; resurrection of the dead
Judgment of Paris, 145n3, 146, 151–53, 154n24, 155–57
judicial ordeals, abolition of, 190
jugement (French term), 7, 153
Jupiter, god and astrological influence, 41, 146–47, 151, 152, 155, 158, 160–61, 162–63, 164, 165, 166, 171, 183
Justice, character in Deguileville, 64, 65, 66, 87, 88, 89–90, 96, 97, 99
Justinian, 41, 44, 47n32
Jutgamen General, mystery play, 52n41

Kay, Sarah, 10n20, 36n7, 39nn13–14, 116n34, 125n57, 131n68, 136, 146n4, 148n10, 161n43, 175n61, 183n71, 186n77, 197n18, 200n30
Kelly, Douglas, 33, 39n14, 40n16, 58n63, 108n9, 161n43, 170n57, 179n66, 183n71, 193, 195n13, 197n20, 198
Kermode, Frank, 25–26, 105n6
Kibler, William, 128n64, 141n89, 148, 153n22, 155nn25–26, 161n43

Lacan, Jacques, 200
Langland, William, *Piers Plowman*, 114
language, in divine judgment, 5–7, 27, 34–38, 41–42, 45–46, 52–56, 59, 67, 147, 184, 204–5, 207. *See also* Advocata Nostra; intercession of the saints; prayer; *rhetor divinus;* rhetoric
Lanoue, D. G., 104, 110nn18–20, 112n25, 113n30, 120n48
Last Judgment, 1–3, 9, 15, 19, 20, 26, 27, 31, 32, 34–38, 98, 111, 131, 138, 139, 143, 147–48, 150, 151, 156, 159, 165, 166, 167, 174–75, 176, 179, 181, 184, 186, 190–91, 195, 201, 205–6. *See also* particular judgment of the soul; resurrection of the dead
Latini, Brunetto: *Livres dou tresor,* 7n13, 42, 57n56; *Rettorica,* 39–40, 41, 42, 43, 56, 163
lawyer, Virgin Mary depicted as. *See* Advocata Nostra
lawyers, divine judgment of, 23, 35
lay readers, 13, 14, 76, 206
Le Fèvre, Jean, *Respit de la mort,* 37–38
legal education, 6, 24, 39, 42, 45–46, 49, 57, 59
legal profession, 24, 35, 38–39, 42, 45–46, 57–59. *See also* Advocata Nostra; Basoche; lawyers, divine judgment of; rhetoric
Le Poirier, Mahieu, *Baillieu d'Amours,* 154, 163n48
Levinas, Emmanuel, 27–28, 33, 201–7
Leys d'amors, 9
Liber vitae (Book of Life), 15–16, 22, 140, 192, 198, 206
Lille, *puy* of, 177
Lollards. *See* Wycliffites
Lucian, 49n39
Luxembourg (Belgian province), 108–9
Lydgate, John, 10; *Fall of Princes,* 104n3
lyric composition, 10n20, 38, 39, 40, 43, 44, 57, 58, 60, 66, 67, 91, 102, 117, 124, 136, 141, 144–45, 148n11, 149, 154, 157, 164, 167, 171n59, 173, 174, 178, 185, 186, 189, 193, 200n30

Machaut, Guillaume de, 5, 10, 14, 22–23, 29, 40n16, 60, 67, 91–92, 100, 102–43, 145, 146, 148, 149, 150, 163, 165, 168, 170, 177, 178, 185, 187, 190–91, 192, 193, 197, 198, 199, 205, 206, 207; *Confort d'ami,* 209n11, 140–41; *Dit de la fleur de lis et de la marguerite,* 185n76; *Dit de l'alerion,* 124, 128n63; *Dit du lyon,* 128n6; *Fonteinne amoureuse,* 119n44, 141, 154n24, 156–57; General Prologue, 128n63; *Jugement* poems, 21n47, 31–32, 101, 102–43, 145, 152, 153, 156, 157, 161, 162, 167n54, 172, 174, 186–87, 191; "Lay de plour," 21n47, 103, 139–40; *Messe de Nostre Dame,* 102, 141, 178; motets, 141, 178; *Prise d'Alexandrie,* 141; *Remede de fortune,* 124, 128n63, 136n79, 141, 144, 154n24; *Voir dit,* 125n57, 141, 144, 154n24, 157n38

manuscripts, compilation of, 10, 14, 16, 21–22, 29, 31, 60n68, 61–62, 68, 88, 89, 96, 97, 99, 101, 102, 103n3, 106, 108, 124–25, 127–28, 142, 145n2, 148, 149, 173, 185–86, 187, 206. *See also* corpus of the author

Marian poetry. *See* devotional poetry; *jongleurs* of Arras; confraternities

Mars, astrological influence discussed in Froissart, 159–60, 161, 166n51, 171

Matheolus, judged by Christine de Pizan, 195

Mathieu-Castellani, Gisèle, 1n1, 3–4, 6n10, 26, 27, 38n12, 85, 150, 190, 200. *See also scène judiciaire de l'autobiographie*

Matthew, Gospel of, 17, 26, 105, 170

Maupeu, Philippe, 4n8, 68n18, 70n21, 71nn22–24, 73n26, 74n27, 75, 76n35, 77nn37–39, 78n40, 79nn43–44, 83n47, 84n49, 86, 87n56, 89n59

McGrady, Deborah, 125n55, 125n57, 128n64, 135n72, 141n91, 206

memento mori, 117–18, 120, 121, 131, 139, 172

Mercury, god and astrological influence in Froissart, 152–53, 158–59

Michael, Saint, archangel and character in Deguileville, 64–65, 66, 69, 80, 87, 97, 98, 174

Miracle de Pierre le Changeur, 50–52, 59, 63, 65, 178

Misericorde (Mercy), character in Deguileville, 64, 66, 96

money. *See* capital

Montaigne, Michel de, 3; *Essais,* 138n82, 198–99

Montpellier, as center of legal culture, 42

mos italicus, legal philosophy, 49

motet: and Machaut, 141, 178; and Froissart, 178

Mystère du Jour du Jugement, 35n6, 53

names. *See* signatures and naming

names and things, in medieval semiotics, 82–83

narrators. *See* first-person voice; persona of the author

nunc stans, 53, 161, 205, 206

Occitan language, 36, 37n9, 38, 40n17, 42, 52n41, 59, 163n48. *See also* Cardenal, Peire; *Leys d'amors;* troubadours

Ockham, William of, 187n79

œuvre (French term), 20, 29, 100, 141, 186, 206. *See also* corpus of the author

Old and New Laws, 49, 52, 61, 99, 182, 184

Old and New Testaments, 48–49, 61, 82, 165, 179–82, 184

opinion, 7, 191, 193; of authors, 7, 12, 99, 130; in Christine de Pizan, 33, 193, 195–96, 197; in Deguileville, 199; in heavenly court, 52–53; in Froissart, 157, 161, 162, 184, 199; in Jean Gerson, 196–97; in Machaut, 106–7, 126–27, 131, 132, 136–37, 138, 140, 157, 161, 162, 170, 199; in Montaigne, 198–99; of readers, 4, 7, 26, 98, 99, 112, 130

Origen, 54

original sin, 45, 75, 156

Orléans, as center of legal learning, 42, 133n71

Ovid: *Ars amatoria*, 86; judged by Christine de Pizan, 195; and Deguileville, 86–87; *Ibis*, 86; *Tristia*, 86n55

Ovide moralisé, 22, 146, 155, 156n32, 156n35, 183

Papal Schism, 196

Papka, Claudia Rattazzi, 114

Paris: Christine de Pizan in, 193; confraternal drama in, 58, 59–60; Guillaume d'Auvergne bishop of, 43; Parliament of, 37; University of, 19, 42, 113n26

Paris, mythological figure. *See* Judgment of Paris

particular judgment of the soul, 9, 65, 69, 88, 98, 115, 206. *See also* Last Judgment

particulars, judgment of, 134–36, 137. *See also* universality in judgment

pastoral duty of the poet, 9, 23–24, 80, 143, 161, 165, 181

pathos, in the Virgin Mary's rhetoric, 47–48, 49n39. *See also* Advocata Nostra

patronage: literary, 13–14, 31, 32, 101, 103, 104n3, 105, 106, 108, 109, 110, 111, 112, 118, 119, 120, 131, 132, 136, 137, 140–41, 143, 144n1, 148, 149, 150, 151, 156, 157, 161, 165–66, 170–72, 173, 175, 184, 186, 187, 190, 193; saintly, 59n65, 60, 67, 101, 184. *See also* names *of individual patrons;* intercession of the saints.

Payen, Jean-Charles, 10n20, 191

penitence. *See* repentance

persona of the author, 10, 11, 12, 14, 22, 30, 67–68, 69, 70, 72–75, 84, 88, 91–92, 99–100, 103, 105, 107, 114n32, 124, 125–26, 142, 144, 148, 157, 161, 162, 178, 186, 189, 192. *See also* first-person voice; rhetoric; subjectivity

Peter Lombard, 26n60

Petrarch (Francesco Petrarca), 10, 29, 183; *Rime sparse*, 29n66, 185n74

Philippa de Hainaut (queen of England), patron of Froissart, 170, 171, 186

Philozophie, character in Froissart, 167–75, 176, 181, 184

Picard language, 42, 57, 117n63

pilgrimage, 62, 70, 72, 74, 76, 88–89, 99. *See also* Deguileville, Guillaume de

Planche, Alice, 179–80, 181n68

Plato of Tivoli, translator of Ptolemy, 146n5

polyphony, in Machaut's music, 102, 141, 178

Pomel, Fabienne, 64n3, 64n5, 65n7, 67n12, 68n15, 69nn19–20, 75, 76n34, 77n37, 79n43, 85n51, 86n55, 90n61, 99n82

prayer, 15n31, 21, 24, 30, 43, 53, 54–56, 58, 60, 66, 67, 95, 100, 139–40, 147, 164–65, 166n51, 177, 178–85, 189

procès (French term), 4n7, 27, 28, 32, 38, 42, 54, 56, 70, 87n56, 101, 120, 123n51, 128, 143, 151, 190–91, 197, 201, 205

Procès de Paradis, 97n80, 99n82

Processus Sathane infernalis contra genus humanum, 45, 47n32, 49

prose, 40, 44, 56, 71, 76, 141, 144, 161, 186, 193

Psalms, 15, 97n80

pseudo-autobiography, 11–12, 14–15, 23, 29, 61, 67, 68n18, 69, 84, 100, 106, 128, 147, 150, 151, 161, 186, 192, 193, 200. *See also* autobiography; De Looze, Laurence; first-person voice; Gybbon-Monypenny, G. B.; persona of the author

psychostasis. *See* scales, imagery of

Ptolemy, 146, 158, 179. *See also* ages of man

purgatory, 9, 21n47, 41, 63, 64n4, 66, 97, 136, 206, 207

puys. *See the* names *of individual host cities;* confraternities; *jongleurs* of Arras

Querelle de la Rose, 21n47, 77

Quintilian, 49n39

Raison: character in Christine de Pizan, 194–95; in Deguileville, 64, 77, 78, 81–84; in Guillaume de Lorris, 77; in Jean de Meun, 78, 82, 83; in Machaut, 131, 135–36

Raoul de Brienne (constable of France), 118–19

Raoul de Houdenc, *Songe d'enfer*, 64n3

redemption, divine, 45, 52, 75n29, 97, 99, 177–85

Reed, Thomas L., Jr., 157, 162n47

Regnier (Régnier), Jean, *Fortunes et adversitez*, 192

Reims, Machaut in, 102, 114, 178

repentance, 12, 15–16, 18–19, 21, 34, 37, 41, 55, 67, 72, 74, 78, 91n62, 92, 96, 117–18, 138, 150, 162, 165, 167, 168, 169, 170, 176, 181, 189, 191, 198–99. *See also* confession, sacrament; confessional discourse

responsibility: of authors, 5, 8, 9, 10, 11, 13, 22, 24, 26, 31, 33, 66, 69, 75, 79, 91, 100, 105, 107, 108, 122, 125, 126n61, 130, 131, 139, 150, 170, 172, 189, 205; in Levinas, 27, 201, 202, 203–4, 205; of readers, 8, 9, 13, 24–25, 83, 100, 191, 192. *See also* ethics; pastoral duty of the poet

resurrection of the dead, 9, 34, 64, 98–99, 120, 174. *See also* Last Judgment

Revelation, Book of, 15, 26, 110, 113

reverdie (trope), 116–17, 140

rewriting: by authors of others' material, 20, 62, 136n79, 143, 157, 162, 183n71, 196; by authors of own material, 9, 32, 61, 71–79, 84, 86, 94, 96, 97, 98, 106–7, 109, 116, 127, 128, 130, 131, 132, 137, 138, 139–40, 143, 174, 177, 182, 184, 191, 205; and the courts of love, 123n51; as spiritual allegory, 16, 22, 23, 49, 52, 61, 98, 139, 184, 191. See also *correctio*, spiritual metaphor

rhetor divinus, 24, 30, 34–61, 67, 95–96, 99, 100, 101, 196. *See also* Guillaume d'Auvergne

rhetoric: and Brunetto Latini, 39–40, 42, 56, 163; and Christine de Pizan, 195n12, 196; and classical influence, 24, 39–40, 42, 47, 54–56; and confraternities, 58, 59–60, 67, 101; and culture of the Artois, 57–59; and Dante, 40–41, 42, 43; and Deguileville, 42, 62, 66–69, 80, 95–96, 98, 99, 138; divine, 24, 30, 36n6, 38, 42, 54–56, 59–60, 61, 66–69, 95, 98, 99, 138, 139, 177, 189; and ethics, 5, 60; and Froissart, 161, 163, 169–70, 177, 189; and Guillaume d'Auvergne, 43, 54–56, 59, 95; and Guillaume le Clerc, 169; legal, 24, 33, 35–38, 38–39, 43, 45, 47n33, 48n34, 52, 54–56, 57, 59, 61, 67, 95, 101, 163, 189; and Machaut, 101, 131, 134, 137; and poetic authority, 24, 40, 43–44, 58, 67, 206; and poetic subjectivity, 11, 12, 13, 35–38, 66–67, 99–100; and saintly advocacy, 30, 44, 45–54, 59–60, 62, 67, 139; and self-defense/apologetics, 80, 95–96, 193. *See also* Advocata Nostra; Alighieri, Dante; apologetic discourse; Cicero, rhetoric of; confraternities; Guillaume d'Auvergne; *jongleurs* of Arras; Latini, Brunetto; *Leys d'amors*; *rhetor divinus*; second rhetoric; subjectivity

Rhetorica ad Herrenium (Ad Herrenium), 55

Robert of Flamborough, *Summa de poenitentia*, 35n5

Root, Jerry, 12–13, 104, 110n16, 118n39, 122n50

Rouen, 58

Rousseau, Jean-Jacques, 1–3, 4, 11, 13, 31, 74, 198n22, 199–200

Rude Entendement, character in Deguileville, 80–84, 93, 97–98, 99

Rutebeuf, 12, 14, 18–19, 21, 24, 61, 138, 170n58

Saint Anthony's fire, 58

Satan, 6, 18, 19, 30, 31, 44–49, 50–52, 61, 64, 66, 68, 70, 72, 81n46, 87, 88–90, 92–95, 96, 97, 98, 99. *See also* Devil's Rights

Saturn, god and astrological influence, 82, 158, 160, 161

scales, imagery of, 52n41, 87, 96, 131–32

scène judiciaire de l'autobiographie, 3–4, 8, 25, 85–86, 106, 150, 188, 190, 191, 196, 199, 200. *See also* Mathieu-Castellani, Gisèle

Schüssler, Rudolf, 197

scribes. *See* copyists

second rhetoric, poetry as, 38, 42–43, 56, 58, 59, 67. *See also ars poetica;* rhetoric

self-defense. *See* apologetic discourse

self-representation. *See* persona of the author

Senior, Matthew, 12n28, 13, 41n21

sententia diffinitiva (legal term), 129

signatures and naming, 10, 22, 41–42, 65, 68, 69, 70, 84, 88, 97, 117, 118, 126, 142, 153n22, 167n53, 170–71, 192

single-author compilation. *See* manuscripts, compilation of

subjectivity: in judgment, 7, 136, 186, 193, 199; personal and authorial, 4, 8, 10, 11, 12–13, 24, 27–28, 30–31, 33, 40–41, 49, 55, 65, 67, 70, 74n27, 126n61, 130, 138, 139, 142, 149, 161, 177, 179, 183n71, 184, 186–87, 189, 191, 192, 193, 197, 198, 199, 200–207 . *See also* first-person voice; persona of the author; pseudo-autobiography

Sun, astrological influence discussed in Froissart, 159, 160, 161, 171

Symes, Carol, 22n49, 57–58

Synderesis, character in Deguileville, 64, 90–92, 96; faculty of, distinguished from conscience, 64n5

Talents, Parable of, 17. *See also* Guillaume le Clerc, *Besant de Dieu*

Taylor, Scott L., 45n29, 49

Tertullian, 54

testament: legal document, 16; used as poetic form, 21, 24, 91n62, 150, 166–67, 171, 173, 175, 181, 192

texte scriptible. See Barthes, Roland

tiers (French term), 26, 27, 101, 172, 190, 202, 203n40. *See* Mathieu-Castellani, Gisèle; Levinas, Emmanuel

Toulouse, legal learning in, 42, 59. *See also Leys d'amors*

Tournai, *puy* of, 177

troisième personne, in Levinas, 203

Trois Morts et les Trois Vifs, legend, 117–18

troubadours, 10n20, 36–37, 38–39, 40, 163n48, 200n30. *See also* Cardenal, Peire; Occitan language

Tuscan language, 39, 43

Tutivillus (demon), 48–49, 61

universality in judgment, 135–36, 202–3. *See also* particulars, judgment of

Valenciennes, *puy* of, 177

Venus, goddess and character, 78, 79, 88, 89, 146–47, 151, 152–54, 155, 156–59, 160, 161, 164, 167, 175–76, 178, 179, 181

vernacular writing, 9, 10, 13, 14, 22, 23, 24, 25, 28, 29, 30, 38, 39, 40, 42, 43, 56, 57, 58, 60, 61–62, 67, 78, 99, 100, 114, 124, 137, 142, 143, 163, 170, 187, 189, 193, 196

Vilain qui conquist paradis par plait, 35n6

Villon, François, *Lais* and *Testament,* 192

Virgin Mary, 18, 19, 30, 32, 37, 44, 45–52, 53, 55, 56, 57, 58n62, 59–60, 61, 62, 64, 66, 67, 94, 95, 139, 145, 147, 164–65, 171, 178–79, 180, 184. See also *Advocata Nostra*

vocation of poetry, 23–24, 30, 43, 58–59, 128n63, 151–52, 153, 157, 187–88

Voie de Paradis, 64n3

Voltaire, *Sentiment des citoyens,* 2, 199

Watriquet de Couvin, 14, 22

Wenceslas I (duke of Luxembourg), patron of Froissart, 148, 171

women, judgment of, 123n51, 137. *See also* female readers and audience members

Wycliffites (Lollards), 12n28, 196

Zink, Michel, 12–13, 17n38, 18nn39–40, 60, 116n35, 149n13

INTERVENTIONS: NEW STUDIES IN MEDIEVAL CULTURE
Ethan Knapp, Series Editor

Interventions: New Studies in Medieval Culture publishes theoretically informed work in medieval literary and cultural studies. We are interested both in studies of medieval culture and in work on the continuing importance of medieval tropes and topics in contemporary intellectual life.

Eschatological Subjects: Divine and Literary Judgment in Fourteenth-Century French Poetry
J. M. MOREAU

Chaucer's (Anti-)Eroticisms and the Queer Middle Ages
TISON PUGH

Trading Tongues: Merchants, Multilingualism, and Medieval Literature
JONATHAN HSY

Translating Troy: Provincial Politics in Alliterative Romance
ALEX MUELLER

Fictions of Evidence: Witnessing, Literature, and Community in the Late Middle Ages
JAMIE K. TAYLOR

Answerable Style: The Idea of the Literary in Medieval England
EDITED BY FRANK GRADY AND ANDREW GALLOWAY

Scribal Authorship and the Writing of History in Medieval England
MATTHEW FISHER

Fashioning Change: The Trope of Clothing in High- and Late-Medieval England
ANDREA DENNY-BROWN

Form and Reform: Reading across the Fifteenth Century
EDITED BY SHANNON GAYK AND KATHLEEN TONRY

How to Make a Human: Animals and Violence in the Middle Ages
KARL STEEL

Revivalist Fantasy: Alliterative Verse and Nationalist Literary History
RANDY P. SCHIFF

Inventing Womanhood: Gender and Language in Later Middle English Writing
TARA WILLIAMS

Body Against Soul: Gender and Sowlehele *in Middle English Allegory*
MASHA RASKOLNIKOV

www.ingramcontent.com/pod-product-compliance
Lightning Source LLC
Chambersburg PA
CBHW021304240426
43669CB00041B/95